DEMOCRATIC EDUCATION

DEMOCRATIC EDUCATION

With a New Preface and Epilogue

Amy Gutmann

PRINCETON UNIVERSITY PRESS

PRINCETON, NEW JERSEY

Published by Princeton University Press, 41 William Street,
Princeton, New Jersey 08540
In the United Kingdom: Princeton University Press,
Chichester, West Sussex

Library of Congress Cataloging-in-Publication Data

Gutmann, Amy.
Democratic education / Amy Gutmann, with a new preface and
epilogue.
p.   cm.
"First printing of the revised paperback edition" — T.p. verso.
Includes bibliographical references and index.
ISBN 0-691-07736-3 (cloth : alk. paper). — ISBN 0-691-00916-3
(pbk. : alk. paper)
1. Education — Aims and objectives — United States.
2. Democracy — United States.   3. Education and state — United
States — Citizen participation.   I. Title.
LA217.2.G88   1999
370'.973 — dc21   98-43566

First printing of the revised paperback edition, 1999

The paper used in this publication meets the minimum requirements
of ANSI/NISO Z39.48-1992 (R1997) (*Permanence of Paper*)

http://pup.princeton.edu

Printed in the United States of America

7   9   10   8

ISBN-13: 978-0-691-00916-2 (pbk.)

TO THE MEMORY OF
BEATRICE GUTMANN
1913–1984

CONTENTS

PREFACE TO THE REVISED EDITION

The central question in the political theory of education—How should citizens be educated, and by whom?—has become even more prominent since the first edition of *Democratic Education* appeared ten years ago. The question has become more prominent in practice and in theory. Education tops the list of politically salient issues in American politics, ranking above even the economy, employment, and crime. Many more political philosophers are now addressing the most salient issues in the politics of education: the content of education, its distribution, and the distribution of educational authority.

As societies have become more interdependent than ever, educational issues have become increasingly international. Debates abound about whether the content of education should be more multicultural and whether schools should try to cultivate cosmopolitan rather than patriotic sensibilities among students. At the same time, the demand for less public control and more parental control over schooling has also become more prominent, especially in the United States.

One response to the conflicting demands placed on education is to let parents decide for their own children how to resolve such conflicts. Even this seemingly nonpolitical response—let parents decide—requires a political decision by citizens and their accountable representatives to distribute public resources to parents and let them spend those resources on the publicly accredited education of their choice. It also requires a political decision about what should count as a publicly accredited education. Except by abolishing mandatory schooling, there is no way of avoiding a political decision about the content of schooling, its distribution, and the distribution of educational authority. And even the decision to abolish mandatory schooling would of course be a political decision. A political decision would similarly be required to institute the system of civic minimalism, which is the latest and strongest defense of parental choice.

The Epilogue begins by examining the case for civic minimalism. Civic minimalists argue that parental authority over publicly subsidized schooling may be limited only by what is essential to civic education in a liberal democracy. Citizens (or their representatives) may mandate the civic minimum, they argue, but no more. Public decisions over schooling more generally may extend no further than mandating the civic minimum. Parents must be given the right to

determine the rest of their children's schooling (at public expense): ·
which school conforms to their idea of a good education and which
parts of the curriculum do not. Parents, civic minimalists argue,
should therefore have the right to exempt their children from any
part of the school curriculum as long as the education that they wish
to substitute satisfies the civic minimum.

Whoever makes decisions concerning the curriculum of elementary
and secondary schools in a constitutional democracy must confront
the question of what constitutes a good education. In the Epilogue, I
therefore also address two important issues that have gained greatly
in prominence in recent years concerning what constitutes a good
education. What is the appropriate response of democratic education
to the challenge of multiculturalism? Should schools try to cultivate
patriotic sentiments or cosmopolitan sentiments among students?

These and other controversial issues of democratic education raise
general questions about democracy and democratic citizenship. *Democratic Education*, therefore, calls for a complementary conception of
democracy. One of the aims of *Democracy and Disagreement*, which
I coauthored with Dennis Thompson, is to provide such a conception.[1] The conception of democratic education developed in *Democracy and Disagreement* supports the account of democratic education
in this book, and also pursues the implications of its basic principles
beyond education.

What is the democratic ideal that complements democratic education? A guiding principle of deliberative democracy is reciprocity
among free and equal individuals: citizens and their accountable representatives owe one another justifications for the laws that collectively bind them. A democracy is deliberative to the extent that citizens and their accountable representatives offer one another morally
defensible reasons for mutually binding laws in an ongoing process
of mutual justification. To the extent that a democracy is not deliberative, it treats people as objects of legislation, as passive subjects to
be ruled, rather than as citizens who take part in governance by accepting or rejecting the reasons they and their accountable representatives offer for the laws and policies that mutually bind them.

Deliberative democracy underscores the importance of publicly
supported education that develops the capacity to deliberate among
all children as future free and equal citizens. The most justifiable way

---

[1] *Democracy and Disagreement* (Cambridge, MA: Harvard University Press, 1996).
As Nancy Rosenblum wrote in her review of *Democractic Education* in the *American
Political Science Review*: "*Democratic Education* succeeds in its contest with liberal
and conservative theorists over who should control education and why. It calls for a
complementary account of democratic citizenship."

of making mutually binding decisions in a representative democracy—including decisions not to deliberate about some matters—is by deliberative decision making, where the decision makers are accountable to the people who are most affected by their decisions. Deliberative decision making and accountability presuppose a citizenry whose education prepares them to deliberate, and to evaluate the results of the deliberations of their representatives. A primary aim of publicly mandated schooling is therefore to cultivate the skills and virtues of deliberation.

Why should deliberation be considered primary even for public education when the opportunity for most citizens to live a good life today requires many more basic skills and virtues, such as numeracy, literacy, and nonviolence? Deliberation is not a single skill or virtue. It calls upon skills of literacy, numeracy, and critical thinking, as well as contextual knowledge, understanding, and appreciation of other people's perspectives. The virtues that deliberation encompasses include veracity, nonviolence, practical judgment, civic integrity and magnanimity. By cultivating these and other deliberative skills and virtues, a democratic society helps secure both the basic opportunity of individuals and its collective capacity to pursue justice.

The willingness to deliberate about mutually binding matters distinguishes democratic citizens from self-interested citizens, who argue merely to advance their own interests, and deferential citizens, who turn themselves into passive subjects by failing to argue, out of deference to political authority. Justice is far more likely to be served by democratic citizens who reason together in search of mutually justifiable decisions than it is by people who are uninterested in politics or interested in it only for the sake of power. Even when deliberative citizens continue to disagree, as they often will, their effort to reach mutually justifiable decisions manifests mutual respect. Because ongoing disagreement among reasonable people of good will is inevitable in any free society, mutual respect is an important virtue. Deliberation manifests mutual respect since it demonstrates a good faith effort to find mutually acceptable terms of social cooperation, not merely terms that are acceptable only to the most powerful, or for that matter to the most articulate.

Democratic Education argues that a necessary condition of an adequate civic education is to cultivate the skills and virtues of deliberative citizenship. It does not follow that cultivating deliberative citizenship should be the focus of all educational institutions or all educators. Parents, the primary educators of children, need not focus on educating their children for citizenship. Universities need not primarily aim at educating democratic citizens. Deliberative citizens

may be the unintended by-product of educational efforts that aim at
something else. A good liberal arts education, for example, is likely
to cultivate many deliberative skills and virtues out of a commitment
to critical inquiry.

Democratic Education offers a principled defense of schooling
whose aim is to teach the skills and virtues of democratic deliberation within a social context where educational authority is shared
among parents, citizens, and professional educators. Citizens are
morally and constitutionally free to support public schooling that
teaches children to deliberate. Suppose that a majority of citizens
defended a more comprehensive authority for parents than *Democratic Education* recommends? By the principles of a deliberative democracy, citizens could legitimately cede more comprehensive educational authority to parents, as long as parents did not thereby
infringe upon the basic liberty or opportunity of their children as
future free and equal citizens or upon anybody else's basic liberties or
opportunities.

Whether citizens in a deliberative democracy would be wise to
cede parents more educational authority is a separate question from
whether citizens have the right to do so. The reasons offered by
Democratic Education regarding why children, for example, would
not be well served by ceding comprehensive authority to any single
educational agent—parents, citizens, or professional educators—
are intended as contributions to a democratic debate. A more principled democratic debate on this and other controversial issues of education is itself an important part of what *Democratic Education*,
along with the conception of deliberative democracy that complements it, recommends.

Amy Gutmann
August 29, 1998

DEMOCRATIC EDUCATION

BACK TO BASICS

When citizens rule in a democracy, they determine, among other things, how future citizens will be educated. Democratic education is therefore a political as well as an educational ideal. Because being educated as a child entails being ruled, "you cannot be a ruler unless you have first been ruled."[1] Because being a democratic citizen entails ruling, the ideal of democratic education is being ruled, then ruling. Education not only sets the stage for democratic politics, it plays a central role in it. Its dual role poses one of the primary moral problems of politics: Who should share the authority to influence the way democratic citizens are educated?

To answer this question, I develop in considerable detail a democratic theory of education. But before developing that theory, I must answer three challenges to the idea that a democratic theory of education is worth developing. First: Why rely on a *theory* to decide who should exercise authority over education? Second: Why a *democratic* theory? Finally: Why focus on *education*?

WHY A THEORY?

"There are two human inventions which may be considered more difficult than any others—the art of government, and the art of education; and people still contend as to their very meaning."[2] We can exercise the art of education, Kant argued, either unreflectively, "without plan, ruled by given circumstances,"[3] or theoretically, with the aid of principles. Must educational policy rest on a principled theory? Why not settle for making educational policy less reflectively, as we often have in the past? Without any principled plan, we could strengthen our science and math curriculum in reaction to Sputnik, desegregate some schools and fund more compensatory education in reaction to the civil rights movement, and go "back to basics" in reaction to declining SAT scores.

Consider the recent back-to-basics movement in American educa-

---

[1] Aristotle, *The Politics of Aristotle*, trans. Ernest Barker (London: Oxford University Press, 1971), p. 105 (1277b).

[2] Immanuel Kant, *Kant on Education (Ueber Padagogik)*, trans. Annette Churton (Boston: D. C. Heath and Co., 1900), p. 12.

[3] Ibid., p. 13.

tion. In the absence of a theory, how might the call to go back to basics be defended? The most common and direct defense is that schools will better educate children by concentrating on reading, writing, history, mathematics, and science rather than on music, art, sex education, and so on. Having invoked the concept of a "better" education, we must ask "better" with respect to what purposes? Without a principled theory of education, an answer is not obvious. Neither, therefore, is the rationality of going back to basics.

This point is not simply academic. Consider the widely publicized recommendation by the National Commission on Excellence in Education for instituting the "New Basics." In making its recommendation, the Commission noted that "if only to keep and improve on the slim competitive edge we still retain in world markets, we must dedicate ourselves to the reform of our educational system for the benefit of all—old and young alike, affluent and poor, majority and minority."[4] Although the tone of the report is set by this statement, the Commission also notes that our concern for education "goes well beyond matters such as industry and commerce . . . [to include] the intellectual, moral, and spiritual strengths of our people which knit together the very fabric of our society."[5] If our educational purposes are this broad, it is not clear why the new basics do not also include art history, sex education, racial integration, and the avoidance of academic tracking. A rigorous course in high-school chemistry may not contribute more to the moral and spiritual strength of students than a racially integrated classroom or an equally rigorous course in art history. The problem is not that the reforms recommended by the Commission are necessarily wrong, but that we cannot judge them without a more principled understanding of our educational purposes.

The Commission may have had a political reason for not engaging in a more principled analysis: the desire to achieve public consensus. The "basics" appear to provide a least common denominator for agreeing on a national agenda for education. If we agree on the basics, we can temporarily set aside our deeper disagreements on more controversial issues, such as racial integration and sex education, and get on with the work of improving our schools. But do we agree on the basics? A greater proportion of citizens may approve of teaching American history than sex education in schools (although 82 percent of the Ameri-

---

[4] National Commission on Excellence in Education, *A Nation At Risk: The Imperative for Educational Reform* (Washington, D.C.: U.S. Government Printing Office, April 1983), p. 7.
[5] Ibid.

can public approves of sex education[6]), but *how* schools teach sex education and American history matters more to most citizens than *whether* schools teach these subjects, and there is no consensus on how either American history or sex education should be taught. There is, in this crucial sense, no consensus on teaching even the "basics."

Were there a consensus, it would not constitute a decisive reason for dispensing with a principled analysis of our educational problems. The charter of the Commission "directed it to pay particular attention to teenage youth."[7] The Report therefore focuses on high-school education, yet it makes no mention (for example) of the educational problems created by a rapidly rising pregnancy rate among unmarried teenage girls,[8] and therefore totally neglects the question of how schools might best deal with the problem. Although the teenage pregnancy rate has risen more rapidly in recent years than SAT scores have fallen, the Commission concentrated exclusively on the latter problem. If public commissions put avoidance of political controversy ahead of principled analysis, they are bound to fail in the task for which they are best equipped: improving the quality of American education not directly by changing school policy, but indirectly by improving the quality of our public deliberations over education.

In a democracy, political disagreement is not something that we should generally seek to avoid. Political controversies over our educational problems are a particularly important source of social progress because they have the potential for educating so many citizens. By not taking principled positions, commissions may avoid converting some of our disagreements into full-fledged political controversies. But we pay a very high price for their avoidance: we neglect educational alternatives that may be better than those to which we have become accustomed or that may aid us in understanding how to improve our schools before we reach the point of crisis, when our reactions are likely to be less reflective because we have so little time to deliberate.

Some members of the Commission may have had another reason for avoiding a principled analysis of our educational problems. They may have believed that the government's legitimate educational role does not extend to what might be called "moral education." On this view, the government should stay away from subjects such as sex education, since courses in sex education cannot possibly be neutral with regard to

---

[6] Reported in Joel H. Spring, *American Education: An Introduction to Social and Political Aspects* (New York: Longman, 1985), p. 133.

[7] *A Nation at Risk*, p. 2.

[8] For a discussion of the dimensions of the problem, see Hyman Rodman, Susan Lewis, and Saralyn Griffith, *The Sexual Rights of Adolescents* (New York: Columbia University Press, 1984).

morality, and moral education is properly a private, not a public, concern.[9] Sex education should therefore be provided by parents, not by public schools. Whatever one thinks of this conclusion, it clearly presupposes a theory, a principled political theory, about the legitimate role of government in education. Unless the theory is articulated, citizens cannot assess its principled merits or its policy implications. Even a brief account of the theory suggests a problem with this rationale for the Commission's recommendations. If one embraces the principle that moral education is the domain of the family rather than the state, then the basics must not include the teaching of history or biology (insofar as it includes evolution) any more than sex education or racial integration. States cannot even support schools without engaging in moral education.

All significant policy prescriptions presuppose a theory, a political theory, of the proper role of government in education. When the theory remains implicit, we cannot adequately judge its principles or the policy prescriptions that flow from them. The attractions of avoiding theory are, as we have just seen, superficial. We do not collectively know good educational policy when we see it; we cannot make good educational policy by avoiding political controversy; nor can we make principled educational policy without exposing our principles and investigating their implications.

Why a Democratic Theory?

To defend the need for a theory of education, however, is not to defend any particular theory. Why a *democratic* theory of education? It will take an entire book to defend a democratic theory in detail. But by extending the example of sex education, I can briefly explain the rationale for developing a democratic theory.

For many years, the teachers in Fairfax County, Virginia, were not permitted to discuss contraception, abortion, masturbation, homosexuality, or rape (the "Big Five," as they were called) in their classrooms. Student were required to submit any questions about these topics in writing. The policy provoked "five years of turbulent debate" in Fairfax County. In 1981, the Fairfax County School Board changed the policy by an 8-to-2 vote, authorizing the introduction of a new elective biology course that discusses the previously prohibited issues, along with other topics related to "family life." The school board's decision

[9] See, for example, "Sex Education in Public Schools?—Interview with Jacqueline Kasun": "Q: Why shouldn't schools teach about sexual choices? A: Because such choices pertain to values, and schools should leave the teaching of values to the family and the church." *U.S. News and World Report*, vol. 89, no. 14 (October 1980): 89.

gave parents "the right to choose whether their children will take either the new sex education course or one or two other courses designed as alternatives" (which do not discuss the "Big Five"). The controversy over sex education in Fairfax County has not ended, but a school survey found that 75 percent of parents and an even greater majority of students favored the new elective course.[10]

Existing theories of education suggest different reactions to this example that either neglect the problem of authority that it poses or denigrate the democratic authority that it exemplifies. Conventional philosophical approaches typically neglect the problem of authority. Utilitarianism, which assumes that the purpose of education is to make the mind "as far as possible, an operative cause of happiness," provides an indeterminate standard for deciding whether sex education is conducive to the pursuit of happiness.[11] Rights theories can more straightforwardly support sex education as a means of preparing children for choice among competing conceptions of the good life, although they have difficulty accounting for the greater value we typically accord to quality rather than quantity of choice.[12] Conceptual approaches, which derive standards (such as rationality, openness to criticism, and so on) from the very meaning of the term "education," can defend sex education courses insofar as they are, properly speaking, educational, and criticize opponents of such courses as opposed not just to sex education but to education per se.[13] These philosophical approaches can aid us in articulating a moral ideal or a conceptual understanding of education,[14] but they give us no guidance in answering the question of who should make educational policy.

[10] *The Washington Post*, May 15, 1981, pp. A1, A28.

[11] W. H. Burston, ed., *James Mill on Education* (Cambridge: Cambridge University Press, 1969), p. 41. For a contemporary utilitarian approach to education, see R. M. Hare, "Opportunity for What?: Some Remarks on Current Disputes about Equality in Education," *Oxford Review of Education*, vol. 3, no. 3 (1977): 207-216.

[12] For a more thorough critique of utilitarian and rights theories of education, see Amy Gutmann, "What's the Use of Going to School?: The Problem of Education in Utilitarian and Rights Theories," in Amartya Sen and Bernard Williams, eds., *Utilitarianism and Beyond* (Cambridge: Cambridge University Press, 1982), pp. 261-77.

[13] The purest conceptual approach is John Wilson, *Preface to the Philosophy of Education* (London: Routledge and Kegan Paul, 1979). See also P. H. Hirst and R. S. Peters, *The Logic of Education* (London: Routledge and Kegan Paul, 1970); R. S. Peters, *Ethics and Education* (London: Allen and Unwin, 1966); R. S. Peters, ed., *The Concept of Education* (London: Routledge and Kegan Paul, 1967); P. H. Hirst, "Liberal Education and the Nature of Knowledge," in *Education and the Development of Reason*, ed. R. F. Dearden, P. H. Hirst, and R. S. Peters (London: Routledge and Kegan Paul, 1972), pp. 391-414.

[14] There is, for example, a large but perhaps not very fruitful debate between conceptual and normative analysis. One need not claim that a conceptual analysis of education

Conventional political approaches often give us the wrong guidance. Conservative theories of education object in principle to courses on sex education on grounds that the state should stay out of those aspects of moral education that directly affect the private realm of the family.[15] Because parents are the appropriate educational authorities in that realm, they should decide how their children are sexually educated. What if a majority of parents want public schools to teach their children about sex, as apparently was the case in Fairfax County, at least in 1981? The conservative position on parental authority must then support a more expansive role for democratic authority, even over sex education, than is commonly acknowledged, provided the majority does not force students to take courses against their parents' wishes (as the Fairfax County School Board did not). Conservative theories of education therefore cannot consistently support the view that a *democratic* state must stay out of moral education, even as it directly affects the family. This apparent inconsistency in conservative theories of education points toward the need for a more subtle specification of the realm of legitimate democratic authority.[16]

Liberal theories of education, which aim at developing individual autonomy, would criticize just that part of the new policy of the Fairfax County School Board that conservatives could applaud.[17] Under the new policy, parents are permitted to restrict what their children learn about sex in school. By liberal standards, the School Board should have voted to give *all* teenagers, not just those who received parental permission, the opportunity "to begin to assume responsibility for the course of their own lives, and to understand that responsibility goes far further than the pleasures of the moment."[18] If all future citizens must be taught to assume responsibility for their lives, sex education courses should not be limited to only those students whose parents approve of it or to only those schools whose boards are educationally enlightened.

---

is wrong to recognize that it is not enough to invoke the concept to criticize (so-called) educational practices that are repressive. One must argue the case for why such practices should not be repressive, and why repressive practices should not be authorized, even by (otherwise) legitimate political authorities.

[15] Some conservatives focus on the specific objections of the parents who oppose the courses. Parents who oppose sex education often argue that it "encourage[s] pregnancies by implying that sexual activity is acceptable." (*The Washington Post*, May 15, 1981, p. A28.) There is no empirical evidence to support this claim and some evidence to doubt it. I therefore concentrate on the more plausible and principled version of conservative theory.

[16] See Chapter Four on "Sex Education and Sexist Education."

[17] For such a theory, see Bruce Ackerman, *Social Justice in the Liberal State* (New York and London: Yale University Press, 1980), esp. pp. 139-67.

[18] *The Washington Post*, May 15, 1981, p. A28.

The federal government should mandate the permissive policy for all students in all schools, public and private. When liberals authorize the federal government to make educational policy for local communities if but only if its views are right, they do not take democracy seriously, at either the local or the federal level.

Liberal political theories might become more philosophical, and simply avoid the question of authority, arguing only for the best educational policy "in principle" or the policy most recommended "by reason." Liberal theories may thereby guide individuals in formulating their own educational ideals, but they cannot give adequate guidance to communities in deciding what educational policies to pursue. The more philosophical liberal theories become, the less they face up to the facts of life in our society: that reasonable people disagree over what forms of freedom are worth cultivating, and therefore over what constitutes the best education, in principle as well as in practice.[19]

Functionalist theories of education pride themselves on facing up to the facts of social reproduction. One of the most prominent functionalist theories suggests that schooling in a capitalist society serves to reproduce the social inequalities necessary to maintain the capitalist mode of production.[20] Viewed in this theoretical light, the Fairfax County School Board's new policy (that made sex education an elective course, based on parental preference) is one among several educational means to reproduce existing class divisions, in this case, between middle-class women, who must defer childbearing to compete in the professional workforce, and working-class women, who must bear

[19] Liberal theories can also become more democratic and defend those educational policies for a community that are necessary for democratic deliberation. Such a liberal theory, fully developed, would converge with the democratic theory that I shall defend. For a suggestion of such a theory, see Israel Scheffler, "Moral Education and the Democratic Ideal," in *Reason and Teaching* (London: Routledge and Kegan Paul, 1973), p. 142.

[20] See Samuel Bowles and Herbert Gintis, *Schooling in Capitalist America: Educational Reform and the Contradictions of Economic Life* (New York: Basic Books, 1976), e.g., p. 48: "The educational system serves—through the correspondence of its social relations with those of economic life—to reproduce economic inequality and to distort personal development. . . . It is precisely because of its role as producer of an alienated and stratified labor force that the educational system has developed its repressive and unequal structure. In the history of U.S. education, it is the integrative function which has dominated the purpose of schooling, to the detriment of the other liberal objectives." See also Joel H. Spring, *Education and the Rise of the Corporate State* (Boston: Beacon Press, 1972), esp. p. 151: "Schools tend to reinforce and strengthen existing social structures and social stratification." Other functionalist analyses of schools include Colin Greer, *The Great School Legend* (New York: Basic Books, 1972); Clarence Karier, Paul Violas, and Joel H. Spring, *Roots of Crisis: American Education in the Twentieth Century* (Chicago: Rand McNally, 1973); and Michael B. Katz, *Class, Bureaucracy, and Schools: The Illusion of Educational Change in America* (New York: Praeger, 1971).

children early to maintain the reserve army of the unemployed. Functionalist theories do not claim that educational authorities intended these outcomes, nor do they specify the mechanism by which the unintended outcomes are produced.[21] The primary evidence supporting the claims of functionalism is the stability of the system (in this case, capitalism) that educational policy (intentionally or unintentionally) supports.

Whereas liberal and conservative political theories assume that the best educational policies *must* be implemented, functionalist theories assume that they *cannot* be, regardless of the results of democratic deliberations. The latter assumption is no more plausible than the former. The demands of the capitalist economy did not change sufficiently between 1976 and 1981 to explain the different outcomes of the Fairfax County School Board's deliberations, nor can the equally great differences between the policies of Fairfax County and other school boards be explained by the differing regional demands of capitalism. Even if the School Board's decisions did serve to stabilize the capitalist economy, this fact would not suffice as an explanation either of why the Board passed these specific policies or of what the primary purpose of their policies were. If one assumes that all educational policies that do not result in the overthrow of capitalism function to preserve it, then virtually any educational policy can fit into this functional explanation, but at the price of misunderstanding the significance of most educational policies to the people who supported them.[22] Alternatively, functionalist theories could treat local controversies over school curricula as insignificant, epiphenomenal episodes in the making of educational policy, but only at the price of converting the theory into a tautology.[23]

Despite appearances, functionalist theories are similar to conventional philosophical theories in being profoundly apolitical. By invok-

[21] For a general critique of functionalism, see Jon Elster, "Marxism, Functionalism, and Game Theory," *Theory and Society*, vol. 11 (1982): 453-82; and Elster, *Sour Grapes: Studies in the Subversion of Rationality* (Cambridge: Cambridge University Press, 1983), pp. 101-108. For a more specific critique of functionalist analyses of schools, see David K. Cohen and Bella H. Rosenberg, "Functions and Fantasies: Understanding Schools in Capitalist America," *History of Education Quarterly* (Summer 1977): 113-37. For two recent sympathetic critiques of Bowles and Gintis, see Ira Katznelson and Margaret Weir, *Schooling for All: Class, Race, and the Decline of the Democratic Ideal* (New York: Basic Books, 1985), esp. pp. 17-23, 46-48; and Martin Carnoy and Henry M. Levin, *Schooling and Work in the Democratic State* (Stanford, Calif.: Stanford University Press, 1985), esp. pp. 18-22.

[22] For such a criticism on historical grounds, see Rush Welter, "Reason, Rhetoric, and Reality in American Educational History," *The Review of Education*, vol. 2 (January/February 1976): 94-96.

[23] See Diane Ravitch, *The Revisionists Revised: A Critique of the Radical Attack on the Schools* (New York: Basic Books, 1978), pp. 146-47.

ing an intuitively implausible and empirically unverified form of deter-
minism, functionalist theories never pose, let alone answer, the
question of how citizens should resolve their disagreements over educational policy. Liberal theories, in their more political version, are
profoundly undemocratic: they answer the question by suggesting that
we need a philosopher-king (or a philosopher-queen, if they are truly
liberal) to impose the correct educational policies, which support individual autonomy, on all misguided parents and citizens. Conservative
theories suffer from a variant of both problems. They depoliticize education by placing it as much as possible in the province of parental authority, and at the same time they deny parents the democratic authority to implement educational policies that require state support. In
contrast to these theories, a democratic theory faces up to the fact of
difference in our moral ideals of education by looking toward democratic deliberations not only as a means to reconciling those differences, but also as an important part of democratic education.

The most distinctive feature of a democratic theory of education is
that it makes a democratic virtue out of our inevitable disagreement
over educational problems. The democratic virtue, too simply stated, is
that we can publicly debate educational problems in a way much more
likely to increase our understanding of education and each other than
if we were to leave the management of schools, as Kant suggests, "to
depend entirely upon the judgment of the most enlightened experts."[24]
The policies that result from our democratic deliberations will not always be the right ones, but they will be more enlightened—by the values and concerns of the many communities that constitute a democracy—than those that would be made by unaccountable educational
experts.

The primary aim of a democratic theory of education is not to offer
solutions to all the problems plaguing our educational institutions, but
to consider ways of resolving those problems that are compatible with
a commitment to democratic values. A democratic theory of education
provides principles that, in the face of our social disagreements, help us
judge (a) who should have authority to make decisions about education, and (b) what the moral boundaries of that authority are.

A democratic theory is not a substitute for a moral ideal of education. In a democratic society, we bring our moral ideals of education to
bear on how we raise our children, on who we support for school
boards, and on what educational policies we advocate. But we cannot
simply translate our own moral ideals of education, however objective
they are, into public policy. Only in a society in which all other citizens

[24] Kant, *Kant on Education*, p. 17.

agreed with me would my moral ideal simply translate into a political ideal. But such a society would have little need for politics as we now know it. The administration of persons would, as Engels (and later Lenin) imagined, be replaced by the administration of things. To create such a society, someone would have to establish an educational tyranny, a tyranny that would be unworkable without the simultaneous creation of a political tyranny as well. There is no morally acceptable way to achieve social agreement on a moral ideal of education, at least in our lifetimes. We can do better to try instead to find the fairest ways for reconciling our disagreements, and for enriching our collective life by democratically debating them. We may even find ourselves modifying our moral ideals of education in the process of participating in democratic debates and of publicly reconciling our differences.

This separation between a moral and a political ideal of education is often hard to accept. It is hardest to accept when we are convinced not only of the correctness of our moral ideal but also of the beneficial social consequences that would follow from its implementation. Many feminists, myself included, are firmly committed to the ideal of an egalitarian division of labor between parents with regard to childrearing. We have, moreover, good reason to believe that women, men, and democratic politics would benefit were the nuclear family to become more egalitarian in this respect. One might therefore argue that the ideal of an egalitarian family is a political as well as a moral ideal. But it is not a political ideal in the stricter sense that I identified above: the moral ideal of an egalitarian family does not simply translate into a political ideal that sanctions state intervention into the family for the sake of making it more egalitarian.

Although few feminists explicitly defend direct political intervention into the family, some suggest that until we achieve an egalitarian family structure, neither democratic education nor democratic politics is possible. This position may seem more benign, but it has a similarly troubling implication: that until the family is transformed into our moral ideal, deliberative political processes and their results possess no democratic authority. The feminist view of the family properly serves as a moral ideal not over but within democratic politics, an ideal that should lead us to support policies (such as subsidized childcare and sexually unstereotyped schooling) that stimulate the creation of more egalitarian families. Democratic principles give parents a great deal of room to exercise discretion in structuring their families and educating their children. Of course, room still remains for scholars and citizens to discuss how parents should raise their children. I give no such advice, not because it would be wrong to give it, but because I wish to concentrate on questions concerning how democratic governments should furnish the educational room unoccupied by parental discretion. Among those questions is what democratic governments should do to overcome gender biases in the content and structure of schooling and culture.

We need to theorize about education, and the theory we need is democratic, but why do we need a *new* democratic theory of education? The most influential theory of this century—John Dewey's—is itself explicitly democratic. The democratic theory that I develop is inspired by Dewey, but it also diverges from Dewey in at least one way. Dewey correctly emphasized the need to enlarge the range of our outlook on education beyond "an individualistic standpoint, as something between teacher and pupil, or between teacher and parent." But what should that broader, presumptively democratic standpoint be? In a sentence more often quoted than questioned, Dewey concluded that "what the best and wisest parent wants for his own child, that must the community want for all of its children."[25] The idea that a community should not settle for less than the best education for all its children is, and should be, intuitively appealing. A democratic society is responsible for educating not just some but all children for citizenship. But "must" the community want for all its children "what the best and wisest parent wants for his own child"?

Consider what the best and wisest parents, on one understanding, would want for their child. They would want her:

> to read and write fluently; to speak articulately, to listen carefully; to learn to participate in the give-and-take of group discussion; to learn self-discipline and to develop the capacity for deferred gratification; to read and appreciate good literature; to have a strong knowledge of history, both of our own nation and of others; to appreciate the value of a free, democratic society; to understand science, mathematics, technology, and the natural world; to become engaged in the arts, both as a participant and as one capable of appreciating aesthetic excellence. . . . [S]uch parents would also want a good program of physical education and perhaps even competence in a foreign language.[26]

Must every local community want this and only this curriculum for its children? Although Dewey's aim is admirable, translating what the best and wisest parents want into what a community *must* want is not an acceptable way to enlarge our outlook on education, to be less individ-

---

[25] John Dewey, "The School and Society" [1900] in *"The Child and the Curriculum" and "The School and Society"* (Chicago: University of Chicago, 1956), p. 7.

[26] Diane Ravitch, "A Good School," in *The Schools We Deserve: Reflections on the Educational Crises of Our Time* (New York: Basic Books, 1985), p. 277.

ualistic. Would any other ideal, acted upon, destroy democracy, as Dewey goes on to argue? If democracy includes the right of citizens to deliberate collectively about how to educate future citizens, then we might arrive at a very different conclusion: that the enforcement of any moral ideal of education, whether it be liberal or conservative, without the consent of citizens subverts democracy.

Yet this criticism is surely too simple. Problems—specifically, the threat of democratic repression and discrimination—remain. Citizens and public officials can use democratic processes to destroy democracy. They can undermine the intellectual foundations of future democratic deliberations by implementing educational policies that either repress unpopular (but rational) ways of thinking or exclude some future citizens from an education adequate for participating in democratic politics. A democratic society must not be constrained to legislate what the wisest parents want for their child, yet it must be constrained *not* to legislate policies that render democracy repressive or discriminatory. A democratic theory of education recognizes the importance of empowering citizens to make educational policy and also of constraining their choices among policies in accordance with those principles—of nonrepression and nondiscrimination—that preserve the intellectual and social foundations of democratic deliberations. A society that empowers citizens to make educational policy, moderated by these two principled constraints, realizes the democratic ideal of education.

WHY FOCUS ON EDUCATION?

The ideal helps define the scope of a democratic theory of education. A democratic theory of education focuses on what might be called "conscious social reproduction"—the ways in which citizens are or should be empowered to influence the education that in turn shapes the political values, attitudes, and modes of behavior of future citizens. Since the democratic ideal of education is that of *conscious* social reproduction, a democratic theory focuses on practices of deliberate instruction by individuals and on the educative influences of institutions designed at least partly for educational purposes.

Education may be more broadly defined to include every social influence that makes us who we are. The inclusiveness of the broad definition is intellectually satisfying. Almost every major political philosopher who wrote about education began with the broad definition, but few if any employed it in their subsequent analysis.[27] When one begins

[27] For example, see Rousseau's understanding in *Emile*, cited at the beginning of Chapter One. A contemporary example is Israel Scheffler, "Moral Education and the Democratic Ideal," in *Reason and Teaching*, pp. 139-40.

with the broad definition, it is much easier to extol the significance of education than it is to say anything systematic about it.[28]

Most political scientists who write about education subsume it under the concept of political socialization. Political socialization is typically understood to include the processes by which democratic societies transmit political values, attitudes, and modes of behavior to citizens.[29] Since many of these processes are unintended, political socialization studies tend to focus on what might be called "unconscious social reproduction." The focus of political socialization studies makes sense as long as their aim is to explain the processes by which societies perpetuate themselves. If one's aim is instead to understand how members of a democratic society should participate in consciously shaping its future, then it is important not to assimilate education with political socialization.[30] When education is so assimilated, it is easy to lose sight of the distinctive virtue of a democratic society, that it authorizes citizens to influence how their society reproduces itself.

On the other hand, when education is distinguished from political socialization, it is hard to resist the temptation to focus entirely on schooling, since it is our most deliberate form of human instruction. I try to resist this temptation without succumbing to the opposite, even more troubling one of regarding schools as an insignificant part of what American education is or should be. Among the many myths about American education in recent years has been the view that schooling

[28] But systematic analysis is not impossible. Historians of American education have made significant contributions to our understanding of the educative role of institutions other than schools, especially after Bernard Bailyn's critique of "an excess of writing along certain lines and an almost undue clarity of direction" in historical writing about schooling. See Bernard Bailyn, *Education in the Forming of American Society* (New York: Vintage, 1960), p. 4. Education, according to Bailyn, is "the entire process by which a culture transmits itself across the generations . . ." (p. 14). Compare Lawrence Cremin (who has probably written more extensively and systematically about American education than any other contemporary historian): education is "the *deliberate*, systematic, and sustained effort to transmit, evoke, or acquire knowledge, attitudes, values, skill, or sensibilities, as well as any outcomes of that effort." (Emphasis added.) Lawrence A. Cremin, *Traditions of American Education* (New York: Basic Books, 1977), p. 134.

[29] Because its subject is so vast, the literature on political socialization defies simple summary. For a broad definition and overview of the field, see Fred I. Greenstein, "Socialization: Political Socialization," *International Encyclopedia of the Social Sciences* (New York: Macmillan, 1968), 14: 551-55. See also Richard E. Dawson and Kenneth Prewitt, *Political Socialization* (Boston: Little, Brown and Co., 1969); Kenneth P. Langton, *Political Socialization* (New York: Oxford University Press, 1969); and Roberta S. Sigel, *Learning About Politics: A Reader in Political Socialization* (New York: Random House, 1970).

[30] For another reason not to assimilate education and socialization, see David Nyberg and Kieran Egan, *The Erosion of Education: Socialization and the Schools* (New York: Teachers College Press, 1981), pp. 2-5.

does not matter very much—except perhaps for the pleasure it gives children while they experience it—because it makes little or no difference to how income, work, or even intelligence gets distributed in our society. Like most myths, this one has no apparent author but a lot of social influence.[31] Unlike some myths, the myth of the moral insignificance of schooling distorts rather than illuminates our social condition. Its prophecy—of inevitable disillusionment with even our best efforts to educate citizens through schooling—is self-fulfilling because it pays exclusive attention to the question of whether schools *equalize* and neglects the question of whether they *improve* the political and personal lives of citizens.

We can appreciate the centrality of schooling to democratic education and still recognize that there is much more to democratic education than schooling. Institutions other than schools—libraries, for example—can contribute to democratic education, and other institutions—television, for example—can detract from it. This much may be obvious, although the implications of the obvious are often avoided for the sake of making discussions of education more manageable. By focusing our inquiry beyond schooling on the central political question of how authority over educational institutions should be allocated in a democratic society, we can avoid perpetuating the false impression that democratic education ends with schooling.

Translating Theory into Practice

Authority over education is the theoretical issue that organizes this book.[32] The central question posed by democratic education is: Who should have authority to shape the education of future citizens? In Chapter One, I defend the principled outlines of a democratic answer to this question against three of the most influential nondemocratic theories of states and education.

The rest of *Democratic Education* is an attempt to explore the practical implications for educational policy in the United States today of

[31] The two works most often identified with this view are Christopher Jencks, et al., *Inequality: A Reassessment of the Effect of Family and Schooling in America* (New York: Basic Books, 1972); and James S. Coleman et al., *Report on Equality of Educational Opportunity* (Washington, D.C.: U.S. Government Printing Office, 1966). See esp. Jencks, pp. 29, 256.

[32] I rely upon a common meaning of authority, "the right to command, or give an ultimate decision" (*Oxford English Dictionary*). Authority may or may not involve the "appeal to an impersonal normative order or value system which regulates behavior basically because of acceptance of it on the part of those who comply" (Peters, *Ethics and Education*, p. 239). Compare David Nyberg, *Power Over Power* (Ithaca, N.Y.: Cornell University Press, 1981), pp. 63-91.

going back to theoretical basics. The method of translating theory into practice is akin to what John Rawls calls "reflective equilibrium," but it does not require us to separate ourselves from our particular interests or our moral convictions by entering an original position.[33] At the same time as we explore the implications of democratic principles for educational practice, we refine the principles in light of their practical implications.

Political theorists are likely to be as skeptical of the practical part of this enterprise as policymakers (and perhaps also historians[34]) are of the theory. The translation of political principles into practice, however, is no less essential to defending a political theory than to evaluating educational practices. The best defense of this theoretical claim also lies in practice rather than in theory. When we consider the liberal principle of equal educational opportunity, for example, we find that its practical implications conflict with some of our firmest convictions.[35] We then must either change our convictions or revise our understanding of the principle. In theory, it is possible that the liberal principle rests on foundations firm enough to withstand the force of our convictions. In practice, this is not the case. Our convictions here constitute the firmest foundations of our theoretical understanding. We therefore have no better alternative but to revise our principled understanding of

[33] See John Rawls, *A Theory of Justice* (Cambridge, Mass.: Harvard University Press, 1971), esp. pp. 20 ff., 48-51.

[34] I am not sure how to account for the skepticism of many historians towards political theory. Perhaps the transhistorical and transcultural claims of many political theories engender the skepticism. I make no such claims for this theory of democratic education. I claim only that the principles of democratic education can aid Americans today in assessing the value of our educational practices by holding those practices up to a set of standards that we can publicly defend. I do not try (nor am I equipped) to contribute an account of the past successes and failures of democratic education in the United States. Yet most historical accounts of success and failure presuppose a set of normative standards, which need to be explicitly elaborated before they can be fully understood. I hope to help further this understanding. Historical accounts, on the other hand, can help theorists understand the practical implications of our normative standards. I have relied (often implicitly) on many historical accounts of past practices of American education in developing my understanding of democratic education. Among those that have most affected my thinking are: Lawrence A. Cremin, *The Transformation of the School: Progressivism in American Education, 1876-1957* (New York: Vintage Books, 1964); Cremin, *American Education: The National Experience, 1783-1876* (New York: Harper and Row, 1980); Paul E. Peterson, *The Politics of School Reform 1870-1940* (Chicago: University of Chicago Press, 1985); Diane Ravitch, *The Great School Wars: New York City, 1805-1973* (New York: Basic Books, 1974); Ravitch, *The Troubled Crusade: American Education 1945-1980* (New York: Basic Books, 1983); and Rush Welter, *Popular Education and Democratic Thought in America* (New York: Columbia University Press, 1962).

[35] See Chapter Five on "Interpreting Equal Educational Opportunity."

equal educational opportunity. In general, we cannot understand a political theory or use its principles to evaluate existing practices until we engage in the process of formulating its principles, translating them into practices, and judging the practices against our convictions.

I begin this process with an extensive discussion of elementary and secondary ("primary") schooling in the United States. I consider its purposes in Chapter Two. An understanding of the democratic purposes of primary schooling provides the groundwork for discussions in the following three chapters of the dimensions of democratic participation (Chapter Three), the limits of democratic authority (Chapter Four), and the distribution of educational resources in school systems (Chapter Five).

Higher education is distinguished from primary education by its distinctive democratic purposes. Chapter Six considers those purposes and how universities should be governed consistently with them. Chapter Seven discusses the controversy over preferential admissions in the context of a broader discussion of university admissions and financial aid.

Chapter Eight considers the extent to which institutions other than schools—libraries and television in particular—can educate children. A central question, once again, is the relationship between the democratic purposes of these institutions and the way a democratic society should allocate authority over them.

Chapter Nine looks at three ways in which governmental authority can be enlisted to extend democratic education for adults: by more broadly distributing opportunities to influence and appreciate high culture, by increasing the access of adults to higher education, and by offering illiterate adults a second chance at primary education.

In the Conclusion, I show how a theory of democratic education makes sense of the claim that politics itself is a form of education. A more robust democratic politics, I argue, would render the concerns of democratic education not less but more important. Just as we need a more democratic politics to further democratic education, so we need a more democratic education to further democratic politics. If we value either, we must pursue both.

CHAPTER ONE
STATES AND EDUCATION

"We are born weak, we need strength; helpless, we need aid; foolish, we need reason. All that we lack at birth, that we need when we come to man's estate, is the gift of education." So broadly understood as what we learn "from nature, from men, and from things,"[1] the gift of education may make us who we are, but is not ours to give. Like Rousseau, we therefore direct our concern to that portion of education most amenable to our influence: the conscious efforts of men and women to inform the intellect and to shape the character of less educated people. And we naturally begin by asking what the purposes of human education should be—what kind of people should human education seek to create?

Perhaps the most commonly articulated answer is relativistic. "The citizens of a state should always be educated to suit the constitution of their state," Aristotle argued.[2] "The laws of education must be relative to the principles of government,"[3] Montesquieu agreed, as did Durkheim and several more contemporary social theorists.

Many moralists react unfavorably to the mere mention of relativism because they associate it with the view, properly called "subjectivism," that claims morality to be nothing more than personal opinion. Aristotle, Montesquieu, and Durkheim reject subjectivism for the far more defensible view that the deepest, shared moral commitments of a society—its "constitution" in Aristotelian terms or "political principles" in Montesquieu's more modern sense—serve as the standard for determining the justice of its educational practices. Conservatism is the moral hazard of this form of relativism. Does justice demand that citizens be educated to suit the constitution of their society if that constitution supports cruelty and injustice? The strongest formulation of educational relativism suggests not, or at least not necessarily. Education must be guided by the *principles*, not the practices, of a regime. Edu-

---

[1] Jean Jacques Rousseau, *Emile, or On Education*, trans. Barbara Foxley (New York: Everyman, 1972), p. 6.

[2] *The Politics of Aristotle*, ed. and trans. by Ernest Barker (London: Oxford University Press, 1958), p. 332 (1337a).

[3] Montesquieu, *The Spirit of the Laws*, trans. Thomas Nugent (London, 1750), 1: 42. Cf. *The Writings of Benjamin Franklin*, ed. Albert H. Smyth (New York and London, 1905-1907), 10: 97-105; and Emile Durkheim, *Moral Education* (New York: Free Press, 1961), *passim*.

cational relativism is conservative not in the narrow sense of maintaining the status quo, but in the broad sense of supporting existing social ideals.

The problem of reinforcing cruelty and injustice through education arises only in the event that the principles (not the practices) of a society support cruelty and injustice. This problem may be rare, but it is not merely hypothetical. Some societies—slave societies of the past and South Africa today, for example—probably rest on racist principles. Any credible form of educational relativism must either find critical principles within even the most thoroughly racist societies or recognize limits to the principles that are justifiable by a society's internal understandings.[4] When societies or the most powerful groups within them transgress those limits by, for example, committing themselves to racist principles, revolution or civil war becomes a precondition of moral education.

Many unjust societies, however, are not morally dedicated to cruelty or injustice. Marxist principles, for example, provide ample grounds for Soviet dissidents to condemn virtually all the practices of Soviet regimes that strike many Americans as cruel or unjust. On the regime's interpretation of Marxism, criticism may become impossible. But "the education of a citizen in the spirit of his constitution does not consist in his doing the actions in which the partisans of oligarchy, or the adherents of democracy, delight. It consists in his doing the actions by which an oligarchy, or a democracy, will be enabled to survive."[5] Relativism, according to Aristotle's formulation, does not require us to accept the moral interpretation of the ruling class as the morally ruling interpretation.

But what interpretation should rule? How do we determine the prin-

---

[4] Even the most thoroughly racist societies typically generate internal criticism. Consider the interpretation of apartheid by the dissident Afrikaner, André Brink. Having characterized apartheid as "an extension of an entire value system, embracing all the territories of social experience, economics, philosophy, morality and above all religion," Brink argues that "the dissident is fighting to assert the most positive and creative aspects of his heritage. . . . In summary, apartheid, as I see it, denies what is best in the Afrikaner himself. . . . What it denies is the Afrikaner's reverence for life, his romanticism, his sense of the mystical, his deep attachment to the earth, his generosity, his compassion. . . . The dissident struggles in the name of what the Afrikaner could and should have become *in the light of his own history*. . . ." André Brink, *Writing in a State of Siege: Essays on Politics and Literature* (New York: Summit Books, 1983), pp. 19-20. Emphasis added.

I set aside here the question of how relativism could develop the theoretical resources either to choose "what is best" within a culture or to set limits on the acceptance of internally generated principles. The democratic theory developed below provides a set of limits (in the constraints of nonrepression and nondiscrimination) consistent with, but not derivable from, relativism.

[5] *The Politics of Aristotle*, p. 233 (1310a).

ciples of a particular society, or its constitution, in Aristotle's sense? This question poses a greater challenge to relativism than the charge of conservatism once one recognizes that the "members of a society are unlikely to agree about what the constitution, in Aristotle's broad sense, actually is, or what it is becoming, or what it should be. Nor are they likely to agree about what character type will best sustain it or how that type might best be produced."[6] If this is the case, then believing in educational relativism is compatible with believing in any one of a wide range of incompatible interpretations of educational justice. So whether or not we accept the basic tenet of educational relativism (that citizens should be educated according to the political principles of their society), we must use some form of philosophical analysis to defend a set of principles or to determine which set of principles and whose interpretation of them ought to rule. The controversy over relativism— or at least educational relativism—is best set aside if we are to make any progress in analyzing the purposes of education.

The form of analysis that follows might best be called dialectical, although I hesitate to call it such.[7] It begins by evaluating the most commonly held theories concerning educational purposes, authorities, and distributions, not simply for the sake of criticism but to develop a better theory, which integrates the strengths while avoiding the weaknesses of the standard views. The method will not satisfy strict foundationalists, who believe that any defensible political theory must begin by discovering some unquestionable or self-evident starting point, and build from the ground up (so to speak). I fear that even were I to discover such a starting point, I could not possibly build enough upon it to speak about educational issues of any political moment before this book, or my life, ended. The fear of foundationalists is the reverse, of course: that so much moral talk about politics and education is indefensible because it does not refer back to basic principles. Yet my dialectical method is not without foundations in this sense: it enables me to defend an internally consistent and intuitively acceptable set of basic premises and principles, basic at least with respect to our society.

An important advantage of this method over strict foundationalism

---

[6] Michael Walzer, *Spheres of Justice* (New York: Basic Books, 1983), p. 197.

[7] The reason for my hesitation is not that suggested by one of my high-school civics books, which defined dialectic as "the Communist manner of reasoning—a convenient substitute for standard logic." See Roger Swearingen, *The World of Communism* (New York: Houghton Mifflin, 1962), p. 247. Rather, I hesitate because the Aristotelian sense of the term has been all but lost in our ordinary language. Although the dialectical method cannot establish scientific knowledge (which must be based on truth, not just opinion), according to Aristotle, "dialectic is a process of criticism wherein lies the path to the principles of all inquiries." *Topica*, in *The Works of Aristotle*, trans. W. D. Ross, vol. 1 (Oxford: Oxford University Press, 1928), 101b3.

is that one can arrive at a democratic theory of education without first defending a conception of human nature upon which theories of education are typically constructed. The fallacy of relying on deductions from axioms of human nature is that most of the politically significant features of human character are products of our education. If education is what gives us our distinctive character, then we cannot determine the purposes of education by invoking an a priori theory of human nature. "Nature" may set the bounds beyond which a society cannot accomplish its educational purposes. But the constraints of nature surely leave societies a vast choice among competing educational purposes. Education may aim to *perfect* human nature by developing its potentialities, to *deflect* it into serving socially useful purposes, or to *defeat* it by repressing those inclinations that are socially destructive.[8] We can choose among and give content to these aims only by developing a normative theory of what the educational purposes of our society should be.

We have inherited not one but several such normative theories, which compete for our allegiance and account for many of our social disagreements as well as our personal uncertainties concerning the purposes of education. Three of the most distinct and distinguished of these theories can be drawn from interpretations of Plato, John Locke, and John Stuart Mill.[9] I call them (for reasons that will become apparent) the theories of the *family state*, the *state of families*, and the *state of individuals*. Despite their differences, each treats questions of education (its purposes, distributions, and authorities) as part of a principled *political* theory. That is the tradition within which I work, although I reject—or at least modify—the principles suggested by each of these theories in favor of a more democratic theory, which (I argue) supplies a more adequate ground for determining educational purposes, authority, and the distribution of educational goods for our society.

THE FAMILY STATE

Can we speak meaningfully about a good education without knowing what a just society and a virtuous person are? Socrates poses this challenge to the Sophists in the *Protagoras*. Like most of Socrates's

---

[8] Robert Fullinwider suggested this trilogy to me.

[9] It should go without saying that my aim in constructing these theories is not to offer an interpretation of Plato, Locke, and Mill that is faithful to their intentions or to the full range of their arguments. My aim is rather to *use* their theories to illuminate the principles underlying three of the most common and compelling political understandings of education in our society.

questions, it has remained unanswered after twenty-five centuries. But it is still worth re-asking.

In his critique of the Sophists and in the *Republic*, Plato suggests that we cannot speak about a good education without knowing what justice and virtue really are, rather than what a society assumes that they are by virtue of their shared social understandings. Justice, Socrates suggests, is the concurrent realization of individual and social good. Since the good life for individuals entails contributing to the social good, there is no necessary conflict between what is good for us and what is good for our society—provided our society is just. The defining feature of the family state is that it claims exclusive educational authority as a means of establishing a harmony—one might say, a constitutive relation—between individual and social good based on knowledge. Defenders of the family state expect to create a level of like-mindedness and camaraderie among citizens that most of us expect to find only within families (and now perhaps not even there).[10] The purpose of education in the family state is to cultivate that unity by teaching all educable children what the (sole) good life is for them and by inculcating in them a desire to pursue the good life above all inferior ones. Citizens of a well-ordered family state learn that they cannot realize their own good except by contributing to the social good, and they are also educated to desire only what is good for themselves and their society.

One need not accept Plato's view of natural human inequality to take seriously his theoretical defense of the family state. Once we discount this view, we can find in Plato the most cogent defense of the view that state authority over education is necessary for establishing a harmony between individual virtue and social justice. Unless children learn to associate their own good with the social good, a peaceful and prosperous society will be impossible. Unless the social good that they are taught is worthy of pursuit, they will grow to be unfulfilled and dissatisfied with the society that miseducated them. All states that claim less than absolute authority over the education of children will therefore degenerate out of internal disharmony.

It is important to emphasize that Plato's family state provides no sup-

---

[10] That we no longer assume (it may never have been accurate to do so) that families are "havens in a heartless world" does not prevent us from retaining the ideal of family life as a realm where parents and children identify their own good with the good of the whole. We are (perhaps increasingly) tempted to think along Platonic lines, however, that this identification is not sufficient to creating an ideal family life. A just division of work, of emotional support, and of the other rewards and burdens of family life between husband and wife may be another necessary part of our ideal. For better or for worse, the condition of familial justice may have become a prerequisite to achieving the condition of a harmonious identification of wills. Compare Michael J. Sandel, *Liberalism and the Limits of Justice* (New York: Cambridge University Press, 1982), pp. 33-34 and *passim*.

port for any educational authority that teaches children a way of life that cannot be rationally defended as morally superior to other ways of life. The state may not argue simply: "Because we wish to achieve social harmony, we shall indoctrinate all children to believe that *our* way of life is best." A reasonable response then would surely be: "But why should you have the authority to impose *your* way of thinking on the next generation. Why shouldn't I have the authority to impose *my* way?" And, of course, there will be many other reasonable people whose responses will be the same, but whose conceptions of the good life will be at odds with both mine and that of the state's educational authorities. On the Platonic argument, it is essential to the justice of the state's educational claims that its conception of the good life for every person be the *right* one.

Before pursuing the Platonic argument, we might consider a non-Platonic form of the family state, where educational authority is based not on the state's greater wisdom but on its status as the "political" parent of all its citizens. When the Laws and the Constitution of Athens speak to Socrates in the *Crito* of his duty to obey, they claim not that they are right but that they have a right to rule him: "Did we not give you life in the first place? Was it not through us that your father married your mother and begot you? . . . [S]ince you have been born and brought up and educated, can you deny, in the first place, that you were our child and servant, both you and your ancestors?"[11] The advantage of resting the authority of the family state on parental imagery is obvious: the state need not claim greater wisdom; it need only claim that it begot, brought up, and educated its citizens. This imagery is suggestive in some situations, but its moral force is doubtful as a defense of a state's right to educate—or to rule more generally—in disregard of the best interests or the moral convictions of its citizens. Because a family state is at best the *artificial* parent of its citizens, it must create the conditions under which citizens are bound to honor and obey it. The moral force of parental imagery in politics (as suggested by Socrates's subsequent arguments in the *Crito* concerning the freedom available to Athenian citizens) varies either with the degree to which the wisdom of a state exceeds that of its citizens or with the fit between the goods pursued by a state and those valued by its citizens.[12] A state that lacks wisdom or that rules against the moral convictions of most citizens cannot credibly claim parental status. Not even natural parents, moreover, may properly assert an absolute right to educate their children. I argue this

---

[11] *Crito*, in *The Last Days of Socrates*, trans. Hugh Tredennick (Harmondsworth: Penguin Books, 1970), pp. 90-91 (50b-51c).

[12] Ibid., pp. 92-93 (51c-52e).

later against the state of families, but need not pursue it here because citizens, after all, are not children, and states are at most metaphorical, not real, parents of their citizens.

The Platonic family state therefore rightly rejects the relativism of the non-Platonic family state, which would ground education on the mere opinions of state authorities, as readily as it rejects the subjectivism of Sophists, which defines a good education as one that simply satisfies the preferences of students. States that assume a parental role to educate according to false opinion are no better than Sophists who assume a professorial role to teach children virtue without knowing what virtue is. Indeed, sophistical states are worse because they wield more power.

But the Platonic family state has its own problems. The most obvious one is the difficulty of determining the best constitution for any society and the correct conception of the good for any person. Although this is a very serious problem, I shall not pursue it because it is not necessarily decisive for my argument.[13] After all, neither do we know that a single conception of justice and the good *cannot* be discovered. Even if discovery is improbable, the possibility of discovering something so valuable may justify subordinating other values to the search—perhaps even the freedoms of individuals to pursue what they believe to be a good life and to support what they believe to be a good society. Unless we can establish the value of these freedoms, we shall lack a sufficient moral argument against the claims of the family state. An argument based solely on skepticism about the possibility of discovering virtue and justice is not only inadequate but dangerous, because skepticism can also be used to defeat the claim that personal and political freedoms are valuable human goods.

The more telling criticism of the family state proceeds by accepting the possibility that someone sufficiently wise and conscientious might discover the good. She would then try to convince the rest of us that she had discovered *the* good, not just another contestable theory of the good, and the good for *us*, not just the good appropriate to some other people. It's possible that a few of us—an unusually open-minded or uncommitted few—might be convinced, but most of us (as Plato realized) would not; and we would refuse to relinquish all authority over the education of our children to the philosopher-queen (or the state).

In order to create a just family state, the philosopher therefore must wipe the social slate clean by exiling "all those in the city who happen to be older than ten; and taking over their children, . . . rear them—far

[13] See, for example, Karl Popper, *The Open Society and Its Enemies* (Princeton, N.J.: Princeton University Press, 1971), vol. 1, chs. 3 and 9, pp. 18-34, 157-68.

away from those dispositions they now have from their parents. . . ."[14]
That is an exorbitantly high price to pay for realizing a just society. Socrates himself on behalf of the philosopher recoils from the idea, suggesting that "he won't be willing to mind the political things . . . in his
fatherland unless some divine chance coincidentally comes to pass."[15]

This objection to the family state is not a purely practical one—
pointing to the impossibility of realizing a just society in an unjust
world. Even if the philosopher-queen is right in claiming that a certain
kind of life is objectively good, she is wrong in assuming that the objectively good is good for those of us who are too old or too miseducated
to identify the objectively good with what is good for our own lives.
"That may be the best life to which people—educated from birth in the
proper manner—can aspire," we might admit, "but it's not the good
life for *us*. And don't we have a claim to living a life that is good for
us?" The objectively good life, defined as the life that is best for people
who are rightly educated from birth, need not be the good life, or even
the closest approximation of the good life, for people who have been
wrongly educated. Could my personal identity be sustained were someone to succeed in imposing upon me (perhaps through brainwashing)
the consciousness and life suitable to the contemporary equivalent of a
Platonic guardian? Suppose that a life devoted to the *polis* but deprived
of a family and private property is objectively better than any I would
choose for myself. The question of personal identity still remains: Can
I live this life while still retaining my own identity? People who know
me well will strongly suspect that the answer is "no," even if they cannot offer a theory of personal identity that would confirm their suspi-
cions. If we would have to be stripped of our personal identities to become Platonic guardians, then the best life for *us* is less than the
objectively best on Platonic grounds.

What about a state that lets us live our less-than-objectively good
lives, but that insists on educating our children so they will not face the
same dilemma or create the same problem for the next generation of
citizens? Here a significant variant of the previous problem arises:
"Don't we also have a claim to try to perpetuate the way of life that
seems good to us within our families? After all, an essential part of *our*
good life is imparting an understanding of our values to our children."
We can say something similar about our good as citizens: "Don't we
also have a claim to participate in shaping the basic structure of our society? After all, an essential part of our good is the freedom to share in

   [14] *The Republic of Plato*, trans. Allan Bloom (New York: Basic Books, 1968), p. 220
(541a).
   [15] Ibid., p. 274 (592a).

shaping the society that in turn influences our very evaluation of a family and the degree to which different kinds of families flourish." The Platonic perspective refuses to recognize the force of these claims about *our* good. Yet these claims constitute the most forceful challenge to the philosopher-queen's claim to have discovered the good for us, even if she has discovered what is objectively good for our children. The cycle of imperfection must continue,[16] not merely because the costs of realizing the family state are too great, but because our good must be counted in any claim about what constitutes a just society for us and our children.[17] Our good might conceivably be overridden by the prospects of achieving the objectively good life for our children, but the objectively good is likely to be the fully operative good only for a society of orphaned infants.

If she is perfectly wise, the philosopher-queen must moderate her claims. Perhaps she may claim to know what is good for our children, but surely she may not claim the right to impose that good on them without taking our good, both as parents and as citizens, into account. If we now relax the rather absurd assumption that we can find a perfectly wise philosopher-queen, we shall want some assurance from even the wisest educational authority that our good as parents and as citizens, and not just the good of our children, will be considered in designing the educational system for our society. The only acceptable form of assurance is for parents and citizens both to have a significant share of educational authority.

If one begins with a society whose members all already agree about what is good (say, an entire society of Old Order Amish), then the moral dilemmas of personal identity and transformation costs may never arise. Unlike some contemporary theorists who in their criticisms of liberalism implicitly support a family state, Plato faces up to its more troubling implications. Part of Platonic wisdom is not to assume away the problems of founding a family state, but to recognize that the proc-

---

[16] Alternately, one might argue: If the philosopher-queen could convince us that her claims are correct, then the cycle of imperfection need not continue. But the only context in which she can be said to have convinced us (rather than to have manipulated our views by taking advantage of her monopoly on political power) is democratic. The family state therefore must become democratic to be legitimate.

[17] And, one might add, we can only know our good if our conception is uncoerced. Our conception must, to borrow a phrase from Bernard Williams, "grow from inside human life." The idea of an uncoerced conception of the good life, like the idea of an uncoerced social agreement on an ethical life, "implies free institutions, ones that allow not only for free inquiry but also for diversity of life and some ethical variety." See Bernard Williams, *Ethics and the Limits of Philosophy* (Cambridge, Mass.: Harvard University Press, 1985), pp. 172-73.

ess of creating social agreement on the good comes at a very high price, and to wonder whether the price is worth paying.

Yet Plato ultimately fails to recognize the moral implication of the fact that our attachments to (and disagreements over) the good run so deep, into our earliest education. Even if there is an objective ideal of the good for an imaginary society created out of orphaned infants, our good is relative to our education and the choices we are capable of making for ourselves, our children, and our communities. The objectively good life for us, we might say, must be a life that can fulfill us according to our best moral lights. This, I think, is the truth in educational relativism.[18] As long as we differ not just in our opinions but in our moral convictions about the good life, the state's educational role cannot be defined as realizing *the* good life, objectively defined, for each of its citizens. Neither can educational authorities simply claim that a good education is whatever in their opinion is best for the state.

The family state attempts to constrain our choices among ways of life and educational purposes in a way that is incompatible with our identity as parents and citizens. In its unsuccessful attempt to do so, it successfully demonstrates that we cannot ground our conception of a good education merely on personal or political preferences. Plato presents a forceful case for resting educational authority exclusively with a centralized state, a case grounded on the principle that knowledge should be translated into political power. But even the Platonic case is not sufficiently strong to override the claims of parents and citizens to share in social reproduction, claims to which I return in defending a democratic state of education.

THE STATE OF FAMILIES

States that aspire to the moral unity of families underestimate the strength and deny the legitimacy of the parental impulse to pass values on to children. Radically opposed to the family state is the state of families, which places educational authority exclusively in the hands of parents, thereby permitting parents to predispose their children, through education, to choose a way of life consistent with their familial heritage. Theorists of the state of families typically justify placing educational authority in the hands of parents on grounds either of consequences or of rights. John Locke maintained that parents are the best protectors of their children's future interests. Some Catholic theologians, following Thomas Aquinas, claim that parents have a natural right

---

[18] Cf. Bernard Williams, "The Truth in Relativism," in *Moral Luck* (New York: Cambridge University Press, 1981), pp. 132-43.

to educational authority. Many modern-day defenders of the state of families maintain both, and add another argument: if the state is committed to the freedom of individuals, then it must cede educational authority to parents whose freedom includes the right to pass their own way of life on to their children.[19] Charles Fried, for example, argues that "the right to form one's child's values, one's child's life plan and the right to lavish attention on the child are extensions of the basic right not to be interfered with in doing these things for oneself."[20] Fried bases parental rights over children on "the facts of reproduction" and the absence of a societal right to make choices for children. Fried's denial of a societal right is based on the consequentialist judgment that parents can be relied upon to pursue the best interests of their children.

Although the appeal of the state of families is apparent upon recognizing the defects of a family state, none of these theoretical arguments justifies resting educational authority exclusively—or even primarily—in the hands of parents. It is one thing to recognize the right (and responsibility) of parents to educate their children as members of a family, quite another to claim that this right of familial education extends to a right of parents to insulate their children from exposure to ways of life or thinking that conflict with their own. The consequentialist argument is surely unconvincing: parents cannot be counted upon to equip their children with the intellectual skills necessary for rational deliberation. Some parents, such as the Old Order Amish in America, are morally committed to shielding their children from all knowledge that might lead them to doubt and all worldly influences that might weaken their religious beliefs.[21] Many other parents, less radical in their rejec-

[19] For the former justification, see Milton Friedman, *Capitalism and Freedom* (Chicago: University of Chicago Press, 1962), pp. 85-107; and John E. Coons and Stephen Sugarman, *Education by Choice: The Case for Family Control* (Berkeley: University of California Press, 1978). For the latter, see Thomas Aquinas, *Supplement Summa Theologica un Divini Illius Magistri of His Holiness Pope Pius XI*, and a 1936 encyclical of the Catholic Church, where Aquinas is quoted as saying: "The child is naturally something of the father, . . . so by natural right the child before reaching the age of reason, is under the father's care. Hence it would be contrary to natural justice if any disposition were made concerning [the child] against the will of the parents." (Quoted in Francis Schrag, "The Right to Educate," *School Review*, vol. 79, no. 3 [May 1971]: 363.) Article 41 of the Irish Constitution also "recognizes the Family as the natural primary and fundamental unit group of Society, and as a moral institution, possessing inalienable and imprescriptible rights, antecedent and superior to all positive law." (Quoted in Walter F. Murphy, "An Ordering of Constitutional Values," *Southern California Law Review*, vol. 53, no. 2 [January 1980]: 739.)

[20] Charles Fried, *Right and Wrong* (Cambridge, Mass.: Harvard University Press, 1978), p. 152.

[21] See *Wisconsin v. Yoder*, 406 U.S. 210-11.

tion of modern society, are committed to teaching their children religious and racial intolerance.

To criticize the state of families, however, it is not enough to demonstrate that the perspectives of these parents are *wrong*, for we can never realistically expect any educational authority to be infallible. The strongest argument against the state of families is that neither parents nor a centralized state have a right to exclusive authority over the education of children. Because children are members of both families and states, the educational authority of parents and of polities has to be partial to be justified. We appreciate the danger of permitting a centralized state to monopolize education largely for this reason. The similar danger of placing all authority in the hands of parents may be less widely appreciated, at least in the United States, because support for parental authority over education has been associated historically with Lockean liberalism. Because the Lockean state cedes adult citizens the freedom to choose their own good, many liberals (like Fried) assume that it must also cede parents the freedom to educate their children without state interference.[22] To the worry that parents might abuse their authority, many liberals invoke a secular variant of Locke's response:

> God hath woven into the Principles of Human Nature such a tenderness for their Off-spring, that there is little fear that Parents should use their power with too much rigour; the excess is seldom on the severe side, the strong byass of Nature drawing the other way.[23]

Other liberals, more critical of the state of families, call Locke's premise into question by citing the prevalence of physical child abuse in this country. But one need not dispute Locke's claim about the direction and force of "Nature's byass" to conclude that parental instincts are an insufficient reason for resting educational authority exclusively in the family. The same principle that requires a state to grant adults personal and political freedom also commits it to assuring children an education that makes those freedoms both possible and meaningful in the future. A state makes choice possible by teaching its future citizens respect for opposing points of view and ways of life. It makes choice meaningful by equipping children with the intellectual skills necessary to evaluate ways of life different from that of their parents. History sug-

---

[22] The Lockean argument, therefore, does not depend for its force, as some critics have maintained, on the claim that children are the property of their parents, a claim that Locke himself rejected.

[23] Locke, "The Second Treatise of Government," in *Two Treatises of Government*, intro. Peter Laslett (New York: Cambridge University Press, 1960), ch. 6, sec. 67, p. 355.

gests that without state provision or regulation of education, children will be taught neither mutual respect among persons nor rational deliberation among ways of life. To save their children from future pain, especially the pain of eternal damnation, parents have historically shielded their children from diverse associations, convinced them that all other ways of life are sinful, and implicitly fostered (if not explicitly taught them) disrespect for people who are different. This spirit is inimical to the kind of liberal character that Locke argued that parents should teach their children.[24] The end—moral freedom—that Locke recommends in his *Essay on Education* requires us to question the means—exclusive parental authority—that Locke defends in the *Second Treatise*, once we can assume (as Locke could not) the political possibility of dividing educational authority between families and the state.

This argument against exclusive parental authority depends neither upon parental ignorance nor upon irrationality. From the perspective of individual parents who desire above all to perpetuate their particular way of life, teaching disrespect for differing ways of life need not be irrational even if the outcome turns out to be undesirable. For many deeply religious parents, mutual respect is a public good (in the strict economic sense). As long as they have reason to believe that their religion will continue to be respected, they need not worry about teaching their children to respect other religions. But even if they can foresee a serious threat to their religion in the future, they still have no reason to believe that they can solve (or even ameliorate) the problem by teaching their children to respect the disrespectful.

American history provides an informative example. Many public schools in the mid-nineteenth century were, to say the least, disrespectful of Catholicism. Catholic children who attended these schools were often humiliated, sometimes whipped for refusing to read the King James version of the Bible. Imagine that instead of becoming more respectful, public schools had been abolished, and states had subsidized parents to send their children to the private school of their choice. Protestant parents would have sent their children to Protestant schools, Catholic parents to Catholic schools. The Protestant majority would have continued to educate their children to be disrespectful if not intolerant of Catholics. The religious prejudices of Protestant parents would have been visited on their children, and the social, economic, and political effects of those prejudices would have persisted, probably with considerably less public protest, to this very day. There may be little

[24] For an interpretation of Locke's understanding of liberal character, see Nathan Tarcov, *Locke's Education for Liberty* (Chicago: University of Chicago Press, 1984).

reason today for Catholic parents to worry that privatizing schools will reinstitutionalize bigotry against Catholics, at least in the short run. But one reason that Catholics need not worry is that a state of families today would be built on the moral capital created over almost a century by a public school system. That moral capital is just now being created for blacks and Hispanics, and even more well-established minorities might reasonably fear that returning to a state of families would eventually squander the moral capital created by public schooling.

Like most collective goods, the "costs" of mutual respect among citizens may have to be imposed on everyone to avoid the free-rider problem. But this virtue is a cost only to parents who do not accept its intrinsic moral worth. The state of families can overcome the free-rider problem by violating its basic premise of parental supremacy in education and requiring all parents to let schools teach their children mutual respect. For children who are not yet free (in any case) to make their own choices, teaching the lesson of mutual respect is not a cost. It is both an instrumental good and a good worth valuing on its own account. Teaching mutual respect is instrumental to assuring all children the freedom to choose in the future. It is a good in itself to all citizens who are not yet committed to a way of life that precludes respect for other ways of life.

The state of families mistakenly conflates the welfare of children with the freedom of parents when it assumes that the welfare of children is best defined or secured by the freedom of parents. But the state of families rightly recognizes, as the family state does not, the value of parental freedom, at least to the extent that such freedom does not interfere with the interests of children in becoming mutually respectful citizens of a society that sustains family life. There is no simple solution to the tension between the freedom of parents and the welfare of children. The state may not grant parents absolute authority over their children's education in the name of individual freedom, nor may it claim exclusive educational authority in the name of communal solidarity. That there is no *simple* solution, however, should not deter us from searching for a better solution than that offered by either the family state or the state of families.

The attractions of the state of families are apparent to most Americans: by letting parents educate their own children as they see fit, the state avoids all the political battles that rage over the content of public education. The state of families also appears to foster pluralism by permitting many ways of life to be perpetuated in its midst. But both these attractions are only superficial in a society where many parents would teach racism, for example, in the absence of political pressure to do otherwise. States that abdicate all educational authority to parents sacrifice their most effective and justifiable instrument for securing mutual respect among their citizens.

The "pluralism" commonly identified with the state of families is superficial because its internal variety serves as little more than an ornament for onlookers. Pluralism is an important political value insofar as social diversity enriches our lives by expanding our understanding of differing ways of life. To reap the benefits of social diversity, children must be exposed to ways of life different from their parents and—in the course of their exposure—must embrace certain values, such as mutual respect among persons, that make social diversity both possible and desirable. There is no reason to assume that placing educational authority exclusively in the hands of parents is the best way of achieving these ends, and good reason to reject the claim that, regardless of the consequences for individual citizens or for society as a whole, parents have a natural right to exclusive educational authority over their children. Children are no more the property of their parents than they are the property of the state.

The State of Individuals

"It is in the case of children," John Stuart Mill argued, "that misapplied notions of liberty are a real obstacle to the fulfillment by the State of its duties. One would almost think that a man's children were supposed to be literally, and not metaphorically, a part of himself, so jealous is opinion of the smallest interference of law with his absolute and exclusive control over them. . . ."[25] Having exposed the central flaw in the state of families, Mill defended a more liberal conception of education. "All attempts by the State to bias the conclusions of its citizens on disputed subjects are evil," Mill argued. Some contemporary liberals extend the logic of Mill's argument to defend what I call a state of individuals.[26] They criticize all educational authorities that threaten to

[25] Mill, *On Liberty*, ch. 5, para. 12.

[26] Mill himself suggested an educational policy often associated with the state of families: the government should "leave to parents to obtain the education where and how they pleased, and content itself with helping to pay the school fees of the poorer classes of children . . ." (*On Liberty*, ch. 5, para. 13). There are, however, two significant differences between Mill's defense of private schools and that of the state of families. (1) Mill's preference for private control of schools follows not from a principled defense of parental choice but from an empirical presumption that state control of schools leads to repression ("a despotism over the mind"). Since absolute parental control over education also threatens despotism over children's minds, it is as suspect on Millean grounds. (2) Perhaps for this reason, Mill severely limits the educational authority of parents by (among other things) a system of "public examinations, extending to all children and beginning at an early age." If a child fails the examination, Mill recommends that "the father, unless

bias the choices of children toward some disputed or controversial ways of life and away from others. Their ideal educational authority is one that maximizes future choice without prejudicing children towards any controversial conception of the good life. The state of individuals thus responds to the weakness of both the family state and the state of families by championing the dual goals of *opportunity* for choice and *neutrality* among conceptions of the good life. A just educational authority must not bias children's choices among good lives, but it must provide every child with an opportunity to choose freely and rationally among the widest range of lives.

If neutrality is what we value, then a child must be protected from all—or at least all controversial—social prejudices. Neither parents nor states are capable of fulfilling this educational ideal. Parents are unlikely (and unwilling) to resist a strong human impulse: the desire to pass some of their particular prejudices on to their children. And even the most liberal states are bound to subvert the neutrality principle: they will try, quite understandably, to teach children to appreciate the basic (but disputed) values and the dominant (but controversial) cultural prejudices that hold their society together.[27]

Recognizing the power of these parental and political impulses, some liberals look for an educational authority more impartial than parents or public officials—"experts" or professional educators—motivated solely, or at least predominantly, by the interests of children in learning and unconstrained by parental or political authority. I suspect that were professional educators ever to rule, they would convince everyone, albeit unintentionally, that liberal neutrality is an unlivable ideal. But as long as we focus our critical attention on the detrimental effects of parental and political prejudices, we are likely to overlook the limitations of the neutrality ideal, and the tension between it and the ideal of opportunity. Children may grow to have a greater range of choice (and to live more satisfying lives) if their education is biased by those values favored by their society. Bentham and Kant both recognized this. Kant defended—as one of four essential parts of a basic education—teaching children the kind of "discretion" associated with "refinement" of manners, which "changes according to the ever-changing

---

he has some sufficient ground of excuse, might be subjected to a moderate fine, to be worked out, if necessary, by his labor. . . ." To insure neutrality, the knowledge tested by the examinations should "be confined to facts and positive science exclusively" (ch. 5, para. 14).

[27] I assume from here on the understanding that liberalism aims at neutrality only among disputed or controversial conceptions of the good. I therefore omit further use of the adjectives "disputed" or "controversial."

tastes of different ages."[28] One of the primary aims of education, according to Bentham, was to secure for children "admission into and agreeable intercourse with good company."[29]

Contemporary liberal theorists often invoke the spirit of Bentham, Kant, or Mill to defend the ideal of neutrality, overlooking both its moral limitations and the substantial qualifications that each of these theorists placed on the ideal. All sophisticated liberals recognize the practical limitation of neutrality as an educational ideal: it is, in its fullest form, unrealizable. But most fail to appreciate the value of our resistance to the ideal of unprejudiced individual freedom: the value of our desire to cultivate, and allow communities to cultivate, only a select range of choice for children, to prune and weed their desires and aspirations so they are likely to choose a worthy life and sustain a flourishing society when they mature and are free to choose for themselves. Bruce Ackerman argues:

> Such horticultural imagery has no place in a liberal theory of education. We have no right [and the state has no right] to look upon future citizens as if we were master gardeners who can tell the difference between a pernicious weed and a beautiful flower. A system of liberal education provides children with a sense of the very different lives that could be theirs.[30]

But what *kind* of sense do we want to provide? Of *which* very different lives? Ackerman, like all sensible liberals, recognizes that the capacity for rational choice requires that we place some prior limitations on children's choices. To have a rational sense of what we want to become, we need to know who we are; otherwise our choices will be endless and meaningless.[31] We learn to speak English rather than Urdu, not by choice, but by cultural determination.[32] And this cultural determination limits the range of our future choices, even if it does not uniquely determine who we become. Ackerman identifies this prior determination with the need for "cultural coherence," which he uses to justify the family and its nonneutral education. The need for cultural coherence, Ackerman argues, does not justify "adult pretensions to moral superiority."[33] Neither parents nor the state may shape the character of chil-

---

[28] Kant, *Kant on Education*, p. 19.

[29] Jeremy Bentham, *Chrestomathia* (1816), in *The Works of Jeremy Bentham* (Edinburgh, 1843), p. 10.

[30] Ackerman, *Social Justice*, p. 139.

[31] This is an insight common to critics of liberalism. See, e.g., Sandel, *Liberalism and the Limits of Justice*, esp. pp. 161-65, 168-83.

[32] Ackerman, *Social Justice*, p. 141.

[33] Ibid., p. 148.

dren on the grounds that they can distinguish between better and worse
moral character, yet they may shape children's character for the sake of
cultural coherence, or in order to maximize their future freedom of
choice.

Why, one might ask, should parents and states be free to shape children's character and guide their choices for the sake of cultural coherence but not for the sake of their leading morally good lives? Sometimes
the claim that we know better than children the difference between
morally good and bad lives is not a pretension to moral superiority, but
a reflection of our greater moral maturity. Why, then, should adults resist shaping children's character and guiding their choices on *moral*
grounds?

The resistance of many contemporary liberals to one of our strongest
moral impulses stems, I suspect, from formulating educational purposes and their justifications as a dichotomous choice.[34] Either we must
educate children so that they are free to choose among the widest range
of lives (given the constraints of cultural coherence) because freedom
of choice is the paramount good, or we must educate children so that
they will choose *the* life that we believe is best because leading a virtuous life is the paramount good. Let children define their own identity
or define it for them. Give children liberty or give them virtue. Neither
alternative is acceptable: we legitimately value education not just for
the liberty but also for the virtue that it bestows on children; and the
virtue that we value includes the ability to deliberate among competing
conceptions of the good.

But precisely which virtues do "we" value? No set of virtues remains
undisputed in the United States, or in any modern society that allows
its members to dispute its dominant understandings. The problem in
using education to bias children towards some conceptions of the good
life and away from others stems not from pretense on the part of educators to moral superiority over children but from an assertion on their
part to political authority over other citizens who reject their conception of virtue. Neutrality is no more acceptable a solution to this problem than the use of education to inculcate a nonneutral set of virtues.
Neither choice—to teach or not to teach virtue—is uncontroversial.
Neither avoids the problem of instituting an educational authority
whose aims are not universally accepted among adult citizens. The decision not to teach virtue (or, more accurately, to teach only the virtues
of free choice) faces opposition by citizens who can claim, quite reason-

---

[34] The tendency to dichotomize our moral choices is not unique to advocates of liberal
neutrality. What I call the "tyranny of dualisms" is also common to communitarian critics of liberalism. See my "Communitarian Critics of Liberalism," *Philosophy and Public
Affairs*, vol. 14, no. 5 (Summer 1985): 316-20.

ably, that freedom of choice is not the only, or even the primary, purpose of education. Why should these citizens be forced to defer to the view that children must be educated for freedom rather than for virtue? Liberals might reply that freedom is the *correct* end of education. This reply is inadequate, because being right is neither a necessary nor a sufficient condition for claiming the right to shape the character of future citizens.

Because the educational ideal of free choice commands no *special* political legitimacy, the state of individuals poses the same problem as the family state. Even if liberals could establish that, of all disputed aims of education, neutrality is singularly right, they would still have to establish why being right is a necessary or sufficient condition for ruling. The same argument that holds against the family state holds against the state of individuals: being right is not a necessary or sufficient condition because parents and citizens have a legitimate interest (independent of their "rightness") in passing some of their most salient values on to their children.

Proponents of the state of individuals might argue that they avoid the problem of the family state by offering a principled solution morally distinct from that of the family state: authorize only those authorities whose educational techniques maximize the future freedom of children. They try, as Ackerman does and I once did,[35] to justify pruning children's desires solely on liberal paternalistic grounds: by restricting the freedom of children when they are young, we increase it over their lifetimes. Although the liberal state is often contrasted to the family state, its end of individual freedom is subject to a similar challenge. Why must freedom be the sole end of education, given that most of us value things that conflict with freedom? We value, for example, the moral sensibility that enables us to discriminate between good and bad lives, and the character that inclines us to choose good rather than bad lives.[36] A well-cultivated moral character constrains choice among lives at least as much as it expands choice. Why prevent teachers from cultivating moral character by biasing the choices of children toward good lives and, if necessary, by constraining the range of lives that children are capable of choosing when they mature?

Liberals occasionally reply that the standard of freedom supports such moral education. When teachers or parents admonish children not to be lazy, for example, the implicit purpose of their admonition is to expand the future freedom of children by encouraging them to become

---

[35] See Amy Gutmann, "Children, Paternalism and Education: A Liberal Argument," *Philosophy and Public Affairs*, vol. 9, no. 4 (Summer 1980): 338-58.

[36] For an excellent account of moral freedom, see Susan Wolf, "Asymmetrical Freedom," *The Journal of Philosophy* (1980): 151-66.

the kind of people who have the greatest range of choice later in life.[37] This reply begs two crucial questions: Is such an admonition easier to justify because it furthers the freedom of children rather than cultivates a virtue? Is the aim of educating children for freedom as fully compatible with teaching them virtue as this example suggests?

The answer to each question, I suspect, is "no," because both educational ends—freedom and virtue—are controversial, and neither is inclusive. To establish a privileged place for freedom as *the* aim of education, liberals would have to demonstrate that freedom is the singular social good, a demonstration that cannot succeed in a society where citizens sometimes (one need not claim always) value virtue above freedom. Were freedom of choice an inclusive good such that teaching children to choose entailed teaching them virtue, then the debate between whether to educate for freedom or for virtue would be academic. It's not academic, because an education for freedom and for virtue part company in any society whose citizens are free not to act virtuously, yet it is at least as crucial to cultivate virtue in a free society as it is in one where citizens are constrained to act virtuously. The admonition not to be lazy may serve the cause of cultivating virtue rather than maximizing children's freedom in an affluent society that offers generous benefits to the unemployed, but why should it be any more suspect on this account? Neither aim of education is neutral, and each can exclude the other, at least in some instances. Assuming that some citizens value virtue, others freedom, and the two aims do not support identical pedagogical practices, the more liberal aim cannot claim a privileged political position. Educators need not be bound to maximize the future choices of children if freedom is not the only value.

By what standards then, if any, are educators bound to teach? After criticizing the liberal paternalistic standard—constrain the present freedom of children only if necessary to maximize their future freedom—we are left with the problem of finding another standard that can justify a necessarily nonneutral education in the face of social disagreement concerning what constitutes the proper aim of education. Shifting the grounds of justification from future freedom to some other substantive end—such as happiness, autonomy, intellectual excellence, salvation, or social welfare—only re-creates the same problem. None of these standards is sufficiently inclusive to solve the problem of justification in the face of dissent by citizens whose conception of the good life and the good society threatens to be undermined by the conception of a good (but necessarily nonneutral) education instituted by some (necessarily exclusive) educational authority.

---

[37] Ackerman suggests this rationale in *Social Justice*, pp. 147-49.

Our task therefore is to find a more inclusive ground for justifying nonneutrality in education. We disagree over the relative value of freedom and virtue, the nature of the good life, and the elements of moral character. But our desire to search for a more inclusive ground presupposes a common commitment that is, broadly speaking, political. We are committed to collectively re-creating the society that we share. Although we are not collectively committed to any particular set of educational aims, we are committed to arriving at an agreement on our educational aims (an agreement that could take the form of justifying a diverse set of educational aims and authorities). The substance of this core commitment is conscious social reproduction. As citizens, we aspire to a set of educational practices and authorities of which the following can be said: these are the practices and authorities to which we, acting collectively as a society, have consciously agreed. It follows that a society that supports conscious social reproduction must educate all educable children to be capable of participating in collectively shaping their society.

Conscious social reproduction, like any educational end, is not self-evidently correct or uncontroversial. But it is a minimally problematical end insofar as it leaves maximum room for citizens collectively to shape education in their society. A society committed to conscious social reproduction has a compelling response to those adults who object to the form or the content of education on grounds that it indirectly subverts or directly conflicts with their moral values. "The virtues and moral character we are cultivating," the educational authorities can reply in the first instance, "are necessary to give children the chance collectively to shape their society. The kind of character you are asking us to cultivate would deprive children of that chance, the very chance that legitimates your own claim to educational authority." If the challenge is directed to the teaching of values that directly conflict with those of some citizens, then the response to dissenting adults can take the following form: "The values we are teaching are the product of a collective decision to which you were party. Insofar as that decision deprives no one of the opportunity to participate in future decisions, its outcome is legitimate, even if it is not correct."[38]

I have yet to elaborate and defend the democratic theory of education that would fully justify these responses, but assuming for the moment that this is the kind of defense that any nonneutral education de-

[38] If as a result of the decision, someone is deprived of the opportunity to participate in future decisions, or if the decisionmaking process is not truly collective, then this response is unwarranted. In the first instance (as I later clarify), the content of the decision renders it repressive; in the second, the decisionmaking process is discriminatory.

mands, a substantial truth in the liberal educational ideal would remain: it would be an illegitimate pretension to educational authority on anyone's part to deprive any child of the capacities necessary for choice among good lives. The pretension would be illegitimate for two reasons. First: even if I know that my way of life is best, I cannot translate this claim into the claim that I have a right to impose my way of life on anyone else, even on my own child, at the cost of depriving her of the capacity to choose a good life. Second: many if not all of the capacities necessary for choice among good lives are also necessary for choice among good societies. A necessary (but not sufficient) condition of conscious social reproduction is that citizens have the capacity to deliberate among alternative ways of personal and political life. To put this point in more "liberal" language: a good life and a good society for self-reflective people require (respectively) individual and collective freedom of choice.

But neither a good life nor a good society require *maximizing* freedom of choice. Educational authorities may teach children that religious intolerance and racial bigotry (for example) are wrong without claiming that the justification for their nonneutrality is the future freedom of children. The justification for teaching these virtues is that they constitute the kind of character necessary to create a society committed to conscious social reproduction. We need not claim that this kind of society—a democracy—is justified "*sub specie aeternitatis*"[39] to defend its unique legitimacy for us. Most Americans are committed to sharing sovereignty with each other and almost all who are uncommitted are unwilling to live the kind of life that would result from their rejection of this fundamental democratic premise.

One might still wonder what accounts for the widespread appeal of the liberal ideal of neutrality if it is so mistaken. I suspect that its broad appeal rests on a healthy suspicion of claims to moral superiority among educators. The history of schooling in this country (and every other) is full of false claims by educational authorities to moral superiority. In the course of raising our children, we probably have made some ourselves. Reflecting on these rather frequent lapses, we may become suspicious of all such claims. No credible theory of education, however, supports all assertions of moral superiority or all moral distinctions that adults make in their role as educators. But neither can any credible theory deny the legitimacy of all such claims. A democratic theory of education, I later argue, requires us to challenge the propriety of some claims and distinctions: the claim, for example, that one race is inherently superior to another, or, to take a more controversial ex-

---

[39] Cf. Rawls, *A Theory of Justice*, p. 587.

ample, the claim that a woman's place is in the home. In admitting moral distinctions among lives and characters, we bear the burden of differentiating between legitimate and spurious moral distinctions. The state of individuals promises to relieve citizens of this burden by using education to free all children to make their own discriminations. Yet we have seen that accepting freedom as the goal of education does not provide an escape from the burden of choosing (on some grounds) among the many possible lives that children can be taught to appreciate.

Liberals who still insist on defending neutrality might give a more practical reason for admitting cultural prejudices but not moral discriminations into the educational process: it may be harder to agree collectively on moral discriminations than on cultural prejudices. Requiring that all children be taught English, for example, may at one time in American history have seemed to be less controversial than requiring that they all be taught religious toleration. In order to reach a collective moral agreement on the principles of schooling, on this argument, we must agree not to admit our moral disagreements into our public deliberations over educational means and ends.

Perhaps this argument was once soundly prudential, but its premise is surely very shaky today. If recent political battles over bilingualism are any evidence, teaching cultural prejudice is just as controversial as teaching moral principle, perhaps because our political principles are so closely tied to our cultural prejudices. But even if we grant the premise, the liberal neutrality position fares no better by this reasoning than what one might call the moralist position. To a moralist who believes that a primary purpose of education is to cultivate good character, a view that denies the justice of this educational purpose is just as controversial as a view that offers a direct challenge to the idea that a certain kind of character is good or bad. It makes more sense, on both prudential and democratic grounds, to admit the direct challenge and to take the chance that we might lose the political battle to teach religious toleration as a virtue, for example, rather than give up any chance that education will serve one of its primary purposes—cultivating the kind of character conducive to democratic sovereignty.

A DEMOCRATIC STATE OF EDUCATION

Cultivating character is a legitimate—indeed, an inevitable—function of education. And there are many kinds of moral character—each consistent with conscious social reproduction—that a democratic state may legitimately cultivate. Who should decide what kind of character to cultivate? I have examined and rejected three popular and philosophically forceful answers to this question. Theorists of the family state rest educational authority exclusively in the hands of a centralized state in a mistaken attempt to wed knowledge of the good life with political power. Theorists of the state of families place educational authority exclusively in the hands of parents, on the unfounded assumption that they have a natural right to such authority or that they will thereby maximize the welfare of their children. Theorists of the state of individuals refuse to rest educational authority in any hands without the assurance that the choices of children will not be prejudiced in favor of some ways of life and against others—an assurance that no educator can or should be expected to provide.

If my criticisms are correct, then these three theories are wrong. None provides an adequate foundation for educational authority. Yet each contains a partial truth. States, parents, and professional educators all have important roles to play in cultivating moral character. A democratic state of education recognizes that educational authority must be shared among parents, citizens, and professional educators even though such sharing does not guarantee that power will be wedded to knowledge, that parents can successfully pass their prejudices on to their children, or that education will be neutral among competing conceptions of the good life.

If a democratic state of education does not guarantee virtue based on knowledge, or the autonomy of families, or neutrality among ways of life, what is the value of its premise of shared educational authority? The broad distribution of educational authority among citizens, parents, and professional educators supports the core value of democracy: conscious social reproduction in its most inclusive form. Unlike a family state, a democratic state recognizes the value of parental education in perpetuating particular conceptions of the good life. Unlike a state of families, a democratic state recognizes the value of professional authority in enabling children to appreciate and to evaluate ways of life other than those favored by their families. Unlike a state of individuals, a democratic state recognizes the value of political education in predisposing children to accept those ways of life that are consistent with sharing the rights and responsibilities of citizenship in a democratic society. A democratic state is therefore committed to allocating educational authority in such a way as to provide its members with an education adequate to participating in democratic politics, to choosing among (a limited range of) good lives, and to sharing in the several subcommunities, such as families, that impart identity to the lives of its citizens.

A democratic state of education constrains choice among good lives not only out of necessity but out of a concern for civic virtue. Democratic states can acknowledge two reasons for permitting communities to use education to predispose children toward some ways of life and away from others. One reason is grounded on the value of moral freedom, a value not uniquely associated with democracy. All societies of self-reflective beings must admit the moral value of enabling their members to discern the difference between good and bad ways of life. Children do not learn to discern this difference on the basis of an education that strives for neutrality among ways of life. Children are not taught that bigotry is bad, for example, by offering it as one among many competing conceptions of the good life, and then subjecting it to criticism on grounds that bigots do not admit that other people's conceptions of the good are "equally" good. Children first become the kind of people who are repelled by bigotry, and then they feel the force of the reasons for their repulsion. The liberal reasons to reject bigotry are quite impotent in the absence of such sensibilities: they offer no compelling argument to people who feel no need to treat other people as equals and are willing to live with the consequences of their disrespect. To cultivate in children the character that feels the force of right reason is an essential purpose of education in any society.

The second, more specifically democratic, reason for supporting the nonneutral education of states and families is that the good of children includes not just freedom of choice, but also identification with and participation in the good of their family and the politics of their society. The need for cultural coherence does not fully capture this democratic value, because it would not be enough for a centralized state to choose a set of parents and a coherent cultural orientation at random for children. People, quite naturally, value the specific cultural and political orientations of their society and family more than those of others, even if they cannot provide objective reasons for their preferences. The fact that these cultural orientations are theirs is an adequate (and generalizable) reason. Just as we love our (biological or adopted) children more than those of our friends because they are a part of *our* family, so we differentially value the cultural orientations of our country because it is *ours*. We need not claim moral superiority (or ownership) to say any of this. We need claim only that some ways of life are better than others *for us and our children* because these orientations impart meaning to and enrich the internal life of family and society. To focus exclusively on the value of freedom, or even on the value of moral freedom, neglects the value that parents and citizens may legitimately place on *partially* prejudicing the choices of children by their familial and political heritages.

In authorizing (but not requiring) democratic states and families within them to predispose children to particular ways of life, we integrate the insights of both the family state and the state of families into a democratic theory of education. But in doing so, we do not necessarily avoid the weakness of both theories in sanctioning the imposition of a noncritical consciousness on children. To avoid this weakness, a democratic state must aid children in developing the capacity to understand and to evaluate competing conceptions of the good life and the good society. The value of critical deliberation among good lives and good societies would be neglected by a society that inculcated in children uncritical acceptance of any particular way or ways of (personal and political) life. Children might then be taught to accept uncritically the set of beliefs, say, that supports the view that the only acceptable role for women is to serve men and to raise children. A society that inculcated such a sexist set of values would be undemocratic not because sexist values are wrong (although I have no doubt that they are, at least for our society), but because that society failed to secure any space for educating children to deliberate critically among a range of good lives and good societies. To integrate the value of critical deliberation among good lives, we must defend some principled limits on political and parental authority over education, limits that in practice require parents and states to cede some educational authority to professional educators.

One limit is that of *nonrepression*. The principle of nonrepression prevents the state, and any group within it, from using education to restrict rational deliberation of competing conceptions of the good life and the good society. Nonrepression is not a principle of negative freedom. It secures freedom from interference only to the extent that it forbids using education to restrict *rational* deliberation or consideration of different ways of life. Nonrepression is therefore compatible with the use of education to inculcate those character traits, such as honesty, religious toleration, and mutual respect for persons, that serve as foundations for rational deliberation of differing ways of life. Nor is nonrepression a principle of positive liberty, as commonly understand. Although it secures more than a freedom from interference, the "freedom to" that it secures is not a freedom to pursue the singularly correct way of personal or political life, but the freedom to deliberate rationally among differing ways of life.[40] Rational deliberation should be secured, I have argued, not because it is neutral among all ways of life—even all decent ways of life. Rational deliberation makes some ways of life—such as that of the Old Order Amish—more difficult to pursue insofar as dedication to such lives depends upon resistance to rational deliber-

[40] For a conceptual analysis of freedom that fits my understanding of rational freedom, see Gerald C. MacCallum, Jr., "Negative and Positive Freedom," *Philosophical Review* 76 (1967): 312-34. Reprinted in Richard E. Flathman, ed., *Concepts in Social and Political Philosophy* (New York: Macmillan, 1973), pp. 294-308.

ation. Rational deliberation remains the form of freedom most suitable to a democratic society in which adults must be free to deliberate and disagree but constrained to secure the intellectual grounds for deliberation and disagreement among children. Adults must therefore be prevented from using their present deliberative freedom to undermine the future deliberative freedom of children. Although nonrepression constitutes a limit on democratic authority, its defense thus derives from the primary value of democratic education. Because *conscious* social reproduction is the primary ideal of democratic education, communities must be prevented from using education to stifle rational deliberation of competing conceptions of the good life and the good society.

A second principled limit on legitimate democratic authority, which also follows from the primary value of democratic education, is *nondiscrimination*. For democratic education to support conscious *social* reproduction, all educable children must be educated. Nondiscrimination extends the logic of nonrepression, since states and families can be selectively repressive by excluding entire groups of children from schooling or by denying them an education conducive to deliberation among conceptions of the good life and the good society. Repression has commonly taken the more passive form of discrimination in schooling against racial minorities, girls, and other disfavored groups of children. The effect of discrimination is often to repress, at least temporarily, the capacity and even the desire of these groups to participate in the processes that structure choice among good lives. Nondiscrimination can thus be viewed as the distributional complement to nonrepression. In its most general application to education, nondiscrimination prevents the state, and all groups within it, from denying anyone an educational good on grounds irrelevant to the legitimate social purpose of that good. Applied to those forms of education necessary to prepare children for future citizenship (participation in conscious social reproduction), the nondiscrimination principle becomes a principle of nonexclusion. No educable child may be excluded from an education adequate to participating in the political processes that structure choice among good lives.

Why is a theory that accepts these two principled constraints on popular (and parental) sovereignty properly considered democratic? Democratic citizens are persons partially constituted by subcommunities (such as their family, their work, play, civic, and religious groups), yet free to choose a way of life compatible with their larger communal identity because no single subcommunity commands absolute authority over their education, and because the larger community has equipped them for deliberating and thereby participating in the democratic processes by which choice among good lives and the chance to pursue them are politically structured. The principles of nonrepression and nondiscrimination simultaneously support deliberative freedom and communal self-determination. The form of educational relativism acceptable under these principles is therefore democratic in a significant sense: all citizens must be educated so as to have a chance to share in self-consciously shaping the structure of their society. Democratic education is not neutral among conceptions of the good life, nor does its defense depend on a claim to neutrality. Democratic education is bound to restrict pursuit, although not conscious consideration, of ways of life dependent on the suppression of politically relevant knowledge. Democratic education supports choice among those ways of life that are compatible with conscious social reproduction.

Nondiscrimination requires that *all* educable children be educated adequately to participate as citizens in shaping the future structure of their society. Their democratic participation as adults, in turn, shapes the education of the next generation of children, within the constraints set by nondiscrimination and nonrepression. These principles permit families and other subcommunities to shape but not totally to determine their children's future choices, in part by preventing any single group from monopolizing educational authority and in part by permitting (indeed, obligating) professional educators to develop in children the deliberative capacity to evaluate competing conceptions of good lives and good societies. Democratic education thus appreciates the value of education as a means of creating (or re-creating) cohesive communities and of fostering deliberative choice without elevating either of these partial purposes to an absolute or overriding end.

Like the family state, a democratic state of education tries to teach virtue—not the virtue of the family state (power based upon knowledge), but what might best be called *democratic* virtue: the ability to deliberate, and hence to participate in conscious social reproduction. Like the state of families, a democratic state upholds a degree of parental authority over education, resisting the strong communitarian view that children are creatures of the state. But in recognizing that children are future citizens, the democratic state resists the view, implicit in the state of families, that children are creatures of their parents. Like the state of individuals, a democratic state defends a degree of professional authority over education—not on grounds of liberal neutrality, but to the extent necessary to provide children with the capacity to evaluate those ways of life most favored by parental and political authorities.

In the chapters that follow, I treat the theory just sketched as a guide to moral reasoning rather than as a set of rigid rules from which we can logically derive public policies. The theory of democratic education builds upon a critique of the most influential existing theories rather than upon a closed system of self-evident axioms, an original position, or a neutral dialogue. It makes no claim to being a logically tight system of axioms, principles, and conclusions that flow from them. Nor does it claim to command our allegiance independently of its congruence with our deepest convictions. The distinctive virtue of a democratic theory of education is that its principles and conclusions are compatible with our commitment to share the rights and the obligations of citizenship with people who do not share our complete conception of the good life. To the extent that Americans share (or insist on living in a way that requires us to share) this commitment, a democratic theory of education commands our allegiance.

CHAPTER TWO

THE PURPOSES OF
PRIMARY EDUCATION

"Education, in a great measure, forms the moral characters of men, and morals are the basis of government."[1] The implications of Noah Webster's claim are at least as controversial today as they were in 1790. "Education," Webster argued, "should therefore be the first care of a legislature, not merely the institution of schools but the furnishing of them with the best teachers. . . . I shall almost adore that great man who shall change our practice and opinions and make it respectable for the first and best men to superintend the education of youth." That great man—or woman—has yet to appear. If "it is much easier to introduce and establish an effectual system for preserving morals than to correct by penal statutes the ill effects of a bad system,"[2] then perhaps the United States has taken the harder trail. Or perhaps the trail is less easy to blaze than Webster implied, at least in a society where citizens have diverse commitments, which lead them to disagree over what kind of education is necessary for educating citizens.[3]

"The only practicable method to reform mankind is to begin with children, to banish, if possible, from their company every low-bred, drunken, immoral character."[4] Even if a great leader could follow Webster's method, he could not simultaneously maintain a democratic republic. Citizens of a democratic republic must be free to disagree over what constitutes low-bred and immoral character. Webster's prescription would require the establishment of an educational dictatorship, akin to Plato's Republic, but undoubtedly falling far short of its promise. How many, if any, thoroughly moral men and women have lived in even the best republics? Would any have remained thoroughly moral had they assumed the role of unaccountable educators?

We can, however, revise Webster's claim to make it simultaneously

---

[1] Noah Webster, "On the Education of Youth in America" [1790], in Frederick Rudolph, ed., *Essays on Education in the Early Republic* (Cambridge, Mass.: Harvard University Press, 1965), p. 64.

[2] Ibid.

[3] For a discussion of Webster's many ideas for making the United States an independent nation, see Lawrence A. Cremin, *American Education: The National Experience, 1783-1876* (New York: Harper and Row, 1980), pp. 261-70.

[4] Webster, "On the Education of Youth in America," p. 63.

more realistic and more democratic. Education, in a great measure, forms the moral character of citizens, and moral character along with laws and institutions forms the basis of democratic government. Democratic government, in turn, shapes the education of future citizens, which, in a great measure, forms their moral character. Because democracies must rely on the moral character of parents, teachers, public officials and ordinary citizens to educate future citizens, democratic education begins not only with children who are to be taught but also with citizens who are to be their teachers.

A discussion of democratic education therefore must not lose sight of the role of educators—citizens whose religious, political, and social commitments have already been shaped by their early education. Theorists who claim that a democratic society can be transformed by reforming the education of children often overlook or explicitly bypass the role of citizens in educating the next generation. Like John Stuart Mill, they judge the existing generation "lamentably deficient in goodness and wisdom." Yet Mill argued that even a lamentably deficient generation "is perfectly well able to make the rising generation, as a whole, as good as, and a little better than, itself."[5] A radical critic might reply that a little better is not good enough; it may be worth superseding democracy for the sake of creating a substantially better society.

Whether it is worth superseding democracy depends on a judgment of the moral and practical potential of democratic authority over education. In this and the next two chapters, I explore the potential of democratic authority over primary education, which I take to subsume both elementary and secondary schooling.[6] This chapter examines the democratic purposes of primary education. I begin by defending two purposes, which are often considered to be in conflict, separately essential to democratic education and together constitutive of "deliberation," the development of which constitutes the primary democratic aim of primary education. I then develop this democratic understand-

---

[5] Mill, *On Liberty*, ch. 4, para. 11.

[6] Americans have become accustomed to referring to elementary schooling as "primary" and to high school as "secondary" education. Perhaps this distinction carried more theoretical weight when we were a society in which the demands of literacy—and therefore citizenship—were lower. Today, however, a high-school education is clearly necessary to prepare children adequately for citizenship. When discussing the democratic purposes of education, we should therefore think of high school as part of primary education. In this context, high school is secondary only in the relatively trivial sense of building upon the accomplishments of the elementary-school years. In other contexts, the distinction between different levels of lower education may have more significance, for example, when determining the specific pedagogical techniques that are appropriate to different stages of child development. These more specific pedagogical considerations lie beyond the scope of this book.

ing in the course of criticizing three popular alternative understandings of the purposes of primary education—particularly with regard to moral education.

DELIBERATION AND DEMOCRATIC CHARACTER

Childhood is a natural place to begin a discussion of education: good habits and principles are easier to instill in children than in adults, and governments are more justified in limiting the liberty of children than of adults for the sake of education. But by beginning with childhood, we must not overlook the fact that imperfectly educated citizens must educate future citizens. We cannot assume a perfectly wise philosopher-king, an ideal tutor for every child, or parents who unfailingly teach their children democratic virtue.

Nor can we assume that children are born ready for rational deliberation. The earliest education of children is not and cannot be by precept or reasoning; it must be by discipline and example. Children are first educated by their parents, and so must they continue to be as long as raising children constitutes one of our most valued personal liberties. Barring misfortune, parents typically love and nurture their children, later also reward and punish, praise and blame them for their actions. For most children, the family plays a large role in building character and in teaching basic skills for many years. But early in the lives of most children, their parents begin to share these primary educational functions with other associations: day-care centers, elementary (and then secondary) schools, churches and synagogues, civic organizations, friendship circles, and work groups. As children move outside their original families, their character and their skills are shaped by the examples of those whom they love and respect and by the rules regulating the associations to which they belong.

But training of this "exemplary" sort is only one kind of education, undoubtedly most effective during our childhood. At some fairly early stage in their development, children also become responsive to another kind of education, one that is more intellectual in its effect and rationalist in its method. They learn the three R's largely by direct instruction. They also develop capacities for criticism, rational argument, and decisionmaking by being taught how to think logically, to argue coherently and fairly, and to consider the relevant alternatives before coming to conclusions. Training of this "didactic" sort is democratically desirable because it enables citizens to understand, to communicate, and in some cases to resolve their disagreements. Without this sort of mutual understanding, we could not expect to achieve widespread toleration of dissent and respect for differing ways of life. Nor could we expect minorities to convince majorities, or to be convinced by them, of their point of view. But quite apart from its political function, children will eventually need the capacity for rational deliberation to make hard choices in situations where habits and authorities do not supply clear or consistent guidance. These two facts about our lives—that we disagree about what is good and that we face hard choices as individuals even when we agree as a group—are the basis for an argument that primary education should be both exemplary and didactic. Children must learn not just to *behave* in accordance with authority but to *think* critically about authority if they are to live up to the democratic ideal of sharing political sovereignty as citizens.

People adept at logical reasoning who lack moral character are sophists of the worst sort: they use moral arguments to serve whatever ends they happen to chose for themselves. They do not take morality seriously nor are they able to distinguish between the obvious moral demands and the agonizing dilemmas of life. But people who possess sturdy moral character without a developed capacity for reasoning are ruled only by habit and authority, and are incapable of constituting a society of sovereign citizens. Education in character and in moral reasoning are therefore both necessary, neither sufficient, for creating democratic citizens.

Taken together, inculcating character and teaching moral reasoning do not exhaust the legitimate ends of primary education in a democracy. Citizens value primary education for more than its moral and political purposes. They also value it for helping children learn how to live a good life in the nonmoral sense by teaching them knowledge and appreciation of (among other things) literature, science, history, and sports. These subjects are properly valued not primarily for the sake of imparting cultural coherence to a child's life, but for their place in cultivating a nonmorally good life for children, characterized by a combination of literary appreciation, scientific and historical knowledge, and physical agility. I say little more about these nonmoral ends of education not because they are unimportant (or unproblematic), but because the moral ends are less well understood and more politically problematic. Fortunately, the same education that helps children live a nonmorally good life often aids in the development of good moral character. The logical skills taught by science and mathematics, the interpretive skills taught by literature, the understanding of differing ways of life taught by both history and literature, and even the sportsmanship taught by physical education can contribute to the moral education of citizens.

Although inculcating character and teaching moral reasoning by no means exhaust the purposes of primary education in a democracy, together they constitute its core political purpose: the development of "deliberative," or what I shall interchangeably call "democratic," character. Deliberation is connected, both by definition and practice, with the development of democracy. Deliberation, on the individual level, is defined as "careful consideration with a view to decision" and, on the institutional level, as "consideration and discussion of the reasons for and against a measure by a number of councilors (e.g. in a legislative assembly)."[7]

In practice, the development of deliberative character is essential to realizing the ideal of a democratically sovereign society. Democracy depends on a mutual commitment and trust among its citizens that the laws resulting from the democratic process are to be obeyed except when they violate the basic principles on which democratic sovereignty rests. Deliberative citizens are committed, at least partly through the inculcation of habit, to living up to the routine demands of democratic life, at the same time as they are committed to questioning those demands whenever they appear to threaten the foundational ideals of democratic sovereignty, such as respect for persons. The willingness and ability to deliberate set morally serious people apart from both sophists, who use clever argument to elevate their own interests into self-righteous causes, and traditionalists, who invoke established authority to subordinate their own reason to unjust causes. People who give careful consideration to the morality of laws can be trusted to defend and to respect laws that are not in their self-interest, at the same time as they can be expected to oppose laws that violate democratic principles, and ultimately to disobey them, if necessary, with the intent of changing them by appealing to the conscience of the majority.

Citizens therefore have good reason to wonder how deliberative or democratic character can be developed in children, and who can develop it. I shall focus much (although by no means all) of my concern on the ways in which schools develop, or fail to develop, democratic character. Concern for how schools develop democratic character does not preclude concern for how parents teach—or fail to teach—their children democratic virtues within the family. I concentrate on the role of schools rather than parents in educating citizens not because the parental role is less significant but because the role of schools is subject to more direct political control. Parents command a domain of moral education within the family that is—and should continue to be—largely immune from external control. If there should be a domain for citizens collectively to educate children in the democratic virtues of deliberation, then primary schools occupy a large part of that domain, although they do not monopolize it.

[7] *Oxford English Dictionary.*

AMORALISM

What role should primary schools play in moral education? The simplest answer is none: schools should leave character development and training in moral reasoning to families and voluntary associations, such as churches and synagogues. This is the advice of at least one popular American authority:

> Personally, Miss Manners thinks that the parents of America should offer the school systems a bargain: You teach them English, history, mathematics, and science, and we will . . . look after their souls.[8]

An apparent attraction of this solution is that schools would thereby rid themselves of all the political controversies now surrounding moral education and get on with the task of teaching the "basics"—cognitive skills and factual knowledge.

But children do not leave their souls behind when they go to school, and schools cannot escape looking after children's souls in many significant and subtle ways.[9] Even if schools avoid all courses that deal explicitly with morality or civic education, they still engage in moral education by virtue of their "hidden curriculum," noncurricular practices that serve to develop moral attitudes and character in students.[10] Schools develop moral character at the same time as they try to teach basic cognitive skills, by insisting that students sit in their seats (next to students of different races and religions), raise their hands before speaking, hand in their homework on time, not loiter in the halls, be good sports on the playing field, and abide by many other rules that help define a school's character. We become aware of many more ways in which schools shape moral character only when we consider alternative school practices. In Japanese elementary schools, teachers routinely expect students who have mastered the day's lesson to help teach those who have yet to finish. Every member of the school, including the principal, shares in the chores necessary to keep the school building

---

[8] *The Washington Post*, October 21, 1984, p. H1.

[9] One could, of course, rid schools of moral education by ridding society of schools. But "deschooling society" would only transfer the burdens of moral education in a democracy to other social institutions. The new educational institutions that Ivan Illich describes are intended to do much more than teach cognitive skills and factual knowledge. So, the problem of moral education remains, although Illich's proposed solution is not democratic. See *Deschooling Society* (New York: Harper and Row, 1970).

[10] For the source and explanation of the term "hidden curriculum," see Philip W. Jackson, *Life in Classrooms* (New York: Holt, Rinehart and Winston, 1968). See also David Purpel and Kevin Ryan, "It Comes With the Territory: The Inevitability of Moral Education in the Schools," in David Purpel and Kevin Ryan, eds., *Moral Education . . . It Comes With the Territory* (Berkeley, Calif.: McCutchan, 1976), pp. 44-54.

clean (many schools have no specialized janitorial staff).[11] These prac-tices are lessons in egalitarianism that may never need to be explicitly taught in the curriculum if they are consistently practiced in the class-room. Most elementary schools in the United States teach different moral lessons, but they too engage in moral education simply by not doing what the Japanese schools do. The political choice facing us therefore is not whether schools should engage in moral education, but what sort of moral education they should engage in.

Nor would it be desirable for schools to forswear moral education, even if it were possible for them to do so. Public schools in a democracy should serve our interests as citizens in the moral education of future citizens.[12] Our parental interests are to some extent independent of our role as democratic citizens, and hence the emphasis of moral education within the family is likely to be quite different from that within schools. Most parents want to create a family life that satisfies their emotional and spiritual needs, and allows them to share their particular values with their children. However deep this concern for sharing particular values, it need not imply an equal concern for spreading these values more generally among children. Parents can recognize the advantages of living in a society in which a variety of values are deeply held and they are therefore free to teach their values to their children.

This freedom depends on children being taught widespread and en-during tolerance for different ways of life. Parents acting individually and citizens acting collectively both have valuable and largely comple-mentary roles to play in the moral education of children: the former in teaching children what it means to be committed to particular people and one way of life among many; the latter in teaching responsibilities and rights within a larger and more diverse community. Moral educa-tion in a democracy is best viewed as a shared trust of the family and the polity, mutually beneficial to everyone who appreciates the values of both family life and democratic citizenship.

LIBERAL NEUTRALITY

How can primary schools best fulfill the terms of this trust? Three of the most popular answers in this country find their conceptual homes in the state of individuals, the state of families, and the family state. The answer most consistent with the state of individuals is that schools

---

[11] William K. Cummings, *Education and Equality in Japan* (Princeton, N.J.: Princeton University Press, 1980), pp. 107-132. "Egalitarian education" in Japan is a relatively re-cent product of post-war reforms and is discussed by Cummings as a promising example of how educational institutions might serve a transformative rather than conservative so-cial function.

[12] I discuss the role of private schools in Chapter Four.

should teach the capacity for moral reasoning and choice without pre-disposing children toward any given conception of the good life or to-ward a particular moral character (aside from one defined by this ca-pacity). Just as a liberal state must leave its adult citizens free to choose their own "good" life, so must its schools leave children free to choose their own values. If public schools predisposed citizens towards a par-ticular way of life by educating them as children, the professed neutral-ity of the liberal state would be a cover for the bias of its educational system.

Liberal neutrality supports the educational method of "values clari-fication," which enjoys widespread use in schools throughout the United States. Proponents of values clarification identify two major purposes of moral education within schools. The first is to help stu-dents understand and develop their own values. The second is to teach them respect for the values of others. Advocates of values clarification view it as the pedagogical alternative to indoctrination:

> In place of indoctrination, my associates and I are substituting a *process* approach to the entire area of dealing with values in the schools, which focuses on the process of valuing, not on the trans-mission of the "right" set of values. We call this approach *values clarification*, and it is based on the premise that none of us has the "right" set of values to pass on to other people's children.[13]

Values clarification is often criticized for being value-laden, despite its apparent claim to value neutrality. This criticism is weaker than is generally recognized. Advocates of values clarification need not, and many do not, deny that their defense of values clarification is value-laden:

> If we urge critical thinking, then we value *rationality*. If we sup-port moral reasoning, then we value *justice*. If we advocate diver-gent thinking, then we value *creativity*. If we uphold free choice, then we value autonomy or *freedom*. If we encourage "no-lose" conflict resolution, then we value *equality*. . . . Called before the committee, we can only say that values clarification is not and never has been "value-free."[14]

Proponents of values clarification can admit without fear of self-con-tradiction that they are morally committed to the pedagogical position that teachers should not impose their views on students.

The problem with values clarification is not that it is value-laden, but

---

[13] Sidney B. Simon, "Values Clarification vs. Indoctrination," *Social Education* (De-cember 1971): 902. Reprinted in Purpel and Ryan, eds., *Moral Education*, pp. 126-35.

[14] Howard Kirschenbaum, "Clarifying Values Clarification: Some Theoretical Issues," in Purpel and Ryan, eds., *Moral Education*, p. 122.

that it is laden with the wrong values. Treating every moral opinion as equally worthy encourages children in the false subjectivism that "I have my opinion and you have yours and who's to say who's right?" This moral understanding does not take the demands of democratic justice seriously. The toleration and mutual respect that values clarification teaches is too indiscriminate for even the most ardent democratic to embrace. If children come to school believing that "blacks, Jews, Catholics, and/or homosexuals are inferior beings who shouldn't have the same rights as the rest of us," then it is criticism, not just clarification, of children's values that is needed.

The needed criticism is similar to that which was more generally directed against the state of individuals. Citizens value in children not only the rational capacity to choose but the kind of character that inclines them to choose good over bad lives. The aim of cultivating good character authorizes teachers to respect only a limited range of values professed (or acted upon) by children. Indiscriminate respect for children's values cannot be defended either as an ultimate end or as a tenable means of cultivating good character.

MORALISM

"Moralist" positions, which find their home in the family state, begin where this critique of liberal neutrality leaves off, with a conception of primary education whose explicit purpose is to inculcate character and to restrict children's choices to those that are worthy of pursuit. Moralists, both liberal and conservative, reject freedom of choice as the primary purpose of primary education. They seek to shape a particular kind of moral character that will be constrained—by either habit or reason, or both—to choose a good life.

Conservative Moralism

Just as defenders of the family state disagree over what principles constitute a good society, so moralists disagree over what virtues constitute a good person. Conservative moralists emphasize respect for authority. They defend educational programs often criticized by advocates of liberal neutrality as indoctrination or at least as unduly restrictive of individual freedom: patriotic rituals, dress codes, strict discipline within the classroom, and deference to teachers' opinions. The emphasis on teaching children to respect authority is, I suspect, rooted in a deep pessimism concerning the human disposition to be moral: left free to choose a set of principles to guide their actions, people are as likely to choose immoral as moral ones. This pessimism may underlie the conservative preference for shielding students from false political and religious beliefs, examples of immoral behavior, and indecent language rather than providing them with reasons to criticize and resist such beliefs and behavior. The aim of a conservative moralist education is to teach children to "behave" morally. It is not the process but the result of moral education—moral behavior, not moral reasoning—that matters.

Suppose that the results of moral education are all that matter. We still would be left with the difficult problem of determining which methods of moral education in schools will produce the best moral behavior in children. "It is by exposing our children to good character and inviting its imitation," Secretary of Education William Bennett claims, "that we will transmit to them good character."[15] Teachers and principals, Bennett argues, must not only "articulate ideals and convictions to students" but also "live the difference [between right and wrong, good and bad] in front of pupils." Bennett is "not talking about browbeating students into accepting [a] point of view. This is simply indoctrination, which we all deplore." But he is talking about putting less emphasis on discussing moral issues and more emphasis on inculcating democratic character through "the quiet power of moral example."[16]

Would less emphasis on moral discussion and more on moral example in schools produce the results sought by conservative moralists? While it is true that "the development of intellect has never guaranteed the development of good character,"[17] neither has the development of character (absent intellectual understanding) ever guaranteed good moral behavior. The inadequacy of habitual behavior is acute in modern societies where people confront new problems for which old habits supply insufficient guidance, and all the more acute in modern *democratic* societies where the ultimate court of appeal in politics is popular sovereignty, not past authority.

Since all school programs can be criticized for their insufficiency in producing moral behavior, we must find a standard other than sufficiency by which to judge practices of moral education within schools. One such standard might be comparative advantage: What can schools contribute to moral education more reliably or more efficiently than other educational institutions—such as families and churches? Schools can set moral examples for children, but the influence of even the most exemplary principals and teachers on the character of children is likely

[15] William J. Bennett, "Educators in America: The Three R's," Speech delivered to the National Press Club, Washington, D.C., March 27, 1985.
[16] Ibid.
[17] Ibid.

to be overwhelmed by the much greater influence of parents. Principals and teachers can defend their personal convictions in front of students, but they are unlikely to convince students to accept convictions in deep conflict with those previously inculcated by parents.

Schools have a much greater capacity than most parents and voluntary associations, however, for teaching children to reason out loud about disagreements that arise in democratic politics and to understand the political morality appropriate to a democracy. Since many of the virtues defended by conservatives—honesty, respect for law, fairness, self-discipline—are necessary for students to appreciate the advantages of democratic politics, schools should do their best to inculcate these virtues. But if character is, as Webster defines it, "strength of mind, individuality, independence, moral quality," then teaching students how to defend democracy and to reason about our political disagreements is no less essential to developing moral character than instilling the less intellectual virtues of fidelity, kindness, honesty, respect for law, diligence, and self-discipline. Schools have more of a comparative advantage in teaching the former set of virtues than they do in teaching the latter.

Knowing which pedagogical methods produce moral behavior would not justify implementing those methods in the face of public disagreement. "We must not only justify any morality we teach," one conservative moralist argues, "*but find it already in the consciousness of the American people. . . .* What this implies is a system of moral education that is conservative in *both* form and content."[18] Does agreement on conservative moralist policies already exist' in the *consciousness* of the American people? How, then, might we discover our agreement? If by public deliberation and voting, then citizens should have the authority to produce (or at least try to produce) a *new* moral consciousness. Conservative moralism, in its most defensible form, need not therefore produce—or aim to produce—conservative results.

Some conservative moralists resist this potentially radical argument by resorting to a more hypothetical standard: that there *would* be social agreement upon a conservative program of moral education were American citizens not already corrupted by liberal educational practices and the culture of "secular humanism." Because Americans are corrupted, some conservative moralists are willing to rely on any educational authority capable of instituting the correct kind of moral education in schools. This form of conservative moralism is as paternalistic towards adults as any system of moral education in schools must

[18] Andrew Oldenquist, " 'Indoctrination' and Societal Suicide," *The Public Interest*, no. 63 (Spring 1981): 84.

necessarily be towards children. On democratic grounds, nondemocratic paternalism towards adults is much more problematic than democratic paternalism towards children. The former undermines the possibility of a genuinely democratic society while the latter does not.

Were we able to produce a conservative consensus among the electorate in the United States by ridding public schools of secular humanism, such a consensus still would not suffice to support conservative moralism. We need a justification of conservative pedagogy that is independent of the goal of achieving a conservative consensus. If we cannot find that independent justification in the Constitution or the Bible, both of which are open to reasonable nonconservative interpretations, then perhaps we should look to the democratic process itself, once it is stripped of artificial manipulations by democratically unaccountable authorities. This is a democratically consistent but uncommon line of conservative argument. In committing themselves to a standard of democratic fairness, conservative moralists would open some of their preferred educational policies to criticism on their own grounds: that the intent or effect of policies (such as book banning, which I discuss in Chapter Four) is to deprive the next generation of citizens of their democratic freedom by subjecting them to a repressive education as adolescents.

Liberal Moralism

Liberal moralism shares with its conservative cousin a commitment to inculcating character, but it differs from conservative moralism in identifying *moral autonomy* as the goal of moral education: education should produce in children the desire and capacity to make moral choices based on principles that are generalizable among all persons. Liberal and conservative moralists agree that moral education need not be limited to clarifying whatever values children happen to bring into the classroom, but liberal moralism poses a distinct dilemma: How can schools—or anyone else—teach children to respect moral principles rather than established authority?

Guided by Piaget's work on moral development, John Rawls outlines in Part III of *A Theory of Justice* a three-stage theory of liberal moralist education that might be interpreted as an answer to this question.[19] Children begin to learn morality by following rules because their parents and other authorities issue them. Learning the "morality of authority" is an improvement over anarchy of desire, as most parents re-

[19] John Rawls, *A Theory of Justice* (Cambridge, Mass.: Harvard University Press, 1971).

alize.[20] The second stage of moral development, the "morality of association," is characterized by an acceptance of rules because they are appropriate to fulfilling the roles that individuals play within various associations.[21] Students, friends, and citizens obey moral rules because they thereby benefit the associations of which they are a part, and are benefited in turn. The morality of association is an improvement over the morality of authority because children learn to alter their habits and to criticize established authorities out of empathy for others and a concern for fairness.

The final stage of moral development, the "morality of principle," is characterized by a direct attachment to moral principles themselves. In a just society, Rawls tells us, the morality of principles would be achieved "quite naturally" through our previous associational experiences:

> We develop a desire to apply and to act upon the principles of justice once we realize how social arrangements answering to them have promoted our good and that of those with whom we are affiliated. In due course we come to appreciate the ideal of just human cooperation.[22]

Rawls may be right about the naturalness of learning the morality of principles in a just society. But autonomy surely does not come naturally in a less-than-just society. Yet that is where it seems to be needed most. If our schools could develop in children the morality of principles, they could create citizens committed to furthering justice in the face of injustice, a goal much more pressing in an unjust than in a just society. Liberal moralists like Lawrence Kohlberg therefore have tried to determine what schools can do to lead children to the morality of principle.

Neither Kohlberg nor anybody else, however, has yet discovered a way that schools can succeed in teaching the morality of principle. The most extensive research, conducted by Kohlberg and his associates, demonstrates that good schools are most successful in moving children (roughly) from the morality of authority to the morality of association. Very few sixteen-year-olds (or adults) ever embrace the morality of principle, and there is no evidence to credit schools with this rare accomplishment.[23] Although it is possible that there is a way that schools can teach autonomy, nobody has come even close to finding it.

---

[20] Ibid., pp. 462-67.

[21] Ibid., pp. 467-72.

[22] Ibid., p. 474.

[23] See Moshe M. Blatt and Lawrence Kohlberg, "The Effects of Classroom Moral Discussion Upon Children's Level of Moral Judgment," *Journal of Moral Education*, vol. 4 (1975): 129-62; and Kohlberg and E. Turiel, "Moral Development and Moral Educa-

Most conservative moralists set their moral sights too low, inviting blind obedience to authority; most liberal moralists set them too high, inviting disillusionment with morality. From a democratic perspective, success in teaching the morality of association marks great progress over the morality of authority. Schools that help develop the cooperative moral sentiments—empathy, trust, benevolence, and fairness—contribute a great deal to democratic education. Dewey's ideal of a school whose aim is "not the economic value of the products, but the development of social power and insight" pointed to such a morality.[24] The internally democratic practices of schools like the "School Within a School" in Brookline, Massachusetts—inspired by Kohlberg's theory of moral development—contribute more to the moral development of students than the authority patterns of schools perceived by their students to be autocratic and unfair, or simply boring.[25] What the most successful schools seem to teach, however, is not the morality of principle but the morality of association: the willingness and ability to contribute and to claim one's fair share in cooperative associations.

In a democracy, teaching the morality of association marks great moral progress over teaching the morality of authority because children who learn only the latter lack the capacity (or willingness) to distinguish between fair and unfair, trustworthy and untrustworthy authorities. They also fail to identify with the purposes of social institutions that do not continually serve their self interest or force them to cooperate. They have never learned to judge the commands of authorities or their own actions according to whether they live up to the terms of fair social cooperation. Given the democratic goal of sharing the rights and responsibilities of citizenship, schools that teach children

---

tion," in G. Lesser, ed., *Psychology and Educational Practice* (Chicago: Scott Foreman, 1971), pp. 410-65. Cf. John C. Gibbs, "Kohlberg's States of Moral Judgment: A Constructive Critique," *Harvard Educational Review*, vol. 47, no. 1 (February 1977): 43-61, for reasons to doubt the "naturalness" of Kohlberg's stages 5 and 6 of moral development.

[24] Dewey, "The School and Society," in Dewey, *"The Child and the Curriculum" and "The School and Society,"* p. 18. See also A. S. Neill's account of Summerhill (*Summerhill: A Radical Approach to Child Rearing* [New York: Hart Publishing, 1960]). Although his primary aim is "the bringing of happiness to some few children," Neill also views Summerhill's internal democracy as a school of social virtue: "After all, it is the broad outlook that free children acquire that makes self-government so important" (pp. 23, 55).

[25] See Kohlberg, "The Moral Atmosphere of the School," in N. V. Overley, ed., *The Unstudied Curriculum* (Washington, D.C.: Association for Supervision and Curriculum Development, 1970), pp. 104-127; and Ralph L. Mosher and Paul Sullivan, "A Curriculum for Moral Education for Adolescents," in Purpel and Ryan, eds., *Moral Education*, pp. 235-51. For an insightful description of Brookline's "School Within a School," see Sara Lawrence Lightfoot, *The Good High School: Portraits of Character and Culture* (New York: Basic Books, 1983), pp. 186-90.

the cooperative virtues are uncommonly successful and minimally problematical. Unlike the morality of principle, the morality of association does not incorporate the controversial claim (apparently accepted much more widely by men than by women) that impartiality among persons is the singularly highest moral ideal.[26] Empathy, trust, fairness, and benevolence—virtues at least as common among women as men—mark the morality of association.

Achieving the morality of association is compatible, moreover, with the use (at least in the early stages of schooling) of many of the pedagogical practices advocated by conservative moralists. Just as children learn filial independence after they learn to love and respect their parents, so they may learn political independence after they learn to "love" their president and to be patriotic toward their country.[27] The standards of patriotism and loyalty, like those of love and respect for parents, change as children learn to think critically about politics and to recognize that their civic duties extend beyond voting and obedience to laws. Moral education begins by winning the battle against amoralism and egoism. And ends—if it ends at all—by struggling against uncritical acceptance of the moral habits and opinions that were the spoils of the first victory.

That schools are not terribly effective in teaching autonomy should not surprise us. Since moral autonomy means doing what is right and good *because* it is right and good and not because teachers or any other authorities demand it, some of the most effective lessons in moral autonomy may result from the opportunity to disobey an authority whose commands are not perfectly just or fair.[28] At least, we cannot assume that moral autonomy is best taught by lessons that are planned to develop autonomy by those who teach them. Even if the morality of association is, as both Rawls and Kohlberg suggest, a subordinate philosophical ideal,[29] it still may be the primary political ideal for democratic education within primary schools.[30]

[26] See Carol Gilligan, *In a Different Voice: Psychological Theory and Women's Development* (Cambridge, Mass.: Harvard University Press, 1983).

[27] The evidence is strong that even if schools do not try to teach love for the president or patriotism, children learn it before they learn how to criticize politicians or the results of democratic politics. The pathbreaking work on this subject is Fred I. Greenstein, *Children and Politics* (New Haven: Yale University Press, 1965), see esp. pp. 31-54. See also David Easton and Jack Dennis, *Children in the Political System: Origins of Political Legitimacy* (New York: McGraw-Hill, 1969).

[28] Of course, schools might consider encouraging the development of moral autonomy by permitting students to protest and even disobey some general rules without penalty of expulsion.

[29] Rawls, *A Theory of Justice*, p. 478.

[30] There is a different sense in which the morality of association is a primary ideal of higher education. See Chapter Six: "The Purposes of Higher Education."

If by virtue we mean moral autonomy, then the role of schools in moral education is necessarily a limited one. We have little reason to believe that schools, or anyone else, can teach virtue in this sense. We have, on the other hand, considerable evidence that *democratic* virtue can be taught in many ways—by teaching male and female, Protestant and Catholic, black and white students together from an early age in the same classrooms;[31] by bringing all educable children up to a high minimum standard of learning;[32] by respecting religious and ethnic differences; by teaching American history not just as a series of elections, laws, treaties, and battles, but as lessons in the practice (sometimes successful, sometimes not) of political virtue, lessons that require students to develop and to exercise intellectually disciplined judgment.[33] In these and other ways that I shall discuss here and in subsequent chapters, schools can teach respect among races, religious toleration, patriotism, and political judgment.

But suppose virtue, as Kohlberg understands it, can be taught. And suppose that there exists an educational authority willing and able to teach Kohlberg's version of virtue. Let's call this authority the Moralist Teachers Union, "MTU" for short. The MTU reliably determines school policies according to what is known to be most effective in developing autonomous character. The justification for their authority is that a well-ordered democracy requires autonomous citizens. The MTU therefore claims "academic freedom" from democratic accountability.[34]

Although it is hard to imagine a stronger case for freedom from democratic control, even this case presents two serious problems. The first problem takes the form of a paradox: in order to create sovereign citizens, the MTU must remove one of the most important political decisions from democratic control—the education of future citizens. The second is simply a problem: by using nondemocratic means to achieve the end of democratic self-government, the MTU may teach a lesson

[31] For evidence on the success of cooperative learning structures on racial attitudes, see Robert E. Slavin, "Cooperative Learning and Desegregation," in Willis D. Hawley, ed., *Effective School Desegregation: Equity, Quality, and Feasibility* (Beverly Hills, Calif.: Sage, 1981), pp. 225-44.

[32] See Cummings, *Education and Equality in Japan*.

[33] For an example of teaching along these lines, see Diane Ravitch, *The Schools We Deserve: Reflections on the Educational Crises of Our Time* (New York: Basic Books, 1985), pp. 287-88. For negative examples, see ibid., pp. 112-13.

[34] Instead, the MTU could try to convince citizens of its expertise. Were citizens sufficiently convinced to delegate some of their educational authority to the MTU, it could achieve democratic legitimacy. The justification for its educational authority then would not be merely its competence but also its ability to win the confidence and approval of citizens.

incompatible with the assumption of popular sovereignty upon which its authority supposedly rests.

The MTU places citizens in the unchosen position of perpetual students, and then asks their students to believe that they are sovereign. The education of citizens who support self-government thus stands as strong counter-evidence to their democratic convictions. There is no consistent resolution of the problems raised by schools controlled by the MTU as long as one accepts the premise upon which the MTU is founded. If citizens do not guard the guardians of future citizens, they are not sovereign. Moralists must dispense either with the democratic rationale for moral education or with the assumption that the most legitimate educational authority is one that is most likely to implement the best program of moral education within schools.

We should retain the democratic rationale and dispense with the claim that the most justified educational authority is the one most likely to implement the best moralist program. This is not a hard choice once we drop the two implausible empirical assumptions adopted only to refine our criticism of moralism: (1) educators know how to teach the whole of virtue, and (2) they can be relied upon to teach it. Without these assumptions, the rationale for what one might call democratic moralism provides a forceful critique of those who would deny the legitimacy of democratic authority over schools because democratic authorities cannot be relied upon to pursue the correct educational ends or institute the correct programs. The price of denying democratic authority over schools is dispensing with the democratic purposes of primary education.

Once we realize that the independent philosophical justifications of most educational programs are not sufficiently strong or determinate to override the actual disagreements among citizens, then conservatives and liberals alike, so long as they wish to remain democrats, have no better alternative than to endorse a fair procedure of choosing among programs of moral education. The procedure itself has educational value, and although it does not guarantee the best educational policies in every instance, no undemocratic authority can promise—in principle or in practice—better results on the whole.

PARENTAL CHOICE

Some critics challenge this conclusion by invoking democratic, rather than liberal or conservative, values. They claim that the fairest—and the most democratic—procedure for determining the purposes of primary education is to empower parents rather than communities to choose among schools, and thereby among educational purposes and methods for their children. We do not escape philosophizing about the purposes of primary education, therefore, when we determine that the independent philosophical justifications of amoralism, liberal neutrality, and the various types of moralism are too weak to override our disagreements. We still must wonder what constitutes a fair and democratic procedure for resolving our disagreements. Should parents or democratic communities be the primary authorities to choose among the legitimate purposes and methods of primary education?

This question presupposes what we have already argued, that democratic virtue can be taught. Now we need to know what kinds of schools should be empowered (by whom) to teach it. The United States relies primarily on local public schools, which admit all and only those school-age children residing in a particular geographical area. In the judgment of many critics of public schools, their record in teaching democratic virtue ranges from disappointing to disastrous. Critics have ample evidence to support their charges: public school systems in this country have engaged in educationally unnecessary tracking, they have presided over racial segregation in schools and classrooms, and they have instituted some of the most intellectually deadening methods of teaching American history and civics that one might imagine.

Perhaps schools with less captive clients would do better. Were all parents able to send their children to private schools, perhaps the democratic purposes of education would be better fulfilled. The idea of empowering all parents to choose among schools for their children is in this sense democratic: it increases the incentive for schools to respond to the market choices of middle-class and poor as well as rich parents. The idea may seem even more appealing when we compare the record of public and private schooling in the United States. The evidence is scanty, but it suggests that private schools may on average do better than public schools in bringing all their students up to a relatively high level of learning, in teaching American history and civics in an intellectually challenging manner, and even in racially integrating classrooms. Why not simultaneously increase the option of exiting from public schools and the incentive for all schools to respond to the critical voices of parents by providing "every set of parents with a voucher certificate redeemable for a specified maximum sum per child per year if spent on 'approved' educational services"?

To the extent that advocates of voucher plans focus on the rights of individual parents to control the schooling of their children, they rest their defense on the fundamental premise of the state of families, which we have already called into question. More sophisticated voucher plans, however, make substantial concessions to the democratic purposes of primary education by conditioning certification of voucher schools upon their meeting a set of minimal standards. The most carefully designed and defended voucher plan would constrain all schools that accepted vouchers (a) not to discriminate in their admissions policies against children on grounds of race, socio-economic status, or intelligence, (b) not to require or accept tuition payments above the level set by the vouchers, (c) not to expel students except under certain specified circumstances and then only with due process, (d) to supply a governmental information agency with detailed reports of their governance procedures and the academic achievement, socio-economic status, and racial composition of their student body, and (e) to require a minimum number of hours of instruction with a significant portion devoted to reading and mathematics.[35] This list is meant to be suggestive rather than exhaustive. The essence of the constrained voucher proposal is the following: within some predetermined set of constitutional and legislative constraints, voucher plans would empower parents to choose among schools rather than forcing them to send their children to the local public school, regardless of its quality or their preferences. The democratic virtue of parental empowerment is based on a consequentialist calculation: that schools will improve—they will better serve their democratic purposes—if the guardians of their clients are less captive.

Proponents of the constrained voucher plan put the debate over the purposes of education in a new perspective. Having rejected the claim that parents have an a priori right to control the schooling of their children, the case for a constrained voucher plan rests on an assessment of the consequences of increasing parental choice for fulfilling the purposes of education in a democratic society. John Coons and Stephen Sugarman suggest that the only way of fulfilling the democratic purposes of education is to empower parents to choose among schools that are constrained by the government to satisfy some (but by the logic of their case not all) of the purposes of democratic education. Coons and Sugarman recognize that there is no a priori reason to limit the role of government, as Milton Friedman does, "to assuring that the schools met certain minimum standards such as the inclusion of a minimum content in their programs, much as it now inspects restaurants to assure that they maintain minimum sanitary standards."[36] Based on this logic, the standards that constrain voucher schools must be "minimal" in only two senses: (1) schools should not be constrained any more than

[35] John E. Coons and Stephen D. Sugarman, *Education By Choice: The Case for Family Control* (Berkeley: University of California Press, 1978), pp. 133-89.

[36] Milton Friedman, "The Role of Government in Education," in *Economics and the Public Interest*, ed. by Robert Solo (New Brunswick, N.J.: Rutgers University Press, 1955), pp. 123-45. See also Friedman, *Capitalism and Freedom*, pp. 85-107.

is necessary to satisfy our collective interests in primary education, and (2) schools cannot be constrained to satisfy fully the democratic purposes of education, because a substantial degree of parental control over schooling is necessary to realize those purposes.

Resting as it does on a complicated consequentialist comparison, the claim of the constrained voucher plan defies easy assessment. Were citizens to agree on what consequences count (and how much to count them), it would be very difficult to predict the consequences of a thoroughgoing voucher plan versus an improved public school system. But we do not agree, nor is it likely that we shall ever agree as long as we have the freedom to disagree. On consequentialist grounds, the question of whether to institute a constrained voucher plan or to improve public schools by decentralization coupled with other similarly far-reaching reforms is inherently indeterminate. It is not surprising, therefore, that Coons and Sugarman do not argue the case for vouchers exclusively—or even primarily—on consequentialist grounds. They focus instead on the fact that we disagree over the purposes of primary education:

> If there ever was a national understanding about adult society's responsibility for the young, there is no longer. There remains, nonetheless, a general conviction that a just society makes ample provision for the formal portion of children's education and assures a measure of fairness and rationality in its distribution. But distribution of what? Given the diversity of values among American adults, in what should publicly supported education consist?[37]

Given our inability to agree on common standards, Coons and Sugarman conclude that publicly supported education should reflect the diversity of our values by imposing only a minimal set of common standards on primary schools.

But why should the fact of our disagreement over common standards favor the side that argues for minimizing our common standards? Consider Friedman's comparison of the regulation of schools to that of restaurants. The analogy implies that our common educational standards consist only of preventing schools from physically harming children or fraudulently claiming to educate them. Were our public interest in regulating schools as analogous to our interest in regulating restaurants as Friedman suggests, it would be hard to explain why we should subsidize schooling for every child. A necessary condition for justifying public subsidy of schools—but not of restaurants—is the fact that citizens have an important and common interest in educating future citizens. By

---

[37] Coons and Sugarman, *Education By Choice*, pp. 1-2.

labelling that interest an "externality" of education, Friedman suggests that educating citizens is a side effect, rather than a central purpose or "internality," of schooling. Although Coons and Sugarman do not use Friedman's language, they ultimately fall back upon his vision of schooling as primarily a private rather than a public concern.

To justify public support, the standards to which voucher schools are held must fulfill the public purposes—the "internalities"—of primary education. In keeping with this claim, Coons and Sugarman (unlike Friedman) defend stringent constraints on the admissions processes of voucher schools to ensure that all children—not just white or intellectually talented or well-motivated children—have access to a good education. But are the set of constraints that Coons and Sugarman support sufficient for ensuring that voucher schools satisfy the public purposes of schooling? If a primary purpose of schools is to develop democratic character, then the externalities of education may be more extensive than even a constrained voucher plan admits. The externalities may include, among other things, how children of different intellectual abilities, races, and religions are distributed within classrooms, what subjects are taught and how they are taught, how authority in and over schools is distributed, and so on. The externalities of schooling extend beyond the admissions process, the curriculum, and the authority structure, to encompass almost every aspect of schooling, rendering indefensible the distinction between a publicly mandated "minimum" and parentally chosen standards for voucher schools.

Voucher plans attempt to avoid rather than settle our disagreements over how to develop democratic character through schooling. The attempt succeeds insofar as decisions concerning choice among schools are left to sets of parents, who are more likely to agree with one another than they are with other parents as to what constitutes a good school. The attempt fails insofar as the decisions concerning the constraints to be imposed upon voucher schools must still be collective. The most defensible voucher plans, like Coons and Sugarman's, make room for a set of centrally imposed constraints that reflect our collective interest in primary education. But having admitted the possibility—indeed, the necessity—of imposing a set of collective standards on schools, Coons and Sugarman can no longer rest the case for vouchers on the claim that such plans avoid the need for settling our disagreements over how citizens should be educated.

Minimally constrained voucher plans, like Friedman's, avoid the controversial issue of how schools should educate citizens only at the cost of denying our collective interests in democratic education. Maximally constrained voucher plans, like Coons and Sugarman's, appear to avoid the issue only by shifting our controversies over democratic education from a mixture of local, state, and national politics to a more purely centralized politics. If a voucher plan aims to increase diversity in schooling while providing citizens with more control over how schools educate children, then its effect of relegating collective interests in education to a more centralized politics is counter-productive.

In criticizing voucher plans for not recognizing the primacy of our public interest in schooling, we need not claim that society has a greater interest in the education of children than do parents. The point is rather that parents command a domain other than schools in which they can—and should—seek to educate their children, to develop their moral character and teach them religious or secular standards and skills that they value. We can therefore agree that not even the most extensive constraints upon schools can fully satisfy the democratic purposes of primary education, since parental influence over the education of their children is among those purposes. Turning public schools into a domain of parental authority is not, however, the appropriate means of satisfying this democratic purpose of education. The discretionary domain for education—particularly but not only for moral education—within the family has always been and must continue to be vast within a democratic society. And the existence of this domain of parental discretion provides a partial defense against those who claim that public schooling is a form of democratic tyranny over the mind. The risks of democratic and parental tyranny over moral education are reduced (although they can never be eliminated) by providing two substantially separate domains of control over moral education.

In recognition of our collective interest in schooling, voucher plans can incorporate regulations even more extensive than those advocated by Coons and Sugarman. The more room voucher plans make for regulation, the less room they leave for parental choice. Anyone who defends vouchers on the basis of their educational consequences rather than parental rights can defend this trade-off if necessary to fulfill the collective purposes of primary education. But advocates of vouchers cannot adequately defend the means—centralized governmental regulation—by which their plans constrain citizens to manifest their collective interests in influencing primary education. Were there a self-evident set of such regulations, then centralized governmental control over all voucher schools might be desirable. But there is no single self-evident set of regulations. Our collective interests in the moral education of future citizens might be manifest in many ways: by requiring more civics courses or restructuring schools to become more internally democratic, by increasing graduation requirements or retaining our present requirements and making promotion more difficult, by busing black and white children across district lines or dramatically improving the quality of inner-city schools. Which of these practices (if any) reflect our collective interest in influencing the shape of schooling must be determined to a large extent through democratic deliberations. If the politics of schooling does not leave room for such deliberations, we cannot say that the public constraints on schools—whether minimal or maximal—reflect our collective interests in primary education. The problem with voucher plans is not that they leave too much room for parental choice but that they leave too little room for democratic deliberation.

The appeal of vouchers to many Americans who are not otherwise committed to a state of families stems, I suspect, from three facts. One is that our public schools, especially in many of our largest cities, are so centralized and bureaucratized that parents along with other citizens actually exercise very little democratic control over local schools. The second is that only poor parents lack the option of exiting from public schools, and this seems unfair. The third, and most sweeping fact, is that the condition of many public schools today is bleak by any commonsensical standard of what democratic education ought to be.

The proper response to the first problem is to make public school systems less bureaucratic and more democratic. The best response to the second problem is to redistribute income more equitably, which would also overcome many other inequities in the ability of citizens to make use of their freedoms. Were *private* schooling an essential welfare good like health care, then the case for directly subsidizing it would be stronger. But we have already argued that public, not private, schooling is an essential welfare good for children as well as the primary means by which citizens can morally educate future citizens. We have yet to consider whether (and why), given the democratic purposes of education, a democratic society should leave room for private schooling.[38] But based on our considerations so far, we can conclude that the welfare of children and the well-being of democracy can be supported simultaneously by improving education, especially moral education, within public schools rather than by encouraging parents to exit from them. We need not deny the third problem—that the condition of many public schools today is bleak—to recognize that we know of no more effective way, nor is there a more consistently democratic way, of trying to develop democratic character than to improve public schooling.

[38] See Chapter Four on "Private Schools."

CHAPTER THREE

DIMENSIONS OF DEMOCRATIC PARTICIPATION

What structure of authority do democratic principles recommend for primary schools? Even if there were no principled limits on democratic authority, the answer to this question would not be obvious. We would still need to ask which democratic community—local, state, or national—should have authority over schools. Were democratic authority constrained to do whatever is right with regard to education, the answer would also be elusive. Who can be entrusted with implementing the right educational policies? Although we earlier imagined a Moralist Teachers' Union that implements all the correct educational policies, the MTU was not intended as an alias for either the NEA (National Education Association) or the AFT (American Federation of Teachers). The MTU was created to clarify an argument that democratic control is worth defending even if the educational policies it produces are not always wise.

Democratic control over primary schools is worth defending, but not if its results are repressive or discriminatory. We therefore are left with a variant of both questions concerning authority over primary schools. Which democratic community should determine what school policies? Who along with democratic communities should share control over what happens in primary schools? The first question requires us to consider the multiple levels of democratic authority over schools: we need to ask which educational policies are best determined at the local, which at the state or federal level. The second question requires us to consider the role of professional authority in upholding democratic principles. In answering these questions, another issue arises: what room, if any, remains for students to participate in shaping their own schooling? These three questions begin our inquiry into the distribution of educational authority within a large and complex democratic society.

LEVELS OF DEMOCRATIC CONTROL

Imagine a small and simple democratic city-state with no political subdivisions but substantial differences of opinion among its citizens on religious and political issues: something like a small, modern New England town turned into an independent state. This city-state has a particular identity: its own language, national holidays, literary traditions, social honors and taboos. Part of the social identity of its citizens is based upon this culture, which is widely shared. Yet national identity only partially accounts for the identity of citizens of any nontotalitarian society. Citizens are also members of diverse religious, ethnic, occupational, familial, and friendship groups, each with its own particular subculture. In short, citizens of this small city-state are people with a plurality of social identities: one universal, many particular.

The public schools of this city-state aid in shaping the social identities of future citizens by cultivating or changing the common culture. That common culture has two components: shared beliefs and practices *particular* to this city-state (such as speaking English and celebrating Thanksgiving) and those *essential* to any democratic society (such as religious toleration and respect for the dignity of persons). Democratic control over public schools is the primary means by which citizens can collectively cultivate the first set of practices, common among members of their society but particular when compared to the practices of other democratic societies. Democratic control is unlikely to be an adequate means of securing the second set of practices, which follow from the principles of nonrepression and nondiscrimination and constrain democracy in its own name. The temptations are great for democratic majorities or their representatives, once in power, to control what is taught within the classroom. The principled constraints on democratic authority make room within schools for the educational authority of teachers, exercising professional standards. As long as the school board institutes nonrepressive and nondiscriminatory policies, even if those policies are not the wisest ones, it can claim the right to be wrong on democratic grounds. But it cannot claim the right to repress challenges to its political perspective by forcing teachers to profess doctrines inimical to their intellectual standards.

Even in an extremely small city-state, therefore, the ideal of democracy both empowers and constrains community control over education. The most significant difference between such a state and our own is the scope of community. In a small city-state, one democratically elected board could be the primary body responsible for making collective decisions concerning public schooling. The authority of that school board would be final in all those cases—but only in those cases—where its policies do not violate the principles of nonrepression and nondiscrimination. The concept of "community control" would therefore convey a reasonably accurate understanding of the nature of educational authority. In an extremely small society, democratic control can be effective, and the effects of democratic decisionmaking significant.

Members of the school board are held accountable for their policies by voters. Voters have relatively easy access to information about the school board's policies and how the schools are run on the basis of those policies. Because the lines of accountability are so short and clearly drawn, policies can make a discernible difference in how schools are run—provided local school politics remains competitive and conducive to public deliberation, so that school board members do not defer as a matter of course to the administrators of schools. The proviso is essential: even (or perhaps especially) in a small community, democratic control over schools depends on the existence of competitive and deliberative structures that make members of the school board accountable to citizens.[1]

Now expand the size of our imaginary society and its school system beyond what one school board can effectively control and still be effectively controlled by citizens. Later we ask who should share control with democratic bodies over public schools, but for now concentrate on the question of how authority should be apportioned among democratic bodies at the national, state, and local levels.

In a small city-state, the same elected officials who set the standards of public schooling can also oversee implementation, and directly account to the electorate for the perceived shortcomings of their educational policies. In a larger society, the lines of control over public schooling must be longer and electoral accountability more attenuated. Determining the optimal balance between local control and centralized authority over education becomes an issue of enormous complexity. The two simplest solutions are unacceptable. At one extreme, delegating to local school boards full control over public schooling would reduce the United States to a collection of democratic city-states, totally neglecting our collective interest in a common education. At the other extreme, centralizing all control at the national level would eliminate any effective democratic control over schools, leaving bureaucrats, administrators, and teachers in *de facto* control.

A federal system of government holds out the promise of finding a middle ground between these two unacceptable extremes. One aim of federalism is to preserve local democratic control over schools within

---

[1] For a description of existing political structures, some of which mitigate against democratic control over local schools, and an analysis of how democratic control might be improved, see L. Harmon Zeigler, M. Kent Jennings, and G. Wayne Peak, *Governing American Schools: Political Interaction in Local School Districts* (North Scituate, Mass.: Duxbury, 1974), esp. pp. 242–61. A book that appeared too late for me to take account of its exploration of local participation and accountability is Ann Bastian, Norm Fruchter, Marilyn Gittell, Colin Greer, and Kenneth Haskins, *Choosing Equality: The Case for Democratic Schooling* (Philadelphia: Temple University Press, 1986).

limits set by the aims of cultivating a common culture and teaching essential democratic values, limits that might be better safeguarded by higher levels of government. Preserving a realm of local democratic control over schools not only makes control more effective but permits the content of education to vary, as it should, with local circumstances and local democratic preferences. The more effective the control that citizens have over school policies, moreover, the more likely they are to support them. Yet another, more general advantage is that local control facilitates the participation of citizens in political activities beyond the simple act of voting.

Placing political limits on local educational authority also has its advantages from a democratic perspective. Unlimited local control can readily subvert two of the primary purposes of democratic education—to teach essential democratic values and to cultivate a common culture. More inclusive democratic bodies can constrain less inclusive ones to uphold both sets of standards—those that are essential to the justice of any democratic society and those that serve to unite and distinguish us from other democratic societies. So constrained, local school boards should be free to decide how to implement these standards and what further standards to set.

Suppose Congress required all schools to teach American history, religious toleration, racial and sexual equality, the three R's, and the rights and obligations of citizenship. Because of the size and structure of our federal system, states might serve not only as mediators of federal regulations but also as democratic communities in their own right, adding their own educational requirements: that state holidays, state history, and other democratically authorized requirements be taught.[2] Local school boards would remain free to set their own standards within the constraints set by national and state standards, as well as to use their discretion in deciding how to implement federal and state standards.

For federal and state standards to be compatible with local demo-

---

[2] Professional educators often criticize existing state requirements for being vague or "trivializ[ing] the mission of public education." Ernest L. Boyer, *High School: A Report on Secondary Education in America* (New York: Harper and Row, 1983), p. 58. Support for this criticism is ample: California requires the teaching of "kindness towards domestic pets"; Wisconsin requires instruction in "the true and comparative vitamin content . . . and health values of dairy products"; Maine requires public schools to "teach virtue and morality for not less than one-half hour per week." Although these requirements verge on the ridiculous, others (indeed most) do not—many states, like California, require instruction in "the principles of a free government." Pitched at the level of principle, state requirements such as this one are bound to be vague, but public acknowledgment of educational principle is part of the purpose of democratic education. For a partial list of state requirements, see Boyer, *High School*, pp. 58-59.

cratic control, they must not together exhaust the scope of educational policies that matter to citizens. Local school boards must retain substantial control and freedom to exercise their discretion over education within their school districts, subject to the strictures of democratic accountability. So construed, local implementation of both centrally and locally determined educational standards makes diversity of public schooling possible without destroying the moral unity of a democratic society. To preserve the benefits of local control, school districts must be kept small enough for effective democratic control to be possible.

This picture of political control over schools is still too simple, but it helps highlight two essential aspects of educational authority in a complex society, one of which is often overlooked in discussions of democratic control over schools. In anything but a tiny city-state, community control over schools cannot be identified with local control because there are several democratic communities that have a legitimate role to play in determining school policy. For the same reason, federal and state control must not be all-encompassing, otherwise local democratic control over schools is rendered meaningless. Local public schools play a legitimate role in reflecting and responding to the more particular collective preferences of face-to-face communities, a purpose that few other political institutions can serve as effectively in our society.

DEMOCRATIC PROFESSIONALISM

At all levels of government, citizens have a legitimate interest in teaching children a civic culture; democratic politics is the proper means for shaping that culture; and primary schools are the proper institutions for teaching it.[3] But schools that serve simply to perpetuate the beliefs held by dominant majorities—whether at the federal, state, or local level—are agents of political repression. Education is not democratic if citizens do not collectively influence the purposes of primary schooling nor if they control the content of classroom teaching so as to repress reasonable challenges to dominant political perspectives.

The picture of educational authority divided among federal, state, and local levels of government is therefore too simple for a specific reason. Without institutionalized challenges to political authority, governmental control over primary schooling could easily establish, as John

[3] A civic culture includes those common beliefs and practices that are essential to any democratic society and those that are particular to our democratic society. For the source of the term, see Gabriel Almond and Sidney Verba, *The Civic Culture: Political Attitudes and Democracy in Five Nations* (Boston: Little, Brown and Co., 1965).

Stuart Mill feared it would, a "despotism over the mind."[4] At all levels of American government, political control over schools is challenged—and often shared—by other authorities: parents and parent-teacher associations, teachers and teachers' unions, accrediting associations, private foundations, civic groups and lobbying organizations (other than teachers' unions).[5] Although all of these groups help shape what happens in American schools, the challenge posed by teachers and teachers' unions is by far the most significant in upholding the principle of nonrepression against democratic authority. The division between democratic and nondemocratic control over primary schooling depends most crucially on the educational role we attribute to teachers and teachers' unions.

What role should we attribute to teachers? We might conceive of their role as supporting a complementary division of labor between popular authority and expertise: democratic governments perpetuating a common culture, teachers cultivating the capacity for critical reflection on that culture. In short, teachers serve to shed critical light on a democratically created culture. On this conception, the claim to educational expertise by teachers is both relative—to the role played by democratic governments in cultivating a common culture—and partial—it does not comprehend all of what matters in primary education. The professional responsibility of teachers is to uphold the principle of nonrepression by cultivating the capacity for democratic deliberation.

The principle of nonrepression therefore not only constrains democratic authority, it also supplies democratic content to the concept of professionalism among teachers, requiring biology teachers, for example, to resist communal pressures to teach creationism instead of evolution, and social-studies teachers to develop their students' capacity to criticize popular policies from the perspective of mutually shared principles. More generally, nonrepression obligates teachers—at the same time as it authorizes them—to further democratic education by supporting the intellectual and emotional preconditions for democratic deliberation among future generations of citizens.[6] Prominent among those preconditions are two that Dewey defended as prototypically democratic—the recognition of common interests among citizens, and

[4] Mill, *On Liberty*, ch. 5, para. 13.

[5] For a description of the role of accrediting associations, lobbying organizations (other than teachers' unions), and private foundations, see Spring, *American Education*, pp. 222-32.

[6] Similarly, the principle of nondiscrimination requires teachers to further democratic education—at times against the will of democratic citizens—by teaching all students according to their educational needs and abilities, rather than according to their class, race, or religion.

the related commitment to reconsider our individual interests in light of understanding the interests of others. To further these preconditions of democratic deliberation among their students, teachers must be sufficiently connected to their communities to understand the commitments that their students bring to school, and sufficiently detached to cultivate among their students the critical distance necessary to reconsider commitments in the face of conflicting ones.

Understood as the degree of autonomy—or insulation from external control—necessary to fulfill the democratic functions of office, professionalism completes rather than competes with democracy. On this prescriptive understanding of professionalism, the most prominent professions in our society have too much autonomy. Doctors and lawyers often claim, in the name of professionalism, authority over the rest of us far in excess of what their professional expertise warrants. Too much autonomy leads to "the insolence of office."[7] Too little autonomy, on the other hand, leads to what one might call "the ossification of office," from which, by almost all accounts, the teaching profession in the United States suffers. The rewards of professionalism—the pleasures of performance, high salary, status, and the exercise of authority over other people—are offered to a far smaller degree to far fewer teachers than in any of the other major professions in our society.[8] The medical and legal professions suffer from a surplus of all but the first reward, while the teaching profession suffers from a deficit in all four categories.

The source of the first (and most serious) deficit—too few pleasures of performance—is surely not that teaching is an inherently unsatisfying or a socially unimportant profession. Even with its present problems, a majority of teachers say that they chose their career for its inherent satisfactions: they had a strong desire to teach, to serve society, or to be part of what they consider a worthy profession.[9] Yet most teachers who begin with a sense of intellectual mission lose it after several years of teaching, and either continue to teach in an uninspired, routinized way or leave the profession to avoid intellectual stultification and emotional despair.[10] A variety of recent studies support Sey-

[7] Walzer, *Spheres of Justice*, p. 155.

[8] For a discussion of the rewards of professionalism, see ibid., pp. 155-60.

[9] John I. Goodlad, *A Place Called School: Prospects for the Future* (New York: McGraw-Hill, 1984), p. 171.

[10] See Seymour B. Sarason, *The Culture of the School and the Problem of Change* (Boston: Allyn and Bacon, 1971), pp. 161-73. For other reports, see Myron Brenton, *What's Happened to Teacher?* (New York: Avon Books, 1970); Dan Lortie, *School Teacher: A Sociological Study* (Chicago: University of Chicago Press, 1975); and Gertrude McPherson, *Small Town Teacher* (Cambridge, Mass.: Harvard University Press, 1972).

mour Sarason's findings that the structure of schools made the daily work of most teachers so routinized that "without exception, those who have been teaching for five or more years admitted that they no longer experienced their work with the enthusiasm, excitement, sense of mission, and challenge that they once did."[11]

The salaries of teachers are also low, so low that many must moonlight in the summers when they (and their students) would be better off were they able to use summers to continue their education, to plan next year's courses, or to relax and thereby avoid the primary occupational hazard of teaching, early "burn-out." Teachers' salaries are far lower than those of comparably educated professionals.[12] Relative to other salaried workers, teachers' salaries have increased very little in recent years, although much more has been demanded of them: to cope with the effects of racial tensions and economic blight in our inner cities, an increased divorce rate among parents, the rise of drug use and unwanted pregnancies among teenagers, and so on.[13] Current salary levels attract more than enough applicants to fill teaching positions, but the quality of applicants is, by all accounts, low. The relatively poor pay of teachers discourages the best college students from entering the profession, and the slow rate of salary increases encourages the best teachers to leave.[14] Low salaries coupled with little autonomy on the job all but guarantee low social status.

The ossification of office, like the insolence of office, therefore has structural sources: little control over work, low pay, and low social status. The teaching conditions in most public primary schools make it all but impossible for teachers to develop a positive sense of professionalism: "an ethical code, a social bond, a pattern of mutual recognition

---

[11] Sarason, *The Culture of the School and the Problem of Change*, p. 163.

[12] For a comparison of teachers' salaries with those of other professionals, and a report on the downward trend of their real income over the past ten years, see Theodore R. Sizer, *Horace's Compromise: The Dilemma of the American High School* (Boston: Houghton Mifflin, 1984), p. 185; and Boyer, *High School*, pp. 165-71.

[13] Those who deny that teachers are underpaid often compare public- with private-school teachers who earn even less but may be more committed to professional standards. Private-school teachers may earn less on average than public-school teachers, but they are also more insulated from these problems by virtue of the fact that their schools are selective and much freer to expel problem students of all kinds than public schools, by democratic understanding, can be. Put into this context, the model of the dedicated private-school teacher, who works for very little because she gets so much satisfaction (if not status) from her role, reinforces rather than undermines the claim that we need to pay public-school teachers more to make up for their more demanding and less satisfying work.

[14] For two detailed descriptions (and excellent discussions) of the dimensions of this problem, see Boyer, *High School*, pp. 165-74; and Sizer, *Horace's Compromise*, pp. 183-87.

and self-discipline."[15] Instead, most public schools encourage ossification by discouraging intellectual creativity:

> In the worst schools, teachers are demeaned and infantilized by
> administrators who view them as custodians, guardians, or unin-
> spired technicians. In less grotesque settings, teachers are left alone
> with little adult interaction and minimal attention is given to their
> needs for support, reward, and criticism.[16]

Even in many of the best schools, the work load of full-time teachers is
so great as to require them continually to compromise their judgment
of what constitutes good teaching.[17] Far more than doctors or lawyers,
teachers make compromises in their professional standards for causes
that are often entirely beyond their personal control: too many students, too little preparation time for teaching, too much administrative
work, too little money to support their families. Some of these causes,
however, may be within the collective power of teachers—organized by
teachers' unions—to change.[18]

TEACHERS' UNIONS

Democratic authority stands between teachers and the insolence of office, but it also often promotes the ossification of office, by saddling
teachers with heavy teaching schedules, crowded classrooms, low salaries, little time for collegial consultation, threats to their intellectual
independence in the classroom, and/or rigid rules governing what and
how to teach. The failure of democratic communities to support conditions under which the teaching profession would suffer neither from
the insolence nor from the ossification of office legitimates the organization of teachers into unions. The principle of nonrepression defines
the democratic purpose of teachers' unions: to pressure democratic
communities to create the conditions under which teachers can cultivate the capacity among students for critical reflection on democratic
culture. It does not follow that all claims to educational authority or

[15] Walzer, *Spheres of Justice*, p. 155. For a detailed description and explanation of the
"negative" senses of professionalism, see Magali Sarfatti Larson, *The Rise of Professionalism: A Sociological Analysis* (Berkeley: University of California Press, 1977).

[16] Lightfoot, *The Good High School*, p. 334.

[17] See Sizer's account of Horace Smith in *Horace's Compromise*, pp. 9-21. See also
Goodlad, *A Place Called School*, esp. pp. 193-95; and Boyer, *High School*, pp. 155-61.

[18] For informative histories of the two major American teachers' unions, see William
Edward Eaton, *The American Federation of Teachers 1916-1961: A History of the
Movement* (Carbondale, Ill.: Southern Illinois University Press, 1975); and Edgar Wes-
ley, *NEA: The First Hundred Years* (New York: Harper and Brothers, 1957). See also
Spring, *American Education*, pp. 208-222.

challenges to democratic control by teachers' unions are legitimate. We still need to ask how much authority unions should be granted over what school policies.

There is surely not a single correct answer to this question, but the democratic conception of professionalism provides principled guidance in avoiding two theoretically elegant but politically dangerous answers, which reflect alternative visions of democracy. One vision, of what one might call "directed" democracy, sanctions the authority of unions over democratic communities to the extent that unions better represent educational expertise, even if unions thereby control the form and content of public schooling. The other vision, of "strong" democracy,[19] sanctions all policies that result from negotiations between democratic communities and unions, even if the policies leave teachers with little or no autonomy in the classroom. The democratic conception of professionalism offers a critique of both visions and an alternative. The alternative is that teachers' unions be granted enough educational authority to overcome ossification of office but not so much as to convert teaching into a profession that, like medicine or law, is characterized by insolence of office. Union claims of educational expertise cannot in itself carry sufficient moral weight to override democratic authority. As the example of the MTU suggested, being an expert in education is neither a necessary nor a sufficient condition for claiming authority over education in a democracy. The more compelling claim available to teachers' unions is that greater professional control over schooling is a necessary condition for upholding the principle of nonrepression. When democratic control over primary schools is so absolute as to render teachers unable to exercise intellectual discretion in their work, (1) few independent-minded people are attracted to teaching, (2) those who are attracted are frustrated in their attempts to think creatively and independently, and (3) those who either willingly or reluctantly conform to the demands of democratic authority teach an undemocratic lesson to their students—of intellectual deference to democratic authority. A democratic conception of professionalism supports those union claims to educational authority necessary to cultivating a democratically tempered sense of professional mission among teachers.

The strongest rationale for the earliest demands of teachers' unions—for greater teacher participation in the administration of schools and the determination of educational policies—was this need

[19] Benjamin Barber uses the same term, although in a broader sense than I am using it here. See his *Strong Democracy: Participatory Politics for a New Age* (Berkeley: University of California Press, 1984).

to cede teachers more control over their work.[20] When most of these demands were denied, the newly formed American Federation of Teachers directed its efforts toward establishing rights of collective bargaining with school boards, rights that they used to demand better pay and pensions for teachers on grounds that "their professional and social standing is far too low to enable them to produce effective results in teaching."[21] This rationale for better pay still makes sense. Paying elementary and secondary teachers more is a necessary (but not sufficient[22]) way to raise their quality, not because income is the sole measure of the status of teachers, but because the average salary of teachers today is *so* low as to discourage college graduates who have other options from choosing teaching as a career.

The pressing need to pay all teachers more is not good grounds for unions to oppose policies that would pay some teachers more than others on the basis of their better teaching. The institution of merit pay is another way of mitigating the ossification of office among the best teachers. If teaching is a profession, it must have a set of standards by which teachers can be judged better and worse. Unions can play an important role in preventing merit pay from becoming a political tool of administrators by elaborating those standards and insisting on their use in the evaluation of teachers. But to oppose merit pay on the grounds that all teachers should be paid more or that no teachers should be subject to external evaluation is a form of professional insolence: an attempt to shield teachers from legitimate external evaluation. As long as the standards used to judge some teachers better than others are relevant to their social functions, the institution of merit pay can support the professionalism of teachers. Unions threaten to abuse their authority when they oppose the institution of merit pay, although they use it well in demanding better pay for all teachers.

Raising teachers' salaries—across the board and on the basis of merit—is an obvious (probably even a necessary) means of supporting the professionalism of teachers, but certainly not a sufficient means. Democratic education depends not only upon attracting intellectually talented people with a sense of professional mission to teaching, but also upon cultivating and sustaining that sense during their careers as teachers.[23] Unions therefore do not fulfill their democratic function just

---

[20] Spring, *American Education*, pp. 215-16.

[21] Ibid.

[22] One reason why raising teachers' salaries is not a sufficient way to increase their quality is that school systems must be willing and able to select the best teachers from among the larger supply.

[23] For the problems of sustaining a sense of professional mission among experienced teachers, see Jackson, *Life in Classrooms*, ch. 4; Brenton, *What's Happened to*

by demanding more money for teachers. They must also demand that schools be structured so as to sustain teachers in cultivating the capacity for critical deliberation in their classrooms. The limitations on democratic authority over schools suggested by this professional purpose are significant. To support professionalism among teachers, democratic communities must delegate a substantial degree of control over what happens in classrooms. Although a school board may establish the curriculum, it must not dictate how teachers choose to teach the established curriculum, as long as they do not discriminate against students or repress reasonable points of view. Although a school board may control the textbooks teachers use, it may not control how teachers use those textbooks (within the same principled constraints).[24] The rationale for so limiting democratic authority is straightforward: if primary school teachers cannot exercise intellectual independence in their classrooms, they cannot teach students to be intellectually independent.[25]

Too much independence, however, can be as bad as too little. If one thinks only of the best teachers, those with high intellectual standards and humane values, it may be hard to imagine the dangers of granting teachers too much "academic freedom." When one thinks less selectively of public primary-school teachers, who now number about 2.5 million, the dangers of too much freedom are less difficult to discern. In the early years of public schooling in New York City, teachers resisted pressure by the Public School Society to abolish corporal punishment. After several unsuccessful attempts at abolition, the Public School Society managed to convince teachers not to cane children on the head.[26] Although the United Federation of Teachers in New York City has never championed the cause of corporal punishment, it has championed—and won—a form of tenure for teachers that makes it extremely difficult for schools to dismiss incompetent or ineffective teachers:

Teacher?; Sizer, *Horace's Compromise*; Lortie, *School Teacher*; and Goodlad, *A Place Called School*.

[24] Although democratic communities *may* unilaterally select textbooks, they would be wise to consult with teachers and leave them with a considerable range of choice, for the sake of both choosing better texts and retaining good teachers. "It's fine to talk about getting new and talented people into teaching through higher salaries or other means," Saul Cooperman, the New Jersey Commissioner of Education recently commented. "But unless you can also get these teachers more involved in choosing curricula, selecting textbooks and shaping grading policies, they may not stay around very long." *The New York Times*, Sunday, April 27, 1986, section 1, p. 32.

[25] "Teachers must feel inspired and committed to educational goals in order to be in a position to light the fire in students." Lightfoot, *The Good High School*, p. 339.

[26] Carl F. Kaestle, *The Evolution of an Urban School System: New York City, 1750-1850* (Cambridge, Mass.: Harvard University Press, 1973), pp. 180-81.

"principals . . . shift a teacher to another school rather than go through the time-consuming dismissal procedure, which involved formal charges, substantiated evidence, and professional witnesses."[27] The union's tenure rules have protected not only good teachers against punitive transfers or dismissals, but also incompetent and ineffective teachers against legitimate sanctions by local school districts.[28] If there is a solution to this problem, it does not lie in giving school boards the authority, claimed by the demonstration districts in New York City in the late 1960s, to dismiss teachers without cause or review.[29] A solution is more likely to lie in the institution of impartial review procedures, dominated by neither union nor school board.[30]

Although professionalism among public-school teachers does not require absolute authority within the classroom, it requires more authority outside the classroom than most teachers now have. Good schools treat teachers with what Sara Lightfoot calls "respectful regard." Principals of such schools invite teachers to participate as members of a profession—not only individually in the classroom but collectively in the school as a whole—in shaping the curriculum, disciplinary codes, graduation requirements, and their own working conditions.[31] Teachers in good schools exemplify an important aspect of the democratic ideal of professionalism: the primary reward of their work is not high pay or social status, but the pleasures of performance and the satisfactions of social service. Their work is demanding but undemeaning, other-regarding but not other-directed.

The ability of unions to create these conditions of "respectful regard" for teachers may be limited both by their self-understanding and by their legally sanctioned operation as collective-bargaining agents of employees with management. If the democratic ideal of professionalism suggests that school boards and principals treat teachers as partners in determining school policy, then it also suggests that unions demand fewer fixed policies regarding curriculum, discipline, and work schedules, and more participatory structures within which teachers can

[27] Ravitch, *The Great School Wars*, p. 318.

[28] Ibid.

[29] Ibid., p. 356.

[30] The "Yeshiva Plan" outlined such a procedure for empowering local school boards in New York City to fire teachers while protecting teachers against arbitrary dismissal. The plan was initially approved by union and community representatives, but the UFT withdrew their approval when the central Board of Education decided not to give the demonstration districts any additional funds to support improvements in educational services (smaller classes, a new reading program, a training program for community leaders by teachers and one for teachers by community leaders, and additional professional services). See ibid., pp. 313-19.

[31] Lightfoot, *The Good High School*, pp. 334-42.

join administrators and members of school boards in shaping these policies. The law may create a substantial disincentive to such a reorien-
tation of union demands. Were unions successful in elevating teachers
to the status of sharing in the "management" or "ownership" of
schools, courts might rescind the right of unions to represent teachers
in collective bargaining over salaries and other working conditions. Although there has never been a test case with regard to public schools,
the Supreme Court in 1980 ruled (in a 5-to-4 decision) against faculty
members who were organizing a union at Yeshiva University on
grounds that they were not employees but managers, who were "substantially and pervasively operating the enterprise."[32] Were public-
school teachers ever to participate as extensively as college professors
in shaping their work, such a decision would be a much bigger blow to
unionism than to professionalism.[33] The gain in professional autonomy
and status among public-school teachers would overwhelm the loss in
union bargaining rights. But the prospects of such a loss may deter
unions from fighting as hard for structural changes as they do for economic improvements in the status of teachers.

Teachers' unions are ideally an interim solution to the problem of
professional ossification, but the interim is likely to last a long time
given the obstacles now standing in the way of teachers gaining a
greater role in shaping school policy. Many of the most difficult obstacles to overcome have been erected not by local communities but by
city, state, and federal governments in the form of regulations governing (among other things) curriculum, hiring and firing standards, salary
and workload of teachers, the academic calendar, and the education of
handicapped and other disadvantaged children. Some of these obstacles—such as the federal requirement to provide adequate schooling for
all handicapped children—should not be overcome until local educational authorities can be trusted to carry out the educational purposes
that the requirements are intended to serve. Other obstacles ought not
to be so considered: regulations concerning minimum graduation requirements are appropriately set by more centralized political authorities and interfere very little, if at all, with the ability of teachers to exercise substantial control over their work. At John F. Kennedy High
School in the Bronx, for example, "it is not the numbers of state or city
required courses that cause rancor among teachers and administrators.

<hr />

[32] *National Labor Relations Board v. Yeshiva University*, 444 U.S. No. 78-857, pp.
679-91 (1979). See George W. Angell, ed., *Faculty and Teacher Bargaining: The Impact
of Unions on Education* (Lexington, Mass.: D. C. Heath, 1981).

[33] In ruling against unionism at Yeshiva, the Court found that professors determined
curriculum, grading systems, graduation standards, academic calendars, and course
schedules, and were consulted in all hiring, tenure, firing, and promotion decisions.

They seem to be perceived as relatively neutral guidelines shaped by a convincing intellectual rationale. . . ."[34] Most good schools, like Kennedy, supplement the state and city requirements.

Other requirements, however, are unnecessary barriers to achieving an appropriate degree of autonomy for teachers. At Kennedy High School, "the complaints surrounding external regulation tend to be focused on the requirements of staff responsibilities. . . ." The city requires monthly departmental and faculty meetings, teacher supervision, and evaluation of written lesson plans. The union has successfully resisted some of these requirements; its contract gives teachers the right not to comply with requests for written lesson plans, for example. By its regulations, the city tries to prevent teachers from shirking some of their duties. By its resistance, the union tries to prevent the city from overworking teachers or imposing unreasonable requirements on them. The city's regulations call for the union's resistance, but without externally imposed regulation or resistance, teachers would be better able to achieve a sense of professional autonomy and probably would be more willing to work harder. As one teacher at Kennedy High put it: "Somehow the edict from on high makes us all respond like resistant children who would rather go out and play."[35]

Edicts from the federal government elicit the most criticism. The criticism is often too sweeping, since some federal requirements—such as those that prevent schools from excluding disadvantaged children from an adequate education—have the compelling democratic rationale of overcoming discrimination.[36] The criticism is well directed, however, at other federal regulations, such as the *Lau* Remedies and the 1978 Amendments to the Bilingual Education Act of 1968 (Title VII of the Elementary and Secondary School Act of 1965).[37] Although neither repressive nor discriminatory, the *Lau* Remedies and the 1978 Amendments put the federal government in a doubly inappropriate position,

[34] Lightfoot, *The Good High School*, pp. 112-13.

[35] Ibid., p. 113.

[36] For an elaboration of the rationale for federal aid and protection of the handicapped, see Chapter Five.

[37] For a brief history and annotated bibliography of bilingual education in the United States, see Alba N. Ambert and Sarah E. Melendez, *Bilingual Education: A Sourcebook* (New York: Garland Publishing, 1985). For criticism of the *Lau* Remedies and the Amendments, see Ravitch, *The Troubled Crusade*, p. 276; and Noel Epstein, *Language, Ethnicity and the Schools: Policy Alternatives for Bilingual-Bicultural Education* (Washington, D.C.: Institute for Educational Leadership, 1977). For support, see Ricardo Otheguy, "Thinking About Bilingual Education: A Critical Appraisal," *Harvard Educational Review*, vol. 52, no. 3 (August 1982): 301-314; and Raymond V. Padilla, ed., *Theory, Technology and Public Policy on Bilingual Education* (Rosslyn, Va.: National Clearinghouse for Bilingual Education, 1983).

first, of dictating a pedagogical approach of disputed and unproven efficacy to teachers[38] and second, of superseding the diverse views of ethnic communities on the value of bilingual education (versus alternatives such as more intensive English instruction) in public schools.[39] If bilingual education is valued as means of teaching English to non-English-speaking children, but bilingual techniques have not been proven generally more effective than other techniques (such as intensive English instruction), then teachers should play a substantial role in determining which pedagogical methods are used for different groups of students.[40] If bilingualism also is valued for enabling ethnic communities to preserve their cultural heritage and identity, then those communities—rather than the federal government—should be empowered to decide whether and how they wish to preserve their culture through bilingual education.[41]

The *Lau* Remedies and the 1978 Amendments signaled a shift of federal involvement in bilingual education from financially supporting all pedagogical programs that met "the special language skill needs of national origin-minority group children"[42] to requiring public schools to educate all groups of limited-English-speaking students bilingually as a condition of receiving federal support. In the course of this shift, the federal government limited the autonomy of teachers without furthering the self-determination of ethnic communities. The *Lau* Remedies and the 1978 Amendments left teachers with considerably less collec-

[38] Bilingual education actually subsumes several different pedagogical approaches, which are united by a commitment to teaching non-English-speaking children at least partly in their native language. See William Mackey, "A Typology of Bilingual Education," in *Bilingual Schooling in the United States: A Source Book for Educational Personnel*, ed. Francesco Cordasco (New York: McGraw-Hill, 1976), pp. 72-90; and Otheguy, "Thinking About Bilingual Education," pp. 301-314. For the mixed evidence on the effectiveness of bilingualism as a means of teaching English, see Iris C. Rotberg, "Some Legal and Research Considerations in Establishing Federal Policy in Bilingual Education," *Harvard Educational Review*, vol. 52 (May 1982): 148-68.

[39] For different perspectives on bilingual education among and within ethnic communities, see Dena Kleiman, "Views Vary on Approach to a Bilingual Education," *New York Times*, March 3, 1979. For a particular account of the transformation of one Hispanic child who learns to speak English, see Richard Rodriguez, *Hunger of Memory: The Education of Richard Rodriguez* (Boston: Godine, 1981).

[40] For a review of the evidence on the effectiveness of bilingualism compared to intensive instruction in English among different types of students, see Rotberg, "Some Legal and Research Considerations," pp. 155-63.

[41] For a "pluralist" defense of bilingual education, see James A. Banks, *Multiethnic Education: Theory and Practice* (Boston: Allyn and Bacon, 1981), esp. pp. 159-78.

[42] Samuel Pottinger, "Identification of Discrimination and Denial of Services on the Basis of National Origin," Memorandum, Office of Civil Rights, U.S. Dept. of Health, Education, and Welfare, May 25, 1970. Quoted in Rotberg, "Some Legal and Research Considerations," p. 151.

tive influence over the shape of schooling and ethnic communities with little (if any) more.[43]

While the conflict over community control in New York City illustrated the tension between teachers' autonomy and local democratic authority, the controversy over bilingualism illustrates the tension between centralized authority and *both* teachers' autonomy and local democratic control. The latter tension is more pervasive today than the former, and probably more destructive of professional autonomy. As school districts in the United States have consolidated over the past fifty years (from over 127,000 in 1932 to under 17,000 in 1982), their administrations have expanded.[44] Layers of administrative decisions now insulate the policies of school boards and the preferences of ethnic communities within local school districts from the potentially critical perspective of teachers, and vice versa, overwhelming a potentially creative tension within democratic education between communal and professional authority, whereby communities and teachers are encouraged to take each others' educational priorities and programs seriously.

We cannot return to the small schoolhouse of the nineteenth century, nor would we be wise to abolish educational administration. Large school districts have some significant advantages over small ones, such as the ability to offer a broader curriculum and therefore to meet the needs of a wider variety of students. And administrators perform some valuable functions, not the least of which include easing the administrative burdens of teachers. But the advantages of large administrations are often offset by more significant disadvantages, such as the insulation of school policies from public scrutiny, the demoralization of teachers, and the alienation of students. One way of combining the advantages of bigness with those of smallness, suggested by Ernest Boyer in his recent study of American high schools, is to organize large schools into several smaller "schools-within-a-school."[45] It is important to recognize, however, that the smallness of the subunits themselves would be insufficient to overcome the problems of professionalism created by large administrations, unless those subunits were also to a significant extent professionally self-governing and accountable to a

[43] Cf. Abigail M. Thernstrom, "E Pluribus Plura—Congress and Bilingual Education," *The Public Interest*, vol. 60 (Summer 1980): 21. Thernstrom interprets Title VII as a "victory for the Hispanic community" and a sign of their political power. Yet she also recognizes that their "representation both in Congress and state legislatures is poor." One might therefore be more skeptical as to whether federally mandated bilingual education constitutes a victory for the Hispanic community (is there a single Hispanic community?) or a sign of *its* political power.

[44] See Boyer, *High School*, p. 233.

[45] Ibid., p. 235.

public for their educational policies. So conceived, schools-within-a-school can prevent educational bureaucracies from destroying professional autonomy while creating the potential for more local participation in the making of school policy. By empowering both teachers and concerned citizens in local communities, schools-within-a-school can preserve the democratically healthy tension between professional and communal judgment.

DEMOCRACY WITHIN SCHOOLS

The professionalism of teachers, properly defined, serves as a safeguard against repression and discrimination. But professionalism, even on this democratic definition, erects another obstacle to democratic education. The professional autonomy of teachers stands in tension with democratic education to the extent that teachers invoke their professional competence to deny students any influence in shaping the form or content of their own education. The solution to this problem cannot be to give students equal control over the conditions of their schooling. Students lack the competence necessary to share equally in making many decisions. Ceding them equal control on all issues would mean denying teachers even a minimal degree of professional autonomy. The problem of authority within schools, therefore, does not lend itself to the democratic solution of political equality. Yet neither does it lend itself to the most apparent alternative to democratic rule: professional autonomy based upon competence. Insofar as professional autonomy teaches deference to authority, it teaches a lesson in conflict with the conditions of democratic deliberation.

Whether professional authority teaches deference to authority or respect for high intellectual standards is partly an empirical question concerning the effects of different methods of teaching, partly a normative question of what professionalism requires. One way of answering the empirical question is to investigate the extent to which schools that are more internally democratic support the development of more democratic values among students. This investigation runs up against the obvious empirical difficulty of controlling in a nonexperimental setting for the many other variables that also distinguish more from less democratic schools or students who choose to participate in more democratic schools-within-a-school from those who do not. A student from Brookline's School Within a School—where students share authority with teachers over a remarkably wide range of decisions—comments that "in SWS people care about learning. There is a real sense of community." Although this sentiment is widely shared among SWS students, one cannot assume that it is a product of SWS schooling. SWS students tend to be "a much more homogeneous group than the diversity reflected in the school at large."[46] They probably enter SWS with a commitment—or at least a predisposition—to participation.[47]

Students who are predisposed neither to participation nor to learning present the greater challenge to a democratic conception of teaching because their negative attitude toward schooling can readily reinforce a purely disciplinary method of teaching: teachers assert their authority, first to produce order, and then to funnel a body of knowledge into students. Some teachers who are not otherwise committed to the disciplinary method use it when they teach students in the lowest academic tracks.[48] The disciplinary method may be the easiest way to educate students who do not want to be educated. Perhaps more importantly, if education fails, disorder does not ensue (at least not in the classroom). A disciplinary approach therefore recommends itself over "nondirective guidance, which, in gist, means copping out—abdicating the teachers' responsibilities and leaving pupils to work out their own 'development.' " But, as Harry Eckstein points out: "One style will hardly shape democratic character; the other will not shape anything at all."[49]

In practice, however, teachers' options are not this stark even in classrooms of unmotivated students. Teachers committed to a more participatory approach appear to be more successful both in getting their students to work and in increasing their commitment to learning than teachers who take a more disciplinary approach.[50] Participatory approaches aim to increase students' commitment to learning by building upon and extending their existing interests in intellectually productive ways.[51] As one teacher self-consciously committed to a participatory approach commented:

> I personally feel that if a class is upset about something, that it's almost impossible for me to have them swallow anything

[46] Lightfoot, *The Good High School*, pp. 187-88.

[47] Democratic schools that include young children, such as Summerhill, seem to self-select according to parental commitment, which undoubtedly affects the predisposition of children. See Neill, *Summerhill*, p. 16.

[48] See Mary Haywood Metz, *Classrooms and Corridors: The Crisis of Authority in Desegregated Secondary Schools* (Berkeley: University of California Press, 1978), pp. 59-62, 101-110. Metz calls this method "proto-authority."

[49] Harry Eckstein, "Civic Inclusion and Its Discontents," *Daedalus*, vol. 113, no. 4 (Fall 1984): 122.

[50] See Metz, *Classrooms and Corridors*, pp. 115-16. What I call the participatory approach is similar to what Metz calls the developmental approach.

[51] Ibid., pp. 40-41. Compare Alfred North Whitehead, "The Rhythmic Claims of Freedom and Discipline," in *The Aims of Education and Other Essays* (New York: The Free Press, 1967), pp. 29-41.

[else]. . . . So I have made the decision that if I see something that my students want to talk about, we will talk about it. I will leave them with the decision. Many times I can suggest to them many titles of books that are pertinent to what they are talking about. In which case they would be a lot more interested in reading that maybe, or discussing that, and I can bring that in.[52]

To the extent that a participatory approach builds upon students' interests and elicits their commitment to learning, it may be considered more democratic than a disciplinary approach.

By the same criteria, school practices outside the classroom may be considered more or less democratic. The day after Martin Luther King was assassinated, one desegregated junior high school in Berkeley held an assembly exclusively under faculty initiative and planning, while a second, with a similar student body, turned over the plans for its assembly primarily to the students. In the first school, the program was largely nonparticipatory. Most of the students on stage were white and almost exclusively from the high academic tracks. The program in the second school, by contrast, "provided for more audience participation. It was universally praised as a moving experience, even by the 'old guard' teachers. The usually restless and noisy assembly audience was attentive and quiet even through a period of silent meditation."[53] The participants, chosen by the students, were a more diverse group. Although the second school was less orderly, even its lower-track students were more engaged in its life. The students generally seemed "more independent, reflective and insightful about their education, and in many cases more directly responsive to the activities and conditions which support the fulfillment of the school's educational goals." But they were also (according to one sympathetic observer) more disorderly and "arrogant" than students in the first school.[54]

The choice of a participatory approach may not bring all good things in its wake. Ideally, students in the second school would also be orderly and humble. A participatory approach gives priority to cultivating self-esteem and social commitment over humility and order, a priority presumed by the democratic goal of educating citizens willing and able to participate in politics. But because not all good things go together in education any more than in life, this priority is not absolute; it should be overridden when disorder and arrogance are so great as to threaten the very enterprise of education within schools.[55]

[52] Metz, *Classrooms and Corridors*, p. 37.
[53] Ibid., pp. 231-32.
[54] Ibid., p. 228.
[55] This priority *is* overridden even in the most self-consciously democratic of schools,

Existing studies are by no means definitive in their findings of the educative effects of more democratic methods. More empirical data would help us judge the effect of democracy within schools on cultivating participatory virtues—a sense of social commitment, political efficacy, a desire to participate in politics, respect for opposing points of view, critical distance from authority, and so on. Were teachers to discover that more democratic methods better stimulated the development of these virtues, they would still have to consider how much emphasis to give to developing them. The purposes of primary education—even the democratic purposes—are not exhausted by the successful cultivation of the participatory virtues. The disciplinary virtues—the imparting of knowledge and instilling of emotional along with intellectual discipline—are also among the purposes of democratic education, and apparently they are not always most effectively taught by the most democratic methods, especially among those students least committed to learning. The question of how much democracy within schools is democratically desirable remains doubly difficult to answer, therefore, because we have incomplete data on the educative effects of more democratic methods and because we rightly value the disciplinary as well as the participatory purposes of primary education.

Without more empirical evidence, we cannot say precisely how much democracy in schools is desirable, but we can say something significant about the way the professional standards of teachers should and should not be defined. Many teachers conceive of teaching the participatory virtues as lying beyond—or at best on the periphery of—their professional obligations, the core of their professional obligation being to teach what I have called the disciplinary virtues. This understanding is based on two misconceptions, one related to the means and the other to the ends of democratic education. Students generally learn best when they have a prior commitment to what they are being required to learn.[56] Many, perhaps most, students enter school lacking such a prior commitment.[57] Permitting students to participate in determining aspects of their education generally serves to develop a commitment on

---

such as Summerhill. "For example, one safety rule is that kids under a certain age may not possess matches or knives. These safety rules are arbitrary, and are not subject to change by the weekly General Meeting." Joshua Popenoe, *Inside Summerhill* (New York: Hart Publishing, 1970), p. 28.

[56] The Coleman Report, for example, found that "of all the variables measured in the survey, the attitudes of student interest in school, self concept, and sense of environmental control show the strongest relation to achievement." James S. Coleman et al., *Equality of Educational Opportunity*, p. 319.

[57] For the problems of getting students involved in their work, and additional evidence of the relationship between involvement and learning, see Jackson, *Life in Classrooms*, pp. 85-111. See also Metz, *Classrooms and Corridors*, esp. pp. 91-144.

their part to learning.[58] Among the least motivated students, however, a participatory method can entail compromising what many teachers consider the demands of professional competence. In the study cited above, teachers committed to the participatory approach occasionally allowed their lower-track students to engage in some classroom activities that were "not officially acceptable" (but harmless) in order to elicit concentrated effort for those academic activities the teachers deemed educationally most important. The additional work and concentration that such teachers thereby elicited from lower-track students was, according to Mary Metz, "modest, not miraculous." Yet the participatory teachers, Metz comments, "got their students to work seriously for a larger proportion of their time in class than did teachers who officially required them to work all the time but were pushed by constant disruptions into using up their resources for control on matters other than directly academic effort."[59] Metz's study suggests that more democratic methods may be a means of motivating students to develop even the disciplinary virtues.

The ends of democratic education are, of course, not limited to teaching disciplinary as distinct from participatory virtues. Even the ability to think critically about politics is an incomplete virtue from a democratic perspective. If primary schooling leaves students with a capacity for political criticism but no capacity for political participation or sense of social commitment, either because it fails to cultivate their sense of political efficacy or because it succeeds in teaching them deference to authority, then it will have neglected to cultivate a virtue essential to democracy.[60] Although we lack enough evidence to say how much internal democracy is necessary to cultivate participatory virtues among students, the low levels of political participation in our society and the high levels of autocracy within most schools point to the conclusion that the cultivation of participatory virtues should become more prominent among the purposes of primary schooling, especially

[58] "For apart from the fact that fruitful suggestions may develop from such discussions [between students and teacher], there is at least one thing that is known about learning, which is that it tends to improve if the learners begin to feel involved in and responsible for their learning situation." R. S. Peters, *Authority, Responsibility and Education* (London: George Allen and Unwin, 1973), p. 49.

[59] *Classrooms and Corridors*, pp. 115-16. Metz's analysis suggests that the results in the lower tracks might have been less modest than it appeared, since once students were successful they were moved into the next higher track. Her further observation fuels the case against tracking: those who might have become leaders and exemplars for the rest of the class were "drawn upward and out leaving the bottom tracks always populated with the slow or unwilling" (p. 116).

[60] R. S. Peters makes a similar argument in *Authority, Responsibility and Education*, esp. pp. 51-52.

as children mature intellectually and emotionally, and become more capable of engaging in free and equal discussion with teachers and their peers.

How much internal democratization of schools is desirable in a democracy? Dewey conceived of an ideal, democratic school as a "miniature community, an embryonic society,"[61] but he never specified which structures of a democratic school correspond to those of a democratic society. If the Laboratory School at the University of Chicago under Dewey's leadership from 1896-1903 is evidence of the structures he would support, then Dewey's characterization of school as a miniature democratic community is misleading.[62] Dewey treated teachers at the Lab School as colleagues: they met with him weekly to discuss curriculum and other educational matters. Teachers also had a free period daily to discuss their work with other teachers. Students did not have the same freedom, authority, or influence as teachers over the curriculum or the structure of their schooling, but they too were encouraged to engage in far more collective deliberation and decisionmaking than is common in most primary schools. Classes at the Lab School often began with "council meetings" in which teachers discussed past work and planned future work with students. The youngest students were given the daily responsibility of collectively distributing and carrying out important tasks. Judging by its efforts to teach participatory virtues, the Lab School was more democratic than all but a few American schools.[63] It was an embryonic democratic society because it elicited a commitment to learning and cultivated the prototypically democratic virtues among its students, not because it treated them as the political or intellectual equals of its teachers. The most internally democratic schools typically balance the participatory and the disciplinary purposes of education, leaving some significant educational decisions— such as the content of the curriculum and the standards for promotion—largely (but often not entirely) to the determination of teachers and administrators.[64]

[61] "The School and Society," in Dewey, *"The Child and the Curriculum" and "The School and Society,"* p. 18.

[62] For a detailed description of the "Dewey School," see K. C. Mayhew and A. C. Edwards, *The Dewey School* (New York: Atherton, 1966). See also Sarason's favorable discussion in *The Culture of the School and the Problem of Change,* pp. 195-211.

[63] Although the Lab School was less internally democratic than Summerhill, even Summerhill significantly constrains internal democracy. The General Meeting, for example, does not hire and fire teachers.

[64] Cf. Metz, *Classrooms and Corridors,* pp. 118-19: "This attraction of competent teachers to roughly similar [developmental] styles suggests that competent teaching may require an assumption that teacher and student share goals—or perhaps better it may re-

That an ideal democratic school is not as democratic as an ideal democratic society should not disenchant us either with schooling or democracy, since democracies depend on schools to prepare students for citizenship. Were students ready for citizenship, compulsory schooling—along with many other educational practices that deny students the same rights as citizens—would be unjustifiable. It would, on the other hand, be remarkable if the best way to prepare students for citizenship were to deny them both individual and collective influence in shaping their own education. The most democratic schools, like Dewey's Lab School and Brookline's "School within a School," do not look like miniature societies, at least not like miniature democratic societies: teachers have much more authority, both formal and informal, than democratic legislators have, or ideally should have. But these schools do come close to living up to the educational standard dictated by democratic values: democratize schools to the extent necessary to cultivate the participatory along with the disciplinary virtues of democratic character. If, as Dewey argued, a democratic society requires that citizens have "a personal interest in social relationships and control, and the habits of mind which secure social changes without introducing disorder,"[65] then a substantial degree of democracy within schools will be useful, probably even necessary (although undoubtedly not sufficient), to creating democratic citizens.

---

quire the creation of such sharing in actuality. It may also require that a middle ground be struck between total dominance of the teacher and predominance of the student."

[65] John Dewey, *Democracy and Education* (1916) (New York: The Free Press, 1966), p. 99.

CHAPTER FOUR

THE LIMITS OF
DEMOCRATIC AUTHORITY

The democratic purposes of primary schooling constrain as well as empower democratic communities, but not in the name of parental choice, liberal autonomy, or conservative virtue. The principles of nonrepression and nondiscrimination limit democratic authority in the name of democracy itself. A society is undemocratic—it cannot engage in conscious social reproduction—if it restricts rational deliberation or excludes some educable citizens from an adequate education. Nonrepression and nondiscrimination are therefore intrinsic to the ideal of a democratic society, as parental choice, liberal autonomy, and conservative virtue are not. Chapter One developed a theoretical defense of this suggestion. This chapter refines our understanding of the principled limits on democratic authority by examining some actual cases, taken from common practices of primary schooling in the United States.

If our understanding is accurate, the constraints of nonrepression and nondiscrimination, properly interpreted, are necessary and sufficient for establishing an ideal of democratic education. Both claims are controversial. A "strong" democrat would argue that the constraints are not necessary, that the ideal of democratic education is fulfilled whenever majorities control education, even if the results of their decisions are repressive or discriminatory.[1] To the extent that democrats place limits on the legitimate outcomes of majoritarian decisionmaking, the strong democrat argues, they devalue the very process that they profess to defend.

The strong democrat's critique of the constraints could be compelling only if (a) majoritarian decisionmaking were all that we valued about democracy, and (b) democracy did not extend over time. Neither is the case. We value democracy not primarily as a pure process that defines what is just, nor as a perfect process that guarantees justice (defined by some nonprocedural standard).[2] Rather, we value democracy because it is the best way by which we can discover what a community

[1] Cf. Benjamin Barber, *Strong Democracy*. Again, Barber uses the term "strong democracy" in a broader sense than I am using it here.

[2] For a discussion of the difference between pure and perfect procedural justice, see Rawls, *A Theory of Justice*, pp. 84-88.

values for itself and its children. If democracy did not extend over time, we might best discover what a community values on any particular occasion by collective deliberation followed by unconstrained majority rule. The temporal dimension of democracy requires us to ask whether the results of majority rule make future decisions undemocratic either by restricting citizens' capacity for deliberation in the future or by excluding some citizens from full participation in future deliberations. The question is all the more pressing to ask of decisionmaking with regard to education, because educational policies can stifle the capacity and even the desire for deliberation.

A "directed" democrat accepts the constraints as necessary but rejects the claim that they are sufficient. Rousseau's claim that "the general will is always in the right" appears implausible until one notices all the qualifications and constraints he places on actual democratic decisions.[3] Directed democrats imagine additional ways of educating and then constraining democratic bodies to make their decisions achieve Rousseau's ideal of the general will, which is always in the right. But even the most manipulative education (consider the one Rousseau recommends for Emile) and the cleverest set of constraints (consider those Rousseau recommends to the legislator) cannot guarantee correct results. The best democratic bodies, like the best juries, will sometimes make mistakes, even when their decisions are not repressive or discriminatory. Rousseau's position still presents a formidable challenge: after all, the mistakes of majorities (like those of juries) are serious, and they are not suffered only by those who make them. Why should a political philosophy sanction mistakes if it can imagine ways in which a society can realize a general will that is always in the right?

Were democratic decisionmaking valued exclusively as a procedure for achieving correct outcomes, the directed democrat's position would be more forceful. But, unlike a jury trial, democracy is valuable for far more than its capacity to achieve correct outcomes.[4] It is also valuable for enabling societies to govern themselves, rather than to be governed by an intelligence unrelated to their nature, such as Rousseau's legislator.[5] If democracies are to govern themselves, they must remain free to

---

[3] Jean Jacques Rousseau, *The Social Contract*, trans. G.D.H. Cole (New York: E. P. Dutton, 1950), bk. 1, ch. 4 (p. 29).

[4] This contrast with jury trials is exaggerated, since they are not valued exclusively as imperfect procedures for achieving just verdicts. Tocqueville, among others, also valued them as schools of democratic citizenship. For the purposes of this argument, however, I have assumed that jury trials are valued exclusively as imperfect procedures for achieving just verdicts. To the extent that they are also valued as schools of citizenship, the more general defense of democracy is strengthened.

[5] Rousseau, *Social Contract*, bk. 2, ch. 7.

make mistakes in educating their children, as long as those mistakes do not discriminate against some children or prevent others from governing themselves freely in the future.[6] The promise of the principles of nonrepression and nondiscrimination is just this: to support a strong democracy without sanctioning majority tyranny or sacrificing self-government in the future.

To judge whether the promise can be fulfilled, we need to look at the practical implications of these principled limits. With regard to public schools, I shall examine three pairs of policies that raise the problem of repression, but in different ways and to different degrees. The first pair of policies—banning library books and approving textbooks—illustrates the problem of direct repression. The second pair—teaching creationism and civics—raises the more difficult problem of indirect repression. The third pair—sex education and sexist education—introduces a still more complex conflict between what might be called "repressive nondiscrimination" and "discriminatory nonrepression." Although the first practice in each pair is more controversial, the second is at least as troubling for democratic education.

Distinct problems arise with regard to private schools, whose very existence entails further limits on democratic authority. The most prominent problem is whether the principle of nondiscrimination permits private schooling. I shall begin by arguing that it does, and end by arguing that public schools should accommodate internal dissent among students and distinguish between practices of moral and sectarian education for some of the same reasons that recommend a realm for private schooling.

BANNING AND APPROVING BOOKS

Decisions by local school boards to ban books from public-school libraries are among the most direct and open violations of the principle of nonrepression.[7] Even if the school board's intention is to lay the foundation of human decency and patriotism by banning books, it should not attempt to achieve this end by shielding students from understanding why some people use indecent language, hold radical po-

[6] Because the effects of educational policies are often impossible to discern before it is too late, we must often judge intent rather than results. For a defense and clarification of proper judicial use of the standard of intent, see John Hart Ely, *Democracy and Distrust: A Theory of Judicial Review* (Cambridge, Mass.: Harvard University Press, 1980), pp. 136-70.

[7] See, e.g., *Board of Education, Island Trees Union Free School District No. 26, et al. v. Pico, By His Next Friend Pico, et al.*, 457 U.S. 863-73 (1981).

litical views, and break laws. Such understanding constitutes an important part of what it means to be an informed citizen.

But this criticism of book banning does not translate directly into a political position denying local school boards the authority to ban books. A position on democratic control over school libraries and classrooms is not of a piece with that which properly denies majorities the right to restrict free speech for adults. The same critics who deny local school boards authority to ban books admit that school librarians have the authority to select books according to what they think is most educationally suitable for students, and many also argue that children may be barred from buying pornographic books and viewing pornographic movies that adults have a constitutional right to read and see. Even if majorities are unwise to pass more restrictive speech policies for children and adolescents, they may be acting within the range of legitimate discretion given our educational aims with regard to children, our incomplete knowledge of how to achieve those aims, and our commitment to democratic control over education.

I say "may" because the crucial test of the legitimacy—as distinguished from the correctness or the wisdom—of a policy of book banning by local school boards is whether the policy is nonrepressive. Nonrepression protects the foundations of democratic politics by preventing states, and any group within them, from restricting rational deliberation of competing conceptions of the good life and good society. Applied to schooling, nonrepression prohibits educational authorities from shielding students from reasonable (not correct or uncontroversial) political views represented by the adult citizenry or from censoring reasonable challenges to those views. More generally applied to democratic politics, nonrepression prevents anyone from destroying "institutions and practices that guarantee the democratic character of the popular will: assembly, debate, elections, and so on."[8] Without the chance to assemble, debate, and elect, even well-educated citizens cannot engage in conscious social reproduction.

School board decisions to ban books often fail the more general as well as the more specific conditions of nonrepression. Many decisions to ban books are made or applied in an "erratic, arbitrary and freewheeling manner."[9] Typically, a few parents inform several members of a school board that a few books in the school library contain profane language. The board members bring this to the attention of the entire board, which then votes, with little deliberation, to ban the books. This

[8] Michael Walzer, "Philosophy and Democracy," *Political Theory*, vol. 9, no. 3 (August 1981): 384.

[9] *Pico v. Board of Education, Island Trees Union Free School District No. 26*, 638 F.2d 404 (1980) at 416.

was roughly the process by which the School Board of Island Trees Union Free School District in New York banned several books for the use of profanities and obscenities, for explicit sexual allusions, depictions of deviant sex, the glorification of sex and drugs, ungrammatical usage, and excerpts offensive to racial, religious or ethnic groups. The Board passed over many other books that fell into these categories.

Suppose the Board were required to apply its professed policy consistently? A consistently applied policy would be legitimate if it were the result of deliberative democratic procedures, and banned only those books that served, either by their intent or their effect on students, to glorify abhorrent ways of life. Were a book banning policy to satisfy these democratic standards, then we could consistently criticize a school board's decision while recognizing its democratic "right to be wrong." But efforts by local school districts to ban books have rarely if ever passed the standard of democratic legitimacy. They are rarely the outcome of deliberative proceedings. They are not consistently applied, and the banned books do not glorify abhorrent ways of life.

The inconsistent nature of the typical case of book banning risks repression in the more specific sense: by leaving librarians and teachers without guidelines for exercising their residual authority, haphazard policies have a chilling effect on educators. The principle of nonrepression therefore gives democrats good reasons to advocate overturning most if not all book-banning decisions. But these reasons leave room for recognizing the possibility that book-banning policies *could* be the legitimate outcome of democratic decisionmaking, even if they rarely are.

Although textbook control by states is less frequently criticized than local book banning, it is also a direct and common form of censorship, one that has considerably more widespread educational consequences than local book banning. In many states, the board of education, the superintendent of schools, or a special review committee decides which among many history textbooks are suitable for use in public schools.[10] Some states leave a lot of discretion to local school districts. Others— such as Mississippi and Texas—constrain the choice of local schools very narrowly. For many years, the Mississippi State Textbook Purchasing Board approved only one ninth-grade state history. The Board's decision was eventually challenged in court on grounds that its only approved text "denigrated black Mississippians and championed white supremacy."[11] But the authority of the State Board to approve

[10] I rely on Frances FitzGerald's account in *America Revised: History Schoolbooks in the 20th Century* (New York: Random House, 1980).

[11] Ibid., p. 52.

texts remained unchallenged. The reasons for allowing states to approve high-school textbooks are generally that (1) someone must select the texts that school children use, (2) state boards have more time and access to experts in the field, and (3) centralized selection of texts exposes many children to a common historical perspective. State approval of textbooks thereby promises both to raise academic standards and to create common moral standards of public education.

The actual practices of state selection, however, often fly in the face of their justification. Some states, such as Mississippi, use state selection of history textbooks to protect contestable political perspectives against intellectual challenge. Other selection practices, such as those of Texas, have consequences that extend far beyond the single state's policy. The Texas State Textbook Committee controls such a large share of the national market in textbooks that the pressure it exerts on publishers to censor texts also changes the content of texts available for use in other states. In response to pressure from the Texas Committee in the 1960s, various publishers dropped references to Pete Seeger and Langston Hughes, and deleted passages saying that World War II might have been avoided had the United States joined the League of Nations and that some countries would occasionally disagree with us. Combinations of like-minded smaller states can exert a similar influence:

> The fact that most of the former Confederate states have state-level adoptions has meant that until recently conservative white school boards have imposed their racial prejudices not only on the children in their states but on children throughout the nation.[12]

But the effects of centralized textbook selection are not always for the worse and not only a product of state-wide selection. Civil rights groups in the 1960s successfully pressured the school boards and textbook councils of several very large cities to drop texts that were racially and religiously biased. As a consequence of their pressure, textbooks finally started to depict the United States as a multi-racial society. We cannot conclude that centralized textbook selection necessarily, or even generally, has bad educational outcomes. But we can still question the wisdom of placing this particular educational decision in the hands of centralized authorities. Given the limited impact of history courses on the ideology of high-school students,[13] the political and ed-

[12] Ibid., p. 57.

[13] See M. Kent Jennings, Kenneth P. Langton, and Richard G. Niemi, "Effects of High School Civics Curriculum," in M. Kent Jennings and Richard G. Niemi, *The Political Character of Adolescence: The Influence of Families and Schools* (Princeton, N.J.: Princeton University Press, 1974), pp. 181-206.

ucational value of the process of textbook selection may be as important as the resulting policy.

Shifting our concern from the policy to the process, we would judge various methods of textbook selection, first, by their openness to citizen participation, and second, by their potential to open citizens to the merits of unpopular points of view. Such a standard would lead us to criticize textbook committees that were closed to broad citizen participation. It would also lead us to prefer participatory boards that took seriously the opinions of teachers and historians to those that considered only the opinions of their constituents. Restructuring the process of textbook selection would further the democratic education of citizens by challenging their ways of viewing the world at the same time as it authorized them to influence the moral education of children in a nonrepressive manner.

The most effective means of avoiding direct repression may therefore be indirect: to restructure the process by which democratic decisions are made rather than to constrain decisions after they have been made. Restructuring the process rather than constraining its outcomes is likely to have the additional, unintended advantage of furthering the education of adults, while they further the education of children.

TEACHING CREATIONISM AND CIVICS

Democratic communities should have a broad range of authority over education, yet even the best democratic structures will not guarantee legitimate, let alone just, outcomes. So the question remains: How far should democratic authority extend? Instances of direct repression—such as the banning by Island Trees School Board of *Soul on Ice, The Fixer*, and *Slaughterhouse Five*—are the easiest to discern. Instances of indirect repression—where the broader political implications of the policy rather than the policy itself are repressive—raise more difficult problems for the application of democratic principles.

May a school board mandate balanced treatment of creationism along with evolution within high-school biology classes? The simplest reason to say "no" is that decisions concerning what theories are taught in the classroom are a matter of professional, not democratic, authority. We cannot know whether the simplest reason is right, however, until we ask why the realm of professional authority should extend (just?) this far. To answer this question, we must—as usual—rely on a political theory.

Is it within the legitimate authority of a democratic community to insist that biology teachers give the theory of divine creation balanced treatment with the theory of evolution in their classrooms? Suppose all citizens in a democracy shared a similar religious conviction, a conviction which led them to reject all scientific theories and knowledge that conflicted with divine revelation and the literal interpretation of the Bible. Teaching creationism might be compatible with *their* democratic standards. But a policy of equal time or balanced treatment for creationism in our society is much more problematic than a policy of teaching only creationism would be in this hypothetical society. Unlike citizens of the hypothetical society, we do not share a similar religious conviction against accepting the methods and results of scientific reasoning. On the contrary, our ability to agree upon a body of knowledge worthy of transmitting to future generations depends in significant measure upon widespread acceptance of scientific standards of evidence and verification.

The religions that reject evolution as a valid scientific theory also reject the secular standards of reasoning that make evolution clearly superior as a theory to creationism.[14] Only by putting religious faith above reason can someone believe that the entire fossil record (in which more primitive animals are found at lower geological levels and less primitive ones at higher levels) was created at the time of the Great Flood, by animals attempting to save themselves from drowning, the more advanced ones making it to higher ground and the less advanced ones getting stuck at lower levels. As one critic of creationism points out:

> Now this explanation is, of course, *logically possible*—i.e., its description is not self-contradictory. But can anything more positive be said in favor of it? Is there one single *reason* for believing it to be true? *Of course not!* (There is religious prejudice, but that is a cause for belief rather than a reason.) How incredible to imagine, for example, that not a single higher animal *tripped*, fell way down, and got drowned (and thus fossilized) at a lower level![15]

The scientific case against creationism is straightforward. The democratic case is complex. We cannot conclude that, having determined that the evidence favors evolutionary theory over creationism, "we will know what belongs in the classroom and what does not."[16] Reason

[14] For a discussion of those standards and the grounds upon which they are rejected by proponents of creationism, see "Creationism in Schools: The Decision in McLean versus the Arkansas Board of Education," *Science*, vol. 215, no. 4535 (February 19, 1982): 934-43. For an excellent description and critique of "scientific creationism," see Jeffrie G. Murphy, *Evolution, Morality, and the Meaning of Life* (Totowa, N.J.: Rowman and Littlefield, 1982), pp. 34-52.

[15] Jeffrie G. Murphy, *Evolution, Morality, and the Meaning of Life*, p. 51.

[16] Larry Laudan, "Science at the Bar: Causes for Concern," in Jeffrie G. Murphy,

may favor a more balanced account of the Revolutionary War than that offered in most American classrooms, but that fact alone would not deprive schools of the authority to teach the biased "American" account. The distinctly democratic problem with teaching creationism stems from the fact that it (unlike the American account of the Revolution) is believable only on the basis of a sectarian religious faith. Teaching creationism as science—even as one among several reasonable scientific theories—violates the principle of nonrepression in indirectly imposing a sectarian religious view on all children in the guise of science. Teaching creationism as a scientific theory entails teaching children to accept a religious view that takes the words of the Bible to be the literal God-given truth as a scientific explanation of the origins of species. Teaching creationism as a religious rather than a scientific doctrine, on the other hand, is as out of place in a biology classroom as is teaching the Lord's Prayer.

Why not then permit creationism to be taught in public schools, but not as science or in science classes? Would it be repressive to teach children that they can choose *either* to believe in creationism, on the basis of faith in the God-given word of the Bible, or to believe in evolution, on the basis of secular reasoning and scientific evidence? The reasoning behind this "freedom of choice" position has implications that extend beyond the teaching of creationism as an alternative to evolution. Most Americans have reconciled the tenets of their faith with the findings of science. This reconciliation has political as well as intellectual virtues. In a religiously diverse society, secular standards of reasoning accommodate greater agreement upon a common education than religious faith. The case for teaching secular but not religious standards of reasoning does not rest on the claim that secular standards are neutral among all religious beliefs. The case rests instead on the claim that secular standards constitute a better basis upon which to build a common education for citizenship than any set of sectarian religious beliefs— better because secular standards are both a fairer and a firmer basis for peacefully reconciling our differences.

Democratic communities are not in principle bound to teach the truth, although the wisest communities will strive to do so, but they must be bound *not* to teach false doctrines that threaten to undermine the future prospects of a common democratic education. The constitutional prohibition against the establishment of religion creates such a negative boundary, which is subsumable under the more general democratic principle of nonrepression. The rationale for teaching any par-

---

Evolution, Morality, and the Meaning of Life, p. 154. The rest of Laudan's argument against the standard scientific critique of creationism still holds.

ticular religious doctrine in public schools—either as science or as a reasonable alternative to science—conflicts with the rationale for cultivating common, secular standards of reasoning among citizens. To teach creationism *as* science entails not teaching science (which consists of secular standards of inquiry and knowledge). To teach creationism as an alternative to science entails allowing public schools to give equal time to every religious belief firmly held by citizens, even if the belief is unreasonable (as in the case of creationism) or incompatible with basic democratic principles (as in the case of racist doctrines).

The recent demand for equal treatment of creationism is therefore not more benign than the original demand to exclude evolution from biology classes. The logic of both cases would permit the democratic establishment of religion within public schools.[17] The indirect—if not the direct—result of establishing religion in public schools would be to restrict rational deliberation among competing ways of life. The failure to distinguish between believing in creationism based on religious faith and believing in evolution based on scientific evidence therefore reflects not only an epistemological but also a political misperception. If democratic majorities in a religiously diverse society refuse to differentiate between a sectarian and a secular curriculum, they will unintentionally thwart the development of shared intellectual standards among citizens, and discredit public schools in the eyes of citizens whose religious beliefs are not reflected in the established curriculum. A religiously diverse democracy must therefore choose between the disestablishment of religion within public schools and the *de facto*, if not *de jure*, disestablishment of democratic schools.[18]

But public schools need not therefore sacrifice a common moral education for the sake of avoiding repression. Public schools can avoid even indirect repression and still foster what one might call a democratic civil religion: a set of secular beliefs, habits, and ways of thinking that support democratic deliberation and are compatible with a wide variety of religious commitments. Americans have long viewed the study of history and government as a way of inculcating common dem-

[17] See statements by Henry Morris and Duane Gish, director and associate director of the Institute for Creation Research, that neither evolution nor creationism is a science. Reported by Roger Lewin, "Where Is the Science in Creation Science?" *Science*, vol. 215, no. 529 (January 8, 1982): 142-46. For an argument rebutting the creationists' charge of the moral bias in evolutionary theory, see Allen Stairs, "The Case Against Creationism," *QQ: Report from the Center for Philosophy and Public Policy*, University of Maryland, vol. 2, no. 2 (Spring 1982): 9-11.

[18] For a rationale for disestablishing religion similar to the one upon which I rely, see Dennis F. Thompson, "Reasoning, Religion and the Court," in John D. Montgomery and Albert O. Hirschman, eds., *Public Policy*, vol. 21 (Cambridge, Mass.: Harvard University Press, 1967): 358-92.

ocratic virtues in citizens. Webster criticized schools after the Revolution for the "inexcusable" defect of teaching students the history of Greece, Rome, and Great Britain, while neglecting that of the United States. "[E]very child in America," Webster argued, "should be acquainted with his own country. . . . As soon as he opens his lips, he should rehearse the history of his own country; he should lisp the praise of liberty and of those illustrious heroes and statesmen who have wrought a revolution in her favor." Although we no longer criticize our schools for requiring students to memorize "the declamations of Demosthenes and Cicero or debates upon some political question in the British Parliament,"[19] many Americans share with Webster a similar expectation, that schooling "should increase the student's knowledge about political institutions and processes, make him a more interested and loyal (but not superpatriotic) citizen, and increase his understanding of his own rights and the civil rights of others."[20]

When students who have taken such courses are tested for political knowledge, political interest, sense of political efficacy, political trust, and civic tolerance, the findings offer "strikingly little support for the impact of the curriculum." Although students who have taken high-school civics courses tend to score slightly higher on these and other measures, "the increments are so minuscule as to raise serious questions about the utility of investing in government courses in the senior high school, at least as these courses are presently constituted."[21] Nor does the empirical evidence bear out those critics who claim that the source of the problem lies in the shift away from teaching history towards teaching government or "contemporary problems" courses. The same study that found little impact of civics courses on civic virtue also found that "the impact of the history curriculum under the same control conditions . . . was as low or lower than the civics curriculum."[22] A significant exception to these negative results is that civics courses increased the political knowledge, interest, and sense of political efficacy of black students from less-educated families,[23] thereby narrowing the

[19] Noah Webster, "On the Education of Youth in America," pp. 64-65.

[20] Jennings, Langton, and Niemi, "Effects of the High School Civics Curriculum," p. 181. For a contemporary scholarly defense, in the republican tradition, of civic education, see Richard M. Battistoni, *Public Schooling and the Education of Democratic Citizens* (Jackson: University Press of Mississippi, 1985).

[21] Ibid., p. 191. Furthermore, it seems that "virtually all of the small contribution that the curriculum makes in yielding positive results emanates from those students who were (in most instances) just finishing their civics course as the school year headed into its final weeks" (p. 192).

[22] Ibid.

[23] Ibid., pp. 194-206.

gap in political knowledge and efficacy between white and black students.

This conclusion is consistent with the claim that civics courses can have even more widespread significance. Empirical studies measure the results of civics and history courses as they are, not as they might be. And they measure only some, not all, of the results that are relevant to the concern for fostering democratic virtue. Only a small minority of high-school history or civics teachers take as one of their major goals to challenge their students to think critically about history or politics.[24] Empirical studies cannot measure the educational potential of restructured civics courses, nor do they measure whether courses, as they are presently structured, have an impact on how students "process political materials, or how they search for political answers."[25]

Other observers of American education offer evidence that the goal of making high-school history and civics intellectually challenging for students is not a utopian fantasy. Diane Ravitch describes a course, taught in a public high school in Brooklyn, that might serve as a model for civic education at the secondary-school level. On the day Ravitch observed this American history class, the students were discussing whether it was moral for the United States to drop the atomic bomb on Japan:

> The lesson was taught in a Socratic manner. Bruckner did not lecture. He asked questions and kept up a rapid-fire dialogue among the students. "Why?" "How do you know?" "What does this mean?" ... By the time the class was finished, the students had covered a great deal of material about American foreign and domestic politics during World War II; they had argued heatedly; most of them had tried out different points of view, seeing the problem from different angles.[26]

The most relevant result of such a course from the perspective of democratic education would not be an increase in political trust, efficacy, or even historical knowledge, but an increase in the ability of students to *reason*, collectively and critically, about politics, an ability that is no less essential to democratic citizenship by virtue of being difficult to measure by survey research.[27] The ability is so essential to democratic

[24] M. Kent Jennings, Lee H. Ehman, and Richard G. Niemi, "Social Studies Teachers and Their Pupils," in *The Political Character of Adolescence*, p. 226.

[25] Ibid.

[26] Diane Ravitch, *The Schools We Deserve: Reflections on the Educational Crises of Our Times* (New York: Basic Books, 1985), p. 288.

[27] Although Morris Janowitz reports on some surveys that "indicate that students in classrooms exposed to moderate-to-frequent amounts of classroom discussion about

education that one might question whether civics courses that succeeded in increasing political trust, efficacy, and knowledge but failed
to increase the ability of students to reason about politics were indirectly repressive. How can a civics course legitimately teach teenagers
to trust their government more without also teaching them to think
about what kind of government is worth trusting?

If history and civics courses do not teach students to reason about
politics, we should perhaps be grateful that they are not a major source
of political socialization. Perhaps it is inevitable that they are not. Most
theories of child development converge on the conclusion that early socialization shapes the fundamental moral and political values of children to a much greater extent than subsequent schooling. This conclusion is compatible with the claim that history and civics courses can and
should teach democratic virtue, so long as we understand democratic
virtue to include the willingness and ability of citizens to reason collectively and critically about politics. However students have been social-
ized outside of school, there should be room within school for them to
develop the capacity to discuss and defend their political commitments
with people who do not share them. Schools that cultivate the capacity
for critical deliberation need not convert a single student from the Republican to the Democratic Party, or vice versa, to foster democratic
virtue. Schools that fail to cultivate this capacity do not foster democratic virtue even when their students demonstrate the highest degree
of political trust, efficacy, and knowledge.

SEX EDUCATION AND SEXIST EDUCATION

The political problem of how to teach civic responsibility pales in comparison with that of how to teach sexual responsibility to teenagers.
Sex is difficult to discuss under the best of circumstances, but we do not
even agree what the best circumstances are. Conservatives typically
claim that only parents should teach (only their own) children about
sex, while liberals argue that schools have as much authority to teach
students sexual responsibility as they do civic responsibility.

To the conservative claim that sex education should remain part of
the private realm of the family, liberals respond that parents are often
ill-equipped or reluctant to teach their children about sex. Offering sex
education in schools supplements rather than supplants the educational authority of parents. Conservatives reply that when schools in-

---

politics did better than those without such discussion." Students exposed to political discussion in the classroom demonstrated both better reasoning capacities and more factual
knowledge. See Janowitz, *The Reconstruction of Patriotism: Education for Civic Consciousness* (Chicago: University of Chicago Press, 1983), p. 154.

form teenagers about the availability of contraception and abortion, they undermine the authority of those parents who believe that these are not legitimate alternatives to abstention. Liberals respond that informing teenagers of the availability of contraception or abortion is not equivalent to sanctioning its use. By being informed of their choices and forewarned of the consequences of those choices, teenagers are taught to take responsibility for their sexual behavior. Conservatives deny that sex should be taught as a matter of choice or that teenagers are old enough to take responsibility for their sexual behavior. Even if teenagers were old enough, it would be up to their parents to teach them the meaning of sexual responsibility. The controversy continues, liberals emphasizing the need to educate teenagers to make informed choices about their own lives and conservatives emphasizing the need for the state to stay out of the private realm of parental right and responsibility.

There is no way of resolving the controversy between conservatives and liberals on sex education by moving back and forth between the fundamentally different moral foundations of the state of families and the state of individuals. Even separately considered, these foundations lend only shaky support to conservative and liberal views regarding sex education in schools. Conservatives insist that the state stay out of sex education for the sake of preserving parental authority, but the vast majority of parents say that they want public schools to teach their teenagers about sex. Liberals insist that the state offer sex education for the sake of giving teenagers an unbiased choice among ways to live their own lives, but teachers cannot present teenagers with a neutral account of the choice among abstinence, contraception, and abortion. Agnosticism about the significance of sex is no more neutral than agnosticism about the existence of God. Whether or not teachers remain agnostic in the classroom, the content of sex education courses is bound to conflict with the convictions of some parents.

Seeing that sex is even more private (in the sense of intimate) than religion and at least as controversial, a democrat might be tempted to ban sex education along with religious education from public schools so they could get on with the work of teaching subjects such as civics that fall squarely within the public realm. Teaching about sex is, of course, not the same as teaching sex, just as teaching about religion is not the same as teaching religion. The most ardent advocate of the separation of church and state could consistently admit a course on comparative religion in the public-school curriculum. The distinction between teaching sex and teaching about sex is considerably harder, however, to sustain in practice. Perhaps because sex is so intimate, it is more difficult to teach about sex without teaching an attitude toward sex than it is to teach about religion without teaching an attitude toward religion (although the latter is not easy either). The strongest case for banning courses on sex education from public schools (regardless of democratic will) rests on an appreciation of the intimacy of the subject matter.

But the strongest case is not strong enough. One-dimensional distinctions between the private and public realm are too simple to determine whether sex (or religious[28]) education belongs in public schools. It does not follow that because sex is the most intimate realm of human activity, discussions of the nature and consequences of sexual activity must be excluded from public schools, as conservatives often claim. Nor does it follow that because sexual activity among teenagers profoundly affects the interests of other people (most obviously and importantly, the often abused children of unwed teenage mothers[29]), sex education must be mandatory, as liberals often claim. Neither policy prescription follows from these facts about human sexual activity—at least not without democratic deliberation and decisionmaking.

With democratic deliberation and decisionmaking, either conservative or liberal policy prescription would be legitimate. Because sex is the most intimate realm of human activity, one might conclude that public school is the wrong place to teach children about sex: classroom discussions desanctify sex, therefore sex education should remain entirely in the realm of familial responsibility, even if parents sometimes fail in fulfilling their responsibility. Most citizens today apparently do not reach this conclusion, perhaps because they do not believe in the sanctity of sex or (more likely) because they believe that sex education in schools is not a cause of its desanctification. Liberals who reject the conservative position on parental autonomy often support mandatory sex education in schools, to insure that all teenagers are informed of their choices with regard to sexual activity, even over their parents' opposition.

Although both conservative and liberal policies, if democratically sanctioned, would be legitimate, neither would be wise. The rationale behind the conservative policy of banning sex education from schools confuses cause and effect. Were sex perceived as a sacred activity by most adolescents, there would be considerably less need for sex education in schools than there now is. Although sex education courses do not cause the higher incidence of sexual activity among teenagers, they still can be plausibly construed as reaffirming the desanctification of

---

[28] I discuss the rationale for excluding religious—but not moral—education from public schools in the section "Separating Moral from Religious Education" below.

[29] *The New York Times*, October 23, 1982, p. A9.

sex.[30] Conservatives are unwise to attempt to restore the sanctity of sex by banning sex education from public schools, but they are not acting as agents of repression or discrimination in opposing educational policies that reaffirm the desanctification of sex. They may legitimately oppose sex education in schools as long as they recognize the legitimacy of democratically sanctioned policies supporting sex education.

Were it democratically sanctioned, the liberal policy of mandating sex education for all adolescents regardless of parental preference would also be legitimate but unwise for a reason related to the source of conservative opposition to sex education in schools. Mandatory sex education is as offensive to parents who believe in the sanctity of sex as mandatory prayer is to parents who do not believe in God. It does not follow that mandatory sex education is a repressive (and hence illegitimate) policy: teenagers, not their parents, are required to take sex education courses and they may neither believe in the sanctity of sex nor oppose its desanctification. But even if the vast majority of teenagers do not hold their parents' beliefs about sex, mandating sex education would be unwise were it to lead conservative parents to flee the public schools. A better policy would be to allow parents to exempt their children from taking such courses, and rely upon the informal teachings of friends to educate those adolescents who are not themselves committed to their parents' point of view. One of the few things most of us have learned from experience is that adolescents learn more about sex from their friends than from their parents or teachers.

A democratically sanctioned policy of requiring sex education in public schools with a provision for exempting students whose parents (or who themselves[31]) are opposed on principled grounds would be both legitimate and wise. It would be legitimate because the decision of whether to offer sex education in schools must by its very nature be a public one. It would be wise because teenage pregnancy is a public problem, a far greater public problem in this country than in most other Western democracies. The pregnancy rate among American teenagers is more than twice as high as that among Canadian, French, Swedish,

[30] The rates of sexual activity among teenagers are roughly the same in the United States, France, Great Britain, the Netherlands, Sweden, and Canada, although exposure to sex education courses is significantly greater in many of these countries. Those countries with the lowest rates of teenage pregnancy do not have the highest abortion rates. (The United States has by far the highest abortion rate, along with the highest pregnancy rate.) The lowest rates of teenage pregnancy occur in those countries with liberal attitudes toward sex, easily accessible contraceptive services, and comprehensive programs in sex education. *The New York Times*, March 13, 1985, p. A1.

[31] For the principled defense of exempting adolescents from school practices that violate their moral principles, see the section "Dissent Within Public Schools" below.

or British and Welsh teenagers.[32] Almost 100 out of every 1,000 American girls between the ages of 15 and 19 become pregnant. The abortion rate among American teenagers is also at least twice as high as it is in any of these countries (60 out of every 1,000 teenagers in the United States compared to 30 for Sweden). Pregnant teenage girls are on average poorer and drop out of school at far higher rates than other American teenagers. Teenage mothers also have higher rates of child abuse than other mothers. In New Orleans, teenage mothers account for about 30 percent of the child abuse cases. As the head of that City's child abuse unit commented: "With teen-age mothers the problem is primarily in the area of physical abuse and neglect. They don't have parenting skills, they don't have resources and they don't know how to obtain resources."[33]

The high incidence of child abuse among teenage mothers in New Orleans is just one among many illustrations of the limitations of considering sex education (or parenting, more generally) simply a private matter. One need not doubt that sexual activity per se is among the most intimate of human activities—and therefore not properly subject to state regulation—to recognize that the many public consequences of sexual activity among teenagers make it an appropriate subject of public education. Nor need one believe that decisions to offer (or not to offer) sex education courses can be morally neutral between liberal and conservative perspectives to endorse democratic decisionmaking as the legitimate means of deciding whether and how to offer sex education in public schools.

Sex education touches on the broader and more complex issue of sexist education. Although the term "sexist" is often used very loosely, I use it to characterize a specific set of educational practices: those that serve, often unintentionally, to restrict the quality or quantity of democratic education received by girls (or women) relative to that received by boys (or men).[34] The state law that banned sex education in Louisiana schools from 1970 to 1979 is, on this understanding, a sexist policy. Although the Louisiana Legislature did not make its decision for the sake of restricting the education of teenage girls, the policy pre-

---

[32] Although pregnancy rates among black American teenagers are much higher than among whites, the American rate would still be twice as high as any other Western democracies were black teenagers excluded from the calculation. *The New York Times*, March 13, 1985, p. A1.

[33] *The New York Times*, October 23, 1982, p. A9.

[34] This understanding does not commit me to a functionalist theory (criticized in the Introduction). The claim concerning sexist education is not that all, or even most, school policies serve to reinforce the subordination of women in our society, but only that those that do function in this way deserve special scrutiny.

vented schools from offering information (about contraception, for example) that some teenage girls would have used to prevent pregnancy and to stay in school longer. The educational opportunities open to teenage boys were less directly affected by the absence of this information, although the quality of their education probably also suffered as a result of the Legislature's restrictive policy.

The Louisiana legislature lifted its ban on sex education in 1979, but a substantial minority of school districts in the United States still do not offer any sex education, and many of those districts that do avoid controversial topics such as contraception, rape and sexual abuse, masturbation, abortion, and homosexuality.[35] Even those school districts in the United States that offer comprehensive courses in sex education for the purpose of promoting "rational and informed decision making about sexuality"[36] may do so in the context of an otherwise sexist education.

The problem of sexist education in American schools is therefore best illustrated by an issue other than that of sex education. Consider the following statistics concerning educational authority in the American school system: 84 percent of elementary-school teachers are female, while 99 percent of school superintendents and 97 percent of high school principals are male.[37] Although some studies use these statistics to illustrate the problem of sex discrimination in hiring, it is unlikely that the gross disproportion of women and men in elementary-school teaching and high-school administration results primarily from discrimination in hiring or promotion practices. One need not deny the existence of discrimination against women in school administration[38]

[35] *The New York Times*, October 23, 1982, p. A9.

[36] "The What and Why of Sex Education in the Nation's Schools," *The Urban Institute: Policy and Research Report*, vol. 14, no. 3 (December 1984): 8. For a more complete account of the availability of sex education in American schools, see Freya L. Sonenstein and Karen J. Pittman, "The What and Why of Sex Education: Describing and Explaining Program Content and Coverage in City Schools," and "The Availability of Sex Education in City School Districts," Research Reports for the Urban Institute, P.O. Box 7273, Dept. C., Washington, D.C. 20044.

[37] Patricia O'Reilly and Kathryn Borman, "Sexism and Sex Discrimination in Education," *Theory Into Practice*, vol. 23, no. 2 (Spring 1984): 110. See also Letty Cottin Pogrebin, *Growing Up Free: Raising Your Child in the 80's* (New York: McGraw-Hill, 1980), p. 491.

[38] There is ample historical evidence of discrimination against women for positions of authority within the profession, especially during its early years. Until 1866, for example, the National Education Association excluded women teachers from membership. Not until 1910 did it elect a woman president (Ella Flagg Young), and then only after an unprecedented minority nomination from the floor of the convention. For further evidence of past discrimination against women in the NEA and elsewhere in the profession, see David B. Tyack, *The One Best System: A History of American Urban Education* (Cam-

to recognize that, even in the absence of discrimination, a far greater proportion of women than men would choose elementary-school teaching (and a far greater proportion of men than women would choose school administration).

The disproportionality is related to the different gender roles that men and women have traditionally assumed and continue to assume within the American family, for complicated causes that are still not fully understood. But this much is apparent: elementary-school teaching is a career more attractive to adults who see themselves as nurturers of children, who place a high premium on being at home with their children after school and during the summer, who do not assume that they must be the primary breadwinners in their families, and who do not depend for their self-esteem on moving steadily up a career ladder or exercising authority over other adults. Many more women than men in our society fit this description. There are surely additional and deeper causes for the disproportionality of women in elementary-school teaching and men in administration, but one need not uncover those causes to analyze this example of sexism in education.

The problem is roughly the following: as long as women are hired as elementary-school teachers in far greater proportions than men, and men are hired as school administrators in far greater proportions than women, schools will teach children that "men rule women and women rule children."[39] Why shouldn't schools teach this lesson, someone might ask, if it reflects the social reality of gender preferences rather than discriminatory hiring practices?[40] A preliminary answer is that schools do not simply reflect, they perpetuate the social reality of gen-

---

bridge, Mass.: Harvard University Press, 1974), pp. 59-71, 255-68; and David Tyack and Elisabeth Hansot, *Managers of Virtue: Public School Leadership in America, 1820-1980* (New York: Basic Books, 1982), pp. 180-201. Tyack and Hansot note that "as school administrators women often fared better when they were elected by their fellow citizens—male and female—than when they were appointed by a male board or superior" (p. 189).

[39] Pogrebin, *Growing Up Free*, p. 491.

[40] Alternatively, one might ask: if schools shouldn't teach this lesson, why should parents? Although the moral argument against reinforcing sex stereotyping applies to parents as well as schools, it cannot justify direct political intervention into the family for the sake of supporting gender-neutral education. A governmental body cannot ensure that children are educated in a gender-neutral way without violating one of the most basic liberties of parents: the choice of how to share childrearing and what (if any) work to do outside the family. The intimacy of the family is a barrier to realizing the ideal of a thoroughly gender-neutral education, but it need not prevent democratic governments from instituting policies, such as subsidized childcare, for the sake of achieving more egalitarian gender relations, although it does not permit direct state intervention for the same sake. For a further discussion of this distinction, see the section in the Conclusion: "Democratic Education and Democratic Theory."

der preferences when they educate children in a system in which men rule women and women rule children. The authority structure within schools serves as an additional lesson in the nature of "normal" gender relations. Girls learn that it is normal for them to rule children, but abnormal for them to rule men. Boys learn the opposite lesson. The democratic problem lies not in the content of either lesson per se, but in its repressive nature: the lessons reinforce uncritical acceptance of an established set of sex stereotypes and unreflective rejection of reasonable (and otherwise available) alternatives.

What structure of gender preferences, then, should schools support? This question would not be so difficult to answer were there only one rather than two principled limits on democratic decisionmaking. From the perspective of the principle of nondiscrimination, school districts should continue to hire as many more women as elementary-school teachers and men as administrators as there are more qualified women interested in elementary-school teaching and more qualified men interested in administration. The principle of nonrepression, taken alone, generates an incompatible answer: school districts should hire women and men as elementary-school teachers and administrators in more equal proportions to prevent schools from teaching girls that it is abnormal for them to aspire to positions of authority over men and boys that it is abnormal for them to aspire to teaching young children (or to be "ruled" by women).

Given that the two principled constraints on democratic decision-making yield conflicting conclusions, what should schools do? Should they avoid sexual discrimination in hiring at the risk of repressing rational deliberation over gender roles among children? Or should they avoid repressing rational deliberation at the risk of sexual discrimination in hiring? If schools must choose between "repressive nondiscrimination" or "discriminatory nonrepression," then neither alternative is preferable on democratic grounds.

There may be a less stark and more acceptable alternative, however: to admit gender as a qualification for administration and teaching until there are enough men and women in both positions to break down their sex stereotyping. This policy has the potential for overcoming the repressive effects of sexual stereotyping without violating the principle of nondiscrimination. The principle of nondiscrimination requires that the qualifications set for jobs be relevant to their legitimate social functions. One of the social functions of school teachers and administrators is to enable children to deliberate rationally among good lives. Sex stereotyping in these jobs is a formidable obstacle to this end if the overwhelming proportion of women among elementary-school teachers and men among school administrators reinforces sex stereotypes, which in turn has the effect of repressing consideration among both female and male students of ways of life that diverge from these stereotypes. Assuming that this account of the social function of educational authority is accurate, then sex is not an irrelevant consideration in hiring. Preferring women who are basically qualified to men for administrative positions and preferring men who are basically qualified to women for elementary school teachers need not violate the principle of nondiscrimination as long as the sex stereotyping of these jobs remains an obstacle to nonrepressive education.

The specifics of the case for counting sex as a qualification are crucial to its justification. The rationale of counting sex as a qualification is to overcome the repressive nature of sex stereotyping, not to insure that men and women are represented in equal proportions in each job category. When teaching and administration are no longer sex stereotyped, sex therefore ceases to be a relevant qualification, regardless of whether women and men choose teaching and administration in equal proportions. Even before sex stereotyping is broken, the sex of a candidate cannot be considered the only relevant qualification. It would be both counter-productive and unfair to hire men as elementary-school teachers and women as administrators who lack the full range of necessary qualifications.

The educational rationale for breaking sex stereotyping implicates not only the authority structure but also the curriculum of schools. Because most discussions of sexism in education concentrate on the curriculum, I have focused on the authority structure.[41] Breaking sex stereotypes in the curriculum is equally important but simpler to justify. It should be obvious that no democratic principle prevents teachers from paying more attention to women in history and literature or from adopting gender-neutral language. The practical obstacles that stand in the way of curricular reform make it even more important that we discover as many principled ways as possible to overcome sex bias in schooling.

Private Schools

Is access to private schooling a necessary or desirable limit on democratic authority over primary education? In Chapter Two, I argued that

[41] For informative examples of sex bias in curricula, see Pogrebin, *Growing Up Free*, pp. 491-518. For discussions of sex bias in academic disciplines, see Dale Spender, *Men's Studies Modified: The Impact of Feminism on the Academic Disciplines* (Oxford: Pergamon Press, 1981). Spender's essay in this volume, "Education: The Patriarchal Paradigm and the Response to Feminism" (pp. 155-73), connects the problem of male authority to curriculum bias.

the democratic purposes of education provide a defense against voucher proposals, which would subsidize parental choice of private schools. I emphasized there that a primary purpose of schools is to cultivate common democratic values among all children, regardless of their academic ability, class, race, religion or sex. The question now arises: Should parents even be *permitted* to send their children to private schools, which claim a right to cultivate particular values and select students according to their ability, class, religion, race, and sex? A democrat must reject the simplest reason for sanctioning private schools—that parents have a "natural right" to control the education of their children. Democratic education is a shared trust of parents and polity. Only in a state of families is it natural to assume that parents have an exclusive right to control the education of their children regardless of democratic will.

Rejecting private education as a parental right, however, does not necessarily entail rejecting private education. The question still remains open as to whether democracies should prohibit parents from sending their children to private schools. One of the strongest cases for "prohibitionism" is that private schools will siphon off the most affluent and the academically best students, leaving public schools with a student body that is disproportionately poor, economically and academically. Having taken their children out of public schools, the most affluent parents—who also tend to be the most politically influential—will oppose increased spending on public schools. The quality of public schooling will therefore decline even further. As more and more parents pull their children out of public schools, public schools will be increasingly incapable of fulfilling their democratic purposes. By this logic, private schooling must be prohibited so as to fulfill the democratic purposes of public schooling. While a prohibitionist policy deprives dissatisfied parents of the freedom to take their children out of public schools, it supports their freedom to participate as citizens in the control of public schools.

Prohibitionism therefore relies heavily on the consequentialist claim that the results of prohibiting private schooling will be better on balance for democracy than the results of any alternative policy. To decide whether this claim is compelling, we need to answer some difficult questions: Will public schools improve if they have no competition? Will they do better in furthering democratic purposes if dissatisfied citizens are prohibited from paying extra to use the private sector? Have private schools in this country, on balance, hurt public schools by siphoning off the best students along with the most politically influential parents rather than aiding public education by serving as exemplars of new educational practices? Once we recognize that the case for prohibitionism requires an affirmative answer to these questions, we must wonder whether the case for maximizing parental voice by abolishing private schools is any stronger than the case for maximizing market choice by providing parents with vouchers.

The primary weakness of the prohibitionist case is not its logic but its empirical presupposition: that private schools serve primarily to siphon off the most affluent and academically best students. The majority of private schools in the United States are religious, not secular, and a majority of these are Catholic. Two-thirds of private-school students attend Catholic schools. Although the median income of parents who send their children to parochial schools is higher than the median of public-school parents, the distribution of income among private-school parents is very broad. Far from siphoning off only the best and the brightest, private schools admit students with almost as broad a range of abilities as public schools. Private schools are more segregated than public ones by religion, but not by class, race, or academic talent.[42] Private schooling in the United States serves primarily to permit Catholic and other religiously committed parents to send their children to schools that teach their faith.

Before advocating the abolition of private schools, we therefore need to ask whether the democratic purposes of primary schools would be better fulfilled were parents forced to send their children to public schools regardless of the strength of their commitment to religious education. The democratic purposes of primary education include teaching children a common set of democratic values that are compatible with a diverse set of religious beliefs. A better alternative to prohibiting private schools would be to devise a system of primary schooling that accommodates private religious schools on the condition that they, like public schools, teach the common set of democratic values. A mixed system of this sort would better fulfill democratic purposes than a purely public one, which refused to permit even the most strongly committed parents to send their children to private schools. This accommodation presupposes that parents who are intensely dissatisfied with the lack of religious or other forms of education in public schools have a legitimate reason for exiting, but not for exempting their children from learning a common set of democratic values.

A mixed system (of public and private schools) should attempt to achieve a rather delicate balance: permitting parents who are intensely dissatisfied with public schools to send their children to private school,

[42] See James S. Coleman, Thomas Hoffer, and Sally Kilgore, *High School Achievement: Public, Catholic, and Private Schools Compared* (New York: Basic Books, 1982), esp. pp. 16-64.

but also trying to develop in all children—regardless of the religious commitments of their parents—a common democratic character. The balance is delicate because it constrains the moral doctrines that private schools may legitimately teach their students (the doctrines must be consistent with developing democratic character) at the same time as it limits the constraints that democratic states may place on private schools (the constraints must be necessary to developing democratic character). A mixed system thus consists of both constraint on private schools and self-restraint on the part of democratic governments. Having sanctioned a private-school sector on the grounds that dissenting parents should be permitted to exit from public schools, democratic legislatures cannot apply exactly the same standards to private schools without taking away with one legislative hand what the other granted. But neither may they exempt private schools from all standards, having recognized the need to provide a common education for all children.

The limits of dissent from public schooling are reasonably set by the educational standards, both curricular and noncurricular, essential to democracy. In the United States, these standards include teaching religious toleration, mutual respect among races, and those cognitive skills necessary for ensuring all children an adequate education.[43] Enforcement of these standards would leave private schools considerably freer than public ones to provide religious training and to experiment with methods of education unavailable within public schools. Private schools would not be bound by the decisions of local school boards, nor would they be constrained by those national and state standards that are not essential to democratic education. On this accommodation, private schools would be subject to fewer public standards and would be freer from local democratic control to determine how to implement those standards to which they are subject, but they would still be responsible for teaching their students a common democratic morality.

Would this delicate balance of democratic and private control over primary education increase or diminish our chances of developing in all children a common democratic character? Much depends upon a difficult counter-factual comparison of what children of dissenting parents would learn were they forced to attend public schools compared to what they would learn in suitably regulated private schools. Perhaps the closest we can come to making an empirically based judgment is to consider the effects of Catholic private schools on democratic education over the past century. Would Catholic children have better learned

<hr>

[43] For a similar conclusion, see Mark G. Yudof, *When Government Speaks* (Berkeley: University of California Press, 1983), p. 23.

the democratic values of religious toleration and respect among races had their parents been forced to send them to public schools? Given the bitter battles that many Catholics clergy and parents were willing to wage against public schools, it is unlikely that they would have resigned themselves to legislation that prevented them from sending their children to parochial schools.[44] Although Catholic schools enroll a smaller proportion of black students than do public schools, black enrollment is far from trivial, and black students are better integrated with white students within Catholic schools than they are within public schools. Catholic schools enroll approximately the same proportion of Hispanic students as do public schools. Like blacks, Hispanic students are also more integrated within Catholic schools than within public schools.[45]

The historical record is far from an ideal experiment to test the hypothesis that a mixed system can secure the purposes of democratic education better than an exclusively public system. For much of their history, (so-called) public schools fell so far short of an ecumenical ideal that most required children to profess specifically Protestant doctrines, inimical to Catholicism. Viewed in this historical context of far from perfectly realized ideals, the case for publicly constrained private schooling is stronger than the logic of prohibitionism admits. Requiring Catholic children to attend secular public schools (or, worse still, Protestant public schools) against the convictions of their parents is less likely to teach the lesson of religious toleration than requiring Catholic schools to teach religious toleration along with other democratic values. The latter is more likely to be perceived as (and to be) a fair compromise between the religious freedom and the secular obligation of parents than the former. At least in the case of Catholic schools, the compromise has not hurt more disadvantaged minorities or hindered the cause of teaching racial toleration.

What if some dissenting parents perceive any compromise of their religious commitments as unfair? Some fundamentalist Christians today reject the constraint of racial nondiscrimination on their private schools as an unfair—and therefore as an unjustified—restriction of their religious freedom. They translate their religious freedom into a right of exclusive control over the education of their children, a translation inconsistent with democratic values. A distinct and more consistently democratic claim available to fundamentalist Christians is that the welfare of democracy does not depend on *all* schools teaching com-

[44] For a detailed account of these battles in New York City, see Ravitch, *The Great School Wars.*
[45] Coleman et al., *High School Achievement*, pp. 28-37.

mon democratic values. As long as the vast majority of schools are non-discriminatory, some schools may be permitted to discriminate on the basis of their religious convictions without undermining widespread acceptance of the democratic value of racial nondiscrimination. Far from being a mere pragmatic accommodation, exempting Christian fundamentalist schools from the requirement of racial nondiscrimination might be viewed as a principled policy of respect for religious convictions required by nonrepression.

The demands of religious nonrepression and racial nondiscrimination conflict in the case of fundamentalist Christians, forcing a hard choice between two democratic standards. Should fundamentalist Christian schools be forced against their religious tenets to admit black students or should they be permitted to discriminate on the socially (but not religiously) irrelevant grounds of race? The fundamentalists' claim of unfairness in imposing racial nondiscrimination on their schools is not in itself unreasonable: unlike most other religions, Christian fundamentalism rejects the value of racial nondiscrimination (along with the social understanding of race) as irrelevant to the distribution of primary education. Enforcing a policy of racial nondiscrimination is "unfair" in the sense that it imposes a greater moral burden on fundamentalist schools than it does, say, on Catholic ones.

This kind of unfairness cannot, however, constitute an injustice in a democratic society whose common standards are secular. Racial nondiscrimination is an essential and widely shared value within our society. To exclude anyone from an education on racial grounds constitutes an injustice by our common standards, an injustice that runs deep in a society suffering from a history of racism. Christian fundamentalists are not just members of a church, they are citizens of *our* society. The democratic standard of nondiscrimination imposes greater constraints on their schools than on Catholic ones, but that imposition can be justified as the price fundamentalists must pay for sharing citizenship in a religiously and racially diverse society. Because the requirements of racial nondiscrimination and religious nonrepression conflict in this case, democratic principles *permit* but do not *require* legislatures to constrain fundamentalist along with all other schools to racial nondiscrimination. If legislatures decide to forbid all schools from discriminating on grounds of race because overcoming racial discrimination is an urgent goal for our society, than fundamentalist schools must comply with that decision, even if the legislative constraint of nondiscrimination imposes a greater burden on fundamentalists (by virtue of their religious convictions) than on other citizens.

Can a democratic state succeed in forcing parochial schools to teach democratic values in the face of intense religious opposition to these values? Probably not entirely. Just as public schools have failed to live up to ideal democratic standards, so publicly regulated private schools will fall short of achieving the ends of democratic education. The crucial question is not whether public regulation will fall short of its ends, but how far short. Will regulation fall so far short as to undermine the case for a mixed system of schools? The historical evidence, again, is inadequate to answer with confidence. Recent attempts to regulate Christian fundamentalist universities, however, lend support to the view that regulation can make a difference in whether a school upholds democratic values. The trustees of Bob Jones University once claimed, no doubt sincerely, that it was against the tenets of their religion to admit black students. When the government threatened to rescind its tax-exempt status if it barred blacks, Bob Jones changed its admissions policy, admitting blacks but forbidding interracial dating and marriage among its student body. In the face of a more recent threat to rescind its tax-exempt status, the trustees of Bob Jones claimed, again apparently sincerely, that interracial dating and marriage were against the tenets of their religion—but this time they did not claim that the Bible forbids them from admitting blacks to study at Bob Jones. Previous governmental regulation not only forced compliance but changed the professed beliefs of fundamentalists who were previously opposed even to admitting blacks to their university. Like toleration, many democratic values may be more effectively taught by the practices of schools rather than by the professions of their teachers. Public regulation therefore may eventually lead even those private schools that once opposed certain democratic values to teach them. Whether public regulations live up to their potential will depend, of course, on how well they are designed and how much democratic will exists to enforce them.

The greater the democratic determination to improve public schools, the fewer parents will exit and the less urgent public regulation of private schools will be from the perspective of promoting democratic values. Parents today choose the exit option for a wide variety of secular and religious reasons. Were education in public schools substantially improved, we would expect parents who send their children to private schools to be more deeply opposed to the secular nature of public education than most are today. In a state of more democratic education, the practical limits to imposing majoritarian standards upon intense minorities may become more paramount than the moral limits. Attempts to impose a primarily secular education upon children whose parents are intensely committed to parochial education may galvanize opposition among those parents and fail to convert children away from the intensely held commitments of their parents.

DISSENT WITHIN PUBLIC SCHOOLS

It is a short step from this argument for permitting dissenting parents to send their children to private schools (even in a more democratic society) to an argument for exempting public-school children from some required practices, such as saluting the flag, that offend the fundamental religious or moral beliefs of their parents. If public schools do not permit such exemptions, they are likely to drive more parents to enroll their children in private schools, where they will be even less exposed to common democratic standards.

The most consistently democratic argument for permitting internal dissent from some practices of moral education in public schools is not, however, the most commonly cited one. It does not assume that children—at least not young children (I shall consider the case of adolescents in a moment)—have a "right" to dissent from school policy or that parents have a "right" to determine how their children are morally educated within school. Citizens share educational authority over children with parents, and primary schooling is the main realm in which citizens exercise their educational authority. One cannot consistently uphold this authority and claim that children or parents have a right of free exercise of religion or of free speech within schools. Public schools would more effectively teach democratic values, however, if they were willing to exempt some children from practices to which their parents object as long as those practices do not require public schools to be discriminatory or repressive. On this argument, public schools should accommodate children who refuse to salute the flag but not those who refuse to sit next to blacks (assuming both refusals are based on principle rather than mere preference). By such selective accommodation, schools may be able to teach both the moral value and the principled limits of democratic dissent without elevating conscientious refusal into a constitutional right of children or of parents acting on their children's behalf.

As children mature, however, the paternalistic ground for denying them the same free exercise rights as adults gradually erodes, and then democratic schools should *as a matter of right* respect their conscientious dissent unless it interferes with the democratic education of others or severely limits their own democratic education (the evidence for which must go beyond the act of dissent itself). Consider the refusal of adolescent Jehovah's Witnesses to salute the flag. By this standard, public schools must recognize their right of refusal. Their refusal to salute the flag is not likely to be significantly less conscientious than that of their parents, and it neither limits their own educational opportunities nor the interferes with anyone else's democratic education. The same standard does not require democratic governments to recognize a "right" of Amish adolescents to leave school after eighth grade if this right would result in a significant shortening of the time that Amish adolescents were exposed to knowledge and ways of thinking essential to democratic deliberation. Nor does the standard permit schools to recognize a "right" of white adolescents not to associate with blacks: recognizing such a right indirectly discriminates against black students.

By respecting conscientious dissent within these principled limits, public schools can offer a valuable lesson in democratic toleration, and also obtain the allegiance of some dissenting minorities. Private schools provide the option of exiting for intense dissenters as well as an incentive for public schools to become more tolerant of internal dissent even when they are not legally obligated to do so.

Separating Moral from Religious Education

Where should public schools in the United States today draw the line in distinguishing moral from religious education? My critique of the claims of creationists suggested that there is no single or simple answer to be offered for all times and all cases. We cannot avoid the hard work of considering the specific facts of different kinds of cases, but we can draw some conclusions concerning what count as good reasons for making the distinction one way rather than another. A conflict between an educational practice and the religious beliefs of some citizens is not a good reason for forbidding schools to institute that practice, whereas a conflict between a religious practice and the principles of nondiscrimination or nonrepression is. The fact that a practice derives from the religious beliefs of only some citizens is not a good reason for excluding it from schools, whereas the fact that a religious practice makes it harder for the school to develop a common deliberative morality among students is a good reason.

This reasoning suggests a somewhat different method of distinguishing acceptable from unacceptable religious practices than that commonly used by the United States Supreme Court. The three-pronged test articulated by Chief Justice Burger in *Lemon v. Kurtzman* is simultaneously too strict and too weak. The first prong of the Court's test— that a religious practice must have a secular legislative purpose—is unexceptionable if only because virtually every religious practice introduced in schools has some secular purpose: to make children more moral, to unite them in some common set of beliefs, or to instill in them respect for religion. To deny that these are secular purposes would also entail denying public schools the authority to engage in moral education.

The second prong of the Court's test—that a practice must not have the principal or primary effect of advancing or inhibiting religion—is too strict. Even if a primary effect of a prohibition on teaching creationism in public schools is to inhibit fundamentalist beliefs, public schools may have sufficient reason not to teach creationism: the same principle that admits creationism would allow citizens to destroy public schools. One might then be tempted to reply that inhibiting fundamentalist beliefs is not the principal effect of banning creationism; the principal effect is to teach children good scientific logic. I think we would do well to resist this reply, because we rarely (if ever) have evidence that would support such a causal claim. The reply smuggles a judgment of the primary purpose or intent of a practice into a claim concerning its primary causal effect. If the primary *purpose* of a policy of keeping creationism out of public schools is to insure that schools try to teach democratic deliberation, we should not need to establish the causal claim concerning the primary *effect* of the policy.

The third prong of the Supreme Court's test—that a practice must not foster "an excessive government entanglement with religion"[46]—is too weak, or ambiguous. It begs the crucial question of what counts as "excessive" entanglement. Answering this question requires an understanding of the democratic purposes of primary education. If one of those purposes is to teach a common deliberative morality to all future citizens, then school practices that inhibit this aim—because they are discriminatory or repressive—fail the test of excessive government entanglement. The metaphor of excessive entanglement is therefore misleading: the primary purpose of distinguishing between moral and religious education is not the negative one of avoiding unnecessary governmental involvement with religion but the positive one of enabling public schools to develop democratic character. Insofar as admitting religious practices into public schools inhibits this aim, governments must avoid those practices, but governments need not avoid those practices that do not interfere with the essential purposes of primary education, even if they happen to be religious.

Religious practices that also serve the purpose of developing democratic character are admissible into schools so long as they do not violate the principle of nonrepression. Instead of distinguishing moral from religious education by its subject matter, therefore, we should distinguish relevant from irrelevant reasons for introducing a particular doctrine or instituting a particular practice in public schools—where our standards of relevance are relative to the purposes of primary edu-

---

[46] The standard of "excessive government entanglement" comes from *Walz v. Tax Commission*, 397 U.S. 664 (1970).

cation in a democratic society. This standard of relevant reasons is only a first step, but a significant one, in drawing the line between practices that are admissible into public schools and those that are not. The standard then requires us to conduct a detailed investigation of the purpose of introducing any practice into public schools, and to make a judgment as to whether or not that purpose is consistent with the creation and perpetuation of democratic schools. The standard may not yield a clear answer for every case. Some cases—such as whether laws requiring students to observe a "moment of silence" have a primarily repressive purpose—are hard ones, and recognizing them as such would appropriately temper our political debates.

We can admit the difficulty of deciding hard cases and still defend democratic against sectarian education. If we refuse to make any distinction between the two, democratic schooling will either be overwhelmed by religious repression or undermined by amoralism, alternatives considerably less attractive than living with a degree of uncertainty generated by hard cases. One might add that the willingness to acknowledge and the ability to live with moral uncertainty in such cases are among the significant virtues of democratic character that schools should try to cultivate.

Limiting the Limits

The principles of nonrepression and nondiscrimination thus help us draw the boundaries not only of legitimate democratic authority but also of the public realm of education. The capacity to draw such principled boundaries is crucial to the argument against both strong and directed democracy. The defense of strong democracy collapses once we discover that democracy itself entails certain substantive principles that place specifiable limits on democratic authority over education. Banning books and teaching creationism in public schools are cases that support this claim. Directed democracy is discredited by just the opposite discovery: that the principled limits on democratic authority do not uniquely determine the nature of democratic education. The cases of textbook approval and sex education offer evidence against Rousseau's defense of directed democracy.

If the doubt still lingers that Rousseau was right, that democracy is valuable but only insofar as it yields the right outcomes, perhaps we should reflect briefly on what Rousseau took to be right with regard to the education of women.[47] The limits of democratic authority over ed-

---

[47] For a much more detailed exposition and critique of Rousseau's views on the education of women, see Jane Roland Martin, *Reclaiming a Conversation: The Ideal of the*

ucation are as extensive in Rousseau's *Emile* as they are in Plato's *Republic*, although for radically different reasons. Rousseau tells us to read the *Republic* if we want to see how children should be educated as citizens.[48] Both girls and boys must be taken from their parents at birth to be collectively reared and educated as equals. *Emile*, by contrast, tells us how men and women, rather than citizens, should be educated.[49] While citizens must be educated against nature, in accordance with the needs of society, men and women must be educated against society, in accordance with the needs of their nature: "Sophie ought to be a woman as Emile is a man—that is to say, she ought to have everything which suits the constitution of her species and her sex in order to fill her place in the physical and moral order."[50] It follows from this principle, according to Rousseau, that "the whole education of women ought to relate to men":

> To please men, to be useful to them, to make herself loved and honored by them, to raise them when young, to care for them when grown, to counsel them, to console them, to make their lives agreeable and sweet—these are the duties of women at all times, and they ought to be taught from childhood.[51]

To accept Rousseau's view that democratic and parental authority over education must be constrained by what is right, we need not, of course, accept Rousseau's view of what is right with regard to the education of women. But whose view must we accept? "We" do not agree on what is right with regard to the education of women. Philosophers as wise as Plato and Rousseau were (I am convinced) wrong. How then can philosophers justify constraining democratic or parental authority over education to do what is right? If there is a compelling answer to this question, an answer with the authority to compel citizens and parents to educate children against their convictions but not for the sake of preserving democratic and parental freedoms, it will take someone wiser than Plato or Rousseau to discover it.

Educated Woman (New Haven and London: Yale University Press, 1985), pp. 38-69. See also Susan Moller Okin, *Women in Western Political Thought* (Princeton, N.J.: Princeton University Press, 1979), pp. 99-194.

[48] Rousseau, *Emile*, book 1, p. 40.

[49] Ibid.

[50] Ibid., book 5, p. 357.

[51] Ibid., p. 365.

CHAPTER FIVE

DISTRIBUTING PRIMARY SCHOOLING

If its main purpose is to develop democratic character, how should primary schooling be distributed? It does not require an extended philosophical analysis to say something significant about how schooling should not be distributed: not by the market—children of poor and uninterested parents will not receive it; not by unconstrained democratic decision—children of disfavored minorities will be relegated to inferior schools. This much should be common-sensically clear and is broadly acknowledged in the United States, at least today.

A more positive answer, however, requires a more systematic and sustained analysis, for at least three reasons. On many distributive issues—such as how much government should spend on educating children with learning disabilities—many of us lack clear intuitions. Secondly, even when each of us has clear intuitions—for example, about whether suburban white children should be bused to urban schools for racial integration—our intuitions differ, often quite radically. Thirdly, even when the vast majority agree—as most American citizens apparently did about racial segregation throughout much of our history—their agreement may conflict with democratic principles. Only a clear and defensible standard of distribution can come to our aid in these situations. In the first instance, it can help us arrive at our own well-reasoned conclusions. In the second, it can provide a standard for helping us resolve our social disagreements. In the third, it can prevent us from mistaking social consensus or majority rule for the whole of democratic justice.

The principle of nondiscrimination serves these purposes, but only in a preliminary way. Nondiscrimination prevents states and other groups in society from denying anyone an educational good on grounds irrelevant to the legitimate social purpose of that good. In its application to primary schooling, whose social purpose is to develop democratic character in all citizens, the principle of nondiscrimination becomes a principle of nonexclusion: no educable child may be excluded from an education adequate to participating in the processes that structure choice among good lives. Stated so abstractly, the principle of nonexclusion provides a necessary but not sufficient standard of democratic distribution with regard to primary schooling. A complete distributive standard would tell us (1) what resources a democratic state should devote to primary schooling rather than to other social ends, (2) how those resources should be distributed among children, and (3) how children should be distributed among and within schools.

The most popular standard in American society, if not the most promising, is the ideal of equal educational opportunity. The ideal has many meanings, which may account for its popularity, but for its promise to be fulfilled, it is necessary to determine which, if any, of those meanings provides a defensible standard for distributing democratic schooling.

INTERPRETING EQUAL EDUCATIONAL OPPORTUNITY

In its most liberal interpretation, the principle of equal educational opportunity offers a theoretically simple rule to solve all three distributional problems: The liberal state should devote as many resources to primary schooling as necessary, and distribute those resources, along with children themselves, in such a way as to maximize the life chances of all its future citizens.[1] Call this interpretation of equal educational opportunity *maximization*. A second, more common (and less consistently liberal) interpretation of equal educational opportunity requires the state to distribute educational resources so that the life chances of the least advantaged child are raised as far as possible toward those of the most advantaged. Call this interpretation *equalization*. A third, and perhaps the most common interpretation, requires the state to distribute educational resources in proportion to children's demonstrated natural ability and willingness to learn. Call this interpretation *meritocracy*.

Although each of these interpretations has been repeatedly offered in the literature on education as a distributive standard, none is plausible, once one draws out its practical implications. My aim in elaborating the implications of each interpretation in its pure form is not to belabor this critical point, but to be constructive: to demonstrate the need for a more complex and credible standard, and (more importantly) to begin developing one. I shall develop a more democratic standard for distributing primary schooling after understanding the strengths and weaknesses of each interpretation.

[1] For a popular statement and defense of this interpretation of the opportunity principle, see John W. Gardner, *Excellence: Can We Be Equal and Excellent Too?* (New York: Harper and Brothers, 1961), esp. pp. 75 ff.

Maximization

Maximization requires the state to devote as many resources to education as needed to maximize children's life chances. "Our kind of society," John Gardner argues, "demands the maximum development of individual potentialities *at every level of ability* . . . [so] that each youngster may achieve the best that is in him. . . ."[2] If our kind of society is purely liberal, then Gardner's claim is correct. Maximization supports the fundamental liberal values of free choice and neutrality among different ways of life, and distributes the chance to benefit from these values as equally as possible among all citizens.[3] But if our kind of society is also democratic, then we must look more carefully and critically at maximization.

The hidden weakness of maximization is what may be called the problem of the moral ransom. The rule offers us something morally valuable on the implicit condition that we give up everything else that we value. The state could spend an endless amount on education to increase the life chances of children. Yet its resources are limited, and police protection, public parks, baseball stadiums, and stereo systems are also valuable. The price of using education to maximize the life chances of children would be to forego these other goods.[4]

Someone sympathetic to maximization might try to avoid this criticism by adding a proviso that the state must devote as many resources to education as can maximize children's life chances *provided that the increase in life chances is not trivial*. Though reasonable, this proviso does not save maximization from the problem of the moral ransom. Even if the proviso establishes a theoretical limit to investment in education, there is still no practical limit to what we can now collectively spend to increase children's life chances substantially. Most parents are not willing to make such a sacrifice even for their own children. Perhaps parents should sacrifice even more than they now do for their children's

---

[2] Gardner, *Excellence*, pp. 74-75.

[3] Note that this liberal understanding does not identify the improvement of life chances simply with an increase of income, social status, or political power. Life chances include all opportunities to develop and exercise our human capacities.

[4] A variant of maximization that avoids the problem of the moral ransom is what might be called "proportionality": educate every child to achieve the same proportion of his or her intellectual potential. Proportionality introduces new problems: (1) it offers no standard for setting the proportion; (2) if it did offer a standard, we still would not be able to judge what level of educational achievement represented that proportion of a child's potential; and (3) even if we could judge when achievement was proportional to potential, we would still wonder why some children should be denied enough education to become literate (say) just because they are intellectually less talented than other children.

education, but there is no good reason to obligate them to minimize the other, noneducational pursuits that they value in order to maximize their children's life chances. Nor is there good reason to obligate citizens collectively to invest so much in education as to maximize the life chances of the next generation.

A more promising defense argues that maximization requires many social commitments beyond improving schools, raising teachers' salaries, and funding more educational research and development. Maximization commits the state to providing children and their parents with many other opportunity goods, such as police protection, housing, and health care, without which education could not perform its function of maximizing life chances. Because most cultural goods—public parks and museums, perhaps even stadiums and stereos—are also educational, maximization commits the state to their provision as well. As the number of goods included in maximization increases, the price of its hidden ransom decreases. The reformulated offer, a dedicated liberal could argue, is one that we can but we ought not refuse.

The more inclusive maximization becomes, however, the less guidance it gives for making hard choices among the many valuable opportunity goods, all of which the state cannot possibly provide. There is no limit in sight to the amount the state can spend on improving schools, teachers' salaries, the arts, or popular culture to expand children's choices later in life. Nor is there an apparent limit to the amount the state can spend on police protection, housing, or health care to increase their chances of living a longer life. If proponents make maximization into an inclusive good, analogous to the Aristotelian or the utilitarian conception of happiness, then they must be willing to accept less than the maximum of the many goods—such as better schools—that it includes. Only inclusive goods are plausibly worth maximizing, but they require acceptance of less than the maximum of the many valuable goods that they include. Should the state invest in school buildings or stadiums, or neither, leaving parents with more money to spend on travel? Maximization provides no answer.

There is no intuitively obvious answer with which all citizens could agree, nor has a way been found to derive a single correct answer from some self-evident philosophical principle (or set of principles). These are the conditions under which democratic determination of social priorities makes the most sense. Even if the maximization interpretation of equal educational opportunity is correct, it needs to be supplemented by a democratic standard: states should use fair democratic processes to determine how to expand the life chances of their future citizens.

But maximization is not correct. It relies on a general misconception:

that a society should strive to maximize the goods that it values most. No exclusive earthly good—not even educational opportunity, broadly understood—is so valuable as to be worthy of maximization. If the state need not be committed to using education to maximize children's life chances, then democratic citizens should be free not only to set priorities among all the goods that expand educational opportunity, but also to choose between educational opportunity and all the other goods that it excludes.

Equalization

One way of avoiding the many problems posed by maximization is to interpret equal educational opportunity less liberally and more literally. Since its explicit terms do not mention maximization, equal educational opportunity might be construed to demand only equalization: use education to raise the life chances of the least advantaged (as far as possible) up to those of the most advantaged. The scope of the equal opportunity principle is now significantly narrowed: it says nothing about how much a state should spend on education relative to other goods, or on the education of any particular child except in relation to what it provides for other children. This may already be an important, albeit implicit, liberal concession to democracy. The liberal silence concerning how to determine the distribution of education relative to other social goods leaves room for a democratic determination of priorities, even if it does not demand such a determination. I develop the implications of such a democratic principle by examining the case of school financing.

According to equalization, the educational attainment of children should not differ in any systematic and significant manner with their natural or environmentally determined characteristics.[5] Rightly distributed, education should be used to overcome all environmental and natural causes of differential educational attainment, since these causes of social inequalities are beyond people's control, and therefore "arbitrary from a moral perspective."[6] If "even the willingness to make an effort, to try, . . . is itself dependent upon happy family and social circumstances,"[7] then equal educational opportunity must aim also to equalize effort or the results of unequal effort.

[5] See James S. Fishkin, *Justice, Equal Opportunity, and the Family* (New Haven and London: Yale University Press, 1983), p. 32. Fishkin takes only native characteristics and not environment to be illegitimate correlates of life chances, although both are equally arbitrary from the moral point of view that he is characterizing.

[6] Rawls, *A Theory of Justice*, p. 74.

[7] Ibid.

One sympathetic critic of equalization takes it to be a proper moral ideal. In the absence of any competing moral demands, he argues, the state should try to eliminate all inequalities in life chances that result from morally arbitrary differences; the presence of other moral demands, however, renders the price too high. To equalize educational opportunity, the state would have to intrude so far into family life as to violate the equally important liberal ideal of family autonomy.[8] Liberals cannot simply reformulate the principle of family autonomy to permit as much intrusion as necessary to achieve equalization, because the necessary amount would eliminate one of the life chances that citizens value most—the freedom to educate their own children.

Intuitionism seems to be a plausible way of handling the problem of conflicting liberal ideals. Aware of the weakness of maximization, one can conceive of equalization as just one among several liberal ideals, none of which must be fully realized to satisfy the demands of liberal justice. Liberalism, so conceived, consists of "ideals without an ideal": "How its principles are to be balanced remains an open question to be faced in particular cases as they present themselves."[9]

To be faced by whom? Because it offers no answer to the question of whose intuitions will do the balancing, intuitionism avoids rather than solves the political problem of balancing conflicting ideals. The American polity contains a variety of conflicting moral principles and conflicting moral intuitions. Invoking "American" intuitions, therefore, cannot resolve the conflict between equalizing educational opportunity and respecting family autonomy. Our intuitions on this issue differ, as recent controversies over school financing and busing suggest. How the principles should be balanced will depend upon whose intuitions should do the balancing. Because intuitions also differ over who should make the hard choices between the equalization of educational opportunity and family autonomy, intuitionism itself cannot resolve this moral and political problem.

One might doubt even the more limited claim that while equalization is in itself a worthy moral ideal, in practice it must be balanced against other equally worthy ideals, such as family autonomy. The intuitionist understanding of equalization makes a necessity out of a virtue. Even if equalization did not conflict with other liberal ideals, there is good reason to choose its incomplete rather than its complete realization. Completely realized, equalization requires the state to devote all its educational resources to educationally less able children until they reach either the same level of educational attainment as the more able or the

---

[8] See Fishkin, *Justice, Equal Opportunity, and the Family*, pp. 51-67 and *passim*.
[9] Ibid., pp. 10, 193.

highest level that they are capable of attaining.[10] Given limited educational resources and unlimited capacity for educational innovation, this time may never come, in which case the state would provide no educational resources to the more able.[11] This is an unacceptable consequence, because equality of life chances is not in itself a sufficiently important value to outweigh the value of enabling all children to develop their talents to some socially acceptable degree.

A thought experiment can help show why equalization takes equality too seriously. Suppose we know that every difference in the educational achievement of children is beyond their control and correctable by some expensive, but finite, amount of remedial education. Must we then create an educational system that eliminates all differences among children's educational attainments?

The answer is no, and not because equalization would be socially inefficient. There is good reason to accept many differences in educational attainment.[12] The good reason is that many differences in educational achievement can be eliminated only by eradicating the different intellectual, cultural, and emotional dispositions and attachments of children. Some children are more proficient at (and interested in) cultivating friendships and having fun than they are at learning what schools teach. Such variety among children makes their lives, as well as the lives of others, rich and interesting. Many children, moreover, will live more rewarding lives in an environment where competition is not universal but is partly limited by their predispositions for academic achievement, which (whether culturally or genetically created) are undeserved. A society fully charged with competition and so stripped of diversity would be a less desirable place for children, parents, and probably even teachers to live.

Not all variety, on the other hand, is valuable in a society where children who lack learning do not have a reasonable chance to participate

[10] Alternatively, equalization could be interpreted as minimizing the variance among educational attainments. The unattractiveness of this ideal is apparent when one imagines a policy that actively attempts to suppress intellectual achievement among some students to decrease the variance.

[11] If we assume more than two levels of talent, the rule is to raise the educational accomplishment of the least talented to the level of the next least, and so on. On this assumption, even the average child might be deprived of any educational resources. Compare Jencks et al., *Inequality*, p. 109.

[12] Compare Onora A. O'Neill, "Opportunities, Equalities and Education," *Theory and Decision*, vol. 7 (1976): 290-91. O'Neill argues that our choice between equality of educational opportunity and equality of educational outcome depends on whether we view people as "socially produced" or as "autonomous choosers." My argument suggests that we can criticize the goal of equalizing educational outcomes quite independently of what O'Neill calls our "fundamental conceptions of the human condition."

in making democratic decisions. The democratic truth in equalization is that all children should learn enough to be able not just to live a minimally decent life, but also to participate effectively in the democratic processes by which individual choices are socially structured. *A democratic state, therefore, must take steps to avoid those inequalities that deprive children of educational attainment adequate to participate in the political processes.*

Meritocracy

The democratic truth in equalization reveals the flaw in meritocracy. A meritocracy is dedicated to distributing all educational resources in proportion to natural ability and willingness to learn. In principle, therefore, meritocracy must provide those children with relatively few natural abilities and little inclination to learn with the fewest educational resources and the least educational attention, and those children with the greatest natural abilities and motivation with the most.

In practice, few meritocrats accept the full implications of the standard that they profess. They typically invoke the meritocratic interpretation of equal educational opportunity to argue not against providing an adequate education for all children, but for providing a better education for gifted children instead of concentrating resources on the "average" child and the slow learner. A meritocratic distribution of educational resources, they argue, would give educationally gifted children what they deserve and also give society what it needs: a greater pool of human capital to increase social productivity. The case for meritocracy seems strongest when so used, but the meritocratic standard still proves too much for all but the most ardent meritocrat to accept. In principle, meritocracy does not require—it may even preclude—educating less talented and less motivated children up to a socially basic level of literacy. Furthermore, nothing in the meritocratic interpretation of equal educational opportunity secures an education adequate for democratic citizenship to children who happen to have (whether by nature, nurture, or their own free will) little intellectual talent or motivation.

The democratic truth in equalization—that states must secure an education for all children adequate to participate in the democratic political processes—does not rule out a restricted form of meritocracy in which educational resources above the level that is adequate for citizenship are distributed in proportion to children's demonstrated intellectual ability and willingness to learn. Once all children are guaranteed enough education to participate in politics, a democrat might defend a limited meritocracy on grounds of just deserts: children who demonstrate greater intellectual ability and/or greater motivation deserve to be provided with more education than those who demonstrate less.

A more egalitarian democrat might reasonably challenge this claim: Why do more gifted or motivated children deserve more education if they have done little or nothing to deserve their greater intellectual gifts or motivation? "Because intellectual talent and motivation are fitting bases for deserving education even if they are not themselves deserved," the less egalitarian democrat might reply. "Courageous soldiers deserve Medals of Honor, even if they do not deserve their courage. Similarly, intellectually talented children and highly motivated children deserve more education, even if they do not deserve their greater talents and motivation."[13]

The meritocrat's response still is insufficient to support even a more restricted meritocracy, where education above the "threshold" level necessary for citizenship *must* be distributed, as a matter of justice, in proportion to intellectual merit. Rewarding desert is a reasonable way to distribute educational resources above the threshold level, but surely not the only reasonable way. A good case can be made for the use of education above the minimum to compensate less gifted and less motivated children for their undeserved disadvantages. Another good case can be made for using educational resources above the threshold to develop new skills and interests in all children, which might be useful to society as well as satisfying to citizens in the future. Yet another case can be made for concentrating resources on those students who are both intellectually gifted and motivated, on grounds of social utility rather than of desert: the welfare of society as a whole is most likely to be advanced in this way.

Suppose I made each case fully, compared them, and concluded that the case for rewarding merit is, on balance, the best. Suppose also (for the sake of argument) that I am right. I still cannot conclude that my policy preference should dominate a democratic one, provided the democratic one does not violate the principled constraints on democracy. Being right is neither necessary nor sufficient grounds for com-

[13] See Robert Nozick's argument that "the foundations underlying desert needn't themselves be deserved, *all the way down*." *Anarchy, State and Utopia* (New York: Basic Books, 1974), pp. 224-27. See also Sandel, *Liberalism and the Limits of Justice*, pp. 82-95. The concept of desert is complicated and the philosophical discussions correspondingly inconclusive. For the most complete conceptual analysis, see Joel Feinberg, *Doing and Deserving* (Princeton, N.J.: Princeton University Press, 1970). See also Amy Gutmann, *Liberal Equality* (Cambridge: Cambridge University Press, 1980), pp. 160-67; and Alan Zaitchik, "On Deserving to Deserve," *Philosophy and Public Affairs*, vol. 6 (Summer 1977): 370-88.

manding political authority, by either liberal or democratic standards.[14]

When reasonable alternatives are recognizable, meritocracy is put in
its proper, democratic place. If democratic institutions allocate educational resources *above* the threshold level so as to reward intellectual
desert, then a limited meritocracy is properly part of society's democratic standard for distributing education. The democratic interpretation of meritocracy does not hold that education above the threshold
must be distributed according to desert (regardless of democratic preferences) but that it *may* be so distributed (depending on the results of
fair democratic processes).

The Democratic Standard Stated

The standard of democratic distribution developed so far can be for-
mulated more precisely as two principles. Call the first the *democratic
authorization principle*. It recognizes the mistake in maximization by
granting authority to democratic institutions to determine the priority
of education relative to other social goods. Call the second the *democratic threshold principle*. It avoids the mistakes in both equalization
and meritocracy by specifying that inequalities in the distribution of educational goods can be justified if, but only if, they do not deprive any
child of the ability to participate effectively in the democratic process
(which determines, among other things, the priority of education relative to other social goods). The democratic threshold principle thus
places limits on the legitimate discretion of democratic decisionmaking
established by the authorization principle. The threshold principle establishes a realm of what one might call nondiscretionary democratic
authority. It does so by imposing a moral requirement that democratic
institutions allocate sufficient resources to education to provide all children with an ability adequate to participate in the democratic process.
Democratic institutions still retain the discretionary authority to decide
how much more education to provide above the threshold established
by the second principle.[15]

[14] For two different defenses of this conclusion, see Walzer, "Philosophy and Democ-
racy," pp. 379-99; and Amy Gutmann, "How Liberal Is Democracy," in Douglas
MacLean and Claudia Mills, eds., *Liberalism Reconsidered* (Totowa, N.J.: Rowman and
Allanheld, 1983), pp. 25-50.

[15] Democratic decisions in the discretionary realm—allocating resources above the educational threshold—may indirectly define the threshold. What constitutes an adequate
education for less advantaged children may be relative to the educational attainment of
more advantaged children. This conception of an educational threshold can accommodate the phenomenon of relative deprivation.

Although education above the threshold may be democratically distributed according to meritocratic principles, education below the threshold must not be. Democratic decisionmaking may still be the most effective way to determine the threshold. Whether it is will depend partly on an empirical assessment of how we can best guarantee all children an adequate education, and partly on a normative assessment of what adequacy entails. Since educational adequacy is relative and dependent on the particular social context, the best way of determining what adequacy practically entails may be a democratic decisionmaking process that follows upon public debate and deliberation. But to say that the threshold requirements are more likely to be satisfied by democratic institutions than by nondemocratic institutions is not to say that democratic institutions have moral discretion in deciding whether to provide an adequate level of education for all citizens.

The distinction between the nondiscretionary and discretionary realms of democratic authority is already incorporated in the rationales for some present educational policies. In passing Public Law 94-142 (the "Education for All Handicapped Children Act"), Congress mandated an "appropriate" rather than an optimal level of education for handicapped children, leaving states and local school districts free to provide more (but not less) if they wish. The educational provisions of some state constitutions suggest a threshold requirement. The New Jersey Supreme Court has interpreted Article IV of its state constitution to require the state to guarantee "that educational opportunity which is needed in the contemporary setting to equip a child for his role as a citizen. . . ."[16] In many states, so-called "Foundation Programs" (which guarantee a level of state funding to local school districts) invoke the ideal of providing an adequate educational foundation for school-age children in all school districts. In practice (and perhaps even in political intent), however, most Foundation Programs are funded at levels so low as to leave property-poor districts with far fewer resources than they would need to reach any reasonable estimate of the democratic threshold. Although many of our schools fall far short of satisfying the demands of the threshold, implementing the two-part democratic standard does not require a revolution in our way of thinking about education. Rather, it requires more self-conscious use of that standard in arguing about educational policy, and it requires more work in figuring out how to translate that standard into effective educational reform.

A democratic critic might ask: can a standard dictate a threshold and

[16] 1875 Amendment to Article IV, sec. 7, para. 6 of the New Jersey Constitution of 1844: "The legislature shall provide for the maintenance and support of a thorough and efficient system of free public schools for the instruction of all children in this state between the ages of five and eighteen years."

still remain democratic in any meaningful sense? This question arises again in discussing school finance; it cannot be answered in the abstract. But some reasons may be suggested here for remaining hopeful that the answer is yes. The answer would be no if nondemocratic institutions were more reliable than democratic ones in implementing the threshold and if the threshold were so high as to leave no room for democratic support of more than an adequate education for every child. A nondemocratic authority should then determine the democratic threshold. The threshold having been established, no political space would be left for discretionary democratic authority. (Judging from historical experience, it seems implausible that nondemocratic institutions are more reliable in establishing adequate education for every child than are democratic ones. The educational interests of disadvantaged minorities are often better protected by more centralized than by less centralized democratic bodies, but rarely by nondemocratic ones.)

Would any adequate threshold cost so much as to make discretionary democratic authority obsolete? Given how much federal, state, and local governments now spend on defense, criminal justice, social security, and other welfare goods, it is implausible to claim that if we provided an adequate education for every child, we would have no resources to spend on improving education above the threshold. We might, after democratic deliberation, collectively choose to spend more on missiles or medical care rather than to increase expenditures on schools. Such choices—even if mistaken—would be consistent with the democratic claims of the standard.

The policy implications of the democratic standard of distribution, therefore, are underdetermined in principle. What constitutes a just distribution of democratic education not only may vary among different democratic societies but also may change quite significantly over time in the same society. These changes may occur for two moral reasons, related to the two parts of the democratic standard. The authorization principle suggests that the priority and distribution of education above the threshold level should be open to democratic discretion. The threshold principle suggests that while the threshold itself is not similarly open, it is socially relative as it insists that schools provide all educable children with an education adequate to participate effectively in democratic processes.[17] The more educated most citizens are, the more education each citizen is likely to need to participate effectively in the

---

[17] Compare William Nelson, "Equal Opportunity," *Social Theory and Practice*, vol. 10, no. 2 (Summer 1984): 157-84. Nelson defines equal opportunity on the basis of certain objective conditions of a good life that apply to any society independently of its social understandings (p. 168). Nelson's interpretation of equal opportunity is otherwise similar to mine, although he defends and develops it in a different way.

democratic process. The democratic standard is consistent with the view that there is some absolute minimum of literacy below which no democratic society could be said to provide an adequate education to its citizens. But the standard demands more of democracies than supplying an absolute minimum; the threshold of an ability to participate effectively in democratic politics is likely to demand more and better education for all citizens as the average level and quality of education in our society increases.

The democratic interpretation avoids the counter-intuitive extremism of the standard interpretations of equal educational opportunity and improves upon intuitionism. It does, however, leave a crucial question (to which I return) unanswered: How do we determine the democratic threshold? To put the question more precisely: What kind and level of education is adequate to citizenship in our society today? While I cannot answer this question completely here, there is no reason to fall back on the conventional interpretations of equal educational opportunity that avoid uncertainty by embracing unacceptable ideals.

To examine some of the practical implications of these principles and to provide additional support for the claim that the two-part standard is consistently democratic, I turn to two specific distributional problems: public-school finance and the education of the handicapped.

FINANCING PUBLIC SCHOOLS

What is the best process by which citizens may be authorized to determine the priority of education relative to other goods in our society? Do the results of such a process conflict—in practice even if not in theory—with the goal of establishing a democratic threshold? One way to begin to answer these questions is to evaluate some of the ways in which public elementary and secondary schools are financed in the United States.

Of the more than 200 billion dollars spent on public and private education in the United States during 1981-82, over half (approximately $110 billion, or 3.6 percent of the Gross National Product) was spent on public elementary and secondary education.[18] Although their share of spending has declined dramatically over the century (from 83.2 percent in 1919-20 to 44.6 percent in 1982-83), local governments still shoulder almost half of the financial burden of elementary and secondary public education.[19] Almost half the power to determine the priority of education and hence half the responsibility for distributing educa-

[18] National Center for Education Statistics, *Digest of Education Statistics 1983-84* (Washington, D.C.: U.S. Government Printing Office, 1984).

[19] Ibid.; Edward B. Fiske, "States Gain Wider Influence on School Policy," *The New York Times*, December 2, 1984, pp. 1, 40.

tional opportunity rests, one might conclude, upon democratic decisionmaking at the local level.

From the perspective of a democratic theory of education, one might assume that this pattern is good, although even greater local power would be better. This conclusion would be a hasty one for several reasons. The first two of these reasons are commonly recognized but inconclusive. The third reason is less commonly cited, but more conclusive.

The first reason often given for resisting the conclusion that local funding is optimally democratic is that the property tax, which most local governments use to fund education, allegedly is regressive.[20] Revisionist economists, however, question the regressivity of the property tax. According to Garms, Guthrie, and Pierce, for example: "Anyone who reads carefully the analyses of both sides is struck by the number of assumptions that must be made because of lack of data. . . . [I]t appears that the most we can say at present is that it is by no means certain that the tax is regressive."[21] There are methods, moreover, for overcoming whatever regressivity may exist in the property tax. One such method (the "circuit-breaker") exempts all or part of the property taxes that a family pays above a specified percentage of its income.[22] This criticism of local control, then, is inconclusive.

A second criticism points to the unfair effects of the property tax, not within, but among school districts. Because the tax base of local school districts varies with its propertied wealth, property taxes in a poor district produce many fewer dollars per child than do taxes levied at the same tax rate in a rich district, assuming the same school-age population.[23] One solution to this problem, called *power equalization*, requires the state to supplement and/or redistribute tax revenues so that poor districts receive as many dollars per child as do rich districts for the same tax effort (measured by the rate at which districts are willing to tax their property).[24] Power equalization thus equalizes educational

[20] Roe L. Johns, Edgar L. Morphet, and Kern Alexander, *The Economics and Financing of Education*, 4th ed. (Englewood Cliffs, N.J.: Prentice-Hall, 1983), pp. 95-101: "Approximately 99 percent of all tax revenue raised in fiscally independent school districts comes from property taxes" (p. 100).

[21] Walter I. Garms, James W. Guthrie, and Lawrence C. Pierce, *School Finance: The Economics and Politics of Public Education* (Englewood Cliffs, N.J.: Prentice-Hall, 1978), p. 143.

[22] Ibid., pp. 143-44.

[23] If, as is often the case, the rich district has fewer school-age children, then the disparity is even greater, of course.

[24] For the most comprehensive explanation and defense of "power equalization," see John E. Coons, William H. Clune III, and Stephen D. Sugarman, *Private Wealth and Public Education* (Cambridge, Mass.: Harvard University Press, 1970).

spending for equal local tax efforts. Yet why, one egalitarian critic asks, is unequal tax effort among districts a more legitimate basis on which to deprive children of equal educational opportunity than is the unequal property base of districts?[25] This criticism threatens the liberal interpretation of the equalization standard, but not the democratic one. On liberal grounds, the power equalization plan must be faulted for sanctioning some degree of unequal spending among school districts regardless of the developmental potential of students. On democratic grounds, this plan can be applauded: it combines a substantial degree of local control over school financing with a redistribution of resources that enables poorer districts to raise students up to the threshold. A democrat should support local financial control to the extent that it enables communities to determine the priority of education (above the threshold level) relative to other goods.

Yet does local financial control over education, modified by power equalization, succeed in so empowering local communities? The third reason not to conclude that local funding of education is optimally democratic is the primary one. The power to determine the priority of education relative to other goods requires two related powers: (1) the power to decide how much to spend on education, and (2) the power to decide how much to spend on other, competing social goods. Local governments possess the first power only to a limited degree, and they lack the second power almost entirely. More spending entails more taxing, and the tax base of local governments depends heavily on the location of businesses and affluent households, who can relocate—and often threaten to relocate—if school taxes become significantly higher than in other districts. Local governments lack the power almost entirely to decide how much to spend on competing social goods because they cannot decide to spend less on comparably expensive goods in order to spend more on education. What they possess is the considerably more restricted power to decide how much to tax local property to fund schools within a relatively small range of rates that will not threaten to erode the tax base.

This restriction of local democratic decisionmaking has one very significant consequence for financing education: local referenda on school budgets are by far the most effective and obvious means by which citizens can register their desire to slow down government spending and taxation. Thus, even if they would prefer to limit spending by cutting back not on education but on some other goods were they given the

[25] David A. J. Richards, "Equal Opportunity and School Financing: Toward a Moral Theory of Constitutional Adjudication," *University of Chicago Law Review*, vol. 41, no. 1 (Fall 1973): 66-67, esp. n. 144.

choice, they may vote to decrease funding for schools simply for lack of any other effective vehicle for expressing their wish to reduce government spending.

The problem, from a democratic perspective, lies not in the preferences of citizens, but in the inadequate means available to express those preferences. Because most comparably expensive social goods are funded at the state and federal levels, where citizens have less direct voice, local funding for education is likely to bias the results of the democratic process against spending on education relative to other social goods. This is especially true in an era where federal and state government spending is increasing at a relatively rapid pace. Democratic decisionmaking is now structured in such a way that citizens must ask themselves, "Do we want to tax ourselves more for the sake of education?" rather than, "How much do we want to tax ourselves for education relative to the other social goods that we value?" In this sense, local control over educational funding is less democratic than state control, because it presents citizens and their representatives with a considerably narrower choice.

For the priority of education to be democratically determined, citizens or their elected representatives must have the power to make concurrent funding decisions on competing goods. This would require either that local governments be delegated responsibility for funding a host of noneducational goods, or that the major decisions concerning educational funding be elevated to the state or federal levels. The practical barriers to granting local governments responsibility for many other social goods are so great that the principled objections to this alternative can be safely put aside. Local governments simply cannot afford to fund the construction of super-highways or modern hospitals and health clinics for their residents alone. (Even if some local governments could afford such funding, their resulting tax rates almost certainly would lead businesses to relocate.) The more practical—and democratically defensible—alternative is to make educational funding the primary responsibility of states or the federal government.

The trend has been steadily in this direction over the last sixty years: states accounted for only 16.5 percent of total funding for public schooling in 1919-20 and for 47.4 percent in 1980-81. The federal government's contribution has risen just as dramatically over the same period, from 0 percent to approximately 8 percent. If the argument so far is correct, we should hope that the trend continues, although it has been increasingly criticized on the ground that citizens have a much greater degree of control over decentralized than centralized democratic decisions.

The implication of this criticism is that democracy is more meaningful the greater chance each citizen has to influence decisions. If democracy is only as meaningful as the probability that any single citizen will influence an election, then few elections these days, including local ones, are very meaningful. Beyond that, this measure of meaningfulness is inexplicably narrow.[26] Why not also include a consideration of the importance of the outcomes that citizens can control and the degree to which citizens are motivated to participate in the decisionmaking process? While citizens may have a greater chance of influencing a local election, the net importance of the outcome generally is much greater in state elections than in local elections. These much greater stakes may outweigh the much lower probability of anyone influencing the election.[27]

Why, then, stop at the state level, rather than push for full federal funding of education? Federal funding would have the considerable advantage of placing education on the same level as defense, facilitating the trade-off between better minds and better missiles. It would also eliminate the risk faced by state and local governments that raising taxes for schools might lead to the erosion of their tax bases if businesses were encouraged to relocate to areas where taxes were lower. Critics of centralization, on the other hand, argue that federal funding of schools would diminish both the diversity of educational offerings and the capacity of schools to respond to the particular needs and preferences of local communities.

Would federal control follow federal funding? It is impossible to say with certainty, but the best evidence available—studies of state financing of schools—does not support the conventional wisdom that he who pays the piper calls the tune. The correlation between the amount of state control over local schools and state share of school financing is low: "some states supply state funds with few controls, others with many controls."[28] States, on the other hand, constitutionally can control local education even if they do not pay a cent,[29] and since education

---

[26] The critics may instead be suggesting an indirect connection between more state financing and less democracy: that financing at the state level leads to state control over other local educational decisions. This would be unfortunate from a democratic perspective, but (as I indicate in a moment) the evidence suggests that state financing need not, and often does not, have this consequence.

[27] See Derek Parfit, *Reasons and Persons* (Oxford: Clarendon Press, 1984), p. 74.

[28] Garms, Guthrie, and Pierce, *The Economics and Financing of Education*, p. 152. See also Betsy Levin, Thomas Muller, William J. Scanlon, and Michael A. Cohen, *Public School Finance: Present Disparities and Fiscal Alternatives* (Washington, D.C.: The Urban Institute, 1972), ch. 5.

[29] Southern states prior to 1920, for example, exercised control over local education without financing. See W. Norton Grubb and Stephan Michelson, *States and Schools:*

is legally the responsibility of states, federal aid is the only mechanism by which the federal government can exert control (except when school districts are in violation of the Constitution, as in the case of segregation).[30]

There is, however, little reason to conclude that greater federal funding would significantly decrease diversity among schools. The federal government, like the states, can supply funds with few or many strings attached. Revenue-sharing programs can combine the advantages of taxation at the federal level with control at the local level. The strongest principled arguments against more federal funding are therefore not compelling. The primary reason to focus on the case for more state funding is practical: states already possess full legal authority to tax for education, so shifting school financing further from local school districts to the state requires no constitutional change, only new state legislation that furthers the trend already established.[31]

The shift to more state and federal funding is compatible with preserving some substantial degree of local control over school financing. The democratic standard of distribution gives local districts the freedom to supplement state funds with their own, as long as state and federal governments guarantee a level of funding for all districts sufficient to bring every child to the democratic threshold. Inequalities above this threshold would not be morally suspect. A well-financed Foundations Program, for example, would leave wealthier districts with a greater capacity than poorer ones to raise money above the threshold.[32] Wealthy districts should not be prevented from doing so any more than talented children should be prevented from surpassing the learning threshold. A democratic state is morally required to ensure that all districts reach the financial threshold and that all children reach the learning threshold to the extent possible.[33] In both cases, the decision of whether to equalize above the threshold is a matter of democratic discretion, but reaching the threshold is not.

A critical question remains unanswered: How can the democratic threshold, defined by an adequate level of learning, be translated into dollars? The distributional problem for those who believe in the importance of spending on education is acute: they recognize that while

---

The Political Economy of Public School Finance (Lexington, Mass.: Lexington Books, 1974).

    [30] See Grubb and Michelson, *States and Schools*, pp. 30-33 and p. 38, n. 72.

    [31] For a discussion of the constitutional and legal status of school financing, see Garms, Guthrie, and Pierce, *The Economics and Financing of Education*, pp. 128-30.

    [32] For a detailed discussion and criticism of existing Foundation Programs, see Coons, Clune, and Sugarman, *Private Wealth and Public Education*, pp. 63-160.

    [33] Cf. ibid., p. 72.

more money can make a difference in educational quality, local school districts cannot be counted upon to spend state money to satisfy the standards of the democratic threshold. Those local districts that are irresponsible could use money to fulfill narrowly meritocratic principles, improving the education of only the most advantaged students. Those districts managed incompetently can try, but fail, to better the education of their students. The problem of school financing seems to be a paradox. The closer local school districts come to satisfying the demands of the threshold, the less they need, but the more efficiently they will use, additional state funds. Public officials who care about educational efficiency may have a greater incentive to fund better rather than worse school districts.

Centralized funding of schools is a paradox, however, only if efficiency must trump equity. If considerations of equity must take precedence over efficiency in the allocation of educational resources, as the democratic standard requires, then school funding is not a paradox. It does, however, remain a problem with no obvious solution: How can federal and state governments be obligated to fund local school districts up to the threshold when they cannot be sure that any amount of money will produce an adequate education at the local level? Governments should not be held responsible for goals they cannot realize, any more than individuals should be. Yet to relieve federal and state governments of full responsibility is not to relieve them of all responsibility. States should still provide poorer districts with funds sufficient to educate students up to the threshold, with efficient use of resources. States should also do what they can to see that local districts use their money well.

By what method may states, say, judge what level of financing is sufficient to enable poorer districts to reach the threshold (provided they make good use of their resources)? Consider two reasonable, if not sure, methods, both of which begin by identifying school districts that have succeeded in reaching the educational threshold. By the first method, "leveling down," a state redistributes money from the adequate to the inadequate school districts until either the inadequate districts become adequate or the adequate ones become inadequate. If the adequate districts become inadequate first, then the state stops redistributing and starts allocating more money to the educational system as a whole. The obvious political problem with this alternative is that it penalizes rather than rewards those school districts that provide more than an adequate education for their students.

The second method, "building up," avoids this problem. As with the "leveling down" method, building up begins by identifying an educationally adequate school district to establish a financial threshold. Instead of taking money away from the most affluent districts, however, a state would subsidize inadequate districts with funds necessary to reach the financial threshold. A complete funding formula would be quite complex, taking account of educational needs of disadvantaged children, which are on average more expensive to meet. Even an incomplete formula, however, which would bring average per pupil expenditures on education in inadequate districts up to those in adequate districts, would be an improvement over most state financing programs today. A complete funding formula would not guarantee satisfaction of the democratic standard—responsible distribution and competent delivery of educational services must ultimately rest in local hands.

The democratic virtue of "building up" becomes more apparent when we compare it to "power equalization." In theory, power equalization offers a strict standard: states must enable every school district to raise as much money per student as the *richest* school district for the same tax effort (as measured by its relative tax rate). If it had been put into practice in New Jersey in 1983-84, power equalization would have required the state to give Camden (with more than twice the tax rate as Princeton and one-twentieth the property base) over $10,000 per student. (Princeton spends approximately $5,000 per student. The state average is approximately $3,600.) This requirement is politically infeasible. Most state equalization plans, therefore, like New Jersey's, aim at bringing poorer districts up to the state average of expenditure per pupil. Whereas power equalization in theory demands too much of states, its natural compromise with political reality demands too little. Trenton and Jersey City both spend approximately the state average per pupil, yet there is no reason to *assume* that these school systems are adequately financed. There is, in fact, considerable evidence to the contrary.[34] Thus, power equalization does not demand judgments of the quality of education provided by school systems, but the price of avoiding qualitative judgments is political infeasibility or educational inadequacy.

Because it is less mechanical, the "building up" method is more capable of capturing democratic concern over inequality in school financing. A state identifies adequately funded school districts by judging the

[34] Evidence of inadequate education—compiled by the Education Law Center of New Jersey—includes very low scores in the Minimum Basic Skills and High School Proficiency Tests and very high drop-out rates. Evidence that money might make a difference includes low teachers' salaries, high ratios of students to staff, and poor physical plants relative to districts whose students' scores are higher and drop-out rates lower. See the "Brief for the Plaintiffs" in *Abbott v. Burke*, filed in Superior Court of New Jersey, Chancery Division, Mercer County, 1985. (Available from Education Law Center, Inc., 155 Washington Street, Newark, New Jersey 07102.)

quality of education they provide. The state then concentrates on building up inadequately funded school districts to that threshold level. Whether states should try to raise still more money for schooling so as to make districts even better becomes a matter of democratic discretion. Building up, unlike power equalization, satisfies two necessary conditions of a democratic method of financing: it neither mandates equalization above the threshold against democratic discretion, nor relieves public officials (or citizens) of the responsibility for making substantive judgments about educational adequacy.

The most difficult question may remain: What level of ability or set of accomplishments should count as adequate? It is easy to provide a partial answer: high-school students who have not learned enough to understand the help-wanted ads in their local newspaper, to fill out a check so that it can be cashed, or to address an envelope so that it can be mailed are not adequately educated. These are three commonly employed tests of "functional literacy," defined as attainment of the skills and knowledge essential for effective functioning in one's society. Functional literacy is more typically understood as having the intellectual capacity to get a job and to make a decent living for oneself and one's family.

This understanding of functional illiteracy is simultaneously too weak and too strong to serve as a democratic standard of adequacy. It is too weak insofar as many Americans have the capacity to make a decent living but not the capacity to understand the political issues that structure their future choices and the future choices of their society. Many high-school students—those who can understand the help-wanted ads but not the text of news stories; who can fill out checks but understand nothing about the national economy; who have learned how to mail a letter but not how to think about the social choice between a public and a private post office—lack the prerequisites for effective political participation. Such skills may be necessary, but they are surely not sufficient for being able to participate effectively in American politics. By democratic norms, they are functionally illiterate.

The standard understanding of functional illiteracy is too strong insofar as citizens can be adequately educated—able to analyze the issues that shape their future and the future of their society—and incapable of making a decent living due to structural unemployment in the economy. A more democratic definition of functional literacy requires high-school students to have the intellectual skills and the information that enable them to think about democratic politics and to develop their deliberative skills and their knowledge through practical experience.

Although this definition is quite abstract, it is sufficiently specific to suggest a policy shift in primary schooling in the United States, redirecting concern away from the question of whether high-school graduates can get good jobs and toward the question of whether they have the capacity to deliberate about the political issues that affect their lives—for example, those issues that determine whether a high-school education will be necessary or sufficient for getting good jobs in the future. By redirecting our concern, we focus on the comparative advantage of schools—their ability to improve the capacity and willingness of citizens to think.

It would be a sign of progress in public education in this country if parents were to judge education by more than the threshold of intellectual ability it provides for their children. It is not a sign of progress, however, for schools to be judged primarily by their success in enabling all students to get good jobs or in equalizing their income or educational attainment. Schools are bound to fail by such judgments, for reasons that speak against the prevailing standards by which they are judged, rather than against their democratic purposes. The main problem with primary schooling today is not that it does not compensate for the failures of other social institutions—in not enabling all high-school graduates to get good jobs, for example—but that it does not prepare students for democratic citizenship. If they were educated to exercise the rights and to fulfill the responsibilities of democratic citizenship, these future citizens collectively could decide whether to change the way that social institutions (including schools) structure their life chances.

EDUCATING THE DISADVANTAGED

If this priority—preparation for citizenship—is accepted, the adequacy of financial formulae can be tested only by asking whether the funding of a local school district *taken together with other educational policies* is sufficient to produce results that raise most students up to the threshold. For those students who are socially or biologically handicapped, it might be impossible for states to provide enough schooling to enable them to reach the threshold, or so expensive as to call into question the moral requirement to bring all handicapped children up to the threshold. What, then, does the threshold standard demand?

Consider two cases. The first is that of six-year-old Rebecca Paul.[35] Rebecca's mother and father separated when she was two. She lives with her mother in a poor section of an inner city. Her father, a fore-

[35] This case study is taken from Donald H. Clark, Arlene Goldsmith, and Clementine Pugh, *Those Children* (Belmont, Calif.: Wadsworth Publishing, 1970), pp. 9-39. The authors of the study changed some details to preserve the privacy of the child and her family, but tried to preserve the essential facts of the actual case.

man, makes modest child-support payments. Rebecca's older sister lives at home; her older brother is a drug addict and has spent time in jail and in a drug rehabilitation center. Rebecca's mother, who works as a door-to-door saleswoman, is often not home when Rebecca comes from school. Rebecca is in first grade in her local public school. She is a discipline problem and already has difficulty keeping up with her class, a "slow group," although her IQ is reported to be over 115. Rebecca's school spends considerably more than average per child, by both state and national standards, but Rebecca receives no special services.[36]

The second case is that of Amy Rowley.[37] Like Rebecca, Amy is six years old and attends a first grade in a public school. Her IQ is reported to be 122. But there the similarity ends. Amy's parents are deaf, and so is Amy. She reads at above the second-grade level and is highly motivated to learn. Before Amy entered kindergarten, members of the school staff met with her parents and agreed to assess Amy's special educational needs over the year. Several teachers and administrators took a mini-course in sign language interpretation, and a teletype phone was installed in the school to communicate with Amy's parents at home. At the end of the assessment period, the district's Committee on the Handicapped (a psychologist, a teacher, a doctor, and a parent of a handicapped child) recommended that Amy be provided with an FM wireless hearing aid, the daily services of a certified teacher of the deaf, and the weekly services of a speech therapist. Amy's school provided her with these services beginning in the first grade.

Are Rebecca and Amy receiving an adequate education by democratic standards? The conventional wisdom, supported by the threshold standard as it applies in typical cases, is that schools must do more to help children who are harder to teach than they must do for more talented or more motivated children. Doing more often means spending more. In the case of seriously handicapped children, it almost always means spending more, because seriously handicapped children need special services, a specially trained teacher, and more expensive teaching aids than average children to learn even basic skills. Amy's

---

[36] None except those diagnostic services that were part of compiling the case study itself. All the clinical specialists who interviewed and tested Rebecca were paid for by the study. The actual case study provides no facts about the resources spent at Rebecca's school. I have stipulated above-average spending to help clarify the democratic standard of equal opportunity. The stipulation is reasonable, since Rebecca's school was probably in New York City.

[37] All the details of this case study are factual. They are taken from *Rowley v. Board of Education of Hendrick Hudson, et al.*, 483 F. Supp. 528 (1980); and 632 F. 2d. 945 (1980).

case supports the conventional wisdom. The special services of the speech therapist, for example, make it possible for Amy to acquire the basic skill of normal speech. Before public schools provided such special services, deaf children were taught very little unless their parents were rich enough to afford a private education and motivated enough to provide one (although even money and motivation could not buy mainstreaming, which many public schools now provide).

Given her intelligence and motivation, perhaps Amy could do even better if her school were to spend still more, providing her with a full-time sign interpreter.[38] Let us suppose this is true. Is her school morally required to provide her with one? The threshold principle suggests that it is not. Although Amy's school does not maximize or equalize her educational achievement or reward her extraordinary effort, the education it provides cannot reasonably be considered inadequate for democratic participation. Were Amy's parents to judge her education unacceptable, their dissent would be insufficient to defeat the claim that her education lies within the bounds of discretionary democratic judgment. In reviewing Amy's case, the Supreme Court emphasized that she was learning as much and as quickly as the average child in her class. The Court's claim is sufficient on legal grounds to sustain the school's policy without the judgment that the average child in Amy's school was adequately educated. If this claim is credible (as it was in the actual case), then the Court's judgment is also fully defensible on democratic grounds. Although the threshold principle does not require the school district to spend more, the principle does permit it, as long as increased spending does not result in the deprivation of other children in the district of the threshold level of learning.

Amy's case is not simple, but Rebecca's case is still harder to judge, because much less is known about what it would take for her to behave better and learn more. The panel of psychiatrists and social workers who diagnosed Rebecca's case recommended family counselling. The pediatrician recommended that she take medication to control her hyperactivity. The authors of the case study recommend that Rebecca's teacher try a variety of teaching techniques to help both Rebecca and her classmates get along better, but they also suggest that because she

---

[38] Amy's parents made this case to their school board, then to the Independent Examiner, next to the State Commissioner of Education, and finally, when these appeals failed, to the courts. The Rowleys won their case against the Hendrick Hudson Board of Education in the U.S. District and the Appeals Court. The case ended in the Supreme Court, which reversed the lower-court decision, upholding the local school board's right *not* to provide Amy with a full-time sign interpreter. See *Board of Education of the Hendrick Hudson Central School District v. Amy Rowley*, 458 US 176 (1982). Justice Rehnquist wrote the majority opinion. Justices White, Brennan, and Marshall dissented.

is so deeply troubled, "it is unlikely that a teacher will be able to help Rebecca directly," although they conclude that a perceptive teacher "might sense that this child is deeply troubled and refer her for psychological consultation."[39]

What, then, must Rebecca's school do to help her learn? What is striking about Rebecca's case—as distinct from Amy's case—is not how much her school must spend to educate her, but how little her school can do to overcome her problems. Perhaps an inspired teacher could break through these problems, but no public educational system can depend on hiring miracle workers. Yet there are many more Rebeccas than Amys in the public schools. Rebecca's case reminds us that democratic states cannot rely upon schools alone to help children reach the threshold of learning. States must provide access to a wide range of other goods and services—decent housing, job training and employment for parents, family counselling, day care and after-school programs for children—without which schools cannot possibly succeed in their educational missions.

Schools are not, however, freed from responsibility to help children like Rebecca. They still can help by diagnosing learning problems, developing better teaching techniques for coping with these problems, hiring and training better teachers, and referring parents to people outside the school who can provide additional help. Given Rebecca's learning problems and the fact that her school provides her with no special services at all, it is as implausible to claim that her education is adequate by democratic standards as it is to claim that Amy's education is inadequate. Both children require special services. Because such services cost money, schools must spend more on Amy and Rebecca than they spend on children who lack learning disabilities, just as teachers must pay more attention to any child who is less motivated to learn than to those who lack unusual learning disabilities.

Rebecca's problem is more common and therefore more costly to solve by social policy, but that is not the primary way in which Rebecca poses a much greater challenge to her school than does Amy. The greatest obstacle to solving Rebecca's educational problem is not insufficient spending on schools. Without a well-developed welfare state, which provides ample economic, medical, and social services for disadvantaged families, the special services that schools can provide will fall short of enabling them to reach the threshold. In suggesting that our expectations of schooling must be lowered, critics of the underdeveloped welfare state generally fail to recognize that lowering our expectations is consistent with raising our demands. The more government

---

[39] Clark, Goldsmith, and Pugh, *Those Children*, p. 38.

helps outside the school, the more schools will be able to teach with any set of resources. The less government spends for nonschool services, the more schools must spend to help disadvantaged children learn, if spending helps at all.

Does spending help at all? In the wake of the 1966 (Coleman) *Report on Equality of Educational Opportunity*[40] and Christopher Jencks's subsequent study on inequality,[41] many doubted the value of spending more on schooling for poor children. The Coleman Report found that differences in spending among schools could not account for differences in the average educational attainment of students attending those schools. The Jencks study went one step further: "Eliminating differences between schools would do almost nothing to make adults more equal. Even eliminating differences in the amount of schooling people get would do relatively little to make adults more equal."[42] These findings were frequently cited as evidence that spending more on schools would not equalize opportunity or improve the life chances of children. Jencks explicitly recommended that "we think of school life as an end in itself *rather than* a means to some other end."[43] As he put it: "[S]tudents' and teachers' claims on the public purse are no more legitimate than the claims of . . . manufacturers of supersonic aircraft who want to help their stockholders pay for Caribbean vacations. . . ."[44]

Despite its methodological flaws, Coleman's findings have stood up well against re-analysis, but they do not support the policy conclusion that spending more on schooling for the disadvantaged is futile.[45] The report measured differences in spending only among school districts (and in teacher characteristics among schools). It did not look at how districts distribute their resources among children within schools. Its findings therefore cannot be used to conclude that significant changes in the internal organization of schools—for example, assigning the most experienced and highly paid teachers to the least advantaged children—would make no difference.[46] Its findings cannot even be used to

[40] Coleman et al., *Report on Equality of Educational Opportunity*.

[41] Jencks et al., *Inequality*.

[42] Ibid., p. 16.

[43] Ibid., p. 256. Emphasis added.

[44] Ibid., p. 29.

[45] Nor does Coleman himself claim that they do.

[46] For further precautions on extrapolating policy recommendations from the Coleman Report, see Eric A. Hanushek and John F. Kain, "On the Value of *Equality of Educational Opportunity* as a Guide to Public Policy," in Frederick Mosteller and Daniel P. Moynihan, eds., *On Equality of Educational Opportunity* (New York: Vintage Books, 1972), pp. 116-45. See also Richard J. Murname, *The Impact of School Resources on the Learning of Inner City Children* (Cambridge, Mass.: Ballinger Publishing, 1975), pp. 8-10.

account for the variation that currently exists in the achievement levels of disadvantaged children within different schools or classrooms.

The most striking finding of the Jencks study—that the income inequality among men with the same family background, cognitive skills, educational attainment, and occupational status was "only 12-15 percent less . . . than among random individuals"[47]—suggests only that income inequality cannot be decreased significantly by increasing educational equality. It does not support the conclusion that Amy and Rebecca will have the same capacity for deliberation or participation in democratic politics if they learn less in school as they will if they learn more. Nor does it justify the conclusion that schooling is a consumer good like any other and that it matters only for making children's lives better in the present, not for making it "better in the hereafter."[48] The appeal of this conclusion may stem from a truncated conception of what counts in the "hereafter" and of what opportunity entails. A school that teaches Rebecca how to communicate civilly and Amy how to communicate effectively with her peers would make both their lives better in the hereafter, even if it does nothing to increase their income or to change their occupations. Educational achievement is measured not by level of income (above a certain decent minimum), but by the capacity to deliberate and participate in democratic politics.[49] While the latter is less susceptible to precise measurement, it is not therefore less important. *Inequality* provides evidence that schooling is an ineffective means of equalizing income, not that it is an ineffective means of distributing democratic opportunity.[50]

Although the Coleman and Jencks studies neither refute nor support the possibility that better schooling for disadvantaged children will increase their educational opportunity, subsequent studies make it appear likely that better schooling makes a difference. Richard Murname's study of the classroom experiences of 875 inner-city black

[47] Jencks et al., *Inequality*, p. 226.

[48] Ibid., p. 29.

[49] It is important to note that educational opportunity is only a part of the more inclusive democratic good of opportunity. The more inclusive good requires that all citizens be guaranteed a decent minimum income—preferably through a full employment policy. Schooling is therefore a limited, but not an ineffective, means of equalizing opportunity for the disadvantaged: in a state that lacks a full employment and decent minimum-wage policy, even the best schooling for the least advantaged will leave some able people unemployed or earning less than a decent minimum. Equal *educational* opportunity is only a part, albeit an important part, of equal opportunity.

[50] For an excellent discussion of the limitations of large-scale, cross-sectional surveys of the effects of schooling, see Michael Rutter, Barbara Maughan, Peter Mortimore, Janet Ouston, and Alan Smith, *Fifteen Thousand Hours: Secondary Schools and Their Effects on Children* (Cambridge, Mass.: Harvard University Press, 1979), pp. 3-8.

children demonstrates that "teachers have a critical impact on student achievement."[51] The most effective teachers are costly because they are experienced; yet they need not necessarily be the most experienced and therefore the most costly.[52]

In his three-year study of children in twelve secondary schools in inner-city London, Michael Rutter found that schools "varied markedly with respect to their pupils' behavior, attendance, exam success and delinquency . . . *even after taking into account differences in their intake*" and that these differences in outcome "were systematically and strongly associated with the characteristics of schools as social institutions."[53] Some of the most costly characteristics—such as the school's physical plant, its student-teacher ratio, and its administrative structure—did not correlate with greater achievement. Rutter notes that many characteristics that did correlate—such as the degree of academic emphasis, teacher participation in lessons, their use of incentives and rewards (rather than punishment), and the extent to which students were encouraged to assume responsibility—could be changed by the school staff without additional cost.[54] Such changes, of course, require a staff perceptive enough to realize that they should change and capable enough to know how to change. If worse schools tend to have worse teachers, and if higher salaries are necessary to attract better teachers to such schools, then improving schools along the lines Rutter suggests is likely to be quite costly.

These studies and others converge in concluding that better schools—and more specifically, better teachers within schools—increase the educational achievement of poor children.[55] What they do not tell us, however, is whether schools must spend more to become better than they now are for poor children, or how much better they must become to reach the democratic threshold. The best studies all caution against making policy inferences from their research conclu-

---

[51] Murname, *The Impact of School Resources on the Learning of Inner City Children*, p. 77.

[52] Murname found that the most effective teachers were those who had taught for three to five years, and not longer. He rightly warns against concluding that teaching experience beyond five years does not increase effectiveness. An equally consistent conclusion is that many of the best teachers move out of inner-city schools after five years, or leave the profession. See ibid., pp. 78-80.

[53] Rutter et al., *Fifteen Thousand Hours*, p. 205.

[54] Ibid., pp. 178-79.

[55] See *Do Teachers Make a Difference?* (Washington, D.C.: U.S. Government Printing Office, 1970); Eric A. Hanushek, *Education and Race* (Lexington, Mass.: D. C. Heath and Co., 1972); and Martin T. Katzman, *The Political Economy of Urban Schools* (Cambridge, Mass.: Harvard University Press, 1971).

sions.[56] The most that we can conclude with confidence on the basis of these studies is that (a) better schools do not necessarily spend more than worse ones, and (b) it is likely that schools could improve were they able to afford better teachers.

This may seem inconclusive. It is—for good reason. Whether schools must spend more (and how much more) to teach disadvantaged children depends not only on whether reaching the threshold requires more spending, but also on whether citizens choose to reach the threshold by redistributing existing monies or by raising more money to spend to increase the achievement of disadvantaged children. There is no moral freedom to choose neither to spend more nor to improve the use of existing resources. Democratic principles leave citizens with discretion in deciding *how* but not in deciding *whether* to improve the education of disadvantaged children that now falls below the democratic threshold.

Even spending substantially more on education, however, is not an adequate alternative for those children who are so severely handicapped that no amount of education will raise them to the threshold, or for those whose behavior so disrupts the education of other students that trying to educate them is incompatible with educating other students in the same environment. What must democratic states and schools do for such children? I have already considered the case of a "troubled" child and concluded that the state should provide her (and her family) with access to noneducational supportive services. For some children, however, it is too late for such help. Public schools may not be able to teach the vast majority of children unless they are permitted to place disruptive children in special classes, even if that diminishes their chances of learning. Because their interests are, in this sense, sacrificed to preserve the educational prospects of other children, disruptive children should be isolated only as a last resort or "supreme educational emergency": they must present a clear and substantial threat to the education and/or safety of other children.

Children with brain damage pose a different problem, because even the best social services coupled with the best schooling may not give them the capacity to deliberate and to participate effectively in democratic politics. We cannot owe such children the same democratic opportunities that we owe other children, but we do owe them a good life relative to their capacities, a life good for them (not simply convenient for us). A substantial amount of special education is likely to be a necessary but not sufficient condition for their leading such a life. Brain-damaged children, therefore, need not be educated to the limits of our

[56] For example, Murname, *The Impact of School Resources*, pp. 15, 21, 78-79; and Rutter et al., *Fifteen Thousand Hours*, pp. 180-82.

capacity. Who knows what those limits are? The frontiers of education as of science are ever-expanding. How much and what kind of education we owe such children will depend on their capacities to learn and on our willingness to provide them with noneducational services as they grow older. This standard leaves room for democratic discretion in deciding on the particular combination of schooling and noneducational services to provide brain-damaged children. Any adequate combination, however, is bound to be much more costly and demanding than raising average children up to the normal threshold.

The education of handicapped children generally (even those that are not severely retarded) is so expensive that states cannot be expected to bear that cost by themselves (even if the richer among them should). Education, according to democratic principles, is the responsibility of all levels of government, not just of states or local governments, although traditionally more responsibility has been vested in state and local governments. The case of handicapped children (and disadvantaged children more generally) has recently become, and should continue to be, a partial exception to this rule. Without substantial federal aid earmarked for their education, handicapped children are unlikely to be adequately educated. The federal government, therefore, should play an important financial role in protecting handicapped children.

In passing the "Education for All Handicapped Children Act" (Public Law 94-142) of 1975, Congress began to assume such a role. But the federal government has subsequently assumed much less than full financial responsibility for educating the handicapped—one study estimates that its greatest contribution since 1977 has been only six percent of the total cost.[57] At the same time, it has assumed much more than financial responsibility. Public Law 94-142 imposes many regulations and reporting requirements on local schools: it requires local schools to provide each handicapped child with an "appropriate" education in the "least restrictive educational environment," to create a detailed "individualized education program" (IEP) for each child,[58] to follow certain procedural guidelines in setting up the IEP, and to pro-

[57] John C. Pittenger and Peter Kuriloff, "Educating the Handicapped: Reforming a Radical Law," *The Public Interest*, no. 66 (Winter 1982): 87.

[58] The IEP must include: "(A) a statement of the present levels of educational performance of each child, (B) a statement of annual goals, including short-term instructional objectives, (C) a statement of the specific educational services to be provided to such child, and the extent to which such child will be able to participate in regular educational programs, (D) the projected date for initiation and anticipated duration of such services, and (E) appropriate objective criteria and evaluation procedures and schedules for determining, on at least an annual basis, whether instructional objectives are being achieved" (*Public Law 94-142*, sec. 4).

vide appeal procedures for parents who are dissatisfied with their child's IEP.

Critics of Public Law 94-142 correctly argue that "fairness is costly" and that federal regulations designed to ensure fairness have the effect of bureaucratizing schools.[59] But these critics often recommend remedies that are morally worse, such as eliminating the protections of due process.[60] Before procedural safeguards were instituted, most handicapped children were denied anything approaching an adequate education.[61] Because handicapped children are a particularly needy minority whose education is costly and demanding, they should be provided with protection not due to other children (such as the gifted and talented).[62] Because the educational needs of handicapped children are complex and individualized, they are generally better protected by instituting procedural rather than substantive safeguards at the federal level. The best procedures are those which hold local schools accountable to parents, professionals, and other citizens who are motivated to protect the special educational needs of the handicapped. Procedural safeguards are rarely sufficient to secure justice, but they are often, as in this instance, necessary. Instead of eliminating the procedural safeguards, the federal government should alleviate the burden on schools by paying more to support the educational programs for which it is responsible.[63]

[59] Pittenger and Kuriloff, "Educating the Handicapped," pp. 89-90; and Arthur E. Wise, Legislated Learning: The Bureaucratization of the American Classroom (Berkeley: University of California Press, 1979), pp. 27-28, and passim.

[60] In support of their critique of due process, Pittenger and Kuriloff report that half of the parents (of 50 handicapped children) who asked for due-process hearings said that they "would not willingly go through such an experience again, even if they knew it would improve conditions for their children." But it is hard to know what to conclude from this fact. Half of the parents said they would go through the experience again. Pittenger and Kuriloff also neglect to consider the preventive effect of these procedural safeguards: schools probably treat most handicapped children (whose parents never ask for due-process hearings) better than they otherwise would.

[61] See David Kirp, William Buss, and Peter Kuriloff, "Legal Reform of Special Education: Empirical Studies and Procedural Proposals," California Law Review, vol. 62, no. 1 (January 1974): 42-58 and 117-55.

[62] Pittenger and Kuriloff criticize the procedural safeguards for handicapped children because they are part of an ongoing "procedural revolution" that "has extended due-process protections to the gifted and talented, and already one hears it said that any child ought to be able to challenge the fairness of any major educational decision affecting him. Where will it end? And with what consequences for public education?" ("Educating the Handicapped," pp. 89-90). Unlike violent revolutions, the procedural one can be stopped—democratically—at some socially acceptable point. A good case has yet to be made for the slippery slope argument that our only choice is between granting all children or none the fullest range of due process.

[63] For an extended case study that supports this conclusion, see Richard A. Weatherly,

More money, however, will not make schools less bureaucratized. The reporting requirements are probably the greatest single source of bureaucratization in Public Law 94-142 (and of complaints against the law). If these requirements were all essential to accomplishing the purpose of the law, then it would be hard to choose between improving the education of handicapped children and avoiding the growth of school bureaucracy. We do not face such a hard choice here, because telling teachers *how* (rather than *whom*) to teach is often counter-productive.[64] Good teaching requires flexibility and imagination, which the writing of detailed blueprints discourages.[65] The more detailed the blueprints must be, the less time teachers have for teaching (or for recuperating from its strains). Moreover, federal policymakers possess no special knowledge about how to teach handicapped children, and there is little reason to believe that they will learn much more by gathering the data that they require local schools to supply.[66]

One critic of bureaucratization suggests that the federal government ought therefore to concern itself with "equity" and leave concerns of "productivity" to the schools.[67] This distinction may be misleading. Increasing the educational achievement ("productivity") of handicapped children is an important part of what democratic justice ("equity") demands. Congress should concern itself with whether its legislation is likely to improve the educational achievement of the handicapped. It should not, however, simply assume that detailed federal regulations, which generate an enormous amount of paperwork at the local level, are an effective means to such improvement. Democratic theory establishes a presumption against bureaucracy.[68] In the case of democratic schools, respecting this presumption means that policymakers should not impose regulations and detailed reporting requirements on local schools unless they have good evidence that educational equity cannot be realized otherwise. Good evidence was lacking in the case of Public Law 94-142. Congress would have done better had they provided more money and fewer regulations.[69]

Reforming Special Education: Policy Implementation from State to Street Level (Cambridge, Mass.: MIT Press, 1979), esp. pp. 142-48.

[64] A similar argument applies to federally funded Title I programs for the poor. See Tyack and Hansot, *Managers of Virtue*, pp. 244-46.

[65] Pittenger and Kuriloff, "Educating the Handicapped," p. 90.

[66] Wise, *Legislated Learning*, pp. 53-58.

[67] Ibid., esp. pp. xiv-xv, 52-53, and 206-207.

[68] See Dennis F. Thompson, "Bureaucracy and Democracy," in Graeme Duncan, ed., *Democratic Theory and Practice* (New York: Cambridge University Press, 1983), pp. 235-50.

[69] This is not to say that Congress should have provided all the money and no regulations. Requiring states to direct some of their own money to disadvantaged children (to

By assuming major responsibility for funding the education of the most disadvantaged children, the federal government can help make schooling more democratic. This claim may seem implausible, since centralization is generally not the most effective means to democratization. But the generalization in this case does not hold, for reasons to which I have already alluded. Local school districts should be constrained to educate every child up to the threshold, but they should also be free to spend more money on education than the threshold demands. States are better equipped to provide local school districts with funds necessary to educate average children up to the threshold than they are to provide the funds necessary to educate the most disadvantaged children. This is because educating these children up to the threshold can be extraordinarily costly, and because there is a more effective constituency for special education at the national level than in the 50 states separately. If the federal government contributed more financially to helping disadvantaged children reach the threshold, then state and local governments would be freer to decide what priority to give education above the threshold.

"[E]ducation is so special," Secretary of Education T. H. Bell announced on leaving office, "that it ranks in priority alongside and possibly ahead of the Department of Defense."[70] Not until the federal government increases its role in financing education for the disadvantaged, however, can the priorities of majorities at the state and local levels be morally translated into democratic politics. Bell's claim that "[e]ducation is to state government what defense is to the Federal Government"[71] must be qualified on this account. Like defense, education is a national responsibility. The federal government therefore must not let states and local school districts neglect the educational needs of any children. Unlike defense, education may be best controlled and distributed locally. Consequently, the federal government should limit its role to the protection of otherwise underserved students and limit its protection, if possible, to providing money and instituting procedural safeguards (at least initially at the local level) in case the money is misused. Were the federal government to assume this responsibility, state and local governments would be free to determine how much (more) they want to spend on schooling and how they want to distribute schooling above the threshold.

---

receive federal funds) can encourage economy. Some regulations are necessary to ensure fulfillment of the law's purpose. See Weatherly, *Reforming Special Education*, p. 120.

[70] *The New York Times*, November 9, 1984, p. 1.

[71] *The New York Times*, December 2, 1984, section 1, p. 40.

INTEGRATING SCHOOLS

Children are, among other things, each others' educational resources.[72] The quality of their education depends importantly on how they are distributed among and within schools. "It is no surprise, then, that association and segregation are the most hotly contested issues in the sphere of education."[73] Nor is it surprising that racial integration is the most hotly contested of hotly contested issues in a society where blacks suffer from racial prejudice, poverty, and the lack of political power. What are the implications of the democratic standard for distributing black and white children among and within schools?

The principle of nonexclusion applies to a wide variety of associational issues, ranging from whether schools should "track" students in the same ability groups through an entire educational program to whether school districts should create "magnet" schools that attract the most academically talented students and, according to critics, "demagnetize" the rest of the school district.[74] Whether school systems must be racially integrated is among the more inclusive of these associational issues, because the most thoroughgoing racial integration entails nonexclusive practices both within and among schools. I shall therefore focus on it here. Must school systems be racially integrated against majority will? To answer this question, we must ask what effective racial integration entails. And to answer this question, we must inquire into the purpose of racially integrated education.

Why integrate schools if integration goes against majority will? A compelling reply might begin by describing racial prejudice along with the economic and political status of blacks in the United States today. Although opinion polls show that white attitudes towards blacks have improved over the past twenty years, they also reveal that a substantial degree of racial prejudice, or racism, remains. In 1978, 60 percent of whites reported that they would be concerned about the marriage of a friend or relative to a black (down from 84 percent in 1963); 79 percent said they would be concerned if their own child dated a black (down from 90 percent in 1963); 27 percent would be concerned over a black family moving next door (down from 51 percent in 1963).[75] Even more revealing of racism is the response by 25 percent of whites that blacks

[72] Walzer, *Spheres of Justice*, p. 215.

[73] Ibid.

[74] For a critique of tracking, see Walzer, *Spheres of Justice*, pp. 220-21. For a critique of magnet schools, see Jennifer Hochschild, *The New American Dilemma: Liberal Democracy and School Desegregation* (New Haven, Conn.: Yale University Press, 1984), pp. 70-79.

[75] Louis Harris and Associates, *A Study of Attitudes Toward Racial and Religious Minorities and Toward Women* (New York: Louis Harris and Associates, 1978), p. 15.

"have less native intelligence than whites" and by 15 percent that "blacks are inferior to white people."[76] The judgment that racism is still prevalent in the United States is widely shared by Americans themselves: in 1985, 84 percent of whites (and 94 percent of blacks) agreed that "even though we call America a melting pot of religious and racial minorities, there's still a lot of prejudice against most minority groups."[77]

The perpetuation of any form of prejudice is a serious problem in a democracy because it blocks the development of mutual respect among citizens, but more serious still is the perpetuation of prejudice against an already disadvantaged minority, whose low economic and political position has been created in significant part by past *de facto* and *de jure* discrimination. To cite just one of many revealing statistics on the deprivations of the black population: in 1983, almost half of all black children lived below the poverty line compared to less than one-fifth of white children. (One-fourth of all black children lived below 50 percent of the poverty line compared to only one-twentieth of all white children.)[78] Racial integration of schools would be a less urgent issue in our society were blacks a more privileged minority, such that prejudice did not compound their economic, political, and educational deprivations. School integration is one of the most urgent educational issues today because primary schooling has the potential of improving the racial attitudes of white students along with the educational achievement of black students.

Note what the goal of racial integration need not entail. If the dual

[76] Ibid., p. 16. Some of the most extensive evidence of racist attitudes among American high-school students comes from a 1963 survey of three schools in the Greater New York area: "When teenagers are asked about associating with an unsuccessful black [student], the majority are unwilling to engage in most forms of interaction. The only exceptions are sitting next to a black peer in class and having a black as a speaking acquaintance. Three out of four . . . are unwilling to have a low-status black teenager as a close friend or even as a dinner guest." Charles Y. Glock, Robert Wuthnow, Jane Allyn Piliavin, and Metta Spencer, *Adolescent Prejudice* (New York: Harper and Row, 1975), p. 137. Consider the exceptions: approximately 30 percent of the white students said they would be unwilling even to sit next to a low-status black or be a speaking acquaintance. When asked about their attitudes towards a successful black student, between 30 and 40 percent say that they would be unwilling to invite him home to dinner, sit on the same committee, or be a member of the same club. Between 10 and 20 percent say they would be unwilling to associate with him as a speaking acquaintance, a lunch companion, by sitting next to him in class or attending the same party (ibid., pp. 136-39). Since 1963, such blatant racial prejudice seems to have decreased but has by no means disappeared.

[77] Louis Harris, "Poll Results Contradict Claims That Prejudice Is Increasing" (Orlando, Fla.: Tribune Media Services, February 18, 1985), p. 2.

[78] U.S. Bureau of the Census, "Characteristics of the Population Below the Poverty Level: 1983," *Current Population Reports*, Series P-60, no. 148, pp. 5, 25, 26.

purpose of racial integration is to decrease racial prejudice and to increase the academic achievement of black students, then schools need
not contain a "perfect proportionality" of white and black children
based on their percentages in the country, or the city, or the metropolitan area at issue.[79] Schools must be diverse enough that white children
learn to respect and cooperate with black children. This requirement,
which falls far short of proportionality, still creates a serious problem.
Largely because neighborhoods in cities and suburbs (particularly in
the North) are not racially integrated, students attending neighborhood schools continue *not* to learn the lesson of mutual respect between races: "attending neighborhood schools has a negative impact
on both black and white students' racial attitudes and behaviors."[80]

If children continue to be distributed among schools according to
neighborhoods, the education of black students will continue to be limited in ways that violate the democratic standard of nonexclusion. The
problem is not the one commonly cited by liberal defenders of equal
educational opportunity: integrating schools will not insure black students more income or a greater range of occupational choice. The problem is that not integrating schools perpetuates racial prejudice among
whites, which in turn perpetuates the most damaging cycle of discrimination ever fostered by our society. *De facto* school segregation is
therefore unacceptable by democratic principles even if it is often supported by democratic politics.

Racially segregated schools are precluded by the nonexclusion principle for reasons that return us to the main purpose of primary schooling:
educating democratic citizens. We have already seen that schools are
more than distributors of future opportunities; they also are, and cannot help but be, moral educators of future citizens. In a society where
blacks are still burdened by racial discrimination and prejudice, the demands of moral education are distributive because the best means
available to schools to reduce racial prejudice is thoroughgoing integration. To say that thoroughgoing integration is the best means to
ending racial prejudice is not to say it is a sufficient means. Nor does it
imply that any degree of integration is better than none at all. One can
be committed to the cause of racial integration and reluctant to support
racial integration of schools out of skepticism either as to its effects on
improving racial attitudes or as to the chances of implementing a thoroughgoing form of integration. The two forms of skepticism nourish
each other: the less thorough the integration, the less likely it is that integrated schools will reduce racial prejudice.

[79] Walzer, *Spheres of Justice*, pp. 222-23.
[80] Hochschild, *The New American Dilemma*, p. 59.

Since most attempts to integrate schools, at least in the North, have been less than thorough, such skepticism is warranted. Less warranted is the skepticism concerning the desirability of full-scale integration, were it politically possible. Studies show that racial prejudice is effectively (even if unintentionally) perpetuated by neighborhood schools and effectively reduced by schools in which contact between black and white students "is prolonged, intimate, noncompetitive, between equals in pursuit of common goals, and sanctioned by those in authority."[81] Desegregated schools that eliminate tracking and institute cooperative learning techniques (for which "sophisticated and detailed" instructional packages are available) significantly reduce racial prejudice among their students[82] and increase academic achievement among blacks (without decreasing it among whites): "*when fully and carefully carried out*, mandatory desegregation reduces racial isolation, enhances minority achievement, improves race relations, [and] promotes educational quality."[83] Schooling cannot fully "compensate for society,"[84] but the preponderance of empirical evidence suggests that schools can contribute to reducing the social stigma of being black and raising the academic achievement of black children above the democratic threshold at the same time that they make both black and white students more comfortable in racially integrated settings.[85]

Where there is a way, however, there is not necessarily a will. Or more accurately, there are often not enough wills to make the way either practically or morally simple. Teachers typically resist changing

---

[81] Nancy St. John, "The Effects of School Desegregation on Children," in *Race and Schooling in the City*, ed. Adam Yarmolinsky, Lance Liebman, and Corinne S. Schelling (Cambridge, Mass.: Harvard University Press, 1981), p. 92. St. John is reporting the conclusions of Gordon W. Allport, *The Nature of Prejudice* (Reading, Mass.: Addison Wesley, 1954), and Yehuda Amir, "Contact Hypothesis in Ethnic Relations," *Psychological Bulletin*, vol. 71, pp. 319-42. See also the more specific findings of Robert E. Slavin and Nancy A. Madden, "School Practices That Improve Race Relations," *American Educational Research Journal*, vol. 16, no. 2 (Spring 1979): 169-80.

[82] See Hochschild, *The New American Dilemma*, pp. 46-91. For the use of cooperative learning techniques, see David W. Johnson and Roger Johnson, *Learning Together and Alone: Cooperation, Competition and Individualization* (Englewood Cliffs, N.J.: Prentice-Hall, 1975); and Robert E. Slavin, *Cooperative Learning* (New York: Longman, 1982).

[83] Hochschild, *The New American Dilemma*, pp. 91, 177.

[84] Basil Bernstein, "Education Cannot Compensate for Society," *New Society* (February 26, 1970): 344-77.

[85] For experimental evidence on the long-term effects of desegregation, see Robert L. Crain, Jennifer A. Hawes, Randi L. Miller, and Janet R. Peichert, "A Longitudinal Study of a Metropolitan Voluntary Desegregation Plan," Washington, D.C.: National Institute of Education, October 1984. See also Jomills Henry Braddock II, Robert L. Crain, and James M. McPartland, "A Long-Term View of School Desegregation: Some Recent Studies of Graduates as Adults," *Phi Delta Kappan*, vol. 66, no. 4 (December 1984): 259-64.

their teaching methods, often on the well-intentioned misperception that their obligation is to impart knowledge, not to develop the moral character of their students. Principals generally find it easier to leave well enough alone rather than to restructure an entire school against the resistance of their staff. Although the racial prejudice that is left standing is not really "well enough" for a democratic society, it does not always manifest itself in ways that disrupt the normal workings of schools, especially of those that are not integrated.

Many suburban school boards and legislators refuse to support plans for effective desegregation not because they are racist but because a majority of their constituents vehemently oppose metropolitan-wide busing.[86] The opposition of their constituents need not be attributed to racism either. Why would middle-class white parents who live in the suburbs of a predominantly black city, whose children go to a predominantly white but otherwise good neighborhood school, decide to support a metropolitan-wide integration plan—unless they had the firmest moral commitment to furthering integration or reducing racism? One might attribute opposition to "forced busing" per se to racism, or at least to irrationality, insofar as all busing is involuntary and "over 50 percent of all American school children are bussed to school for nonracial reasons" without the least bit of protest by white parents.[87] White opposition to metropolitan-wide desegregation need not be either racist or irrational, however, since white parents living in middle-class neighborhoods have something substantial to lose for their children if, as is often the case, desegregation plans are not throroughgoing and therefore do not decrease racism among white students or increase the academic achievement of black students. Studies show that desegregation in its minimal form—busing black and/or white students to achieve "racial balance" but making no substantial changes in the way students are educated within schools—may augment racial prejudice and decrease the educational achievement of black students.[88] White and black parents living in poor neighborhoods also have something substantial to lose: their community schools.

Teachers, principals, legislators, and ordinary citizens all have excuses—I have just suggested some good ones—for not supporting desegregation under these circumstances. Should the finding that partial desegregation often does more harm than good to both black and white children be taken as reason not just to excuse but to justify opposition

---

[86] "Among whites [in 1978], an overwhelming 85-9% majority . . . oppose busing, not significantly different from the consistent opposition of whites to busing since the idea was first launched in the 1960's." Harris and Associates, *A Study of Attitudes*, p. 37.

[87] Hochschild, *The New American Dilemma*, p. 62.

[88] Ibid., pp. 50-51, 91.

to desegregation? Suppose white middle-class suburban parents argued the following: "We would support school desegregation if our support would make its success likely. Because so many other people oppose integration, our support is more likely to further some half-hearted desegregation plan, which will do more harm than good to both black and white children. Our morally best course of action is therefore to oppose desegregation." Were our only political alternatives to support or to oppose desegregation, then this reasoning would be compelling.[89] After all, citizens as well as public officials should take the consequences of their actions into account when deciding what public positions to support. What these parents neglect to consider, however, are the alternatives involving social coordination that would make their actions more effective in furthering full-fledged school desegregation. They might, for example, publicly support or campaign for public officials committed to whole-hearted desegregation, and speak out against both officials who oppose integration and those who support only half-hearted desegregation plans.[90] Unlike private citizens, public officials possess the power to coordinate many of the hands necessary to make integration work.[91]

Not many candidates for elected office, however, stand on platforms favoring desegregation. They oppose desegregation, they often say (if pressed), because the vast majority of voters in their district oppose it. Yet of those citizens whose children have been bused for racial integration, 6 out of 10 report the experience to have been "very satisfactory"; 8 out of 10 report an overall positive reaction; and "no more than 8% of the blacks and 16% of the whites feel that having their children

[89] We might still be suspicious of such reasoning because it is easy for a middle-class parent simply to *assume* that all others are staunchly opposed to desegregation and therefore that his support could only serve to bring about some half-hearted desegregation plan that is worse than no plan at all—when in fact other middle-class parents feel the same way and would support desegregation if they realized that the source of a good deal of the opposition was similar. The only way to know what other parents really think is for all parents publicly to speak their true and full minds on the subject. But, as I point out below, the problem with this reasoning goes well beyond such strategic considerations, which in practice are probably indeterminate.

[90] Black parents might make a much better case for justifying opposition to desegregation because they fear that their children will be stigmatized even further in the early stages of even a successful desegregation plan. "Why should we take the risk that our children suffer still more?" they might ask. The question is not easy to answer, except on thoroughgoing consequentialist grounds. Most black parents, however, do not ask this question, at least not rhetorically, probably because their children's education is already so bad that the risk seems worth taking. Collective efforts on the part of public officials and democratic citizens can minimize this risk.

[91] My argument here is influenced by Derek Parfit's discussion of the second "mistake in moral mathematics" in *Reasons and Persons*, pp. 70-73.

bused has not been a satisfactory experience."[92] We must be cautious in interpreting this evidence, since it does not include the (presumably) unchanged attitudes of parents who sent their children to private school or who moved to avoid busing. Yet the satisfaction expressed by both black and white parents of bused children is surely significant, and the most common reason expressed by these parents for their satisfaction—the lack of problems or complaints from their children—may increase the significance of this finding. Perhaps a substantial proportion of parents whose children have not been bused would also change their attitude toward busing were they to discover few problems or complaints from their own children. (I shall not rest any conclusion on this speculation, however, since it may well be mistaken.) The second most common reason given by black parents for their satisfaction is that their children learn more; the second most common reason given by white parents is that black and white "children learn to live with each other."[93] Not only is the retrospective response to busing almost as overwhelmingly favorable as the prospective response is unfavorable, but the reasons for the favorable retrospective response also reflect the democratic purposes of busing: busing has the potential for increasing the academic achievement of black students and decreasing the racial prejudice of white students.

The difference between "before" and "after" responses suggests that busing may be an issue on which politicians would do well—morally well, that is—to act as temporary trustees of the public interest, educating citizens to civic virtue by enacting a policy that they prospectively fear but retrospectively endorse. There are two problems with this piece of advice. The first is that we lack sufficient evidence to decide whether and to what degree thoroughgoing integration would also shift the attitudes of those parents who oppose busing and are presently intent on avoiding it for their children, even at great cost. (We do not even know how many parents today fit into this category. The evidence on why parents of school-age children "flee" from inner cities and send their children to private schools is still quite inconclusive.[94]) The second, and more insurmountable, problem is that politicians who pub-

[92] See Harris, *A Study of Attitudes*, pp. 30. Cf. p. 37: Even blacks oppose busing, although by a narrow 43%-42% margin (in 1978). Whites overwhelmingly oppose it, by a wide 85%-9% margin.

[93] Harris, *A Study of Attitudes*, p. 39.

[94] For some evidence, see Michael W. Giles, Douglas S. Gatlin, and Everett F. Cataldo, "The Impact of Busing on White Flight," *Social Science Quarterly*, vol. 55 (1974): 493-501; and Jeffrey A. Raffel, Nancy J. Colmer, and Donald J. Berry, "Public Opinion Toward the Public Schools of Northern New Castle County" (Newark, Del.: College of Urban Affairs and Public Policy, 1983), esp. pp. 86-93.

licly support busing may never get elected since it is such an unpopular issue. The incentives of electoral politics run counter to democratic principles in this case, making it more important that politicians recognize a moral responsibility to educate their constituents by exercising leadership—but doubtful that they will get elected if they do so. School desegregation is difficult to enact democratically. Yet having experienced it, the majority of parents may approve of it.

One can begin to construct a tentative case for judicial enforcement of desegregation upon its democratic rationale, the educability of public opinion concerning desegregation, and the electoral obstacles to its implementation:

(1) Insofar as it increases the academic achievement of black students and decreases the racial prejudice of white students, thoroughgoing school desegregation fulfills two of the essential purposes of primary schooling in our society.
(2) Citizens overwhelmingly oppose thoroughgoing school desegregation before it is implemented, but seem to support it after experiencing its effects.
(3) Judges, by virtue of their greater insulation from popular pressure, are in a better practical position than legislators to enact desegregation.[95] They are also in a good—even if not the best—moral position, because thoroughgoing desegregation is often necessary to fulfill the distributive requirements of a democratic education.

This case for judicial enforcement of desegregation is obviously (and, I suspect, necessarily, given the available evidence) tentative and incomplete. It would take another book to defend the role that I have just attributed to courts in a democratic society. Short of writing that book,[96] I can mention a misunderstanding that might lead someone to suppose that judges undermine rather than support democracy when they mandate desegregation. One might identify democracy merely with majority rule, and therefore conclude that "if most citizens choose not to grant the rest of the citizens their full rights [by supporting school desegregation], then perhaps democracy must give way to liberalism."[97] No misunderstanding need arise here if one means to say

[95] Whether courts have the capacity to enforce thoroughgoing desegregation is a controversial issue, which I cannot settle here. A compelling case for the affirmative can be found in Michael Rebell and Arthur Block, *Educational Policy Making and the Courts: An Empirical Study of Judicial Activism* (Chicago: University of Chicago Press, 1982), pp. 199-216. For a summary of the evidence, see Hochschild, *The New American Dilemma*, pp. 131-41.

[96] Or repeating the arguments that I made in "How Liberal Is Democracy?" pp. 25-50.

[97] Hochschild, *The New American Dilemma*, p. 145.

only that majority rule must give way to judicial enforcement of certain basic rights. But if one means to claim that a commitment to democracy is incompatible with support for judicially mandated school desegregation,[98] then identifying "democracy" with "majority rule" is misleading. Most theories of democracy—and certainly all those that can pass as credible interpretations of our Constitution—authorize judicial constraints on the rule of majorities (or pluralities) in the name of fulfilling the demands of democratic justice. The relevant question from the perspective of defending democracy, then, is not whether court-ordered desegregation constrains majority rule but whether it is consistent with the demands of democratic justice. I have suggested some reasons for thinking that it is, and that a commitment to school desegregation does not require us to choose between liberalism and democracy. In the case of school desegregation, democracy leads us in a liberal direction—with a difference, a difference that poses a serious dilemma for democrats, especially for democratic judges.

The difference is that democrats must regret not only the present prejudice and the past discrimination that create the need for mandatory desegregation, but also the intrusions upon local community that are its effect. Because local school politics is a democratic good, permitting citizens to give shape to their own community, "democratic" judges will not impose orders on local districts beyond what is necessary to institute an effective form of school desegregation. Local schools are the preferred democratic pattern of associating school-age children. By participating in local school politics, adults can learn the skills as well as reap the communitarian benefits of democratic citizenship.[99] By attending local schools, children also can learn to identify with a community bigger than their family but small enough to feel at "home" in. Although these democratic goods need not be totally lost when schools desegregate by court order, they can be.

The democratic value of community suggests that judges not impose unnecessary orders on local districts, but the evidence on effective desegregation suggests that only the most thoroughgoing plans are likely to succeed in achieving the democratic value of integration. In this tension between the values of local community and racial integration lies perhaps the greatest dilemma of democratic education in our time. Critics and supporters of desegregation alike agree that "moving chil-

[98] For an argument along these lines, see ibid., pp. 9-11, 40-44, 144-45, and esp. 199-200.

[99] "For politics is always territorially based; and the neighborhood . . . is historically the first, and still the most immediate and obvious, base for democratic politics. People are most likely to be knowledgeable and concerned, active and effective, when they are close to home, among friends and familiar enemies." Walzer, *Spheres of Justice*, p. 225.

dren around like checkers will not in itself improve matters."[100] Busing may in fact decrease rather than increase racial understanding (as well as the academic achievement of blacks) if it is done haphazardly and without the cooperation of local schools or communities.[101] Judges often have another option: they can permit a school district to design its own desegregation plan within the range of plans compatible with the goals of decreasing racial prejudice and increasing the achievement of black students. If the district's first plan is unacceptable, judges can insist that it try again.

If districts repeatedly fail to develop adequate plans, however, should judges impose plans on them?[102] At the very least, judges should try to draw up their plans in consultation with the most cooperative members of the community. But even the best judges may fail to enlist the cooperation of the most powerful groups in an intransigent community. They then face a hard choice, between imposing a complete plan on a community against its will or permitting the community to implement its own, inadequate plan. Neither choice guarantees good results.

If the best existing evidence is correct—that not integrating schools guarantees bad results—then perhaps judges should impose thorough-going plans on intransigent communities, in the hope that communities will be reconstituted on more democratic ground after being deconstituted. This is what apparently happened to the metropolitan area of Charlotte-Mecklenburg, after being subject to court-ordered desegregation. "Charlotte-Mecklenburg's proudest achievement of past 20 years," The Charlotte Observer noted in reaction to a speech by President Reagan, "is not the city's impressive new skyline or its strong, growing economy. Its proudest achievement is its fully integrated public school system." The editorial is a small but significant piece of evi-

---

[100] Nancy St. John, "The Effects of School Desegregation on Children," pp. 86-90. See also Nancy St. John, School Desegregation: Outcomes for Children (New York: Wiley Interscience, 1975).

[101] See esp. Robert L. Crain and Rita E. Mahard, "Desegregation and Black Achievement: A Review of the Research," Law and Contemporary Problems, vol. 42, no. 3 (Summer 1978): 17-56. Also see Meyer Weinberg, "The Relationship between School Desegregation and Academic Achievement: A Review of the Research," Law and Contemporary Problems, vol. 39, no. 2 (Spring 1975): 240-70 (but see St. John's criticism in "The Effects of School Desegregation on Children," p. 88). For a useful summary of the studies and a note of caution on interpreting their findings, see Willis D. Hawley, "Increasing the Effectiveness of School Desegregation: Lessons from the Research," in Yarmolinsky et al., Race and Schooling in the City, pp. 150-52.

[102] See for important examples, David L. Kirp, Just Schools: The Idea of Racial Equality in American Education (Berkeley: University of California Press, 1982); and Ralph Cavanaugh and Austin Sarat, "Thinking about Courts: Toward and Beyond a Jurisprudence of Judicial Competence," Law and Society Review, vol. 14, no. 2 (Winter 1980): 371-420.

dence that, far from being forever lost, communities can be reconstituted, on more democratic ground, by court-ordered desegregation.[103]

But is reconstitution a realistic hope for larger Northern cities, such as Detroit, Boston, New York, and Chicago? Many of the people committed to reconstituting South Boston by integrating its schools gave up that belief, reluctantly, after years of court-ordered busing. Anthony Lukas's account of Colin and Joan Diver, two of the most committed residents of the South End, who finally moved their family to Newton, makes it hard to discount such disillusionment as the product of class interest or lack of political imagination. Colin came to believe that

> only by providing jobs and other economic opportunities for the deprived—black and white alike—could the city reduce the deep sense of grievance harbored by both communities, alleviate some of the antisocial behavior grounded in such resentments, and begin to close the terrible gap betweeen the rich and the poor, the suburb and the city, the hopeful and the hopeless.[104]

But if economic development and redistribution are politically no more feasible than busing, then the dilemma remains. "Surely, [the critics of Judge Garrity] argued, there must be some way, while preserving the plaintiffs' constitutional rights, to prevent Boston's schools from becoming the preserve of the black and the poor."[105] If there is some way for cities such as Boston to be reconstituted with racially integrated schools, it (surely) has yet to be found.

THE DEMANDS OF DEMOCRATIC OPPORTUNITY

Democratic standards require neither that the "inputs" nor the "outcomes" of education be equalized. We need not spend the same amount on every child's education nor produce equal educational results among children or groups of children. The democratic interpretation of equal educational opportunity requires instead that all educable children learn enough to participate effectively in the democratic process. It also authorizes democratic communities to determine the nature of schooling above the threshold. What constitutes an education adequate to democratic participation will vary over time as well as among dem-

---

[103] "You sometimes speak of a 'shining city on a hill,' Mr. President," the editorial concluded. "You visited one briefly on Monday, but you didn't understand, or seem to care, what makes it shine." Reprinted in *The Washington Post*, October 10, 1984, p. A15.

[104] J. Anthony Lukas, *Common Ground: A Turbulent Decade in the Lives of Three American Families* (New York: Alfred A. Knopf, 1985), p. 650.

[105] Ibid.

ocratic societies; but that should not stop us from trying to determine what the democratic standard demands of our society.

The demands of the threshold principle are considerable: states should take greater responsibility for financing primary education or for making more effective use of existing resources; the content of education should be reoriented toward teaching students the skills of democratic deliberation; and the federal government should give local schools more money for educating handicapped children. The authorization principle permits democratic institutions to determine how much to spend and how to distribute education above the threshold. The demands of this principle are primarily procedural: federal agencies and courts should not assume any more control over school politics than is necessary to satisfy the threshold principle; state politicians should place school finance more squarely on the political agenda; and local school districts should have the option of spending more on their children's education.

The demands of the democratic standard go beyond what is commonly considered "school politics." The success of schools in educating children of the poor up to the threshold depends on the success of the state in doing more for poor parents—creating more jobs, better housing, more community services, better childcare, and so on. Schools cannot be relieved of all responsibility when other institutions let children down, but neither can they compensate for society. Schools can, however, contribute to democratic education by associating children over extensive periods of time in ways conducive to overcoming racial prejudice.

CHAPTER SIX

THE PURPOSES
OF HIGHER EDUCATION

Higher education cannot succeed unless lower education does. If high schools are not educating most students up to the democratic threshold, then many colleges and universities will continue the primary education of their students. Many American colleges have already assumed this role: most community colleges offer high-school graduates a second chance at achieving basic literacy, often for the explicit sake of helping them get a job. The fact that most American colleges compete for students rather than vice versa reinforces this market perspective on higher education. The perspective is both pedagogically and morally uncomfortable. Most professors are neither trained nor motivated to teach either basic literacy or job skills. Many students who could benefit from an extended high-school education are effectively excluded from receiving one, because even community colleges are costly, if only by virtue of the income that students from poor families must forego to attend them.

If college education is to be part of primary education, it should be made free and compulsory. One might argue that the time has come in the United States for an extension of compulsory schooling, since every increase in compulsory schooling so far has been a step towards equalizing democratic citizenship by excluding fewer children from a more adequate primary education. Twelve years of schooling may not be enough time to cultivate the character and teach the basic skills of democratic citizenship.[1] Then why not require a college education in the name of nonexclusion?

There are at least two reasons to look for a better alternative. First, colleges are unlikely to succeed for students after high school has failed them. Most poorly educated students needed better, not more, schooling. Second, even if college could succeed in adequately educating all

[1] Most school-leaving age laws today stop just short of the normal age of completing high school. A further extension of compulsory education to coincide with the normal age of high-school graduation might be yet another victory for democratic citizenship. Although a much larger proportion of citizens in the 1980s than in the 1970s completed four years of high school, a substantial minority (13.8 percent of citizens between the ages of 25 and 29 in 1982) still lack a high-school education. See *Digest of Educational Statistics 1983-84* (Washington, D.C.: U.S. Government Printing Office, 1984), p. 13.

students, its success would come at a very high price, and not just in dollars. "For some children, beyond a certain age, school is a kind of prison (but they have done nothing to deserve imprisonment). . . ."[2] Making college part of primary education would extend the prison sentence of many young people after they have ceased to be children. Were a college education necessary for the sake of citizenship, the extended sentence could be justified. But until we do more—much more—to improve the first twelve years of schooling, we cannot conclude that a college education is necessary.

A far better option than to extend compulsory schooling into college is to improve earlier education and, if necessary, to begin compulsory schooling at an earlier age (when it also can serve as childcare for working parents). The alternative of making college compulsory is morally worse and politically no more feasible—it would be a victory not for citizenship but for schooling, and a further imposition on adolescents of an unnecessary tendency to make a college degree necessary for living a good life in our society.

Schooling does not stop serving democracy, however, when it ceases to be compulsory—or when all educable citizens reach the democratic threshold. Its purposes change. Higher education should not be necessary for inculcating basic democratic virtues, such as toleration, truth-telling, and a predisposition to nonviolence. I doubt whether it can be. If adolescents have not developed these character traits by the time they reach college, it is probably too late for professors to inculcate them by "preaching, witnessing, [and] setting a good example" for their students. If, as Mark Lilla argues, "this is the only way students can understand, in a complex way, what their roles will be in a democracy and what virtue is in those roles," then that understanding had better precede their college education.[3]

There is, I have already argued, another, equally complex and intellectually more challenging way in which students can be taught to understand the moral demands of democratic life. While not a substitute for character training, learning how to think carefully and critically about political problems, to articulate one's views and defend them before people with whom one disagrees is a form of moral education to which young adults are more receptive and for which universities are well suited. Many of the same arguments for teaching primary-school students to deliberate hold for college students, for whom engaging in a "bit of 'indoctrination' in the virtues of democracy" is less likely to

[2] Walzer, *Spheres of Justice*, pp. 207-208.
[3] Lilla, "Ethos, 'Ethics,' and Public Service," *The Public Interest*, no. 63 (Spring 1981): 17.

be effective.[4] Not only is this reason for democratic control (the inculcation of common values) missing, but there are other reasons—rooted
in the democratic purposes of universities—that support a case for the
relative autonomy of universities from democratic control.[5]

The relative autonomy of a university is rooted in its primary demo-
cratic purpose: protection against the threat of democratic tyranny.
The threat of democratic tyranny was most eloquently characterized by
Tocqueville:

> [I]n democratic republics . . . tyranny . . . leaves the body alone
> and goes straight for the soul. The master no longer says: "Think
> like me or you die." He does say: "You are free not to think as I
> do; you can keep your life and property and all; but from this day
> you are a stranger among us. . . . You will remain among men, but
> you will lose your rights to count as one. When you approach your
> fellows, they will shun you as an impure being, and even those who
> believe in your innocence will abandon you too, lest they in turn
> be shunned. Go in peace. I have given you your life, but it is a life
> worse than death.[6]

Control of the creation of ideas—whether by a majority or a minority—subverts the ideal of *conscious* social reproduction at the heart of
democratic education and democratic politics. As institutional sanctuaries for free scholarly inquiry, universities can help prevent such subversion. They can provide a realm where new and unorthodox ideas are
judged on their intellectual merits; where the men and women who defend such ideas, provided they defend them well, are not strangers but
valuable members of a community. Universities thereby serve democracy as sanctuaries of nonrepression. In addition to creating and funding universities, democratic governments can further this primary pur-

---

[4] Ibid. For extended analyses of the reasons for teaching applied ethics at the university
level, see Derek Bok, *Beyond the Ivory Tower: Social Responsibilities of the Modern
University* (Cambridge, Mass.: Harvard University Press, 1982), pp. 116-35; Daniel Callahan and Sissela Bok, eds., *Ethics Teaching in Higher Education* (New York: Plenum
Press, 1980); and Dennis Thompson, "Political Theory and Political Judgment," *PS*, vol.
17, no. 2 (Spring 1984): 193-97.

[5] A case can also be made (although I do not make it here) for the relative autonomy
of professional schools. To determine precisely what the relative autonomy of professional schools—as distinct from that of universities—entails, one would consider the
partly distinct democratic purposes of professional education. Because law schools, for
example, serve as educators of both technically competent lawyers and critical legal
scholars, one might conclude that the standard of relative autonomy justifies state licens-
ing of lawyers but not control of the content of legal education.

[6] Alexis de Tocqueville, *Democracy in America* (1848), trans. George Lawrence, ed.
J. P. Mayer (Garden City, N.Y.: Doubleday and Co., 1969), vol. 1, pt. 2, ch. 7, pp. 255-56.

pose of higher education in two ways: by respecting what is commonly called the "academic freedom" of scholars, and by respecting what might be called the "freedom of the academy."

ACADEMIC FREEDOM AND FREEDOM OF THE ACADEMY

What is academic freedom, and what does it demand of democracies? As derived from the German concept of *Lehrfreiheit*, academic freedom is neither a universal right of citizenship nor a contractual right of university employees. It is perhaps best understood as a special right tied to the particular office of scholar, similar in form (but different in content) to the particular rights of priests, doctors, lawyers, and journalists. The core of academic freedom is the freedom of scholars to assess existing theories, established institutions, and widely held beliefs according to the canons of truth adopted by their academic disciplines, without fear of sanction by anyone if they arrive at unpopular conclusions. Academic freedom allows scholars to follow their autonomous judgment wherever it leads them, provided that they remain within the bounds of scholarly standards of inquiry.

The proviso of remaining within the bounds of scholarly standards is sometimes overlooked,[7] but it is necessary to justify the social office that scholars occupy, and to distinguish academic freedom from the more general freedoms of citizens to think, speak, and publish their ideas. If academic freedom knew no scholarly bounds, the freedom of scholars would be indistinguishable from these more general freedoms. These general freedoms also apply to scholars in their role as citizens, but academic freedom is more demanding—of scholars and therefore of their society. Scholars must recognize a duty to observe scholarly standards of inquiry as a condition of their social office.[8] (I return to

[7] Clark Kerr, for example, confuses academic freedom with the freedom of a professor to do as he pleases, and therefore mistakenly concludes that a professor has more academic freedom in a multiversity than in any other university because "he has a choice of roles and mixtures of roles to suit his taste as never before. He need not leave the Groves for the Acropolis unless he wishes; but he can, if he wishes. He may even become, as some have, essentially a professional man with his home office and basic retainer on the campus of the multiversity but with his clients scattered from coast to coast. He can also even remain the professor of old, as many do. There are several patterns of life from which to choose. So the professor . . . has greater freedom. *Lehrfreiheit*, in the old German sense of the freedom of the professor to do as he pleases, also is triumphant." Were academic freedom "the freedom of the professor to do as he pleases," neither academic freedom nor universities that fostered such freedom would have any special democratic value. Kerr, *The Uses of the University* (Cambridge, Mass.: Harvard University Press, 1982), p. 44.

[8] For an explanation of the (common) understanding of social office on which I rely, see Walzer, *Spheres of Justice*, pp. 129-35: "[A]n office is any position in which the po-

examine the contextual conditions of this duty below.) Democratic citizens must observe an obligation not to restrict the intellectual freedoms of individual scholars or those freedoms of liberal universities that secure an institutional environment conducive to the exercise of scholarly autonomy.

Control of the educational environment within which scholarship and teaching take place is the form of academic freedom most often neglected by its democratic defenders. The historical reason for this neglect is not difficult to discern. Whereas German universities were generally self-governing bodies of scholars who made administrative decisions either collegially or through democratically elected administrators, American universities (with few exceptions) are administered by lay governing boards and administrators chosen by those boards.[9] Therefore, while the scholar's right of academic freedom in the German context could readily be extended to a right collectively to control the academic environment of the university, the academic freedom of faculty in the American context had to be used as a defense *against* the university's legally constituted (lay) administrative authority. Recurrent threats by universities' trustees and administrators to the academic freedom of faculty members made it easy for faculty to overlook their stake in defending their universities against state regulation of educational policies.[10]

Despite this historical neglect, the stake of scholars and citizens in the autonomy of the academy is great—not only because public officials have directly threatened the academic freedom of individual scholars, but also because governmental regulations can indirectly threaten academic freedom by making universities unconducive to good scholarship and teaching. When HUAC and state legislative committees pressured universities in the 1950s to dismiss faculty members for their alleged Communist loyalties or for their failure to testify concerning

---

litical community as a whole takes an interest, choosing the person who holds it or regulating the procedures by which he is chosen" (p. 129).

[9] See Ralph F. Fuchs, "Academic Freedom—Its Basic Philosophy Function, and History," in Hans W. Baade and Robinson O. Everett, eds., *Academic Freedom: The Scholar's Place in Modern Society* (Dobbs Ferry, N.Y.: Oceana Publications, 1964), pp. 5-6; and Richard Hofstadter and Walter Metzger, eds., *The Development of Academic Freedom in the United States* (New York: Columbia University Press, 1955), pp. 383-98. The first systematic formulation of this understanding of academic freedom seems to have been Frederich Paulsen's in *The German Universities and University Study* (1902), trans. F. Thilly and W. W. Elwang (New York: C. Scribner's Sons, 1906), pp. 228-31.

[10] For evidence of such threats, see the AAUP's list of "Censured Administrations, 1930-1968," in Louis Joughin, ed., *Academic Freedom and Tenure: A Handbook of the American Association of University Professors* (Madison: University of Wisconsin Press, 1969), pp. 143-47.

their political beliefs, universities could legitimately assert their autonomy as a means of protecting the academic freedom of their faculty.[11]

Even when the academic freedom of individual faculty members is
not directly at stake, the academic freedom of universities may be. Constraints upon a university's hiring and admissions standards are likely
to affect the future academic standards within disciplines and the environment within which scholarship and teaching take place. Administrative time and money spent complying with state regulations may
be time and money not spent on improving academic departments or
responding to the concerns of faculty and students. Like other large institutions, universities have responsibilities that extend beyond their
specific social function. They therefore cannot claim a "right" to be free
from all external regulations that make it more costly or administratively difficult to pursue their academic goals. But they may claim a
right to be free from those regulations that threaten the very pursuit of
those goals. When governmental regulations threaten to destroy the environment for scholarship and teaching, either by substantially lowering the intellectual quality of faculty and students or by draining essential resources from academic to nonacademic areas, universities
dedicated to free scholarly inquiry can legitimately assert an institutional right to academic freedom, consistent with (indeed, derived
from) the right of their faculty to academic freedom.

Taken together, the academic freedoms of scholars and of liberal universities serve as safeguards against political repression, not just for
scholars but also for citizens. They help prevent a subtle but invidious
form of majority tyranny without substituting a less subtle and worse
form of tyranny—that of the minority—in its place. Democracies can
foster the general freedom of conscious social reproduction within politics by fostering the particular freedom of defending unpopular ideas
within universities, regardless of the political popularity of those conceptions (but not regardless of their scholarly merits).

Scholars and universities that claim academic freedom against interference with their intellectual and institutional pursuits also must acknowledge duties that accompany the right. What duties does devotion
to free scholarly inquiry entail for the individual scholar? Consider
Abraham Flexner's description of the career of Louis Pasteur:

When the prosperity and well-being of France were threatened by
silk-worm disease, by difficulties in the making of wines, in the
brewing of beer, by chicken cholera, hydrophobia, etc., Pasteur

[11] For an account of governmental attacks in the 1950s, see Robert M. MacIver, *Academic Freedom in Our Time* (New York: Columbia University Press, 1955), pp. 46-55,
158-87. For the failure of universities under attack to defend academic freedom, see Ellen
Schrecker, *No Ivory Tower* (New York: Oxford University Press, 1986).

permitted himself to be diverted from his work in order to solve these problems, one after another; having done so, he published his results and returned to his laboratory. His approach was intellectual, no matter whether the subject was poultry, brewing, or chemistry. He did not become consultant to silk-worm growers, wine makers, brewers, or poultry men. . . . The problem solved, his interest and activity ceased. He had indeed served, but he had served like a scientist, and there his service ended.[12]

Flexner does not say precisely what serving "like a scientist"—or, more generally, like a scholar—entails, but his description of Pasteur provides some clues. Although Pasteur pursued knowledge for the sake of serving society, he was sufficiently independent to decide when to leave pressing social problems behind to work on problems that would take longer to solve. Pasteur directed some of his work towards helping particular groups in society, but he did not serve only those groups that could afford to pay for his services. Pasteur did not isolate himself in an "ivory tower," to avoid all influences of the "real world," but he did shield himself from improper influences, those that would impede the exercise of his scholarly judgment.

The duty of a scholar, one might say, is to avoid those influences that are likely to impede—or to give the appearance of impeding—scholarly judgment.[13] What influences constitute impediments to free scholarly judgment? Financial influences are the most obvious, but not all financial influences are improper. It clearly would have been wrong for Pasteur to accept money from the wine-makers had they restricted the methods or results of his research in exchange for payment—in an attempt to use his intellectual authority to persuade the public, say, that wine was good for their health (not that the French needed to be convinced). Such a contract would be tantamount to bribery ("we'll pay you not to exercise your best intellectual judgment") and would clearly violate scholarly autonomy in a way that drawing salary directly from a university does not. Most consulting contracts today are not restricted in this invidious fashion. The more common and complex problem lies not in the influence that a particular consulting contract has on the integrity of one scholar's work but in the way in which the widespread acceptance of consulting contracts can skew the types of problems that scholars pursue—drawing them away from investigating more serious social problems that have fewer immediate pay-offs or

---

[12] Abraham Flexner, *Universities: American, English, German* (New York and London: Oxford University Press, 1930), pp. 131-32.

[13] Avoiding the appearance of improper influence is important because scholarship must be taken seriously to serve its social purpose.

away from equally serious problems that afflict people who cannot afford to hire consultants. Not all types of research contracts interfere with the collective autonomy of scholarship, but many do. The more freedom that contracts give scholars to define their own research problems, the less they interfere with the collective autonomy of scholarship, which provides an intellectual sanctuary against political control of the creation of ideas. The less freedom contracts give scholars, the more suspect they are on these grounds and the greater the need for scholars collectively to limit their right to accept such contracts.

Just as the academic freedom of scholars carries with it an individual duty to resist improper influences, so the freedom of the academy carries with it an institutional duty not to exert improper influences on scholars, for example, by making promotions depend on popularity rather than on the intellectual merits of research and teaching, by failing to defend faculty against political attacks by alumni or trustees, or simply by burdening scholars with too many nonacademic duties. By virtue of their democratic purpose, universities have not only a right to relative autonomy from external political control but also an obligation to create an environment that is conducive to the exercise of scholarly autonomy. When they live up to that obligation (by securing for scholars an intellectual realm free from improper pressures), universities provide an institutional sanctuary against repression, which prevents majorities or coalitions of minorities from controlling the creation of politically relevant ideas. The sanctuary protects democracy not only against its own excesses but also against nondemocratic tyranny.

Because the institutional right of academic freedom ("freedom of the academy") is derived from the democratic value of scholarly autonomy and not from a private property right, the right may be claimed with equal force by public and private universities that are dedicated to defending the scholarly autonomy of their faculty. A state-enforced loyalty oath requirement, for example, does not cease to be problematic when it is applied only within state-owned universities. Nor may private universities invoke their "academic freedom" to defend racially and sexually discriminatory promotion practices. The democratic purpose of a university, not the contractual arrangements between owners and employees, grounds the academic freedom of faculty, as well as the freedom of the academy.

Academic freedom is not a legitimate defense against governmental regulations that are compatible with preserving, or instrumental to achieving, an environment conducive to scholarly autonomy. Some of the most controversial legislation of the past twenty-five years—the Equal Pay Act of 1963, Executive Order 11246 defining affirmative action guidelines for universities, and Title IX forbidding sex discrimination in student athletic programs—limit the authority of universities with regard to important internal practices, but in ways that are compatible with (perhaps even instrumental to) their professed educational purposes. One can therefore agree with the general claim that "an institution which lacks freedom from government interference in the management of its educational functions cannot protect its faculty from government interference with theirs"[14] and yet refuse to shout "Academic Freedom!" whenever a university defends itself against governmental regulation.

In some cases, a conflict arises from the fact that a (so-called) university is committed to certain sectarian religious purposes that are incompatible with both nondiscrimination in the distribution of offices and freedom of scholarly inquiry. The associational purposes of fundamentalist Christian universities whose members "genuinely believe that the Bible forbids interracial dating and marriage"[15] are incompatible with a requirement that tax-exempt institutions not discriminate on the basis of race. The proper defense against governmental regulation by such institutions is not academic freedom, but freedom of association. In these cases, democracies must decide whether the associational freedom of a sectarian academy should be honored against the competing rights of nondiscrimination and free scholarly inquiry. One way of honoring associational freedom without dishonoring nondiscrimination is for governments to allow sectarian academies to discriminate but deprive them of the tax-exempt and the credentialing statuses of universities, statuses rightly reserved for academies of higher learning that respect the academic freedom of their faculty and the principle of nondiscrimination in distributing opportunities to social office.

The autonomy of universities, like that of social institutions more generally, is relative to their democratic purposes. A defense of university autonomy on grounds of free association cannot be conclusive because the democratic purposes of universities include far more than supporting membership in consensual communities. Universities also serve as gatekeepers to many social offices; they have a virtual monopoly on the education necessary for many of the most valued jobs in our society. As gatekeepers, they share responsibility for upholding the democratic principle of nondiscrimination in the distribution of office. Democratic governments therefore properly concern themselves with safeguarding the interests not only of current members of universities but also of students seeking admission to, and academics seeking jobs

---

[14] Dallin Oaks, "A Private University Looks at Government Regulation," *Journal of College and University Law*, vol. 4, no. 1 (February 1976): 3.

[15] *Bob Jones University v. United States*, 461 U.S. 574 (1982) at 580.

within, universities. When the interests of members conflict with those of nonmembers, as they do in the case of sectarian academies that discriminate against blacks, then a democratic state should uphold the more important democratic interest at stake. Because the claim to autonomy is derived from the democratic purposes served by universities, a democratic state does not violate an absolute right of universities when it regulates them for the sake of making the system of universities function more democratically.

The question that must be asked in every case is whether a proposed restriction on their decisionmaking authority will bring universities closer to serving their democratic purposes. In answering this question, the interests both of members and of nonmembers who seek membership in a university must be considered. By virtue of recognizing both sets of interests, legislatures will sometimes be forced to make hard choices in deciding whether and how to regulate universities, and courts may then face equally hard choices in deciding whether regulations that are challenged violate associational freedom or are necessary to protect citizens against unjustified discrimination. Defenders of state regulation point out that universities often invoke academic freedom to rationalize what would otherwise be blatantly discriminatory practices, such as not admitting or hiring blacks. Those who defend universities against state regulation respond that the standard of nondiscrimination taken to its logical extreme leaves little or no room for associational freedom. One need not disagree with either of these claims to defend the relative autonomy of universities based on their democratic purposes. The alternatives of granting universities full autonomy from democratic control or none at all are worse than facing up to the hard choices entailed in establishing a principled middle ground.

EDUCATING OFFICEHOLDERS

In addition to serving as sanctuaries of nonrepression, universities also serve as gatekeepers to many of the most valuable social offices, particularly in the professions. Economists often view the university's gatekeeping function as a piece of its primary purpose: maximizing social value, welfare, or utility (the terms are used interchangeably). The view is apparently attractive. Why, one might ask, should universities not try to maximize social value? The rhetorical force of the question can best be countered by considering how a self-consciously utility-maximizing university would behave with regard to selecting and then educating future officeholders.

The aim of the utilitarian university is most fully elaborated with regard to its function in "screening" students and then "signaling" employers of their relative value by grading, recommending, and certifying them.[16] To maximize social productivity, a utilitarian university does more than educate students. A university education, as Joseph Stiglitz suggests, "provides information as well as skills. . . ." It supplies society with "a 'commodity' for which it is well known that the market 'fails'. . . ."[17]

But how successful are universities in making up for market failure? The best studies tend to agree that although "there is no more consistent social science finding than that of the correlation between educational attainment and higher personal income,"[18] there are few less well understood relationships than that between educational attainment and success in later life, measured by income, occupational status, or any other (more or less meaningful) measure of social contribution.[19] "The voluminous literature on academic variables and later-life success is not worthless . . . ," Robert Klitgaard comments. It teaches us that "[d]efining them as we will, 'later life contributions' are very difficult to forecast."[20] Differences in academic success explain a very small portion of the differences in income, occupational status, or any other (more or less) meaningful measure of social contribution. To the extent that a university education is associated with future success, the data do not indicate whether it is the education, the information, or the mere credential supplied by a university that accounts for the association.

In face of this evidence that universities do not maximize social welfare, economists look for means by which they might. The descriptive model—which measures how well universities screen students according to their future social contribution—is easily translated into a prescriptive model—which recommends ways in which universities can do a better job in predicting future social success. "The problem," Klitgaard concludes, "is not with our objectives [to predict future success]

[16] On screening and signaling, see A. Michael Spence, *Market Signaling* (Cambridge, Mass.: Harvard University Press, 1974); Joseph E. Stiglitz, "The Theory of 'Screening,' Education, and the Distribution of Income," *American Economic Review*, vol. 65, no. 3 (June 1975): 283-300; Kenneth Wolpin, "Education and Screening," *American Economic Review*, vol. 67, no. 5 (December 1977): 949-58; and John G. Riley, "Testing the Educational Screening Hypothesis," *Journal of Political Economy*, vol. 87, no. 5 (October 1979): 227-52.

[17] Stiglitz, "The Theory of 'Screening,' Education, and the Distribution of Income," p. 298.

[18] Douglas M. Windham, "The Benefits and Financing of American Higher Education: Theory, Research, and Policy," no. 80-A19 (Stanford, Calif.: Institute for Research on Educational Finance and Governance, Stanford University, November 1980), p. 5. Quoted in Robert Klitgaard, *Choosing Elites* (New York: Basic Books, 1985), p. 118.

[19] For an excellent summary and analysis of the relevant literature, see Klitgaard, *Choosing Elites*, pp. 116-31.

[20] Ibid., p. 119.

but with what at present can be measured and predicted."[21] But *is* this the problem? Before we advise universities to get on with the task of trying to develop better measurements and make more accurate predictions, we should question the "framework that suggests that . . . the institution [of the university is] . . . a production process whose value added is to be maximized."[22]

Utilitarianism *can* translate all the purposes of universities into positive and negative utilities or into values added or subtracted, but "can" does not imply "ought." As long as they must look for measurable and commensurable values, universities that try to maximize the social value added of their students must take their signals from the job market. If employers are racist or anti-semitic, so will universities be in the guise of maximizing social utility.[23] If the demand for engineers far exceeds the supply while humanities majors are having difficulty finding jobs, then utility-maximizing universities will admit more potential engineers and fewer potential humanists until the job market reaches an equilibrium (or some universities discover that they have a "comparative advantage" in admitting and educating humanists). It is a simplification to describe utility-maximizing universities as being signaled by the market and then signaling it back, but an informative simplification. More complicated utility-maximizing models conceal their fundamental tendency by translating into utilitarian language every purpose a university can serve,[24] except the purpose of *not* maximizing social utility.

There is good reason, however, for making the utilitarian exception the democratic rule. Universities are more likely to serve society well not by adopting the quantified values of the market but by preserving a realm where the nonquantifiable values of intellectual excellence and integrity, and the supporting moral principles of nonrepression and nondiscrimination, flourish. In serving society well by preserving such a realm, a university acts as an educator of officeholders rather than simply a gatekeeper of office. Acting as an educator entails appreciating rather than abolishing the discrepancies between intellectual standards and market practices, since such discrepancies often signal a moral failure of the market rather than an intellectual failure of the university. To

[21] Ibid., p. 184: "I have cited Raymond Cattell's view that the ultimate object is not to select those who will do well in school. In theory, we should also look for those other attributes that go along with success after school. But how might we do that in practice?"

[22] Ibid., pp. 60-61.

[23] For evidence that universities have actually used the market rationale to justify not admitting Jews, see Seymour Martin Lipset, "Political Controversies at Harvard, 1936–1974," in S. M. Lipset and David Riesman, eds., *Education and Politics at Harvard* (New York: McGraw-Hill, 1975), p. 150.

[24] For a sophisticated utilitarian model for admissions policies at elite universities, see Klitgaard, *Choosing Elites*, pp. 61-84.

serve as an educator of officeholders and not just a gatekeeper for the market, a university must distinguish between these two very different kinds of failure.

Far from appearing to maximize social utility, universities that uphold intellectual standards in the face of conflicting social practices may seem to be a source of considerable social disutility. By democratic standards, universities should be a source of social tension as long as a conflict exists between social standards and social practices. Consider the tension as it applies to professional practices. Doctors, lawyers, and politicians are often tempted to deceive the rest of us, more tempted than they would be in a society where the democratic norms of professionalism were better understood and more effectively enforced, although surely they would be tempted even in such a society. Many professionals and politicians in our society not only succumb to temptation when they should not, but profit handsomely by succumbing. Universities can do little to prevent professionals and politicians from profiting by their transgressions, but they can do a great deal to articulate the moral standards of professional and political life that would support public criticism of such transgressions. Universities serve an essential democratic purpose by preserving the tension between social standards and practices and thereby helping citizens contain professional authority within its proper realm. But they can serve that purpose only if they do not take their cues from the market in an effort to maximize social utility.

Utilitarians can accommodate this view of the university by integrating long-range, nonquantifiable considerations into their conception of social utility. But in making their analysis more sophisticated, they often obscure a crucial point about the democratic value of universities: universities do not serve democracy best when they *try* to maximize existing social preferences or to predict (rather than shape) future ones. Universities serve democracies best when they try to establish an environment conducive to creating knowledge that is not immediately useful, appreciating ideas that are not presently popular, and rewarding people who are—and are likely to continue to be—intellectually but not necessarily economically productive.

If this is what "maximizing the social good" requires of universities in a democratic society, then the most sophisticated utilitarians must agree with nonutilitarians that universities should not think in utilitarian terms. Universities that try to maximize social utility are less likely to succeed in doing so than universities that try to serve as sanctuaries of nonrepression and as educators of officeholders, even when they do not appear to be maximizing social utility. If universities serve society best when they resist the temptations to repress unpopular ideas and to discriminate against less marketable but more intellectual students, then utilitarians should recommend that universities not think like utilitarians. Universities are likely to serve democracies better, even by utilitarian standards, when they think like democrats about their social purposes, and act as educators of officeholders rather than mere gatekeepers of office.

Fostering Associational Freedom

Safeguarding academic freedom and educating officeholders are the primary purposes of universities, but not their only socially significant purposes. Universities are also communities of scholars, students, and administrators who share intellectual, educational, and (in some cases) also religious values. Although they are not truly voluntary communities (since so many careers today require a college degree), many students and faculty choose where they want to study or to teach. The relative intellectual worth of various institutions is only one factor in their decisions. Universities are also chosen for the kinds of academic communities they are. In the case of many private universities, trustees first determined the nature of their community, but they rarely remain the sole force behind perpetuating or redefining communal standards. Faculty and students as well as administrators also influence the communal life of their university. They generally have more of an interest in defining communal standards than do nonmembers, at least as long as a university is not threatening the principles of nonrepression and nondiscrimination.

Is there an ideal academic *community* by democratic standards? The most commonly invoked ideal—the ivory tower, all of whose members are dedicated to the pursuit of knowledge for its own sake—is not the most democratic one. The ideal is based on an interpretation of the classical Greek understanding of knowledge and its relation to the good life and the good society: the pursuit of knowledge is the good of the mind, and the good of the mind is the highest good to which humans can aspire and that societies can support. All members of a genuine academic community must be dedicated to the pursuit of knowledge for its own sake, according to this view, not only because no higher purpose exists but also because all other purposes (such as professional education) prevent scholars and students from searching for the most fundamental form of knowledge, which is metaphysical rather than practical.[25]

---

[25] "The aim of higher education is wisdom. Wisdom is knowledge of principles and causes. Metaphysics deals with the highest principles and causes. Therefore metaphysics

The ideal of a community united solely by the pursuit of knowledge for its own sake may have made more sense where it first flourished: within the Athenian *polis*, where much work was reserved for resident aliens (metics), slaves, and women, who were excluded from citizenship.[26] Even with regard to Athens, however, the ideal is not beyond criticism, since many Athenian citizens were artisans who had to work for their living (to what degree they actually shared in ruling is difficult to determine).[27] But whatever one thinks of Athens, consider what it would mean today for a society of citizens who both rule and work to claim that "the only kind of university worth having" is one dedicated solely to the pursuit of knowledge for its own sake.[28] It would mean that most citizens are not worthy of membership in such a community, not because they lack sufficient intellect or motivation to learn but because they lack independent income or they are dedicated to learning for the sake of being socially useful.

Nonexclusive democracies cannot support the claim that genuine academic communities consist only of ivory towers, but they can support the pursuit of knowledge for its own sake within universities, as within individual lives. Many people value lives that depend at least partly on the pursuit of knowledge for its own sake. Many others value being part of a society in which other people live such lives. We therefore need not return to Athens nor await discovery of a deep metaphysical defense of the pursuit of knowledge for its own sake to support communities that are "liberal" in this classical sense of being dedicated to studies that liberate students from the more immediate and material concerns of their daily lives. On a democratic view, ivory towers are desirable rather than necessary features of a community of higher learning.

If there is an ideal university community by democratic standards,

---

is the highest wisdom." Robert Maynard Hutchins, *The Higher Learning in America* (New Haven, Conn.: Yale University Press, 1936), p. 98.

[26] "The freemen were trained in the reflective pursuit of the good life: their education was unspecialized as well as unvocational; its aim was to produce a rounded person with a full understanding of himself and of his place in society and in the cosmos." *General Education in a Free Society: Report of the Harvard Committee* (Cambridge, Mass.: Harvard University Press, 1945), pp. 52-53. The purpose of higher learning in Athenian democracy was not wholly noninstrumental, even if it was wholly unspecialized and unvocational. Knowledge was useful for the *polis*, or at least for a well-governed *polis*. Socrates and the Sophists agreed on this much, although they disagreed on what kind of knowledge was useful, and who was capable of learning it.

[27] For accounts of citizenship and political participation in Athens, see A.H.M. Jones, *Athenian Democracy* (Oxford: Basil Blackwell, 1957), esp. pp. 4-11; and M. I. Finley, *Politics in the Ancient World* (Cambridge: Cambridge University Press, 1983), pp. 70-75.

[28] Hutchins, *The Higher Learning in America*, p. 118.

one might expect it to be democratic. Paul Goodman and Robert Paul Wolff have argued that a genuine "community of learning" must be democratically self-governing.[29] An ideal university community, on their understanding, would consist of a small group of faculty and students who are self-governing and fully autonomous from all external authorities. On this view, self-government within a university is necessary to create commitments that are morally binding on scholars and students just as self-government in a society is necessary to create binding commitments on citizens. Autonomy from external authority is essential because the intellectual commitments of scholars and students are foreign to the loyalties of citizens and public officials. "It is finally this foreignness," Goodman comments, "that makes a university; it is not the level of the studies, the higher learning, the emphasis on theory, or anything like that."[30]

In a society that increasingly renders self-governing communities anachronistic, the "community of learning" is an appealing vision of a university that by virtue of its absolute autonomy from external authority furthers both knowledge and self-government. Given the legal authority of lay trustees and the growth of administration within American universities, it is also a radical vision, summarized by the slogan, "All Power to the Faculty and Students."[31]

The democratic appeal of the autonomous community of learning is limited, however, by the very principles that Goodman and Wolff invoke in its defense. The foreignness of a university and its claim to absolute autonomy from external control are ultimately justified on the grounds that intellectual standards of truth and value inevitably conflict with social standards. The conflict enters the university—only to corrupt it—whenever scholars or students pursue knowledge other than for its own sake. Students must not be graded and certified for entry into the professions. Faculty and students must not be governed by lay trustees and administrators whose commitments extend beyond the university community. Yet these practices could be sanctioned by democratic deliberations within a community of learning: students and faculty might recommend grading and a substantial degree of hierarchical administration for reasons that are not reducible to the corrupting

[29] A true university, according to Wolff, is "a *community of persons* united by collective understandings, by common *and communal* goals, by bonds of reciprocal obligation, and by a flow of sentiment which makes the preservation of the community an object of desire, not merely a matter of prudence or a command of duty." Robert Paul Wolff, *The Ideal of the University* (Boston: Beacon Press, 1969), p. 127. See also Paul Goodman, *The Community of Scholars* (New York: Random House, 1962).

[30] Goodman, *The Community of Scholars*, pp. 5-6.

[31] Wolff, *The Ideal of the University*, p. 133.

pressures of the external world. The argument that democratic communities of learning must be prevented from grading and certifying students depends on a version of the view from the ivory tower: that the highest—or only "pure"—form of knowledge must be pursued for its own sake. The argument that genuine academic communities must eschew any administration collapses with the claim that the commitments of administrators necessarily conflict with those of faculty and students, who pursue knowledge only for its own sake.

The conflict between university and society lies elsewhere, I have argued, not between intellectual and social standards of judgment, but between social *standards* and social *practices*. This tension enters a university in many ways, perhaps the most obvious being when it admits and educates future professionals. A genuine "community of learning," on Goodman's and Wolff's understanding, excludes this tension by refusing to admit students who want to become professionals, or by refusing to grade and certify students. A university that admits the tension must complicate rather than compromise its task of scholarship and teaching. Its scholars are called upon to articulate standards of judgment that apply not just to an ideal world but also to *their* world, and its students are encouraged to pursue knowledge not just for its own sake but for the sake of better serving their society. Public attacks on universities for being sanctuaries for social critics are evidence not of the foreignness of universities, but of one of the ways in which they belong to democracies. As communities of critics, universities make it more difficult for public officials, professionals, and ordinary citizens to disregard their own standards when it happens to be convenient. Universities make it more difficult to the extent that scholars base their judgments on widely shared (although frequently violated) social standards. In excluding scholars and students who are interested in socially useful knowledge, a community of learning therefore misses a democratic opportunity: to cultivate a sense of social responsibility among future professionals and to criticize society on the basis of shared rather than "foreign" standards.

Seizing the opportunity, however, also entails running a risk, which the community of learning avoids. A university that admits the tension between social standards and social practices risks elevating social practices into social standards, thereby serving as apologists for the status quo. Pre-professional students tempt faculty to teach more "practical" courses; government agencies and private businesses seek the services of faculty in search of "practical" answers to their problems. The distinction between seeking knowledge for the sake of serving society and seeking it for the sake of satisfying a social demand is lost by a university that defines itself as a service station for the rest of society.

Communities that pursue knowledge solely for its own sake and those that supply all social demands for knowledge are both unlikely to be sanctuaries of nonrepression. Radical separation from society and radical submersion in it tend to create disinterest in social problems and indifference to critical standards. Ivory towers and communities of learning foster too much intellectual distance, service stations too little.

Many of the most prominent American universities claim to strike a balance between the tendencies of the ivory tower, the community of learning, and the service station: to preserve a place for the pursuit of knowledge for its own sake, to accommodate subcommunities united by common academic and social purposes, and also to open their gates to the pursuit of some but not all socially useful knowledge. Clark Kerr popularized the term "multiversity" to describe this "remarkably effective educational institution. A university anywhere can aim no higher than to be as British as possible for the sake of the undergraduates, as German as possible for the sake of the graduates and the research personnel, as American as possible for the sake of the public at large—and as confused as possible for the sake of the preservation of the whole uneasy balance."[32] If Kerr's defense of the multiversity is correct, even its confusion serves a cause: securing a diversity of educational purposes and of intellectual communities within one institution of higher learning.[33]

Although such diversity is appealing, a multiversity has other, less attractive features. The mark of a multiversity "on the make," Kerr noted, "is a mad scramble for football stars and professional luminaries. The former do little studying and the latter little teaching, and so they form a neat combination of muscle and intellect."[34] Kerr therefore questioned whether the multiversity "has a brain as well as a body."[35]

Derek Bok's more recent discussion of the social responsibilities of a university offers a set of moral standards that would enable a multiversity to secure a brain to its body. The ideal multiversity would "avoid undertaking tasks that other organizations can discharge equally well" and commit itself to supplying only those demands for knowledge that are consistent with "the preservation of academic freedom, the maintenance of high intellectual standards, the protection of academic pursuits from outside interference, the rights of individuals affected by the university not to be harmed in their legitimate interests, [and] the needs of those who stand to benefit from the intellectual services that a

[32] Kerr, *The Uses of the University*, p. 18.
[33] Ibid., p. 118.
[34] Ibid., p. 90.
[35] Ibid., p. 123. For Kerr's analysis of the problems facing multiversities, see pp. 118-23.

vigorous university can perform."[36] Bok's conception of the multiversity is probably the dominant American ideal of a university community. As an ideal, the multiversity combines a variety of intellectual communities within one institution without being unprincipled in its pursuit of knowledge. Multiversities combine liberal arts with career education, and by virtue of their intellectual diversity, tend to be socially diverse as well.

Although multiversities pursue more democratic purposes and include more communities than other universities, more is less for some students and faculty. More choice among undergraduate courses, for example, may reflect the unwillingness of many faculty to teach anything other than specialized courses directly related to their research. Smaller liberal arts colleges with faculties less involved in research and consulting are often better for students primarily interested in getting a good general education and close faculty attention. The faculties of smaller liberal arts colleges are also more likely to reach agreement on basic scholarly standards, such as not sponsoring classified research.

The willingness of major American universities to support classified research is one important piece of evidence against elevating the multiversity into the ideal community of higher learning. Classified research cannot by its very nature satisfy a basic standard of scholarly inquiry: it cannot be placed before other scholars—or the public—for their scrutiny. The demand for classified research, moreover, defies a university to judge the social value of its undertaking. The government agency is, in effect, saying to scholars and universities: "Trust us." Scholars and universities should say in response: "If we trust you, then democratic citizens should not trust us, either for living up to our scholarly standards or for serving the public welfare instead of whomever happens to demand our services." Despite the apparent and irreconcilable conflict between scholarly standards and secretive research, many multiversities cannot reach an internal agreement to restrict classified research. Some even support classified research in the name of academic freedom, thereby reducing academic freedom to an unrestricted license of scholars and universities to pursue knowledge for the sake of politics or profit, without any responsibility to account to a scholarly community for their findings. More diversity within a university is less democratically desirable to the extent that it undermines support for the scholarly standards that justify the rights of academic freedom and the freedom of the academy.[37]

[36] Bok, *Beyond the Ivory Tower*, pp. 76-77, 88. This is only a partial list of Bok's criteria.

[37] "The intellectual world has been fractionalized as interests have become more diverse; and there are fewer common topics of conversation at the faculty clubs. Faculty

Multiversities also fall short of an ideal academic association insofar as their members are excluded from decisionmaking on matters central to their interests and expertise. Some of the same divisions that prevent members of the multiversity from agreeing on substantive issues also lead them to disagree on deliberative procedures by which such issues might be resolved. Quite apart from the level of internal disagreement, the sheer size of multiversities makes it difficult for faculty and students in multiversities to share in policymaking or even to be consulted before others make policy. The "pluralism" of multiversities is therefore a partial rather than an inclusive value: favoring choice among educational offerings over a more intensive, general education; cultivating a faculty that is more involved in research and graduate teaching instead of one that is more involved in undergraduate teaching; offering a more hospitable environment to students and faculty who prefer diversity than to those who prefer to participate in a more democratic community.

One need not think that an ideal university community would be thoroughly democratic to recognize the benefits of more democratization than now exists within most American universities: participation can improve the quality of decisions made by universities on many significant issues, it can be educationally valuable for students, it can make both faculty and students more committed to the university's educational purposes and more united in their understanding of what those purposes are.[38] The community of learning contains an important but inverted insight: participation within universities is desirable not because students and faculty enter with the same intellectual commitments, but because self-government tends to create mutual, and mutually recognized, commitments to scholarly standards.

If participation tends to be the cause rather than the effect of agreement on purpose, then university trustees and administrators need not, and probably should not, be excluded from participating in university governance. The educative effects of participation on trustees and administrators is not an insignificant consideration, although the primary purpose of participation by trustees and administrators is to guard the university's long-term interests, especially its financial interests.[39] On

government has become more cumbersome, more the avocation of active minorities; and there are real questions whether it can work effectively on a large scale, whether it can agree on more than the preservation of the status quo." Kerr, *The Uses of the University*, p. 43.

[38] For a more complete argument to this effect, see Dennis F. Thompson, "Democracy and the Governing of the University," *Annals of the American Academy of Political and Social Science*, vol. 404 (November 1972): 160-62.

[39] For a case for giving nonresident trustees decisionmaking authority over many fiscal

most academic matters, however, faculty have considerably greater competence than trustees and administrators, although on some academic matters—such as assessing the results of teaching that they have experienced—students may be the best judges. Even this very rough and incomplete sketch suggests the need for a wider distribution of authority than typically exists in American universities.

The tendency among many American universities has been to elevate financial guardianship into the controlling consideration of university governance, and therefore to concentrate authority in the hands of trustees and administrators, who govern largely to the exclusion of faculty and students. When students revolted at Columbia in 1969, "there existed no faculty body that could debate important academic issues, generate a consensus about them, and make sure that that consensus took effect. (There was a University Council, but it was dominated by administrators and traditionally had concerned itself with bagatelles.)"[40] A similar problem existed at Berkeley, leading critics along with supporters of the Free Speech Movement to criticize the concentration of authority in administrative hands.[41]

Insofar as fostering free scholarly inquiry is the primary purpose of universities, neither their social value nor their autonomy from external political control varies directly with the degree to which they are internally democratized. But insofar as universities are also valued—and valuable—as communities, whose associational purposes are advanced by faculty and student participation, democratic societies have an interest in supporting a greater degree of self-governance within universities. Many American universities are not self-governing communities

---

matters, see Special Committee on the Structure of the University, *The Governing of Princeton University* (Princeton, N.J.: Princeton University, 1970), pp. 53-57. See esp. p. 54: "The interests of faculty, staff, and students are likely to bias them toward expenditures for present, as opposed to future, needs, and they have direct, personal interests in the outcome of decisions regarding tuition, scholarships, and fellowships, rent subsidies, fringe benefits, and the many services provided by the university, as well as in those regarding salaries. While decisions on all of these matters are likely to be better made if the views of faculty, staff, and students are taken into account, no one should want the making of such decisions to become either an exercise in logrolling or a contest of power among interested parties. The involvement of non-residents in the governing of the university can help to insure that decisions do not become either of these things."

[40] Walter Metzger, "Authority at Columbia," in Immanuel Wallerstein and Paul Starr, eds., *The University Crisis Reader: Confrontation and Counterattack*, vol. 2 (New York: Random House, 1971), pp. 333-34.

[41] "The constitution of the university—the distribution of powers among its various elements—may well be out of joint," Nathan Glazer commented in the context of a critique of the Berkeley student movement. "What Happened at Berkeley," in Seymour Martin Lipset and Sheldon S. Wolin, eds., *The Berkeley Student Revolt: Facts and Interpretations* (Garden City, N.Y.: Doubleday and Co., 1965), p. 301.

in any meaningful sense, but rather are autocratically governed institutions even on issues central to the interests and expertise of their faculty and their students. The two major reasons to respect the autonomy of universities—as a means of securing the academic freedom of their faculty and the associational freedom of their members—both point in the direction of securing a broader distribution of power within universities.

Is there, then, an ideal university community by democratic standards? Yes and no. To the extent that there is an ideal community, it is one whose members are dedicated to free scholarly inquiry and who share authority in a complex pattern that draws on the particular interests and competencies of administrators, faculty, students, and trustees. This ideal serves as a critique of autocratically governed universities that do not secure the academic freedom of their faculty, but it also leaves room for a variety of university communities to flourish, all of which are dedicated to academic freedom but each of which support a different set of intellectual and social commitments.

Consider how the educational commitments of larger and smaller universities typically vary. Larger universities generally offer undergraduates a broader curriculum, smaller liberal arts colleges a more intensive, general education. The faculty of the former may be more involved in research and graduate teaching; those of the latter in undergraduate teaching. Larger universities offer a hospitable environment to students who prefer more social diversity, liberal arts colleges to those who prefer to participate in more face-to-face communities.

In combining secular with religious education, church-run universities add even more diversity among communities of higher learning, a diversity that furthers the primary purpose of higher education insofar as these universities also respect the academic freedom of their faculty (as do many church-run universities in the United States). Because no single kind of university community can offer everything that is democratically valuable in higher education to everyone, the democratic ideal of a university community is best conceived as a "principled pluralism" of universities, each of which is dedicated to nonrepression and nondiscrimination, and all of which together foster freedom of academic association.

CHAPTER SEVEN

DISTRIBUTING HIGHER EDUCATION

Although many Americans think of colleges and universities as selective institutions, most are open to all applicants who have a high-school degree and can afford the tuition. As long as it remains difficult to get an adequate education or a good job without a college degree, there will be reason to support a substantial sector of nonselective community colleges and state universities.[1] But it would be a mistake for democratic governments to support nonselective universities at the expense of selective ones. The primary democratic purposes of the two sets of institutions are distinct. An improved system of primary schools would ideally serve the purpose of providing all citizens with an adequate education. Selective universities ideally serve the purpose of higher education.[2] Neither ideally serve the purpose of guaranteeing good employment. An improved economy along with job-training programs could come closer than either set of institutions in helping most citizens get good jobs.

This chapter focuses on the issue of how higher education within selective universities should be distributed. Although they constitute a minority of the over 3,000 American universities, selective universities raise, for reasons I explore below, some very important issues concerning the distribution of democratic education above the threshold, the most obvious being how universities should decide whom to admit.[3]

Nobody doubts that the freedom to decide "who may be admitted to study" is essential to a university's ability to maintain its own academic and associational standards, but many doubt how absolute this "essen-

---

[1] I use the terms "college" and "university" interchangeably from here on.

[2] Compare Michael Rustin, "The Idea of the Popular University: A Historical Perspective," in Janet Finch and Michael Rustin, *A Degree of Choice?: Higher Education and the Right to Learn* (Harmondsworth: Penguin, 1986), pp. 17-66. Rustin's critical account of higher education in Great Britain points toward the ideal of a comprehensive, nonselective system of higher education.

[3] This discussion applies to both public and private universities. The limits of legitimate state regulation vary, according to my argument, not with the form of ownership but with the (legitimate) purposes to which a university is dedicated. Insofar as publicly owned universities may not be sectarian, the state may prevent them from preferring Protestants, say, to Catholics and Jews. But the same criteria that would make it illegitimate for a public university to discriminate against blacks would also make it illegitimate for a private university to do so.

tial freedom" should be.[4] This doubt raises some of the hardest and most controversial questions concerning the distribution of higher education: Should a university admissions committee have the discretion to discriminate for or against members of disadvantaged groups? In discussing this issue, I focus on the case of blacks. The form of my argument can be extended to other disadvantaged minorities and women, although the discretion available to admissions committees will vary depending on the differing social deprivations of each group and the policies of other universities.

The distribution of higher education also raises difficult questions concerning the positive responsibilities of democratic government. I focus on whether and how democratic governments should make a college education available to academically able students regardless of their family income. Before trying to answer these questions, we need to settle upon a standard for distributing higher education.

NONDISCRIMINATION

The principle of nonexclusion applies to education that is necessary for participating in democratic politics. Because admission to a selective university (or a professional school) is not necessary for democratic freedom, nonexclusion is an inappropriate standard for distributing higher education.[5] We return to the more general democratic principle of nondiscrimination. Nondiscrimination requires that every democratic citizen be treated, not equally, but as an equal with respect to the distribution of university places.[6] All citizens are worthy of consideration on the basis of how much they can contribute to the democratic purposes of higher education.

Although democratic governments do not owe a university educa-

[4] See Justice Frankfurter's often-quoted summary of the "four essential freedoms" of universities in *Sweezy v. New Hampshire*, 354 US 234 at 263: "It is the business of a university to provide that atmosphere which is most conducive to speculation, experiment and creation. It is an atmosphere in which there prevail 'the four essential freedoms' of a university—to determine for itself on academic grounds who may teach, what may be taught, how it shall be taught, and who may be admitted to study."

[5] For the remainder of this section, I use university, college, and higher education to refer to selective colleges and universities.

[6] For example: treating a blind child and a sighted child equally would entail teaching them in the same way, whereas treating them as equals would entail providing them both with schooling appropriate to their educational needs. The distinction is simple but significant, especially in defending egalitarianism against some crass criticism (that it demands "equality of results" rather than "equality of opportunity"). For further elaboration and defense of the distinction, see Ronald Dworkin, "DeFunis v. Sweatt," in Marshall Cohen, Thomas Nagel, and Thomas Scanlon, eds., *Equality and Preferential Treatment* (Princeton, N.J.: Princeton University Press, 1977), pp. 67-68.

tion to every student who succeeds in high school, universities are not therefore free to admit and exclude students arbitrarily. Like professional offices, places in universities are scarce social goods that can be converted into many other social goods, one of the most important being professional offices. Professional offices, in turn, convert into "honor and status, power and prerogative, wealth and comfort."[7] Places in universities are prized, again like professional offices, not just for their exchange value but also, sometimes even primarily, for the satisfactions of the academic and associational experiences themselves. The common nostalgic recollection that "those were the best years of my life" may overlook the ordeals of college life, but it also conveys the commonly satisfying experience of being part of a college community. College is an experience many people prize, even if they do not enjoy it.

Prizing the experience does not give anyone a right to it. Because universities serve as academic communities with their own associational purposes and as gatekeepers to professional and other skilled offices, students must qualify for admission. Even when they qualify, by (for example) demonstrating the ability to do acceptable academic work, they still must compete with other academically qualified students because university places (again, like professional offices) are scarce relative to the number of qualified candidates. Although some students may rightfully be turned down by all universities and no student has a right to be admitted to any, it does not follow that who gets admitted should depend on the unconstrained preferences of university admissions committees. The principle of nondiscrimination applies to the distribution of university places just as it applies to the distribution of professional offices, because both goods are valued for similar reasons, and because nondiscrimination in the distribution of professional offices requires nondiscrimination in the distribution of university places.

The principle of nondiscrimination as it applies to university admissions has two parts. The first stipulates that the qualifications or standards set for university places must be relevant to the legitimate purposes of the university. The second is that all applicants who qualify or satisfy these standards should be given equal consideration for admission.[8] The simplicity of the principle masks the complexity of applying it to judge particular admissions programs.[9] In trying to establish what

[7] Walzer, *Spheres of Justice*, p. 155.

[8] For nonselective universities, only the first part of the nondiscrimination standard is relevant. Nondiscrimination demands that every qualified applicant be admitted.

[9] This discussion of nondiscrimination is taken from Amy Gutmann and Dennis F. Thompson, eds., *Ethics and Politics: Cases and Comments* (Chicago: Nelson-Hall, 1984), ch. 7 ("Equal Opportunity"), p. 171. See also Walzer, *Spheres of Justice*, pp. 143-47, on which my discussion here also relies.

qualifications are relevant to being admitted to a university and what constitutes equal consideration of those who meet those qualifications, the hard work begins.

Relevant Qualifications

What qualifications are relevant for being considered for a place in a university? No one doubts that academic ability is relevant. Unless its title is a mere pretext for tax exemption, the primary purpose of a university is higher education. Students who lack adequate academic ability cannot benefit themselves, their university, or society by attending a selective university. Some critics argue that academic ability therefore is all that is relevant. Universities should pick the *most* academically able applicants among those sufficiently able to qualify for consideration. On this argument, the first part of the nondiscrimination standard—the standard of relevant qualification—completely specifies the second part—the standard of equal consideration. To give every applicant equal consideration entails judging who among the applicants is the most academically able.

The simplest rationale for counting academic ability as the sole qualification is that the pursuit of higher learning is the singular purpose of universities, and the smartest students best enable universities to achieve their purpose. But this rationale, I have already argued, is an incomplete understanding of the legitimate purposes of universities. It neglects the significant role of universities as academic communities and educators of officeholders.

A more compelling reason for counting only academic ability as a qualification would be that the most academically able derive the greatest benefits for themselves, their university, and society from a university education. We have, however, little reason to think that the most academically able actually do derive the greatest benefits from higher education for themselves, their university, and their society. Students who are academically able enough to benefit from a college education may learn more by being in college than more academically able students who learn more on their own. Some of the most academically able may not contribute most to the academic life of universities. They may be less academically stimulating than some less able students. As for benefiting society, academic ability is, by the best accounts, a very poor predictor of social contribution, however it is measured.[10]

---

[10] "Numerous studies reveal that even substantial differences in grades and test scores explain very little of the variations in the success students achieve after graduation, whether success is measured by salary or status or by more refined criteria of accomplishment. It is true that high grades and scores may have a significant bearing on the ability

More accurately, one should say that academic ability "seems" to be a poor predictor of social contribution because it is not clear how either academic ability or social contribution can be measured. We considered some of the problems in trying to measure social contribution in the last chapter, so let me focus here on the problems of measuring academic ability. When universities speak of selecting the academically most able, they generally mean choosing those applicants with the highest weighted average of high-school grades and test scores. This weighted average is the best statistical indicator now available for predicting a student's first-year grades. But these predictions are far from accurate even for the first year (the weighted average accounts for between 5 and 30 percent of the variance in first-year grades) and the correlation between weighted average and grades diminishes substantially over subsequent years,[11] suggesting that grades and test scores do not measure all that there is to academic ability, that academic ability is not all that it takes to succeed in college (or in later life), or that the academic ability of students changes in college, some becoming relatively better and others relatively worse academically. All these inferences are surely correct, and widely accepted when so simply stated, but the implications of these inferences for the admissions policies of universities are not widely appreciated, perhaps because many people consider nonacademic qualifications more subjective and therefore less legitimate grounds for favoring one applicant over another.

Leave the charge of subjectivity aside for a moment and consider the implications of these inferences for university admissions. Being academically able is a relevant qualification, arguably the most relevant qualification given that the pursuit of higher learning is what defines a university. It does not follow that academic ability is best measured by high-school grades and test scores or that it is the only relevant qualification that universities should consider. Even if some universities conceived of themselves solely as "knowledge factories," aiming only to

---

to succeed in research or a few other callings that make unusual intellectual demands. Since universities are legitimately interested in preparing students for such careers, they may well decide to enroll an ample number of applicants who possess exceptional academic aptitude. . . . But universities are also interested in preparing students for many occupations, and in most of them a host of other factors play an important role in determining achievement in later life." Bok, *Beyond the Ivory Tower*, pp. 96-97.

[11] See William H. Angoff, *The College Board Testing Program* (New York: College Entrance Examination Board, 1971), p. 53. In *Beyond the Ivory Tower*, Bok cites this evidence to support a similar conclusion that "such measures are the best we have to meet the threshold goal of screening out applicants who are likely to have trouble meeting the academic standards of the institution. . . . But grades and test scores are much less helpful in deciding whom to admit from a large number of well-qualified applicants" (p. 96). Cf. Klitgaard, *Choosing Elites*, pp. 104-153.

maximize their "intellectual product," they would consider in addition to test scores and grades: evidence of creativity, perseverance, emotional maturity, aesthetic sensibility, and motivation to learn. These qualities are either aspects of academic ability or qualities that support academic success in some fields. They are measured, if at all, only very imperfectly by high-school grades and test scores.[12] It is possible that they cannot be measured or even discerned by admissions committees (a problem to which I return in a moment).

The vast majority of universities self-consciously serve as more than knowledge factories and should be free to consider more than academic ability and its related qualities as qualifications for admission. Most universities legitimately aim to contribute not only knowledge to society, but also people who will use their knowledge to serve society well. Evidence of motivation to help people, honesty, reliability, leadership, and a capacity to work well with others are among the qualifications relevant to a university's purpose as educator of officeholders. Virtually nobody argues that good character is a sufficient qualification for pursuing a professional career.[13] The assumption that all anyone needs is academic ability is almost as absurd.[14]

It is not absurd, however, to argue that judgments of character generally are extremely difficult to make, or at least to make accurately. Members of admissions committees, moreover, may disagree in their evaluation of what constitutes good character or in their interpretation of what the evidence implies about a student's character. Were the College Board to offer a standardized test for character, we would do well to doubt what it measured, other than the ability to take a test. Admissions committees must rely upon evidence that cannot be found in test scores or grades: recommendations written by teachers, most of whom they do not know, evidence of extra-curricular activities and accomplishments reported mostly by students themselves, a personal essay (written with the help of a student's parents or teachers?), and sometimes a short personal interview. These pieces of evidence are obviously incomplete, the product of varying standards of assessments, and sub-

[12] For some examples of how standardized tests may devalue intellectual creativity, see David Owen, None of the Above: Behind the Myth of the Scholastic Aptitude (Boston: Houghton Mifflin, 1985), pp. 33-88. Owen also discusses a method by which some students have been successfully coached to "beat" the tests (pp. 113-40).

[13] Although most professionals—whether in medicine, law, or business—cite nonacademic along with academic qualifications as important to success in their field. See Klitgaard, Choosing Elites, pp. 132 and 240 n. 1.

[14] Almost, I say, because a few professional careers, in theoretical mathematics for example, require almost exclusively intellectual ability. Although universities are the primary source of education in such fields, a very small proportion of college students concentrate in them.

ject to differing interpretations. So are high-school grades. It does not follow that admissions committees therefore should rely exclusively on test scores. It would follow only if test scores gave complete evidence or if all other factors gave no evidence of the qualities that universities legitimately seek in their students. Neither is the case.

It was the case, however, that admissions committees of some of the most selective American universities used subjective standards such as potential social contribution and ability to get along with others as rationales—or rationalizations—for keeping out "socially undesirable" minorities, Jews in particular, despite their high test scores. One way of countering this prejudice was to pressure those committees to rely on grades and test scores rather than judgments of character and potential social contribution. The legitimate purpose of such pressure was to counter prejudice against Jews, not to institute a meritocracy based on testing. A meritocratic system cannot be based on grades and test scores, because grades and test scores cannot measure many of the qualities relevant to the academic life of a university, or to the offices for which universities serve as gatekeepers. Grades and test scores cannot measure intellectual creativity, honesty, aesthetic sensibility, perseverance, motivation to help others, leadership, and many other qualities that would "merit" a student's entry into a university, assuming entry can be merited.

If the best reason for pressuring universities to rely more heavily on grades and test scores was to prevent them from perpetuating prejudice against Jews, then we might reconsider whether the same pressure is warranted today—now that it may prevent universities from overcoming prejudice against blacks, who (unlike Jews) have disproportionately low test scores. The discretion inherent in assessing nonacademic qualifications does not counsel exclusive reliance on test scores and grades. It does warrant making admissions committees more accountable to a larger community for explaining their standards and the results of their deliberations. Admissions committees are generally so unaccountable to larger communities—of faculty, scholars, students, or citizens—that it is almost impossible for an outsider to get good evidence of the criteria they use to make their decisions. Many critics suspect that admissions committees often give weight to the wrong nonacademic characteristics—conformity rather than creativity, ambition rather than motivation to help others, lust for power rather than leadership, good manners rather than good character. Unlike academic ability, these characteristics should not be considered qualifications (and perhaps would not be so considered were admissions committees more accountable).

The simplest—and the strongest—reasons for insisting that selective universities rely exclusively on test scores and/or grades are to minimize the use of such irrelevant nonacademic considerations and to maximize the average academic achievement of student bodies. Substantially higher test scores and high-school grades usually correspond to substantially higher grades during freshman year.[15] Were a university's sole purpose to maximize the academic contribution of its student body, its admissions committee might be well-advised to rely exclusively on test scores and high-school grades. I say "might" for two reasons. First: test scores and high-school grades predict only freshman, not upper-class, grades. Second: were test scores and grades also good predictors of upper-class grades, grade-point average still would be an incomplete measure of a student's academic contribution. Students also contribute to a university's intellectual life by participating in academically oriented extracurricular activities such as editing the student newspaper and debating, often to the detriment of their grade-point average. Some students create more intellectual stimulation on campus by challenging ways of thinking that would otherwise be taken for granted, without themselves being the most successful students. Universities therefore may be able to maximize the academic contribution of their student body not by maximizing the standard academic indicators, but by admitting a more intellectually diverse group of students with less than the highest average test scores and high-school grades.

More critically, universities have aims other than maximizing the academic contribution of their student body, aims that offer additional reasons for not resting admissions decisions exclusively on quantifiable academic qualifications. As gatekeepers of office and educators of officeholders, many nonacademic characteristics of students are relevant qualifications for admissions: motivation to learn and to help others, leadership, honesty, and so on. Most of these qualities are impossible for admissions committees to measure and difficult—but probably not impossible—for them to discern. The same can be said about intellectual creativity, aesthetic sensibility, perseverance, and other significant components of academic ability. The limited ability of admissions committees to judge the character and intellectual aptitude of applicants counsels uncertainty, humility, and even skepticism, but not skepticism selectively directed at nonquantifiable nonacademic qualifications, since test scores and high-school grades are only partial measures of what universities legitimately value.

[15] The increase in freshman grades is even more substantial when increases in high-school grades are included along with increases in test scores. See Klitgaard, *Choosing Elites*, pp. 104-115, 195-209.

Many characteristics of applicants are relevant to the role of universities as communities, depending on the purposes to which they are dedicated. Some private universities aspire to being religious communities, and may therefore consider religious identification as a qualification for admission. Most universities legitimately aspire to diversity, although diversity can be illegitimately invoked to justify a questionable range of admissions policies. Mindless or trivial diversity does not constitute a legitimate goal of university admissions. Such diversity could be achieved considering penmanship style and taste in stereo systems as qualifications. One might wonder whether more commonly considered characteristics—such as athletic talent and place of residence—border on the mindless or trivial. Universities more sensibly seek economic, sexual, racial, religious, and cultural (which only sometimes correlates with geographical) diversity for the sake of significantly enriching their intellectual life.

In considering the qualifications relevant to a university's associational purposes, admissions committees must remember that universities are, above all, *academic* communities. None of the characteristics relevant only to its *associational* purposes should therefore be considered either necessary or sufficient to *qualify* a student for membership. Qualification follows social purpose in this quite specific sense: since the necessary purpose of a university is academic inquiry, a necessary qualification for admission into a university must be academic ability. Insofar as academic inquiry need not completely constitute the social purpose of any university, academic ability need not be a sufficient qualification for admissions. Universities therefore should be constrained to consider academic ability as a necessary or primary qualification for admission, yet free to consider as additional qualifications nonacademic characteristics that are relevant to their social purposes.

Admissions committees therefore can exercise discretion in determining qualifications that are relevant to the particular purposes to which their universities are dedicated. Discretion leaves room to consider a variety of qualifications as relevant, but it does not leave room to neglect academic qualifications, which are relevant to the primary purpose of a university. Nor does discretion leave room for setting qualifications that are irrelevant to those university purposes that can be publicly defended, nor for acting arbitrarily, which effectively precludes the pursuit of any purpose. An admissions committee is free to set nonacademic qualifications within three principled bounds. Each nonacademic qualification must be (1) publicly defensible, (2) related to the purposes to which the university is publicly dedicated, and (3) related to associational purposes that are themselves consistent with the academic purposes that define a university as such. These three criteria leave ample room for different universities to count different characteristics as qualifications (and to weigh the same characteristics differently), depending on their particular associational purposes. A final consideration is whether a particular admissions policy permits the entire system of universities to support its democratic purposes (of nonrepression and nondiscrimination), since it is from these purposes that the academic and associational freedom of every university derives its legitimacy.

Equal Consideration

Having set qualifications that are relevant to its legitimate social purposes, universities then must give equal consideration to all qualified candidates. What does equal consideration entail? The most basic requirement of equal consideration is that similar cases must be treated similarly. Two students who have the same qualifications must both be admitted or both be rejected. If they are both accepted, an applicant whose qualifications all are better must also be accepted. And so on. This logic is very simple, but it is not very useful if few applicants have the same qualifications and most rank high on some qualifications but low on others. Many of the disagreements over who should be admitted concern the relative weight that should be given to different qualifications. How should an admissions committee compare student A with high test scores but few extra-curricular interests to student B with low (but adequate) test scores but many extra-curricular interests, including a great deal of community service? My characterization of the two students is deceptively simple because it is sorely incomplete. Most admissions committees would want to judge, if they could, whether either student had to work against economic, social, or physical hardships. The fact that student B was physically handicapped or from a poor family or black might make a difference in the committee's judgment of her intellectual and moral motivation. The fact that student A was a farm boy from Kansas and very interested in becoming a scholar might make a difference in the committee's judgment of his potential contribution to the intellectual life of the university. The subjectivity and discretion involved in making such judgments is not a good reason to restrict them as long as they are relevant to the social functions of universities.

The two most significant practical requirements of equal consideration are that (a) admissions committees read the folders of *all qualified applicants* and consider their relative qualifications as prospective students and (b) that they take *all relevant qualifications* of each applicant into account in making their decisions. Equal consideration entails considering all the relevant qualifications of every qualified candidate. Neglect of the first requirement leads admissions committees to overlook some qualified applicants, often because they have generalized, perhaps correctly, from their previous experience that applicants of a certain social "type"—farm boys from Kansas, say—are less likely to get admitted than other, easily "typed" applicants. Farm boys from Kansas who are exceptions to this (presumed) rule are therefore denied equal consideration. Neglect of the second requirement often results in overly restrictive definitions of relevant qualifications, designed to perpetuate the university as it presently exists rather than its purposes. An admissions committee from a predominantly white male university may count being from Kansas but not being black or a woman as a relevant qualification, even though racial and sexual diversity are as essential as geographical diversity to satisfying the university's professed purposes.

These two requirements are simple, but far from trivial, as we can see upon considering preferential admissions for blacks. Although they constrain the way that admissions committees must deliberate, these requirements do not determine who among the many qualified applicants must be admitted. The determinate answer results from the undoubtedly difficult and subjective deliberations of admissions committees—constrained by the requirements of relevant reasons and equal consideration.

RACIAL DISCRIMINATIONS

Do the constraints of relevant reasons and equal consideration justify efforts by the state to prevent universities from discriminating either in favor of or against blacks in their admissions policies? The most common liberal answer, based on a commitment to nondiscrimination, is "yes": the state should prevent universities from discriminating both against and in favor of blacks because both policies violate the nondiscrimination standard. This common conclusion is a mistaken inference from the commonly agreed-upon principle. The nondiscrimination standard precludes discrimination *against* blacks but does not preclude all ways of discriminating *in favor of* blacks. It rules out the use of racial *quotas*—strictly understood—that favor blacks, but it does not rule out the most common ways in which many universities now give preference to blacks over otherwise equally qualified applicants. Although the empirical details of this argument are specific to the situation of blacks in the United States today, the form of the argument applies equally well to the case of other disadvantaged minorities and women.

Discriminating Against Blacks

Consider first the case of a fundamentalist Christian university that does not admit blacks because "the sponsors of the University genuinely believe that the Bible forbids interracial dating and marriage."[16] Should the university be allowed to discriminate against blacks on the basis of a sincere religious doctrine that regards "cultural or biological mixing of the races . . . as a violation of God's commands"?[17] The argument of the university's sponsors—that its policy of racial discrimination is relevant to, indeed required by, its religious and associational purposes—is correct, but incomplete. It ignores the other social functions that every university serves by virtue of being a university.

Like all universities, fundamentalist Christian universities serve not just as religious communities but also as gatekeepers to the professions and other high-status jobs. If they count being black as a disqualification for admission, they violate the principle of nondiscrimination in carrying out their function as gatekeepers.[18] The problem is not discrimination per se—Catholic universities may legitimately discriminate against non-Catholics, women's colleges against men in their admissions policies. We must question the social impact of different discriminations before arriving at a conclusion concerning their legitimacy. In the cases of university admissions that discriminate against non-Catholics or men, discrimination by a few universities does not create or perpetuate a problem of religious or sexual discrimination in the distribution of office (if anything, such universities have helped overcome problems of religious and sexual discrimination).

The case of blacks is special in this sense: discrimination against *blacks* by any university *in our society* exacerbates an already egregious social problem. Blacks are underrepresented in professional life as a result not of cultural choice but of a very recent history of economic, social, political, and educational discrimination following a far from ancient history of slavery. The connections between underrepresentation

---

[16] This language is taken from *Bob Jones University v. United States* and *Goldsboro Christian Schools, Inc. v. United States*, 461 U.S. 574 (1982) at 580: "To effectuate these views, Negroes were completely excluded until 1971. From 1971 to May 1975, the University accepted no applications from unmarried Negroes, but did accept applications from Negroes married within their race. . . . Since May 29, 1975, the University has permitted unmarried Negroes to enroll; but a disciplinary rule prohibits interracial dating and marriage" (ibid. at 2022-23). Although the details of the Bob Jones case are different, the issue is the same. Prohibiting interracial dating and marriage is different only in degree from excluding blacks entirely.

[17] Ibid. at 582 (referring to the religious doctrine of Goldsboro Christian Schools).

[18] If serving a social function does not imply serving it "well," then the nondiscrimination standard would not be a moral standard.

in the professions and discrimination are not at all remote. For example, "it was not until 1968 that the American Medical Association banned racial bars to membership in its state and local affiliates." We should not be surprised to learn that "in 1970, as in 1950, slightly over 2 percent of the country's physicians were black, and the ratio of black doctors to the black population was about one-seventh that of white doctors to the white population."[19] More than half of the black doctors, moreover, were educated in two black medical schools (Howard University and Meharry Medical College). One need not therefore support a scheme of proportional group representation in the professions to recognize the problem of perpetuating past discrimination against members of a group, all of whom have suffered in some significant respect from a history of degradation and discrimination.

In the context of such a history, no university can perpetuate racial discrimination and still serve its proper social function as a university. Freedom of association provides universities with a prima facie defense against state regulations that violate its associational purposes, but that defense is inadequate to sustain the case of any American university that discriminates against blacks today. When we imagine a society in which it might be permissible for a university to favor whites over blacks on religious grounds—a society, say, in which whites are the oppressed minority—we recognize immediately how radically different that society would be from ours. Taking account of race is not what constitutes a violation of the nondiscrimination standard. Rather, the standard is violated by taking race into account in order *to exclude blacks* from a university education in a society in which being black means being a member of a severely disadvantaged minority.

The nondiscrimination standard rules out discrimination against blacks not because race is an ascriptive or unearned human characteristic but because counting race as a disqualification is incompatible with the gatekeeping function that universities fulfill in our society.[20] The same reasoning that justifies preventing a fundamentalist Christian university from discriminating *against* blacks therefore does not also justify preventing a professedly liberal university from discriminating

[19] Allan P. Sindler, *Bakke, DeFunis, and Minority Admissions: The Quest for Equal Opportunity* (New York: Longman, 1978), p. 48.

[20] Cf. Chief Justice Burger's opinion in *Bob Jones University v. United States*: "The institution's purpose must not be so at odds with the common community conscience as to undermine any public benefit that might otherwise be conferred" (587). The Court may find it more convenient to rely upon the "common community conscience," but the right (indeed the duty) of the state to prevent universities from discriminating against blacks would be just as strong were the community's conscience less well developed.

in favor of blacks in its admissions policy.[21] To decide whether a democratic government should prevent preferential treatment for blacks, or what is commonly called (by its critics) "reverse discrimination," we need to begin again and ask whether policies favoring blacks violate the nondiscrimination standard.

Discriminating in Favor of Blacks

Consider two hypothetical but not extreme cases, both of which entail preferential treatment for blacks. The admissions committee of Queenston University considers individually all applicants who meet their minimum academic requirements (the weighted average of grades and test scores judged necessary for doing acceptable academic work). Whether an applicant is black is one among many additional characteristics that the admissions committee regards as a qualification. During their final deliberations, the committee decides to admit 100 black applicants, 50 of whom have lower grades and test scores than any of the white applicants whom they have admitted with the exception of 25 football and hockey players, who also meet the minimum academic standards.

Kingston University—otherwise identical to Queenston—sets its academic requirements considerably higher (higher, therefore, than what is necessary to do acceptable academic work). As a result, its regular pool of qualified applicants contains very few blacks or athletes. Kingston therefore sets aside 50 places in its incoming class for the most qualified black students, regardless of whether they satisfy the minimal academic standards set for the rest of the applicant pool. It also sets aside 25 places for athletes. During their final deliberations, Kingston's admissions committee admits 100 black students—50 from their regular and 50 from their special, all black applicant pool.

Should the state prevent either Queenston or Kingston from continuing its preferential admissions program for blacks? Both universities prefer blacks over otherwise better qualified white students. Both also prefer athletes to otherwise better qualified students. Are these preferences per se illegitimate? Although universities are often criticized for admitting athletes with relatively lower academic qualifications, most critics agree that universities have the right to do so (assuming the academic qualifications of athletes are high enough to do acceptable ac-

---

[21] Cf. Mr. Justice Powell's argument in the *Bakke* case: "The guarantee of equal protection cannot mean one thing when applied to one individual and something else when applied to a person of another color. If both are not accorded the same protection, then it is not equal." *Regents of the University of California v. Bakke*, 98 S. Ct. 2733 at 2748 (1978).

ademic work). Yet many of the same critics argue that universities should be prevented from giving blacks preferential treatment on grounds that racial preferences—whatever their effect or intent—are invidious. Is the apparent inconsistency of the critics' position sustainable?

Both Queenston and Kingston Universities think that athletics enhances university life and serves as a way of keeping alumni loyal to the university. They regard the outlook of athletes as complementary to the generally more intense academic outlook of other students (but they would not admit athletes just for this reason). Since the nondiscrimination standard does not require universities to admit the *most* academically qualified students, preferring athletes to more academically qualified students is a legitimate policy that the state should not prohibit.

But the ways in which Queenston and Kingston Universities give preference to athletes differ, and the differences matter from the standpoint of equal consideration. Queenston admits athletes from its general pool of applicants, all of whom meet minimal academic standards and all of whom are individually considered. Kingston admits athletes from a special pool consisting only of athletes. The different procedures might make a difference in the results of the admissions process, since in its deliberations Queenston might discover, say, a talented violinist whose academic ranking was lower than the cut-off point set by Kingston for its regular applicant pool but higher than the academic ranking of five of Kingston's athletes. Because Kingston has a special pool reserved for athletes, it ignores the violinist, while Queenston admits her.[22] The athletes and blacks that Kingston admits could also have significantly lower academic qualifications than those that Queenston admits, since Kingston's special pool, unlike Queenston's regular pool, has no lower limit on academic qualifications.

A utilitarian might try to calculate whether the greater efficiency of Kingston's quota policy makes it "worth" overriding the principle of nondiscrimination. But the nondiscrimination standard is meant to block just this kind of (impossible?) consequentialist calculation. Nondiscrimination still remains a partly consequentialist standard. One reason to consider every qualified applicant is to avoid having any qualified applicant turned down merely by virtue of having been ignored. The use of a special athletic pool indicates either that Kingston admits athletes who are not academically qualified or that it refuses even to consider other potential applicants with similar academic qualifica-

[22] A member of Queenston's admissions committee convincingly argues that she will be a better addition to the university community than another athlete.

tions and similarly relevant nonacademic qualifications. Kingston's special pool for athletes makes its policy of preferential admissions for athletes suspect by the standard of nondiscrimination while Queenston's is not.

We may judge the policies of preferential admissions for blacks in a similar manner. If being black is also a legitimate qualification, then we must reach the same conclusion: Kingston's procedure of creating a special pool for blacks violates equal consideration while Queenston's procedure of giving equal consideration to every applicant who meets minimal standards does not, despite the fact that both prefer blacks over applicants who are otherwise better qualified. I say "otherwise" because what remains at issue is whether being black is a legitimate qualification. It is obviously not the same kind of personal characteristic as is being athletic or musically talented. No one does anything to become black, just as no one does anything to be born to an alumnus of Kingston or to become a farm boy in Kansas, and so to be preferred over more qualified applicants. But, as these examples may indicate, the *kind* of characteristic that being black, athletic, musically talented, the son of an alumnus, or a farm boy from Kansas is—whether it is, for example, an earned or unearned attribute—is not what matters for the purposes of nondiscrimination. What matters is whether the characteristic is a qualification. Is being black relevant to the legitimate social purposes of universities?

Suppose that the administrators, faculty, and students of Queenston largely agree that it is: "In a country where racial problems and misunderstandings are so prominent, all students stand to benefit from the chance to live and work with classmates of other races who can offer differing attitudes and experiences that will challenge and inform others and increase the understanding and tolerance of everyone concerned."[23] Queenston also thinks it can best serve its function as a gatekeeper to the professions by admitting more blacks, as long as they can do acceptable work, because the United States needs more professional blacks both to serve its underserved black communities and to serve as role models for the next generation of blacks who may not otherwise think it reasonable to aspire to professional office. Bringing more blacks into the medicine, law, and other professions, moreover, will make white doctors, lawyers, and other professionals more aware of the special problems and needs of blacks.[24] To recognize its right to give

[23] Bok, *Beyond the Ivory Tower*, p. 99. As a thought experiment, one might substitute "regional" for "racial," and "regions" for "races." The case for diversity seems to me to become much less persuasive.

[24] For a lucid defense of such reasoning, see Richard A. Wasserstrom, "Preferential Treatment," in *Philosophy and Social Issues: Five Studies* (Notre Dame: University of

preference to blacks, we need not think that Queenston's priorities are correct, only that they are relevant to one of its legitimate social functions—which they clearly are.

Why, then, is there so much public resistance to preferential admissions (untied to quotas) for blacks? The simplest, and I think strongest, explanation is historical: we have learned from our history to be suspicious of racial classifications because they have been used almost exclusively to subvert rather than to support democratic justice.[25] In this country, racial discrimination has historically preserved the political power, social status, economic and educational advantage of already privileged white males. Discrimination against blacks after the Civil War added injury to injury. This historical explanation should not prevent us from supporting a racial classification when it is justly used for a just cause, as in the case of Queenston's preferential admissions policy, which aims to create a racially integrated society by means of equal consideration.

A commitment to equal consideration also provides a way around the worry, well expressed by Robert Fullinwider, that preferential policies will become entrenched even after they have outlived their justification:

> Thirty-five years after V-J Day, veterans of World War II are still enjoying employment preferences in state and federal governments. Because of this, women are effectively barred from holding many top level civil service jobs. Here is a preferential program that tolls a substantial cost in the frustrated aspirations of many non-veterans and which effectively discriminates against women; yet, although once given by a majority, the program is a privilege the majority cannot now easily eliminate. The danger that racial preferences will become similarly entrenched should be taken seriously.[26]

This danger is mitigated by (a) making preferential treatment the result of a series of autonomous decisions by universities rather than of a centrally imposed governmental policy, and (b) requiring the procedures of all universities to satisfy the standards of nondiscrimination. This would mean that every year, the admissions committees of every university would have to defend their preferences not only for blacks but also for alumni children, athletes, and farm boys from Kansas above

---

Notre Dame Press, 1980), pp. 55-61. Wasserstrom uses these reasons as a basis for making a more thoroughly consequentialist argument for preferential treatment.

[25] See Dworkin, "DeFunis v. Sweat," pp. 82-83.

[26] Robert K. Fullinwider, *The Reverse Discrimination Controversy: A Moral and Legal Analysis* (Totowa, N.J.: Rowman and Littlefield, 1980), p. 249.

otherwise more qualified applicants. It also means that as our society becomes more egalitarian and the experience of being black becomes less relevant to the educational and social purposes of universities, the case that members of admissions committees make for preferring black applicants over more academically qualified white applicants will become weaker. Taking the problem of entrenchment seriously means taking university autonomy and the demands of nondiscrimination seriously, not opposing preferential treatment on grounds that it may be abused.

Quotas and Qualifications

For the sake of highlighting the value of Queenston's procedure per se, I have assumed in my hypothetical case that it does not produce a result differing dramatically from Kingston's quota system for blacks. In practice, substantially different results are quite likely. Without a quota, Queenston may admit considerably fewer blacks than Kingston admits with one (although Queenston admits more blacks than it would were its qualifications more narrowly academic). Imagine, therefore, that Queenston's admissions committee admits only 70 black applicants, while Kingston's quota secures 100 black admissions. It is only by considering this more realistic (although still simplified) case that advocates of equal consideration face up to the full strength of an argument in favor of quotas.

True, Queenston's procedure brings all applicants capable of doing acceptable work to the attention of the admissions committee. Queenston is therefore less likely to overlook any applicant who would have been admitted to Kingston had she been considered and also less likely to admit students whose academic credentials are inadequate for academic success. But Kingston's policy of setting aside 50 places for blacks (and of setting a higher academic standard than necessary to do acceptable work) is not only more efficient, it guarantees admission to substantially more blacks than Queenston's policy of equal consideration. Under Queenston's policy of equal consideration, more blacks will be admitted than would qualify on narrowly academic criteria, but not nearly as many more as will be admitted by Kingston. The admission of blacks by Queenston depends on the outcome of deliberations that take each qualified candidate's case into consideration. The results of Kingston's policy are not so dependent. Its quota system secures the goal of overcoming the "underrepresentation" of blacks in prestigious universities as Queenston's policy of equal consideration cannot.

The strongest consequentialist defense of quotas begins with this observation: universities that adopt quota systems are likely to contribute more to overcoming racism in the United States simply by admitting and certifying more blacks than universities that abide by the principle of equal consideration, properly understood. The consequentialist accepts nondiscrimination as the correct standard by which university places would be distributed in a just society, but he quickly and correctly notes that ours is far from a just society, particularly (but not only) with regard to the underrepresentation of blacks in "institutions such as the university, legal system, various occupations and corporate structures."[27] As a consequence of having suffered from a history of slavery and discrimination, blacks are not only poorer and less educated than most other social groups, their underrepresentation in positions of prestige and power tends to be self-perpetuating. Seeing fewer blacks in these positions, black children have lower educational and career aspirations than white children. Fewer black doctors and lawyers are available to serve the needs of black communities. Even our intellectual understanding of racial problems may suffer from the underrepresentation of blacks in academia and law, making it still harder for our society to overcome its racist history.[28]

For Richard Wasserstrom, who puts the consequentialist case for quotas most convincingly, the general issue is how a society might "both effectively and fairly move from the existing state of affairs to a closer approximation of the ideal"—an ideal where blacks are no longer underrepresented in the professions by virtue of past discrimination and where racial preferences are therefore no longer necessary or justified.[29] Wasserstrom considers quotas fair and effective means by which we can "break the systemic, exclusionary character of the present arrangement."[30]

We should grant the potential effectiveness of quotas, but worry more about their fairness. Were the only issue how to move our society closer to the ideal, then quotas *might* be justified. (We would still have to worry about the problem of entrenchment). But fairness (as Wasserstrom acknowledges) is yet another moral issue: How should we treat people along the way to a more ideal society? The common critique of quotas rests on the assumption that the most qualified (generally assumed to be the most academically able) *deserve* to be admitted to universities.[31] Wasserstrom stops worrying about fairness when he persua-

---

[27] Wasserstrom, "Preferential Treatment," p. 51.

[28] For a strong defense of these claims with reference to both blacks and women, see Wasserstrom, "Preferential Treatment," pp. 55-60.

[29] Ibid., p. 52.

[30] Ibid., pp. 52-53.

[31] For a more general critique of distribution based on desert, see Walzer, *Spheres of Justice*, pp. 135-39, 143-47.

sively argues that no one *deserves* to be admitted to universities by virtue of being the most academically able or the most qualified.[32] Having demonstrated the weaknesses of the critique based on desert, Wasserstrom concludes that qualifications are relevant but not decisive:

> [The] concern for qualifications is wholly consistent with the claim that race or sex is today also properly relevant when it comes to matters such as admission to college or law school, or entry into the most favored segments of the job market. And that is all that any preferential treatment program—even one with the kind of quota involved in the *Bakke* case—has ever sought to establish.[33]

But that is not all that any preferential treatment program involving quotas must seek to establish. If treating people as equals entails giving *all* qualified applicants equal consideration, then a defense of quotas (whether racial, sexual, or athletic) must demonstrate that their use justifies violating the value of nondiscrimination. The defense cannot simply be that qualified blacks would not otherwise be admitted to universities, since (as I have already argued) a policy of equal consideration admits qualified blacks without quotas. The defense is rather that admissions committees who give equal consideration will not admit *enough* blacks to overcome racism in our society, or at least not overcome it *quickly enough*.

One might wonder *how many* and *how* fast is enough, but this indeterminacy is only a symptom of a more significant problem with the consequentialist argument. The problem is that quotas, unlike nondiscrimination, put universities in the general role of serving society *to the detriment of their publicly acknowledged academic purposes*. This can best be seen by returning to our second hypothetical example. Queenston University decides to admit 70 blacks, after considering the qualifications of every applicant, including the contribution applicants can make to the university and society. What might be said in favor of admitting more? Not that Queenston's admissions committee overlooked the qualifications of any candidate. We are defending a thoroughgoing policy of nondiscrimination, as exemplified by Queenston's dedication to equal consideration, not to existing, highly imperfect admissions policies. Perhaps Queenston's admissions committee undervalued the potential contribution of some black applicants to the university and society. Instituting quotas would not be the best way to overcome this problem either, unless there exists some magical number that would guarantee admission of just those black applicants who would contrib-

---

[32] Wasserstrom, "Preferential Treatment," pp. 71-77.
[33] Ibid., p. 77.

ute more to the university than other applicants. The best way to overcome this problem is for an oversight committee at Queenston University to criticize the admissions committee for undervaluing the
potential contribution of black applicants.

The strongest argument in favor of admitting more blacks by means
of a quota instead of a thoroughgoing policy of nondiscrimination is
that Queenston could thereby help overcome the general problem of
racism in American society simply by certifying more black students as
its graduates. For this argument to have force, however, one must reject
the relative autonomy of the university that I defended in the last chapter. Were Queenston able to defend admitting more blacks on grounds
of their qualifications (in the broadest meaningful sense of the term),
then a process of equal consideration could be devised that did so. If
Queenston is not able to admit more blacks consistently with a practice
of nondiscrimination, then it must dedicate itself to serving society *at
the expense of fulfilling its own institutional purposes* (which are primarily but not exclusively intellectual).

An advocate of quotas could respond that my defense of nondiscrimination works only in theory. In practice, defending quotas is the only
way to insist that admissions committees admit many blacks whom
they should (but will not) admit under a process of equal consideration.
But *who* will insist that admissions committees institute quotas when
they are unwilling to admit more blacks by equal consideration? If university administrators or faculty members are to be the ultimate authorities over admissions, then why do they not then replace a bad admissions committee with people who more fully appreciate the
contribution that blacks can make to the university and society? If governmental intervention is necessary to institute quotas, then even the
most thoroughgoing consequentialist must worry about authorizing
governments to intervene so deeply into university admissions processes as to require that universities admit a specific number of black (or
any other category of) applicants. Universities cease to be relatively autonomous when admissions quotas are imposed by governmental (or
any other outside) authorities.

The "fundamental justificatory claim" of quota systems, Wasserstrom notes, is "not that they should be made a part of the *ongoing* institutional life of the good society, but rather that they should be introduced because they are a way to help bring that society into being."[34]
But quotas, I have argued, are not the only (although they may be the
most efficient) way of helping to bring that society into being. A policy
of nondiscrimination may take more time, but it leaves ample room to

[34] Ibid., pp. 52-53.

give preference to academically qualified blacks who are not the most academically qualified. The case for quotas depends on either denying the relative autonomy of the university, which we have already affirmed, or affirming the value of efficiency over equity, which consequentialists like Wasserstrom want to deny.

To preface their defense of quotas with the proviso that they should not become part of the ongoing institutional life of a good society, sophisticated consequentialists must deny that efficiency outweighs equity. Perhaps setting quotas *for blacks* can be justified only as a transitional policy—on the assumption that there will be no reason for universities to give preference to blacks in a just society. But one must still recognize that the same efficiency argument that justifies the use of racial quotas in an unjust society can justify the use of alumni, athletic, and a variety of other quotas in a just society—especially in a just society where setting aside places for alumni children or athletes does not discriminate against members of groups that are already discriminated against. To consider *all* qualified applicants individually is inefficient when an admissions committee knows that the *most* qualified applicants cluster in discernible groups.

The consequentialist defense of racial quotas seems strongest when it is presented as an inseparable part of a more general policy of preferential admissions. The comparison between Queenston and Kingston Universities suggests that a policy of using quotas can be separated, in practice as well as in theory, from the more general policy of preferential admissions. The general policy is fully defensible by the standard of nondiscrimination, but programs using quotas as a means of giving preference are not. The case for preferential treatment provides insufficient support for quotas, even as a transitional policy, when preferences can be achieved without violating the relative autonomy of the university or the value of equal consideration.[35] We need not—and

---

[35] A more distinctly consequentialist defense of quotas might be that equal consideration does not really matter very much morally. Achieving the good society matters much more. If admissions quotas will get us to the good society faster, then we should not worry about giving all qualified applicants equal consideration along the way. To respond thoroughly to this significantly more radical form of consequentialism would take me far afield, perhaps never to return to higher education. Here I only ask: But why should achieving the good society be all that matters to us morally? Why should we not care a lot about how people are treated along the way? I can imagine some hard cases where we are forced to choose between moving closer to a good society and treating people fairly along the way. But the choice between a policy of preferential admissions based on equal consideration and one based on quotas is not a hard one. We should take advantage of this rare opportunity to move closer to a good society while treating people as equals.

should not—justify quotas for the sake of efficiency in our society if we do not want to justify them in a just society.

Is the case against quotas as strong in reality as in even the more realistic of these two hypothetical examples? In the real world of academia, can adequate progress towards racial integration in universities and American society be achieved without the use of quotas? What constitutes "adequate" progress is, of course, eminently disputable, and disputed among well-meaning persons. One might say that any policy that falls short of full reparations for every black who has suffered in some substantial way from racial discrimination cannot constitute adequate progress. I am inclined to accept this view. But accepting this view is compatible with believing that universities are not the appropriate, or the most effective, agents of reparations. This does not exempt them from responsibility to give preference to blacks who qualify academically and have other special qualifications by virtue of their race. The question then remains: Is it realistic to expect universities to bear such responsibility without imposing quotas upon them?

The most challenging cases come from considering the admissions policies of professional schools rather than undergraduate universities, since the minimal academic qualifications for some professions—such as medicine—are clearly quite high. Are they too high to give preference to blacks within a legitimate policy of nondiscrimination? Historically, most professional schools in the United States have set their minimum academic requirements so high as to make it virtually impossible to admit a class of, say, ten percent black students without drawing from a special pool of less than fully qualified applicants.

In medical school admissions, this problem is probably most pronounced. Reacting to the increased demand for medical education in the 1950s, most medical schools set their "minimum academic qualifications for admissions higher and higher, at levels well above the minimum academic credentials needed to complete the school program satisfactorily." By raising their academic threshold, medical schools eliminated from serious consideration all applicants whose test scores and grades were below a level that was considerably higher than necessary to complete the program successfully. Raising the academic threshold in response to increased demand for medical education, "more than any other factor, froze out minorities from regular admissions and led schools to develop 'special' criteria to ensure their admission."[36]

---

[36] Sindler, *Bakke, DeFunis, and Minority Admissions*, p. 148. Medical school applications more than doubled between 1966 and 1976, while places in medical schools increased by only two-thirds (p. 45).

Were medical schools to reset their academic threshold lower (to their earlier level), they would not need to admit blacks out of a special pool. A widely shared understanding of the social function of medical schools provides good reasons to lower the academic threshold. By their own acknowledgment, most medical schools are dedicated not just to contributing new medical knowledge to society but to educating doctors who will use well-established medical knowledge to help those most in need of medical care. Given the oversupply of specialists (especially surgeons) and undersupply of primary-care physicians in our society, many medical schools want to educate more generalists, especially generalists willing to serve in rural and inner-city areas. The admissions committees of most medical schools already weigh nonacademic characteristics—including motivation, maturity, and moral sensitivity—quite heavily as qualifications for admission. The University of California Medical School at Davis, for example, routinely interviews every qualified applicant and includes an assessment of the applicant's potential contribution to the medical profession as part of a numerical "benchmark" score, which takes account of *all* the applicant's qualifications and is normally used to determine who gets admitted.[37]

If this quite common procedure is legitimate, then there is no moral barrier to medical schools lowering their academic threshold to consider a larger pool of qualified applicants (provided the cutoff remains above what is necessary to complete the program satisfactorily). The barrier is a practical one, of efficiency: by lowering their academic threshold, medical schools would need to take many more applications seriously, not just of black but of other applicants whose records evidenced some of the same qualities—of high personal motivation, public service, emotional maturity, perseverance—that medical schools now claim to value highly in all their applicants.

This argument has broad application, to admissions policies not only at the most selective professional schools and colleges, but also at selective and nonselective state universities that wish to admit more black students. Take the case of a state university whose admissions criterion, as stipulated by law or regulation, is to admit all but only those (in-state) applicants who graduate in the top half of their high-school class. The administratively easier way for this university to give preference to blacks is to have an exception made only for blacks, allowing the university to admit lower-scoring blacks, but no other lower-scoring students. This exception would, however, violate equal treatment. The proper, although administratively harder, way to admit more blacks

[37] Ibid., pp. 51-52.

would be to lower the admissions threshold for all students, and then judge individual cases on the basis of their qualifications.[38]

One need not deny that the costs, in time and effort, of expanding the applicant pool would be considerable to conclude that the benefits would be greater. Were universities and professional schools to expand their applicant pools rather than consider only black candidates whose academic credentials were lower than the unnecessarily high threshold, they would not violate the standard of equal consideration. Judging by a more consequentialist standard, universities would avoid overlooking nonblack applicants whose nonacademic qualifications were unusually high compared to their academic ones and avoid admitting black applicants whose academic qualifications were lower than necessary to do satisfactory work.[39] But they would still be free to prefer black applicants who are academically qualified over white applicants who are academically more qualified.[40] When we look at the real world of university admissions, we see that significant costs are attached to abiding by the standards of nondiscrimination, but these costs are neither practically nor morally prohibitive. Even on consequentialist grounds, the benefits may be greater.

COMPENSATORY COLLEGE EDUCATION

Legitimate efforts by universities to overcome racism by admitting more blacks are not exhausted by the practices of preferential treatment that we have been discussing, which are aimed specifically at blacks. Compensatory programs of college education may also help realize this goal, consistently with the principle of nondiscrimination. Indeed, after discussing the rationale for such programs, we must wonder not just whether they are permitted but whether they are dictated by the principle.

Many students today suffer, through no fault of their own, from a sorely inadequate primary education. Many high schools—especially (but not only) those in predominantly black and Hispanic inner cities—are understaffed, poorly funded, and incapable of giving even their bet-

[38] I am grateful to Michael McPherson for suggesting this example to me.

[39] A quota system, strictly implemented, cannot establish an academic minimum, if it is to guarantee that a certain number of blacks be admitted each year. The University of California Medical School at Davis, for example, established a 2.5 minimum grade point average for its regular applicant pool, but no minimum GPA cutoff for its special minority pool. Sindler, *Bakke, DeFunis, and Minority Admissions*, p. 54.

[40] An additional consequentialist consideration is that the political costs, in the broadest sense, of giving preference to blacks through a policy of equal consideration rather than quotas might be much lower.

ter students the education that they would need to meet the minimal academic standards of most selective colleges. What should selective universities do in the face of lower education that fails for many students to fulfill its democratic purposes? Without a college education, many high-school graduates—particularly (but again not only) those from poor black and Hispanic families—face a more restricted set of job opportunities and a higher risk of unemployment than most Americans would consider acceptable for their own children. Had some of these students received a substantially better high-school education, they probably would have satisfied the minimal academic qualifications for admission to a selective university.[41] Should selective universities admit some of these unqualified students to help them make up for the secondary education of which they were deprived?

One might think that universities are not obligated to admit such students because they are not themselves responsible for their deprivation. But even if selective universities are not themselves responsible for creating the deprivation, they—along with many other institutions—may be responsible for not perpetuating it. A stronger reason not to so obligate selective universities is that they are not, nor could they easily become, well-equipped to fulfill such an obligation and still serve their primary social purpose as institutions of higher learning.

The more pressing question, in any case, is whether universities should be *permitted* to override the demands of nondiscrimination and admit some unqualified students on compensatory grounds. Compensatory education is more easily and commonly defended for young children, who are the legal responsibility of the public school system. Can it be defended on grounds of compensatory justice for college-age students, who are no longer children and no longer the legal responsibility of anyone but their parents?

Discussions of compensatory justice for adults have focused mainly on the issue of preferential hiring rather than college admissions. Several strong arguments have been advanced *against* basing preferential hiring of blacks on compensatory grounds.[42] If the purpose of compensation is to make up for the many ways in which blacks have suffered as a result of past discrimination, then it would be morally better to provide monetary compensation in the form of reparations to all blacks rather than to give a relatively few blacks better jobs than those for

---

[41] I say "probably" because it is obviously very difficult to know what would have been the case. We can, however, make a reasonable guess.

[42] A similar argument may be made for other minorities and women as well, although the argument against using preferential hiring as a means of compensating blacks is the most challenging.

which they are qualified.[43] Compensatory hiring policies fail the "proportionality requirement"—that those who have suffered the most should be compensated the most.[44] Jobs generally go to those blacks who have suffered relatively little from racial discrimination, or at least not to those who have suffered the most. Compensatory programs are also criticized for inequitably distributing costs from the most disadvantaged to the next most disadvantaged group: "Reservation [of office] won't fulfill the Biblical prophecy according to which the last shall be first; it will guarantee, at most, that the last shall be next to last. I don't think that there is any way to avoid this result, except by increasing the number of groups for which offices are reserved and turning the remedial program into something much more systematic and permanent."[45]

Do the same arguments apply to compensatory admissions programs? Preferential admissions programs need not aim to pay blacks back for all their past deprivations in an incommensurable currency. Compensatory college admissions programs can have a more specific and defensible aim: to make up for lost education with a similar currency, more and better education. Universities can try to compensate those students who have been deprived of adequate primary schooling but who have suffered only *to a degree that is remediable by a compensatory college education.* The criticism that the costs of compensatory programs are borne by the next most disadvantaged group applies to programs that reserve university places only for black students. It does not extend to compensatory programs that are open to educationally and economically disadvantaged students regardless of race *whose academic disabilities are likely to be remediable by a compensatory college education.* Programs that are open to all educationally and economically disadvantaged students shift the costs to the next least qualified rather than to the next most disadvantaged. If we are most troubled by the likelihood that similarly disadvantaged students will bear the full costs, then compensatory college programs can be designed to allay the worst of our worries by:

(1) being open to all high-school graduates who have suffered similar educational (and economic) deprivations;
(2) aiming to compensate not all educationally deprived students, but only a select group who stand to benefit most educationally from college; and

[43] For an extended argument against preferential hiring based on compensation, see Robert Amdur, "Compensatory Justice: The Question of Costs," *Political Theory,* vol. 7 (May 1979): 229-44.

[44] Fullinwider, *The Reverse Discrimination Controversy,* p. 54.

[45] Walzer, *Spheres of Justice,* p. 154.

(3) providing remedial education (such as summer courses and individual tutoring) to increase the chances that those who are admitted will succeed in satisfying the university's regular educational standards.

Must an advocate of nondiscrimination oppose such a program of compensatory college education because it discriminates against some fully qualified students, who would otherwise have been admitted? By considering all students who have suffered similar educational deprivations, a compensatory program meets the standard of equal consideration with regard to all applicants who suffer similar educational deprivations. In this sense, it treats all its applicants as equals, and thereby avoids arbitrary racial preferences. By compensating only those students who can still benefit educationally from attending college and by providing them with remedial education, it also avoids instituting a double standard or debasing the value of its educational program for its fully qualified students. A compensatory program does, however, still discriminate against some academically qualified students for the sake of compensating some academically unqualified students for the education they never received.

Does this preference violate the "relevant qualification" requirement of nondiscrimination? It does inasmuch as applicants who fall below the minimal standards for academic success are not qualified for admission to the regular academic program of a university. It does not insofar as a university that offers a remedial program educates all students admitted on compensatory grounds up to a level that then qualifies them for regular admission. To satisfy the nondiscrimination standard, compensatory programs must live up to this theoretically specific and practically demanding purpose: to provide a sufficiently good remedial education to qualify their students for admission to the university's regular academic program. This standard suggests that a university committed to compensatory education should devote enough resources to its remedial program to enable students who pass it to succeed in its regular curriculum. It might then admit students to the university conditionally on their passing the remedial program.

In theory, compensatory admissions programs need not violate the nondiscrimination standard. In practice, many may, by failing to design adequate remedial programs and therefore lowering their regular academic standards to accommodate unqualified students. The best programs of compensatory college education can justify rejecting some qualified applicants for the sake of compensating other potentially qualified applicants for their inadequate primary education. All but the best ones probably cannot be justified, because they predictably fail to enable potentially qualified students to realize their potential. That is all the more reason to recommend the best.

FUNDING HIGHER EDUCATION

Universities can discriminate against well-qualified students without really trying. One might argue that universities cannot help but discriminate against students from poor families, because the short-term costs of going to college are so great. The costs include not only tuition, room, and board, but also the income foregone from not getting a job. Some universities subsidize tuition, room, and board for every needy student who is admitted, but none can afford also to pay them the income they would have earned had they instead taken a full-time job. As long as a college education is costly in this sense, students from poor families are less likely to apply to college than equally able students from rich families, even if they have a good chance of getting a full scholarship if admitted and of earning more money after graduation. The greater short-run sacrifices, which are certain, are likely to overwhelm the greater long-run gains, which are only probable. Students who are pressured by their parents or their economic circumstances to "go out and earn a living" are bound to have less access to a college education, in this sense, than students whose parents are better able or more willing to pay for a college education. As long as less advantaged students are under significantly greater pressure to earn a living rather than continue their education, economic discrimination will be implicit in the institution of higher education.

Universities cannot equalize this pressure, but they can alleviate it by many measures, the most obvious being full scholarship aid to needy students. If they fail to take steps to alleviate it, they are in effect—even if not in intent—discriminating on grounds that are irrelevant to the legitimate social functions of a university. As long as universities are capable of increasing access for poor students without sacrificing their academic standards, the principle of nondiscrimination speaks against implicit as well as explicit discrimination. Yet few American universities (if any) could afford to offer scholarships to all needy students without state support, which has taken several forms: scholarships paid directly to students, subsidized student loans, subsidies paid directly to universities, and tax benefits to universities, parents of students, and benefactors of universities.[46] Even with substantial state

---

[46] See Howard P. Tuckman and Edward Whalen, eds., *Subsidies to Higher Education: The Issues* (New York: Praeger, 1980). For an excellent overview of support for private higher education, see David W. Breneman and Chester E. Finn, Jr., "An Uncertain Future," in David W. Breneman and Chester E. Finn, Jr., eds., *Public Policy and Private*

support—totaling many billion dollars per year—most universities still cannot offer full scholarships to all needy and qualified students. What should universities and governments do in the face of the fact that students from poorer families have considerably less access to a college education and fewer choices among colleges than students from richer families?[47]

Governments could do more to improve public universities, which tend to have the lowest tuitions. And universities could do less to subsidize college education for high-income students in order to do more to subsidize low-income students.[48] Economists usually direct the latter suggestion toward governmental policy with regard to tuitions at public universities, but it applies as well to private universities, whose full tuition also represents only a fraction of the per capita costs of undergraduate education. If public and private universities charged students from affluent families the full cost of a college education, they could use the extra revenues to create more and larger scholarships for students from needy families. Empirical studies indicate that low-income students are, as one might expect, "significantly more sensitive to price than high-income students in deciding whether to attend college."[49]

Higher Education (Washington, D.C.: The Brookings Institution, 1978), pp. 17-48. For a detailed analysis of public support for community colleges, see David W. Breneman and Susan C. Nelson, Financing Community Colleges: An Economic Perspective (Washington, D.C.: The Brookings Institution, 1981). See also Chester E. Finn, Jr., Scholars, Dollars & Bureaucrats (Washington, D.C.: The Brookings Institution, 1978), pp. 8-19.

[47] When I use, for the sake of convenience below, the terms "low income," "poorer," "affluent," and so on to modify "students," the adjectives refer to the characteristics of their families. It is important not to assume that parents always share their wealth with their children.

[48] Many economists arrive at this conclusion by assuming that market pricing would best reveal the social value of higher education. One need not, and I do not, share this assumption to support a policy of higher tuitions. For the economic argument for market pricing, see W. Lee Hansen and Burton A. Weisbrod, "A New Approach to Higher Education Finance," in M. D. Orwig, ed., Financing Higher Education: Alternatives for the Federal Government (Iowa City, Iowa: American College Testing Program, 1971), pp. 117-42; Theodore W. Schultz, Higher Education: The Equity-Efficiency Quandary (Arlington, Va.: IDA Economic Papers, 1973), pp. 21-44; Susan C. Nelson, "Equity and Higher Education Finance: The Case of Community Colleges," in Walter W. McMahon and Terry G. Geske, Financing Education: Overcoming Inefficiency and Inequity (Urbana: University of Illinois Press, 1982), pp. 215-36; and Breneman and Nelson, Financing Community Colleges. For more moderate recommendations along these lines, see Finn, Scholars, Dollars & Bureaucrats, esp. chs. 3-4. Cf. Howard R. Bowen, Financing Higher Education: The Current State of the Debate (Association of American Colleges, 1974), pp. 5-26.

[49] Michael S. McPherson, "The Demand for Higher Education," in David W. Breneman and Chester E. Finn, Jr., eds., Public Policy and Private Higher Education (Washington, D.C.: The Brookings Institution, 1978), p. 183.

Higher tuition coupled with more generous need-based scholarships would increase access to college for poorer students without decreasing it for richer students. Richer students, economists argue, would decide whether and where to go to college on the basis of the true costs and benefits of their education relative to other goods. The extra revenues would be used to equalize the access of poorer students to a college education. A high-tuition, full-scholarship policy thereby promises both equity and efficiency.

Critics rightly claim that it promises too much. Students themselves are generally not those who bear the costs of their college education. It is therefore not clear that the distribution of college education becomes more efficient when parents must pay the full costs of their child's education. "There is no practical way of obtaining a distribution of net benefits (or net burdens) by income classes in such a system," Joseph Pechman points out, "because the persons who receive the benefits are not the same persons who pay the costs."[50] On grounds of efficiency alone, it might be just as reasonable to set tuitions at levels that will elicit the optimal social use of higher education. There is no reason to suppose that social welfare is better optimized by parental choice between summer vacations for themselves and higher education for their children when higher education is unsubsidized than when it is subsidized. A market standard is incapable of telling us in which case the decisions of parents better reflect the net (private and public) benefits of a college education. In either case, agents other than the consumers themselves play the major role in deciding whether (and which) college is a worthwhile investment.

Higher tuitions coupled with full scholarships for students from poor families can also erect new barriers to both entry into and choice among colleges for students whose parents are able but unwilling to pay very much for their college education. By keeping tuitions low, universities lower the external barriers of entry for all students, thereby avoiding the potential inequity of restricting access to more affluent students whose parents are able but unwilling to pay—or pay very much—for their children's college education. Low-tuition public universities have yet another virtue, which may be as hard to explain as it is easy to experience. Low-income students seem to feel more like equal members of a low-tuition university than they do within expensive universities where they are among a minority of students who are fully subsidized. In a tuition-free university, all students enter on the same

---

[50] Joseph A. Pechman, "Note on the Intergenerational Transfer of Public Higher-Education Benefits," in Theodore W. Schultz, ed., *Investment in Education: The Equity-Efficiency Quandary* (Chicago: University of Chicago Press, 1972), p. 256.

footing, so to speak. No one has reason to feel more grateful or beholden to the university than anyone else. This feeling of equal membership seems to have been an important part of what was distinctive about the post-war experience of many children of poor immigrants in attending the then tuition-free City College of New York.

These criticisms moderate the claims rather than defeat the case for a high-tuition, full-scholarship policy. If states are willing to spend only a limited amount of money on subsidizing higher education for students, then such a policy is more defensible than the available alternatives on grounds of equity. States should give priority to subsidizing students from poorer families because they are generally more disadvantaged than students from richer families. By raising college tuitions, states avoid subsidizing many affluent parents who would otherwise contribute to the higher education of their children. A similar sense of equal membership, moreover, may be created within a university whose tuition is so high that most students, not just students from particularly poor families, are subsidized. To create such a sense, scholarship policies within high-tuition universities must establish relatively secure expectations of financial aid among qualified students for the whole of their college careers. These modifications permit a more refined defense of a high-tuition, full-scholarship policy, one that acknowledges a possible moral cost of the policy: discriminating against some richer students to avoid discriminating against poorer students.

This discrimination can be avoided altogether by coupling a high-tuition, full-scholarship policy with a policy of offering loans to students regardless of their family income, and tying repayment requirements to the students' future income. (Loan payments are deferred until after college graduation, and the more a student earns after college, the higher her rate of repayment.) Such loans go a long way towards easing the access problems facing students with rich but stingy parents at the same time as they provide an alternative means of access to college for poor students, although the willingness of students to take on the burden of repaying even an income-calibrated loan may also vary with their present family income. Loans of this sort are risky, but the risks may be worth taking for the sake of increasing access to college for all categories of students.[51]

A more morally troubling risk of a high-tuition, full-scholarship policy is that in times of austerity, the two parts of the policy may be decoupled, public or private universities retaining their high tuitions and

[51] For a more detailed discussion of varieties of feasible loan policies, and their economic strengths and weaknesses, see Lois D. Rice, ed., *Student Loans: Problems and Policy Choices* (New York: College Entrance Examination Board, 1977).

giving up their full scholarships. This risk cannot be eliminated without doing away with democracy or the autonomy of universities, but it can be minimized by policies that tie levels of tuition to levels of support, similar to the way in which cost-of-living indexes tie increases in income to inflation. The commitment to economic nondiscrimination is thereby expressed by a single policy, rather than being the coincidence of two policies with independent rationales. Those who propose to do away with the indexing must not only argue against the commitment that constitutes its rationale, they must also persuade enough people of the merits of a different tuition policy.

The policy with the greatest merits from the standpoint of nondiscrimination is eliminating tuitions almost entirely and subsidizing higher education so heavily as to insure equal access to all qualified students. The defense of a high-tuition, full-scholarship policy presumes that citizens would be unwilling or unable to subsidize higher education in the vast amounts that would be necessary to minimize economic discrimination (or maximize nondiscrimination) in its distribution. From the perspective of democratic theory, this presumption is morally as well as practically safe for two reasons, which we have already considered in other contexts: (1) higher education, unlike primary education, is not a necessary good; and (2) nondiscrimination, like other values, is not worth maximizing.

The second point is worth elaborating, because it raises a rather troubling theoretical problem. Maximizing economic nondiscrimination would mean eliminating all the subtle (and not so subtle) ways in which parental attitudes about money differentially shape children's attitudes about going to college. Eliminating these ways would entail obviously illegitimate intrusions into the domain of the family. So it appears to be a mistake to apply nondiscrimination thoroughly and consistently to resolve the problem of distributing higher education. No more than any other principle should nondiscrimination tyrannize over our common sense, or preempt democratic determination of our priorities. Yet the very purpose of the principle is to constrain democratic decision-making, thereby producing a paradox: a principle intended to constrain democracy must be constrained by it.

The paradox dissolves, however, when we correctly interpret the principle as requiring the elimination not of every barrier to equal access but only of those barriers that are irrelevant to the democratic purposes of higher education. On this interpretation, universities are less responsible for overcoming the unequal academic motivation of students caused by different parental values than are primary schools for overcoming similarly created motivational inequalities. In both cases, the responsibility for equalization extends as far, but only as far, as the sources of inequality interfere with the democratic purposes of schooling. In neither case is complete equalization of opportunity called for. Inherent in the rationale for constraining democracy by nondiscrimination is a democratic limit on interpreting the nondiscrimination principle. The principle should be interpreted in accordance with a publicly defensible distinction betweeen relevant and irrelevant obstacles to access. Subsidizing higher education to the extent of eliminating financial obstacles for all qualified students but not eliminating motivational obstacles is surely one publicly defensible distinction.

Can *any* subsidization of college education be publicly justified, one might ask, in a democratic state that provides little or no financial aid to millions of citizens, who are too poor or poorly educated even to consider going to college?[52] Why not leave higher education to private enterprise and philanthropy as long as primary education is still not adequately funded, and so many citizens are less advantaged than even the poorest college students? From a democratic as well as an economic perspective, the most fundamental challenge to governmental funding of higher education is whether college students should be subsidized at all as long as more urgent social needs remain unmet.

Economists who respond to this challenge typically begin by arguing that higher education is to a significant extent a public good: "the external benefits of higher education are ones which increase the satisfaction of other members of society, but for which, as a practical matter, the educated person cannot be compensated."[53] Although educating teachers, for example, increases the welfare of the entire society by contributing to the training of better physicists, engineers, corporate executives, and citizens, the income of teachers does not reflect their full social contribution. Therefore (this economic argument goes), governments should subsidize higher education for teachers to prevent underinvestment relative to its social benefits. Governments should also invest in primary education because it too is a public as well as a private good. But the economic case for subsidizing higher education does not depend on establishing its greater urgency over other public or mixed (public and private) goods. Governments should subsidize *all* goods that are at least partly public. The argument from fairness therefore points in the direction of more, rather than less, governmental spending.

One might still challenge the rationality of subsidies for higher edu-

---

[52] For a similar challenge, see Finn, *Scholars, Dollars & Bureaucrats*, p. 92.

[53] Roger E. Bolton, "The Economics and Public Financing of Higher Education: An Overview," in *The Economics and Financing of Higher Education in the United States: A Compendium of Papers* (Washington, D.C.: U.S. Government Printing Office, 1969), p. 34.

cation by asking: What, exactly, are its external economic benefits? Economists who are skeptical about the externalities of higher education argue that "[t]he nature and magnitude of the social, as distinct from private, benefits from undergraduate education have never been carefully spelled out, let alone measured; thus, the belief in their significance is rooted in hope rather than in any firm evidence that they do indeed exist."[54] I suspect that this challenge seems much stronger than it would were the debate not cast within an economic model that assumes the need to measure all human goods in a common currency, or else doubt their existence, or at least their significance. Because the economic model so dominates discussions of funding higher education, it is worth trying to answer the challenge on its terms before recasting the debate in more democratic terms.

The external economic benefit of higher education that is most commonly cited is its contribution to economic growth. Highly educated people, Alice Rivlin argues, "have ideas, do research, make discoveries, invent new products and processes and procedures. Usually, anyone can use these basic ideas and discoveries. It is because their originator may get little or none of the increase in income which they create that not enough people may be induced in invest in the expensive education which this kind of creative activity requires."[55] Even the productivity of people without college education increases as a consequence of the new knowledge that more educated people create and diffuse.[56] "Unfortunately—although it is easy to point to highly educated people who have made important contributions to national income for which they have received little personal remuneration—," Rivlin adds, "no one has developed a method of estimating the total return that society is getting, or might get, on its investments in higher education."[57] This failure is unfortunate for the economic model, perhaps even fatal if its purpose is to specify the amount that governments must invest in higher education for an efficient use of social resources. We do not need a model that implausibly assumes that all the benefits of higher education are measurable in a common currency to conclude that some of the benefits of higher education accrue to society rather than to the individ-

[54] Hansen and Weisbrod, "A New Approach to Higher Education Finance," p. 122. See also Friedman, "The Role of Government in Education," p. 134; and Friedman, "The Higher Schooling in America," *The Public Interest* (Spring 1968): 109-112.

[55] Alice Rivlin, *The Role of the Federal Government in Financing Higher Education* (Washington, D.C.: The Brookings Institution, 1961), p. 135.

[56] For an elaboration of this argument, see Bolton, "The Economics and Public Financing of Higher Education: An Overview," pp. 35-49.

[57] Rivlin, *The Role of the Federal Government in Financing Higher Education*, p. 137. Although Rivlin wrote this over twenty years ago, the point is still valid today.

uals that produce them. It still may be reassuring to recognize that the argument for public subsidy of higher education is credible even on the assumptions of the economic model.

Like the economic case for subsidizing higher education, the democratic case does not depend on denying the greater urgency of other goods (such as improving primary education), more urgent because they are more essential to establishing the foundations of a decent democracy. But unlike the economic case, the democratic one distinguishes between the moral imperative for democratic governments to satisfy certain urgent needs (for adequate primary schooling) and their moral discretion in deciding whether to satisfy less urgent needs or public preferences (for expanding higher education).

The democratic defense of public spending, again unlike the economic defense, can account for the importance, even the urgency, of goods whose value cannot be measured by money. Universities contribute to furthering political freedom in a democracy in a way unmeasurable by money. It is no paradox that some goods—such as political freedom—whose public worth is not measurable by money require a great deal of public money to prosper. Without substantial governmental support, universities probably would not survive, and certainly would not flourish in our society. The democratic value of nonrepression is most effectively furthered by universities that are able to attract the most thoughtful among all high-school students, not just among the most affluent. Although a policy of economic nondiscrimination has a high price, its price cannot be equated with its democratic value.

Each of the purposes of universities, properly pursued, is in significant part a public good. The pursuit of knowledge for its own sake contributes to preserving our cultural heritage and also to discovering socially useful knowledge. The moral along with the technical education of officeholders contributes to our welfare in a way that money cannot measure, as does the establishment of academic communities, which serve—among other things—as sanctuaries for nonconformists. That "[t]he nature and magnitude of the social, *as distinct from private*, benefits from undergraduate education have never been carefully . . . measured"[58] is evidence of the largely noneconomic nature, not the nonexistence or insignificance of, the public good of higher education.

If the public good of higher education is, strictly speaking, not measurable by money, how do we decide how much money governments should spend to subsidize higher education? The same way that we decide how much money governments should spend on primary school-

---

[58] Hansen and Weisbrod, "A New Approach to Higher Education Finance," p. 122. Emphasis added.

ing beyond what justice requires—through democratic deliberation and decisionmaking at the appropriate levels of government. On this argument, the precise degree to which higher education is a public as distinct from a private good is largely irrelevant to the question of how much governments should spend on higher education. Were we able to distinguish clearly between the private and public goods of higher education, we still would not be able to price the various parts.

But we need not put a price on all the parts of higher education to answer many of the central questions concerning public subsidy that arise in democratic theory. Consider the question of the extent to which democratic governments should subsidize private along with—or instead of—public universities. To answer this question, we must consider whether a purely public, a purely private, or a mixed system of universities would best serve the democratic purposes of higher education. If—as appears to be the case, at least in this country—private universities are better able to resist political sources of repression, such as McCarthyism, while public universities are better able to resist private sources of discrimination, such as resistance by trustees and alumni to admitting qualified Jews, blacks, and women, then democratic governments have good reason to support a mixed system of higher education, where both private and public universities flourish. Since private universities serve as gatekeepers to the many of the most prized offices in this country, democratic governments should also ensure that their subsidies to private universities do not support economic, racial, sexual, or religious discrimination in the distribution of office. A principled pluralism in higher education depends on respecting the autonomy of private and public universities if but only if they serve their democratic purposes. Although higher education is not a necessary good for every citizen in our society, it is still necessary that it be distributed in a nondiscriminatory manner.

A democratic policy of funding universities therefore cannot rest solely—or even primarily—on a calculation of the *economic* costs and benefits of higher education, but economists still can contribute a great deal to our understanding of how changes in the cost of a college education contribute or detract from achieving nondiscrimination. In practice, it may be impossible fully to satisfy the principle. A low-tuition policy is likely to restrict both access and choice for some students from poor families, unless (as is unlikely and perhaps undesirable) governments and universities are willing to spend the enormous amount necessary to send all qualified students to the college of their choice. A high-tuition, full-scholarship policy coupled with student loans, on the other hand, may constrain the choice of at least a few risk-averse students. The high-tuition, full-scholarship and loan policy is on the whole better, but it still runs a substantial political risk, of losing democratic favor in austere times and becoming simply a high-tuition policy, which would be significantly more discriminatory than a low-tuition policy. There is, however, no way of avoiding the political risk completely without adopting a worse policy or, worse still, abandoning democracy.

CHAPTER EIGHT

EXTRAMURAL EDUCATION

As democratic education does not begin, so it does not end, with the schooling of youth. "It is a commonplace to say," John Dewey said, "that education should not cease when one leaves school."[1] The commonplace has more than one point, just as democratic education has more than one purpose.[2] Good schools stimulate rather than quench the thirst for learning. But even good schools are unlikely to succeed if they are oases of learning in a society otherwise barren of democratic education.

The wisdom that education should not end with the schooling of youth does not tell us whose responsibility education beyond schooling should be. To what extent should a democratic state support institutions other than schools for the purpose of furthering democratic education? This chapter on educating children outside of school and the next on educating adults after school only partially answer this question. To answer it completely, we would have to consider every public institution that contributes—or could contribute—to democratic education. Because such an exhaustive study would be exhausting, if not impossible, it is tempting to acknowledge that institutions other than schools engage in democratic education, and then to put the question aside to focus only on schooling. The temptation is hard to resist for a second reason: most contemporary political controversies over democratic education concentrate on schooling.

If we succumb to the temptation, however, we perpetuate the popular impression that schooling fully constitutes democratic education, an impression that is false even on the strict understanding of education as the deliberate transmission of values and knowledge. To take an obvious example, public libraries try and often succeed in encouraging children to continue reading and learning while they are out of school. Concern for democratic education is also an important element in political controversies other than those over schools, such as recent debates over whether government should regulate commercial television or subsidize art. Our present political controversies, moreover, should

[1] Dewey, *Democracy and Education*, p. 51.

[2] "The point of this commonplace," Dewey argued, "is that the purpose of school education is to insure the continuance of education by organizing the powers that insure growth." Ibid.

not set the limits of our concern for democratic education. Political theory must carry our concern for education beyond both schooling and our present political agenda.

OUTSIDE OF FAMILIES AND SCHOOLS

Imagine for the moment a democratic society that treats public responsibility for education as if it begins and ends with schooling. Schools do their best to teach children for the 15,000 or so hours that they attend between ages 5 and 16, but how children spend their time outside of school is considered a matter of parental and not public responsibility. When parents are unable to fulfill their responsibility because they are too poor, the state provides them with money or a child allowance for food and shelter. When parents flagrantly neglect their responsibility by physically abusing their children, for example, the state intervenes to protect the children and to punish their parents (if punishment is compatible with protection). But parents are legally free and fully responsible morally for educating their children outside of school. For government to intervene in education outside of school would, on this view, be unjustly paternalistic towards parents or detrimental to the welfare of children (or both).

A modified state of families of this sort avoids some of the undemocratic excesses of a pure state of families while preserving a large province for parental authority and responsibility. Schooling becomes the province in which citizens acting collectively through schools can teach all children common values and the skills necessary for political participation. Outside that province, parents acting independently or as part of private subcultures determine how best to educate their own children. Some parents supplement secular with religious schooling, encourage their children to read, and discourage them from watching television. The education of even these children differs depending on the particular religious schools, books, and cultural activities chosen by their parents. Other parents make significantly different choices—not to send their children to a religious school, not to buy them books or to restrict their television viewing. If parents serve, most importantly, as educational examples or role models for their children, then there are as many different ways in which parents educate children as there are ways in which they live their own lives.

So conceived, the modified state of families has substantial moral appeal. It recognizes that there are not one but many good ways of educating children, and that a society in which many forms of education flourish is, to this extent, a freer society than one in which only a few flourish. It also recognizes that parents are generally the best paternalistic agents for their own children because, among available agents, parents care most about the welfare of their own children, and know the most about their individual wants and needs. Even when there is room to doubt whether parental control is serving the best interests of children, parents have a nonpaternalistic right to live their own lives freely. This right includes the right of parents to educate, discipline, and socialize their children as they see fit *within bounds set by democratic standards.*[3] The duties of parents to further the democratic education of their children constrain but certainly do not determine what sort of family life they can choose for themselves and their children. Although parents are not free, for example, to keep their children home from school or to require public schools to teach creationism instead of evolution, they are free to teach their children creationism at home and to forbid them from playing on their Sabbath. The duty that children incur by way of gratitude to respect the ways of life pursued by their parents may itself be an important lesson in democratic education, laying the deepest foundations of mutual respect among persons. Even if the lesson sometimes backfires, there are reasons—rooted in the nonpaternalistic rights of parents to live their own lives—to cede authority in these matters to parents rather than to public agencies.

The shortcomings of the modified state of families may be less apparent than its strengths. Between public authority over what children are taught in school and parental authority over what they are taught at home lies a lot of educational territory—occupied by libraries, bookstores, museums, newspapers, movies, radio, television, and other cultural institutions, many of whose proper titles of ownership are not obvious. It is obvious, however, that the independent decisions of parents cannot determine whether these institutions exist or whether they serve to educate children. Parents can permit or prevent, encourage or discourage their children from going to the library or watching educational television, but they cannot provide access to either resource unless it already exists by virtue of a political decision to provide it. Yet how well children are educated after school depends in large part on their access to such resources, which are beyond the power of individual parents to provide.

How children are educated after school also depends on what one might call the culture of learning—the values and attitudes towards learning that social institutions encourage children to adopt. Although parents can try to create an atmosphere conducive to learning within their family, whether they succeed with any given degree of time,

---

[3] For a liberal defense of nonpaternalistic rights of parents over children, see Gutmann, "Children, Paternalism and Education: A Liberal Argument," pp. 338-58.

money, and emotional energy will depend in large part on the culture that surrounds or, in the case of television, permeates their household—a culture over which parents have very little control even, or especially, when governments forswear regulation. If parents have no more freedom in the absence of governmental support and regulation than they have in its presence, then a democratic state need not be acting paternalistically towards parents when it supports libraries or regulates television for the educational good of children.

To say that governmental support and regulation need not be paternalistic is not to say that it is justified. We began by observing that parents cannot be free to choose the educational alternatives available to their children outside of school, even if they should be free to choose among the alternatives themselves. We still need to ask: Who should choose the alternatives? What should the alternatives be? By starting with a relatively simple and settled case of governmental support and regulation of libraries, we can develop some standards for resolving the more difficult and controversial case of governmental support and regulation of television.

LIBRARIES

"When I was a boy, growing up in a poor district of a large industrial town in Northern England," Richard Hoggart recalls, "my great airhole to a wider imaginative world was the local public library. Luckily, some people more than half a century before had believed that there was more hidden ability in those huddled back-streets than was commonly assumed." Hoggart fears that it now "is fashionable and no doubt comforting to assume that these hidden audiences no longer exist, that all such people have been winkled out of the 'masses' by better educational opportunities. . . ." When as a consequence of this assumption, states stop supplementing the education provided by schools, public education becomes "a one-step-forward-two-steps-backwards business."[4]

This impressionistic account of the importance of public libraries finds empirical support in a recent study of how the educational achievement of children is affected by their summertime activities. The two-year study of sixth and seventh graders in Atlanta, Georgia found that schooling reduces the degree to which the academic achievement of children depends on the socio-economic status of parents. During the summer, the achievement gap between less advantaged children

[4] Richard Hoggart, *An English Temper: Essays on Education, Culture and Communications* (New York: Oxford University Press, 1982), p. 148.

and more advantaged children widens, as children depend to a much greater degree on the educational resources of their parents and local peer culture.[5] Libraries, however, help prevent less advantaged children from learning even less (or forgetting more) over the summer:

> For the young users, the library appears to be a critical source of materials; although young clients are disproportionately drawn from the most advantaged classes, the children of the poor obtain benefits that would not be available in the absence of libraries.[6]

If the democratic ideal is to guarantee every child an adequate but not necessarily an equal education, then the fact that more advantaged children make disproportionate use of libraries should not be counted against them. Without libraries, all children in Atlanta—but particularly black children—would read less and therefore learn less over the summer.[7] Such evidence counts strongly in favor of providing public libraries, over half of whose clientele are children, when schools are still struggling unsuccessfully to educate children up to the democratic threshold. Reading books was the single activity "most strongly and consistently related to summer learning" (regardless of the race or socio-economic status of the child).[8] The proximity of public libraries to children's homes had a direct effect on the number of books children read over the summer: "Had all children lived within seven blocks [of a library], the aggregate amount of reading would have increased substantially. Although reading and library use are linked to socio-economic status, the degree of access enjoyed by children is a critical factor for all socioeconomic groups."[9]

Whether public libraries should exist is a settled question for most Americans, but how well they should be funded and how they should be governed are not settled. The Atlanta study suggests that local governments can do more to further democratic education by providing less advantaged children with easier access to books, either by building

---

[5] Barbara Heyns, *Summer Learning and the Effects of Schooling* (New York: Academic Press, 1978), pp. 185-95 and *passim*.

[6] Ibid., p. 183.

[7] Among the most striking and significant findings of the Atlanta study was that "among black families, reading levels [among children] vary across income levels in the predictable way, yet the chief means of implementing parental influence seems to be through encouraging children to use the library, rather than by providing books at home." Ibid., p. 215.

[8] Ibid., p. 161.

[9] Ibid., p. 178. "It would be possible to argue," Heyns recognizes, "that families with an abiding concern for their children's reading behavior chose to live near libraries, but this seems unlikely. The alternative assertion, that the distribution of libraries shapes the patterns of use by socioeconomic status and race, is more plausible."

more libraries in inner cities or by reaching out from existing libraries with bookmobiles, for example. The principle of nonexclusion suggests that they should do more, so as not to undo the positive effects of schooling by depriving less advantaged children of a summer environment conducive to learning.

An earlier study of the library system in Oakland, California suggests some further reforms in the way cities distribute funds among library branches. The Oakland study found that the lower circulation of books in branches located in lower-income neighborhoods was attributable in part to the fact that the same books were purchased for all branches, regardless of the particular educational needs and interests of local neighborhoods.[10] Although books on jobs and careers, civil rights, state and local government, and basic arithmetic were in much greater demand in low-income than in high-income neighborhoods, all Oakland libraries purchased the kinds of books that were in greatest demand in high-income neighborhoods. The budget for future acquisitions was then determined by past circulation. This policy created a "vicious circle" in which inappropriate book stocks in lower-income areas reduced circulation, leading to fewer book purchases for these branches, leading to still lower circulation.[11] This problem can be alleviated without eliminating professional control on quality by adopting the model of democratic schools, and allowing neighborhoods to elect local library boards, whose authority would be similarly constrained by the principle of nonrepression.[12]

Making libraries more accountable to local citizens may stimulate political controversy. Having more authority over their local library, citizens may be more prone to dispute certain policies, such as the selection of certain books and their circulation to children without parental consent. If a primary aim of libraries is to increase interest in reading books among children, we cannot assume that it would be better to avoid such political controversies, which probably add to rather than detract from children's interest in books.

Critics argue that the majority who support the policies of public li-

[10] Frank Levy, Arnold J. Meltsner, and Aaron Wildavsky, *Urban Outcomes: Schools, Streets, and Libraries* (Berkeley: University of California Press, 1974), p. 195.

[11] Ibid.

[12] The authors of the Oakland study suggest a series of reforms that point in this direction: "The members of the board should come exclusively from the area served; they should have power to select a senior librarian from among those certified and, with this librarian, to choose junior librarians who would be expected to come from the local area. . . . Civil service regulations concerning junior librarians should allow ample latitude in appointment. . . . The board should have the power to allocate its funds among personnel, facilities, and materials subject to periodic auditing and required reports on cost, circulation, and effectiveness." Ibid., p. 215.

braries are imposing their educational values on the parents who oppose them. This is true, but how could it be otherwise? Some values must be imposed in any case—either all children (and citizens) will have access to public libraries or all will not; either all children will be permitted to check out books without their parents' consent or all will not. Were tax revenues not used to support libraries, most parents would have marginally more money to buy books for their own children, but children whose parents did not buy books would have a significantly smaller "airhole to a wider imaginative world." Without access to public libraries, parents must raise their children in a culture that treats books as any other commodity, and children must depend on the purchases of their parents. A community that funds public libraries constrains its citizens in a different way. Although no one is forced to use a library, citizens are forced to pay for them and to live in a society where children have easier access than they otherwise would to books that some parents may find objectionable. The choice between communities must by its very nature be made collectively. Funding public libraries is a prototypically democratic decision: fostering some significant freedoms while restricting others, which are publicly deemed less significant; supplying a good that politics can buy but the market cannot—in the case of libraries, a public culture of learning accessible to all children.

TELEVISION AND DEMOCRATIC EDUCATION

Public libraries rest, rather solidly today, on some of the same democratic foundations needed to build a case for public support and regulation of television. The case for public support of television is more difficult and controversial to mount for many reasons. First and foremost in the minds of many critics is the issue of whether television can contribute, even potentially, to a public culture of learning—a doubt rarely directed towards libraries. Those who argue that the medium is the message and the message of the television medium is intellectual passivity, conclude that it clearly cannot. The argument begins with a common observation: children can't talk back to their television sets, they can only turn them off.[13] By sitting in front of a television set, children learn that it is normal to listen but not to respond, to absorb information but not to inquire, to be loyal or to exit but not to raise their voice in criticism, and so on. Intellectual passivity lends itself to political apathy or mindless protest, neither of which are democratic virtues.

[13] Cf. Richard Sennett, *The Fall of Public Man* (New York: Vintage Books, 1978), p. 283.

Many who argue that watching television is a lesson in political passivity conclude that the existence of television is incompatible with a democratic culture. Their message is one of political despair. Others look forward to the widespread use of interactive cable television, which permits viewers to respond to messages that appear on their screen.[14] Even assuming that children would spend as much time interacting with television as they now spending watching it, the experience in using interactive cable television would surely still fall far short of a lesson in becoming an active citizen. Pressing keys in response to messages that appear on the screen is not likely to develop moral understandings or commitments of the sort stimulated by face-to-face associations with family and friends. Nor is technological interaction a process by which children are likely to learn how to translate their moral understandings or commitments into politics by arguing, negotiating, and compromising with people who have conflicting commitments. If the medium of interactive television translates into the message of democratic citizenship, then the prospects of establishing an active democratic politics are much worse than one could otherwise imagine.

There is, however, reason to doubt a direct translation from the medium to the message. Much of what the critics say about the passive nature of watching television could also be said about reading books. Reading may demand more intellectual effort and imagination, but children can no more talk back to a book than they can to a television set. Like television viewing, reading does not require any of the active intellectual or political virtues that we associate with democratic citizenship. The critics should therefore have similar worries about the effects of reading on democratic character, unless their worries about television are, as I suspect, misplaced onto its form rather than its content. Were more of children's television modeled on "Sesame Street" or "The Adams Chronicles," would there not be less reason to worry that watching television detracts from democratic education?

A recent critic of television suggests that there would be more reason to worry: "The best things on television *are* its junk, and no one and

[14] See, for example, Barber, *Strong Democracy*, p. 274: "The capabilities of the new technology can be used to strengthen civic education, guarantee equal access to information, and tie individuals and institutions into networks that will make real participatory discussion and debate possible across great distances. Thus for the first time we have the opportunity to create artificial town meetings among populations that could not otherwise communicate." If we concentrate upon the effects of interactive cable on adults rather than children, this positive assessment is more understandable. Even then, there is some reason to doubt that the medium will be conducive to democratic deliberation. For a critique of interactive cable, see Jean Elshtain, "Democracy and the QUBE Tube," *The Nation* (August 7-14, 1982): 108-110.

nothing is seriously threatened by it . . . [whereas] television is at its . . . most dangerous when its aspirations are high, when it presents itself as a carrier of important cultural conversations."[15] The medium of television is the metaphor, argues Neil Postman, and the metaphor is Las Vegas. The message of the metaphor is entertainment. But entertainment is not what education is about. By pretending that education is entertaining, " 'Sesame Street' undermines what the traditional idea of schooling represents."[16] The traditional idea of schooling views education as having prerequisites, being perplexing, and requiring exposition. "Sesame Street" has no prerequisites, is (for the most part) unperplexing, and waives the requirement of (at least extended) exposition. Postman therefore "ridicule[s] the hope harbored by some that television can be used to support the literate tradition."

The hope would be ridiculous were it that educational television substitute for schooling. The hope is rather that educational television supplement schooling, especially (but not only) for those children who would otherwise watch cartoons or simply "hang out" rather than read. This much more common hope is far from ridiculous. There is no good evidence for the assertion that educational television "does not ban books, it simply displaces them."[17] On the contrary, there is evidence that educational television helps children, including those from less advantaged families, learn to read.[18] (If television did displace reading, better that the displacement be "Sesame Street" rather than "He-Man.") The reasonable promise of educational television is that it can supplement rather than supplant schooling.

Most television programming falls so far short of fulfilling this promise that most of its supporters defend it not for educating but for entertaining children, or—more generally—for satisfying consumer preferences. Its supporters surely have a point: television is by far the most popular form of entertainment for all ages of Americans. The case for its public support and regulation may appear weaker than the case for public libraries largely due to this fact. As it now exists in the United States, television *is* (with few exceptions) entertainment, and not edification. As such, one might argue, it is appropriately left to the market, which specializes in consumer satisfaction.

This argument is, I suspect, inverted: television is entertaining and not edifying *because* it has been left so largely to the commercial market

[15] Neil Postman, *Amusing Ourselves to Death: Public Discourse in the Age of Show Business* (New York: Viking, 1985), p. 16.

[16] Ibid., p. 143.

[17] Ibid., p. 141.

[18] See, e.g., Edward L. Palmer and Aimee Dorr, eds., *Children and the Faces of Television: Teaching, Violence, Selling* (New York: Academic Press, 1980).

in the United States (or, more accurately, to the market in commercials). In England, where television is to a much greater extent part of the public sector, a much greater proportion of programs are entertaining *and* edifying. The analogy of television with libraries is largely descriptive in the English context, because both institutions aim to educate as well as to entertain. In the American context, the analogy is more prescriptive (and hence more helpful): it suggests that the obstacles to making television more educational are not principled but practical.

The principled case for public television is even stronger than the case for public libraries insofar as the educational potential of television is greater than that of libraries. Children spend much more time watching television than reading library books. After schooling and sleeping, watching television is the activity that occupies the most time of most children in the United States. For preschoolers, watching television is second only to sleeping. School children between the ages of six and eleven average about 26 hours a week, or slightly more than 3½ hours a day.[19] Children from poorer, less educated families tend to watch more television, but the vast majority of all children over the age of four watch some television every day. When they graduate from high school, most children will have spent as much time in front of a television set as they have spent inside a school.

Like libraries, television programming has the potential not only for educating in the strict sense, but also, and perhaps more importantly, for contributing to a culture that supports rather than detracts from democratic schooling. Let me begin with the more limited claim—that the educational potential of television is far from realized. Even this rather modest claim may appear to rest on the false premise that educational programs could hold the attention of as many children as cartoons now do. Although the vast majority of television programs have not aimed to improve either the hearts or the minds of children, a few have tried to educate children. Yet most educational television programs have fallen far behind commercial entertainment programs in the competition for young viewers.[20] The striking exception is "Sesame Street," which aims to educate at the same time as it entertains. "Sesame Street" demonstrates the potential of television to educate a mass audience of black and white, rich and poor children by also entertain-

---

[19] Reported in Richard P. Adler and Ronald J. Faber, "Background: Children's Television Viewing Patterns," in Richard P. Adler et al., *The Effects of Television Advertising on Children* (Lexington, Mass.: Lexington Books, 1980), p. 15.

[20] Kenneth G. O'Bryan, "The Teaching Face: A Historical Perspective," in Palmer and Dorr, *Children and the Faces of Television: Teaching, Violence, Selling*, p. 16.

ing.[21] It also demonstrates how much money and commitment it takes for a children's educational program to succeed in the competition against commercial television.

The success of "Sesame Street" suggests that it is not the medium per se, but the predominantly commercial structure of American television broadcasting that predisposes it against producing popular educational programs for children. To sell advertising, commercial networks concern themselves primarily with how many people watch their programs, rather than with the value of their programming to their viewers. It may therefore be more accurate, as one critic comments, "to regard the advertisers as consumers of viewers, than to regard the viewers as consumers of programs."[22]

This commercial incentive structure places two formidable obstacles in the way of producing educational programs for children. First, only on Saturday mornings does it pay for networks to air programs designed primarily for children, for only then do children constitute more than half of the television audience. Although prime-time programming (on weekday evenings from 8 to 11 p.m.) attracts over 10 million children under the age of 12, they constitute only 13 percent of the prime-time audience.[23] Even the most popular children's programs are likely to lose out in the prime-time competition for advertising.

On Saturday mornings, when children constitute the majority of the television audience, commercial networks still have a large economic incentive not to broadcast educational programs. Cartoons cost much less to produce than educational programs such as "Sesame Street" that can sustain a sufficiently large audience for advertising. Unedifying entertainment for children is generally less costly and less risky by commercial standards to produce than entertaining edification.

The economic costs and risks of educational programming for children seem to be too great to be overcome either by a voluntary commitment on the part of the networks or by nonmandatory guidelines on

[21] For a summary of the research findings on the educational effects of "Sesame Street" and "The Electric Company," see Bruce A. Watkins, Aletha Huston-Stein, and John C. Wright, "Effects of Planned Television Programming," in Palmer and Dorr, eds., *Children and the Faces of Television: Teaching, Violence, Selling*, pp. 49-69.

[22] "Since commercial television derives its revenues from advertisers rather than viewers, the intensity of viewer interest, above that necessary to induce viewing, is irrelevant. . . . What matters is the expected number, and the expected value, of additional sales from exposure to the advertiser's message. That depends almost entirely on the number of viewers, not on their intrinsic interest in the message or the program. . . ." Ronald A. Cass, *Revolution in the Wasteland: Value and Diversity in Television* (Charlottesville: University of Virginia Press, 1981), p. 66.

[23] George A. Comstock et al., *Television and Human Behavior* (New York: Columbia University Press, 1978), p. 112.

the part of the FCC.[24] In the face of the ineffectiveness of its voluntary guidelines, the FCC could require its licensees to produce more educational programming for children, just as it has required stations in the past to produce more public affairs programs—on the legally recognized grounds that television broadcasting is a public trust, which the FCC is authorized to regulate in the public interest.

The FCC has, however, recently been moving in just the opposite direction—towards complete deregulation of its licensees. In one of its most drastic steps towards deregulation, the FCC has exempted all commercial television stations from a longstanding requirement to file detailed logs of what they broadcast.[25] Since stations keep such logs for their own commercial purposes as well as for the FCC, the major effect of the new policy is to prevent the records of stations from being scrutinized by the public or by the FCC when licenses are up for renewal. "What's at stake here," the FCC Chairman argues in defense of deregulation, "is whether the Government trusts the common man to make up his own mind about what to watch or not watch."[26] But paternalism cannot be what is at stake, since the common man or woman is free to make up her mind about what to watch whether or not the FCC regulates commercial programming. In neither case, however, can she determine what programs are broadcast. What is at stake in the FCC decision is whether citizens and public officials have access to the kind of information instrumental to judging whether stations are living up to their public trust, or to FCC guidelines, when they apply for license renewal.

The principal stake in the FCC's decision to deregulate is who determines the public's interest in television. The FCC's legal authority is to regulate broadcasting in the public interest, without becoming a censor or violating rights of free speech. A decision not to regulate because citizens disagree about what constitutes the public interest is a decision to

[24] Most commercial networks have voluntarily adopted a code "to maintain a level of television programming which gives full consideration to the educational, informational, cultural, economic, moral and entertainment needs of the American public" (Code of the National Association of Broadcasting). The guidelines of the 1974 Policy Statement of the Federal Communications Commission also recommended that all its licensees increase the amount of educational programming for children. Yet "the average amount of time devoted to educational children's programs on a per-station basis remained essentially the same for the 1977-78 broadcast season compared with the 1973-74 broadcast season." "In the Matter of Children's Television Programming and Advertising Practices" (Docket No. 19142), *Federal Communications Commission 79-851*, December 28, 1979, p. 143.

[25] David Burnham, "F.C.C. Eases Rules for Broadcast TV," *The New York Times*, June 28, 1984, p. C18.

[26] Ibid.

permit commercial networks to determine the public interest. Neither decision—to regulate or not to regulate—gives parents or children more freedom to make up their minds about what programs they wish to watch or have their children watch on Friday night or Saturday morning. The decision to deregulate gives citizens considerably less freedom to act collectively to shape the structure of television programming and no more freedom as parents or consumers to choose among programs. A principled decision not to regulate must therefore rest on the ground that giving commercial networks complete freedom to determine television programming constitutes the public interest. The educational interest of children would be invisible in this view of the public.

The most formidable objection to FCC regulation of commercial television for educational purposes is practical, not principled.[27] Given the nature of the economic pressures on commercial networks, regulation may elicit only minimal compliance. And minimal compliance—resulting in the airing of low-cost, low-quality educational programs—could do more to discredit the idea of educational television than to educate children. Without substantial financial support by the government, "Sesame Street" and similarly popular educational programs for children would probably never have been produced. Had the Children's Television Workshop been forced to produce programs on a much smaller budget, they probably would not have been successful. When one argues that American television should try harder to educate children, one must also argue for more public funding.

The case for making American television more educational is similar to the case for building more libraries. Funding educational television, like funding libraries, is one among several ways in which democratic governments can increase access to education after school for most children. Although neither decision is dictated by democratic principles, both offer parents more rather than fewer choices among qualitatively different ways to educate their children. More significantly, both policies provide children from poor homes with additional airholes to democratic education.

Television and Democratic Culture

When we expand our view of television's role in democratic education, the comparison with libraries ceases to be very helpful. Unlike libraries,

[27] For the results of a survey of producers that provides evidence of some of those obstacles, see Muriel G. Cantor, "The Role of the Producer in Choosing Children's Television Content," in George A. Comstock, Eli A. Rubinstein, and John P. Murray, eds., *Television and Social Behavior: Reports and Papers*, vol. 1, *Media Content and Control* (Washington, D.C.: U.S. Government Printing Office, 1972), pp. 259-89.

television is an almost irresistible presence in the homes of most children. Television teaches without really trying, and without parents really intending that their children learn what television teaches. The most significant educational effects of television are probably not its deliberately educational purposes. Even, or perhaps especially, when television does not aim to educate, it conveys a popular culture that influences children's attitudes not only about learning but, much more generally, about what kind of life is worth living. Although we are still far from understanding precisely how television alters children's attitudes and behavior, we have little reason to doubt that it does. Hundreds of studies and experiments converge in their findings that television affects children's attitudes, expectations, and even their behavior.[28]

So we may worry whether watching violent programs predisposes children to violence, whether sitting through 20,000 commercial messages fosters more materialism, or whether introducing obscenity would harm them. That children may become more aggressive by watching violence on television was one of the first worries to find extensive empirical confirmation—in a five-volume Report to the Surgeon General's Scientific Advisory Committee published in 1972.[29] The Report discovered that network programming for children, particularly cartoons, contained more violence than programs designed for adults, and that exposure to violence on television was associated with more aggressive behavior by some (though not all) children.[30] Subsequent research confirmed the Report's conclusions.[31] Because it is dif-

[28] "Data from many sources converge to indicate that television affects young persons' attitudes and expectations. There are studies demonstrating that some teenagers turn to television to learn norms about behavior . . . ; that views were affected when there was limited real-life experience with the topic . . . ; that exposure to television is correlated with perceiving the world more in accord with the way it is portrayed in television drama . . . ; that exposure to a program intended to change attitudes about other peoples results in changed attitudes. . . . More than 100 experiments have demonstrated that young children can acquire behavior by observing its portrayal on television." Comstock et al., *Television and Human Behavior*, pp. 262-63. For a summary and evaluation of the evidence on the ways in which television influences children's attitudes and behavior, see pp. 173-287.

[29] The Report found that network programs generally contained a high level of violence and that children's cartoons "were more violent than any other category of program format . . . in 1967. In 1969, they were even more violent, and they increased their lead over other types of programs." George A. Comstock, Eli A. Rubinstein, and John P. Murray, eds., *Television and Social Behavior: Reports and Papers*, vol. 1, *Media Content and Control* (Washington, D.C.: U.S. Government Printing Office, 1972), p. 6.

[30] Surgeon General's Scientific Advisory Committee on Television and Social Behavior, *Television and Growing Up: The Impact of Televised Violence*. Report to the Surgeon General (Washington, D.C.: U.S. Government Printing Office, 1972).

[31] For a summary and evaluation of the evidence on the effects of television violence on children, see Comstock et al., *Television and Human Behavior*, pp. 211-50.

ficult to isolate the long-term effects of television from other social influences, we may never be certain as to how viewing violence affects children's behavior, but the preponderance of evidence suggests that television violence detracts from rather than supports one of the least controversial ends of democratic education, predisposing children to nonviolence.

Television teaches children not only by virtue of its effects on their behavior, but also by conveying the standards of a popular culture. Whether and to what degree that culture is commercial, violent, sexist, or obscene is a reasonable matter for public concern quite apart from the effects that commercials, violence, sexism, and obscenity are likely to have on children's behavior. We may disagree as to whether it is good, bad, or indifferent for children to grow up in a popular culture filled with obscenity, sexism, violence, or commercial messages, but the fact of our disagreement does not undermine the legitimacy of public concern or control over that culture as it affects children.

Television is as closely tied to democratic culture as schooling is to democratic education. The analogy, although limited, properly suggests that among cultural media, television is uniquely powerful and pervasive in our society. It is probably the most influential, it is certainly the most universal culture to which children are exposed. Because television shapes and conveys popular culture, it should be primarily publicly rather than privately controlled. Like public authority over schools, public authority over television should be constrained so as not to be repressive.[32]

The analogy to schooling suggests that television should be primarily public. Whereas the British mix of public and private schools is further from the democratic ideal than ours, the British mix of public and private television networks comes closer to the democratic ideal than does our primarily commercial system. It is impossible to do justice here to the issue of restructuring American broadcasting in conformity to this democratic ideal.[33] Given the unlikelihood that we will dismantle our

[32] One might extend the analogy to cable television as follows: because cable television (like private schools) is well-equipped to respond to and shape the divergent preferences of smaller audiences, it should be freer from public control to compete with the common culture and to satisfy less popular cultural tastes. I return later to consider the special, and increasingly important, role of cable television in contributing to democratic culture.

[33] For a critical discussion of the consequences of a primarily commercial broadcasting system, see the Carnegie Commission on the Future of Public Broadcasting, *A Public Trust: The Report of the Carnegie Commission on the Future of Public Broadcasting* (New York: Bantam, 1979), pp. 21-23: "The United States is the only Western nation relying so exclusively upon advertising effectiveness as the gatekeeper of its broadcasting activities. The consequences of using the public spectrum primarily for commercial purposes are numerous, and increasingly disturbing. The idea of broadcasting as a force in

primarily commercial system, it may be more fruitful to explore whether it is possible to create a more democratic culture with a broadcasting system that remains in significant part commercially supported. Can public regulation of commercially supported broadcasting be justified as a means of creating a more democratic culture for children? This question is hard to answer, in part due to our uncertainty about the effects of program content on children, and in part due to our disagreement as to whether the probable effects are good or bad.

Critics of the "kid vid crusade" against television advertising enlist these two facts—of our empirical uncertainty and our moral disagreement—to argue against regulation. They suggest that governmental agencies are justified in regulating the content of television programming, including commercials, only when (a) they can be certain of the effects of program or commercial content, and (b) there is a social consensus that those effects are sufficiently bad to warrant regulation.[34] Constrained by these standards, the FCC or the FTC will rarely be justified in regulating content, even if they are legally authorized to do so.

But are these the right standards? Let's begin with the problem of empirical uncertainty, which the critics use as support for an argument against an attempt by the FTC to ban "unfair" commercials directed at children (such as those that advertise cereals without mentioning that they are heavily sugared):

> In pursuing its crusade, . . . the FTC no doubt believed it was acting in the best interest of children. However, what is best for children with respect to these social issues is largely indeterminate. Confident, long-term predictions concerning the consequences of alternative policies are impossible to make. . . .[35]

True. But the fact of uncertainty in itself favors neither side in the debate over the governmental regulation. Invoking a general presumption against state intervention and for the "free" market would be unwarranted here, given what we know about the nature of the television medium and the enormous power that commercial networks exert over popular culture. There is no reason to assume that the commercial market—regulated as it must be—will serve us better than a more than minimally regulated market, although there are many reasons to worry

---

the public interest, as a display case for the best of America's creative arts, a forum of public debate—advancing the democratic conversation and enhancing the public imagination—has receded before the inexorable force of audience maximization."

[34] Susan Bartlett Foote and Robert H. Mnookin, "The 'Kid Vid' Crusade," *The Public Interest*, no. 61 (Fall 1980): 90-105.

[35] Ibid., p. 99.

about both unconstrained commercial and unaccountable governmental power.

What, then, should we conclude from the fact of our uncertainty about the effects of television advertising and programming? Like teachers in public schools, members of the FTC and FCC are constrained to make decisions in the midst of uncertainty. They cannot be sure that advertising heavily sugared cereals harms children, but neither can they assume that such advertising (or advertising in general) is harmless. Such circumstances call not for certainty but for the agency's best judgment in assessing the implications of the evidence.[36] Skepticism about the ability of social scientists to demonstrate long-term effects of television advertising or violence on children is surely a sound reaction, but selective skepticism—enlisting uncertainty to cast doubt only on the side of regulation—is not.

The second problem is that even were citizens to agree, say, that watching commercials makes children more materialistic, they would disagree over whether these effects are bad or sufficiently bad to warrant regulation. "Much of the disagreement," critics of regulation point out, ". . . really has to do with conflicts over values. . . . [W]ill children believe what the reformers think they *ought* to believe, or will they be manipulated and exploited into believing the 'wrong' things? The critics and defenders [of television advertising] are really fighting for the minds of the next generation."[37]

Who, then, should win the battle for the minds of the next generation? Why not those who have the right values? The critics of regulation rightly reject this answer, although for the wrong reasons. They suggest (by the scare quotes) that children cannot be manipulated into believing the "wrong" things. We do not have to be skeptical about there being wrong beliefs or bad ways of socializing children to judge this answer inadequate. (Thoroughgoing skeptics should care very little about who wins, since nothing of value is at stake.) There are many wrong ways of socializing children, but there is little reason to believe that there is only one right way. Even if parents choose one of the

---

[36] This case is strongest with regard to commercial speech, for which there is only a weak presumption in favor of freedom from regulation. A stronger presumption exists in favor of protecting noncommercial speech, in which case uncertainty may favor deregulation. How strong the presumption should be (especially with regard to noncommercial speech directed primarily at children) and what kind of evidence can override it are two difficult issues, which neither the critics nor defenders of regulation have adequately addressed. The difficulty is compounded by the fact that television programming serves an educative function with regard to children. I can only flag the problem here; it would take another book, on free speech, to resolve it.

[37] Foote and Mnookin, "The 'Kid Vid' Crusade," pp. 100-101.

wrong ways, it does not follow that anyone who knows a better way has the authority to impose it on someone else's children.

The critics point to this problem of authority when they criticize the FTC for being "prepared to impose [their] view on all American families." Since someone's view or views must be imposed in any case, we cannot criticize the FTC for imposing their considered judgment in the midst of our disagreement. We can criticize their authority to regulate if but only if we have determined that someone else has the authority that they are therefore wrongly usurping. In itself, the fact of our disagreement over values, like that of our empirical uncertainty, speaks neither for nor against governmental regulation of television for children.

The critical question, as the critics correctly point out, is: "Who should decide? To put it more precisely, how should power and responsibility for children be allocated?"[38] We do not escape from disagreement by posing this question, however. Instead we shift the grounds of our disagreement to the level of politics, where we have no choice but to settle upon the best answer that we can collectively discover.

Even from the perspective of the state of families, the best answer— at least in the case of television advertising—is to authorize political regulation. Suppose, as the critics claim, that

> parents, not the state, should be primarily responsible for deciding what is best for their children. Parents are in the best position to know what values they wish to impart to their children; they have more information about their own children and their individual needs; and they are economically and legally responsible for their children. This responsibility includes the right to control to a substantial degree what their children watch on television, buy, read, and eat.[39]

Regardless of whether the FTC regulates television, parents may control what their children watch among the available options. At issue between critics and defenders of the government's right to regulate is not only who should determine those options, but how parental control is best exercised.

Let's begin with the "how." If governmental regulation is illegitimate (or unjust) because it undermines parental control over the options available to children, then unregulated commercial broadcasting must be more legitimate (or just) because it provides parents with more control over the options. But does it? It is surprisingly hard to answer this question. One might argue that unregulated broadcasting provides par-

[38] Ibid.
[39] Ibid.

ents with more control because commercial broadcasters can present a greater range of viewing options. One might, on the other hand, come to a quite different conclusion, that authorizing public regulation adds to the parental options of choosing among channels or turning the television off that of voicing criticisms of existing programs through a public agency.[40] There is no sensible way to compare the options made available by these alternatives without taking into account their value.

The second alternative offers an option of considerable democratic value: authorizing an agency to regulate encourages parents (along with other citizens) to formulate and voice their criticisms. This is one among several significant but ordinary ways in which politics is educative. Of course, parents could voice their criticisms outside of authorized channels. If they did, however, commercial broadcasters would probably not hear them or pay attention to what they heard.[41] Commercial broadcasters want to know—and are best equipped to find out—not how much parents approve of their programs and commercials, but how many viewers are watching (and paying attention to) them.

Making television a more purely competitive market would not solve this problem. Because children constitute only a minority of the audience for all but Saturday morning programming, the content of most programming would still not primarily reflect the preferences of parents for their children. Because television is far from a pure competitive market, parents exercise little market control over even Saturday morning programming. As consumers, they are just as captive as their children to the choices that commercial networks offer them. Only as citizens are they less captive.

By their own premises, the critics should accept the legitimacy of government regulation because it gives parents a greater chance to influence the options available to their children. But parental concerns are not all that should count when public agencies decide whether and how to regulate television. Why presume that only parents are competent to decide what is good for children, or that only parents have a legitimate concern in shaping democratic culture? Competence and con-

[40] The limited evidence that we have suggests that a large majority of parents are critical of commercials on children's television, and would like to have them regulated. The evidence also suggests that a majority would rather put up with the commercials than not have the programs broadcast altogether. Most parents, quite reasonably given these preferences, allow their children to watch commercially sponsored programs despite their preference for fewer or fairer commercials. See the results of survey research reported in Richard P. Adler and Ronald J. Faber, *The Effects of Television Advertising on Children*, pp. 196-201.

[41] Ibid.

cern over democratic culture is as widely distributed as competence and concern over democratic education (neither is equally distributed). Public agencies like the FTC and FCC must reflect upon public and not just parental opinion in deciding whether and how to regulate television programming for children.

Although public opinion surely should be considered, it is not all that should be considered. The FTC and FCC are trustees of the public interest, not just agents of public opinion. One reason to require the FCC and FTC to hold public hearings is to bring public opinion to bear on their deliberations. But as public trustees, members of the FTC and FCC are responsible for using their own best judgment—suitably informed by public debates and deliberations—in deciding whether to regulate television content. To accuse the FTC of having "committed itself to a particular point of view" and of being prepared to "impose that view on the American public" (by regulating commercial broadcasters) is to criticize it for doing its job. If the FTC should be criticized, it is not for trying to impose a particular point of view, but for trying to impose a mistaken—or a repressive—point of view.

If they are democratically authorized and accountable, regulatory agencies, like school boards, have a right to be wrong, but not a right to be repressive. The legitimacy of a regulatory agency per se depends on whether it is suitably authorized and accountable. One might criticize the FTC and FCC on grounds that they are overly insulated from democratic accountability. Opposition, then, ought to be aimed not selectively at regulation rather than deregulation of television, but at the authority of the agencies. The legitimacy of a particular regulation, on the other hand, depends on whether the regulation is repressive, or supports repression. Does a regulation restrict rational consideration of reasonable (not correct or uncontroversial) conceptions of the good life?[42] Would the absence of a regulation support repression by placing too much power over popular culture in a few commercial hands? Rather than dissolving disagreement over regulation, these standards of legitimacy allow us to judge when the results of the deliberations of regulatory agencies should and should not be binding on citizens.

[42] Is this standard too permissive with regard to regulation? One might argue that regulation of speech is repressive if it restricts rational consideration of *any* conceptions of the good life, however reasonable or unreasonable they may be. This more liberal standard would rule out regulation of hard-core (sexist) pornography on television, for example, even if the vast majority of citizens were deeply offended and favored banning such programs. One can appreciate the fear of creeping censorship underlying the more liberal standard and still argue that a democratic government should have the authority to provide less protection to "unreasonable" than to "reasonable" speech in situations where it is not likely to become a creeping censor.

New Technology

What is the cultural significance for children of new television technologies? The multi-channel capacity of cable television already gives most middle-class parents a larger menu of choices for their children and themselves than broadcast television alone offers. Whether the additional choices offered by cable television substantially enhance democratic culture depends on what the choices are. What the choices are depends partly on how cable television is financed. Financing cable television by viewers' subscriptions rather than by advertising creates an economic incentive to diversify programming by channels that appeal to relatively small audiences with similar cultural tastes. Such cable systems—designed with the incentive for what has been called "narrowcasting"—offer educational and commercial-free entertainment channels for children as well as channels designed primarily for adults, specializing in movies, sports, music, politics, and pornography. The specific cable culture to which children are exposed depends on the access provided by their parents.

Although the spread of cable stations signals the end of the peculiar scarcity of television channels, it does not mark the end of the "uniquely pervasive"[43] and influential presence of network television in the lives of most children and adults. If it did, then the advent of cable might require the end of governmental regulation of all television programming. Some critics of regulation argue that the communications revolution requires just that. They support their argument by comparing television with newspapers and by noting how heavily the courts have in the past relied on the fact of scarcity to uphold governmental constraints on program content.[44] Were competing television channels like competing newspapers, the spread of cable should mark the end of justified governmental regulation. But television, as I have already suggested, is a much more powerful and less optional cultural presence than newspapers in the lives of most Americans—and especially in the lives of children. Not the peculiar scarcity of spectrum but the peculiar power of network owners morally grounds governmental regulation of

[43] The source of the expression is Justice Stevens, who referred to radio broadcasting as a "uniquely pervasive presence" in *FCC v. Pacifica Foundation*, 438 US 726 (1978).

[44] Ithiel de Sola Pool goes one step further and argues that the scarcity of television broadcasting was always a political creation rather than a fact of nature, and that governmental regulation of program content has never been justified. See *Technologies of Freedom* (Cambridge, Mass.: Harvard University Press, 1983), pp. 108-150. But Pool also recognizes that cable makes the scarcity argument even less plausible. For an informative discussion of political developments in the recent cable revolution, see pp. 151-88.

television. The power to shape popular culture should not rest primarily in private hands.

But neither should the public power rest in the hands of only one or two federal agencies. Cable has the potential for greater decentralization of public control over television programming by allowing local communities to choose among cable companies and to set the terms for their local franchise. Whether cable can simultaneously realize its potential for diversity and decentralization will probably depend, however, on whether and how it is regulated at the federal level. If the FCC continues to move in the direction of deregulation—allowing cable operators to introduce advertising to their programming and not to support any channels for public access (by local community groups, for example)—then the local competition among cable companies may begin to look more and more like the national competition among broadcast networks. Instead of offering a series of cultural alternatives, cable technology may add only more variations on the already overly dominant theme of commercial culture. Realizing the democratic values of diversity and decentralization, therefore, requires a degree of federal control.

To take the analogy between television and schooling one step further, we might compare the cultural role of cable television to the educational role of private schools. Cable provides the alternative of exit for parents who find network broadcasting objectionable. The alternative is costly, and it serves to supplement rather than to supplant more popular culture. For some of the same reasons that we should try to improve our public school system rather than privatize it, we should press for more and better public control rather than for an unregulated cable system that might make broadcasting obsolete. Unregulated narrowcasting would force children to fall back even more on the cultural preferences of their parents. There are many reasons to criticize the popular culture that commercial broadcasting has created, but rather than move in the direction of a more private and less regulated market in narrowcasting, we should support more and better public control over broadcasting. We cannot just pay, we must also work collectively, for a common democratic culture for children.

One justification of our collective work is paternalistic. We may decide democratically to restrict the freedom of children to watch obscene, violent, or commercial-filled programs. Justice does not require but it permits such paternalism toward children. To restrict the freedom of children for their own good by regulating television, however, also entails restricting the freedom of parents who would not themselves choose to have their freedom or their children's freedom so restricted. So it may seem that to be paternalistic toward children, governmental regulations must also be paternalistic toward at least some parents. Yet it is by no means clear that justice permits paternalism toward parents. So the question of paternalism with regard to parents returns, although it is now more specific: Can paternalism toward those parents who oppose democratically authorized regulations be justified?

The answer depends not on deciding whether paternalism towards adults is justified but rather on clearing up a confusion concerning what counts as paternalism. The rationale for restricting the freedom of parents who oppose regulation is not that their good is thereby furthered, but that the good of their children, or of children more generally, is. Regulation of television therefore need be no more paternalistic toward dissenting parents than it is toward those who support the regulations. Regulation will, of course, place greater restrictions on the freedom of dissenting parents who (let us assume) would rather be able to watch more violent, sexist, obscene, and commercial messages. The justification for restricting their freedom, however, is by no means paternalistic—it is not that their good is thereby furthered. Rather, it is that the good of children is thereby furthered, without violating any of their rights.

A critic might argue: "Aren't you assuming that the good of parents can be separated from the good of their children? If it cannot be, then any regulation that restricts the good of parents for the good of their children is paternalistic not just towards children but also towards those parents who oppose the regulation." We can offer two replies to the critic. The first is that the good of parents can be separated to a significant extent from the good of their children. The theoretical justification for this separation can be found in the argument against the state of families. A state that does not recognize any separation cannot consistently educate or, more generally, regard children as future citizens. Even parents who oppose regulation tend to acknowledge the separation when they argue, for example, that restricting violence on primetime television hurts them (by intruding upon their cultural freedom) more than it helps their children (by predisposing them to nonviolence).

The second reply to the critic is that however closely the interests of parents and children are bound, democratically authorized regulation may still be justified as the least restrictive means by which the majority of parents can act in the best interests of their children. It is not morally better to restrict the freedom of the majority by refusing to regulate than to regulate and thereby restrict the freedom of the minority. An argument in favor of paternalism toward children, not toward parents or adults more generally, carries the burden of justifying regulation of television. Determining whether it can successfully carry that burden against opposition to particular (nonrepressive) policies should be a matter of democratic deliberation. The expanded range of options offered to adults by new cable and video technologies makes the case for paternalism towards children easier to justify against the competing consideration of maintaining cultural freedom for dissenting adults. But the case still needs to be made—convincingly—in a democratic forum.

CHAPTER NINE

EDUCATING ADULTS

Democratic education continues after school not only for children but for adults who learn from books, plays, concerts, museums, newspapers, radio, and even television. "What one knows is, in youth, of little moment; they know enough who know how to learn."[1] But many adults in our society, less fortunate than Henry Adams, do not learn enough in school to continue their education without the aid of more formal instruction. A substantial minority of American citizens are functionally illiterate. They need a second chance at schooling. Many adults who are literate want to further their formal education. Yet the responsibilities of most adults prevent them from going back to school as full-time students. If literate or illiterate adults are to be given a second chance at formal education, it will have to be significantly different from the first.

Adult education therefore poses three very different questions for democratic governments. What should the role of government be in supporting (1) cultural opportunities for adults, (2) higher education for adults who want it, and (3) primary education for adults who need it? I begin with the question of public support for culture and end with the problem of adult illiteracy, which takes us back again to basics.

ADULTS AND DEMOCRATIC CULTURE

Democratic societies can consciously reproduce themselves by providing cultural opportunities for adults as well as children, but many liberal theorists claim that the production and distribution of culture for adults must be left to private, not public authorities. The claim has been rigorously defended most recently by John Rawls. "There is no more justification for using the state apparatus to compel some citizens to pay for unwanted benefits that others desire," Rawls argues, "than there is to force them to reimburse others for their private expenses." If cultural institutions are not necessary for "promoting directly or indirectly the social conditions that secure the equal liberties" or for "advancing in an appropriate way the long-term interests of the least ad-

---

[1] Henry Adams, *The Education of Henry Adams* [1918] (New York: Modern Library, 1931), p. 314.

vantaged," then taxation to support them is unjust, unless it happens to be unanimously approved.[2]

Although the amount of government money that goes to the arts in the United States is small compared to almost any other subsidized sector, the support may not in principle be benign. If Rawls is right, governmental support of culture is unjust because national monuments, paintings, sculpture, museums, opera, theater, public television, and so on are certainly not primary goods. The preferences that cultural goods satisfy are not neutral among conceptions of the good life, nor is their satisfaction necessary to secure equal liberty or to advance the interests of the least advantaged. To tax some citizens to support cultural goods that they neither appreciate nor approve, even if a majority of citizens or their representatives approve of those goods, therefore constitutes an injustice.[3]

This criticism of state support of culture, shared by a wide variety of liberal theorists, is further fueled by Rousseau's view of the relation between democratic politics and the arts. A democratic state, according to Rousseau, should support culture, but only culture whose effect is to create more virtuous men and citizens, since "every useless amusement is an evil for a being whose life is so short and whose time is so precious. . . . A father, a son, a husband, and a citizen have such cherished duties to fulfill that they are left nothing to give to boredom."[4] Most modern forms of culture, the theater being Rousseau's prime example, are worse than useless. They are pernicious because they distract citizens from their duties and ultimately corrupt them into denying their duties altogether. Fearing that an argument from civic virtue would fall on already deafened ears, Rousseau offered another reason (based on "considerations of self-interest and money") against state support of theater. The theater taxes the poor to pay for the entertainment of the rich: "In this way, he who has little pays much, and he who has much pays little; I do not see what great justice can be found in that."[5]

Liberal theorists see an even greater injustice in Rousseau's suggestion of state censorship of all forms of culture except those that create good citizens. Rousseau's family state substitutes the evil of repression

---

[2] Rawls, *A Theory of Justice*, p. 332.

[3] A related objection to subsidized culture, posed but not endorsed by William J. Baumol and William G. Bowen, "is simply that those who want to see [the performing arts] ought to pay the price." *Performing Arts—The Economic Dilemma* (New York: The Twentieth Century Fund, 1966), p. 376.

[4] "J.-J. Rousseau, Citizen of Geneva to Monsieur D'Alembert," in Jean Jacques Rousseau, *Politics and the Arts*, trans. Allan Bloom (Ithaca, N.Y.: Cornell University Press, 1973), p. 16.

[5] Ibid., p. 114.

for that of regressive redistribution. The shared commitment to non-repression commits modern democrats as well as liberals to recommending Rawls over Rousseau.

Democratic Perfectionism

But these are not our only alternatives. Rawls's critique of government subsidy of culture is not decisive, even when it is directed to high culture. Before criticizing Rawls's critique, however, we should account for its philosophical force. The critique seems most forceful when directed against the traditional philosophical way of defending public support for high culture, on grounds of its "intrinsic value."[6] Cultural institutions, on this perfectionist view, are valuable not for what they may incidentally contribute to society—better democratic character, more pleasure among citizens, greater national prosperity or prestige—but for what they are: "difficult, rare, creative achievements that realize the highest human possibilities."[7]

The problem with perfectionism, as Rawls suggests, is that it provides an inadequate response to the criticism that governments should not force citizens to subsidize goods that do not contribute to their own or the public welfare. The claim that citizens must support art because it is intrinsically valuable not only is unlikely to persuade anyone not already convinced, it opens the door to more troubling claims. If the intrinsic value of great art is great enough, it may be invoked as a sufficient ground for restricting the liberty of some citizens to pursue lower forms of culture. It is, as Rawls suggests, both easy and dangerous to fall back on notions of excellence and intrinsic value when appeals to justice fail.[8] No further argument need be given; the claim of the cultured need only be that the uncultured lack the experience, education, imaginative capacity, or intellect to appreciate the intrinsic value of art.[9]

It is neither easy nor dangerous, however, to appeal to the public to support high culture on grounds of its intrinsic value. *Democratic* perfectionism sanctions state subsidy of culture only if it is publicly ap-

---

[6] Cf. Baumol and Bowen, *Performing Arts—the Economic Dilemma*, pp. 370-71, 376-86.

[7] Thomas Nagel, "Symposium on the Public Benefits of the Arts and Humanities," *Art and the Law*, vol. 9, no. 2 (1985): 237.

[8] Rawls, *A Theory of Justice*, p. 331.

[9] All of which may be true, but the point remains that the claim can too easily justify repression if the cultured need not convince the uncultured by further argument of why the art in question warrants public support. For further argument, see the comment by Thomas Nagel in "Symposium on the Public Benefits of the Arts and Humanities," pp. 236-39.

proved, and then only if it satisfies the standards of nonrepression and nondiscrimination. Rousseau realized how hard it would be for public officials "to assemble our citizens and townsmen in general council . . . solemnly to propose that a tax be accorded for the establishment of the theatre," but he incorrectly connected the difficulty of convincing citizens to the danger of the proposal.[10] The difficulty mitigates the danger in a democracy. If public officials must convince their constituents of the merits of cultural subsidies, they cannot claim that their constituents are incapable of appreciating the art that they are being asked to approve. Nor need public officials resort to defending governmental subsidy on tenuous consequentialist grounds—that art alleviates social unrest, relieves the isolation of the elderly, rehabilitates prisoners and mental patients,[11] or makes people happy.[12] Democratic politicians are better advised to "wax eloquent about these treasures of human culture"[13] in the hopes of convincing their constituents that they too value the greatest artistic achievements of civilization sufficiently to want their government to support them. There is, as Thomas Scanlon points out, "nothing objectionable about an argument among equal citizens about what is to be recognized as good."[14] One might add that from a democratic perspective, there is something intrinsically valuable about such public argument.

The democratic case for subsidizing art goes beyond the traditional philosophical understanding of perfectionism in yet another way. Art often helps make a society worthy of the collective pride of citizens. Were its citizens to support the theater, argued the article from d'Alembert's *Encyclopedie* that prompted Rousseau's critical letter, "Geneva would join to the prudence of Lacedaemon the urbanity of Athens. . . . This city, which many Frenchmen consider dull because they are deprived of the theatre, would then become the seat of decent pleasures,

---

[10] Rousseau, "Letter to D'Alembert," pp. 97-98.

[11] For a suitably skeptical critique of these consequentialist claims for governmental support of the arts, see Edward Banfield, *The Democratic Muse: The Visual Arts and the Public Interest* (New York: Basic Books, 1984), pp. 198-202.

[12] Cf. Mark Sagoff, "On the Aesthetic and Economic Value of Art," *The British Journal of Aesthetics*, vol. 21, no. 4 (Autumn 1981): 318-19: "Why should we think . . . that the value of art consists in the pleasure it may produce? It seems to me that any sound cost-benefit study will reveal, moreover, that the pleasures of art are small when compared with those, say, of the gambling den or the massage parlour. (Evolution, after all, has used pleasure to promote procreation, not painting.) The pleasures of art, in sheer firepower, are of very low wattage, in relation to their costs."

[13] Thomas Nagel, "Symposium on the Public Benefits of the Arts and Humanities," p. 237.

[14] Scanlon, "Symposium on the Public Benefits of the Arts and Humanities," p. 170.

just as it is now the seat of philosophy and liberty."[15] Becoming the seat of decent pleasures, or of high culture, is not essential to the creation of a just society, any more than enjoying decent pleasures is essential to becoming a just person. But like individuals, societies that enjoy decent pleasures and appreciate high culture may be more desirable than those that do not.

The collective pride that can be taken from the highest human accomplishments is neither illusory nor inaccessible to ordinary citizens. Most Americans can take pride in the impressive architecture of the National Gallery in Washington and the fact that it is open to anyone who wishes to appreciate its art. Democratic perfectionism adds another intrinsic value to that of artistic excellence: collective identification with high culture. This value must be democratically appreciated and supported to justify public subsidies of culture. It is therefore appropriate for public officials to invoke the value of high culture and collective identification with that culture in making a democratic case for governmental subsidy of art. A necessary (but not sufficient) condition of justifying public support for high culture is that it be democratically approved, but it need not be approved for instrumental reasons.

The Rawlsian challenge to democratic perfectionism might be reformulated as follows: If individual citizens value theaters, opera houses, or art museums, they should support them with their own income or pool their income with others who share their preferences. Even if a well-constituted legislative majority shares their values, it does not have a right to use the coercive apparatus of the state to force citizens who do not share these values to support the arts. Recall Rawls's general formulation of the argument: "There is no more justification for using the state apparatus to compel some citizens to pay for unwanted benefits that others desire than there is to force them to reimburse others for their private expenses."[16] Art institutions are not necessary for "promoting directly or indirectly the social conditions that secure the equal liberties" or for "advancing in an appropriate way the long-term interests of the least advantaged."[17] Therefore taxation to support the arts is unjust (unless it happens to be unanimously approved).[18] Providing culture for adults is different from providing education or

---

[15] Quoted in Rousseau's "Letter to d'Alembert," p. 4.

[16] Rawls, A Theory of Justice, p. 283.

[17] Ibid., p. 332.

[18] If any group of citizens unanimously agree to tax themselves to support the arts, they can use the coercive machinery of the state "to overcome the problems of isolation and assurance." It is essential, however, that "no one is taxed without his consent." Ibid., p. 331.

even culture for children. The latter is necessary for fair equality of opportunity; the former is not.[19]

Although fair equality of opportunity requires, according to Rawls, that similarly motivated citizens have "similar chances of education and *culture*,"[20] the considerable expense of unsubsidized art, such as the opera, does not constitute a reason for governmental subsidy. Instead, it adds further force to the Rawlsian argument for redistributing income. Nor can a plausible case be made that opera—or high culture generally—serves the long-term interests of the least advantaged. The interests of the least advantaged, according to Rawls, must be judged by those "primary goods" that people "generally want in order to achieve their ends whatever they are."[21] Governments cannot count opera or even art museums among those goods. Rawls is therefore consistent in concluding that "the social resources necessary to support associations dedicated to advancing the arts and sciences and culture generally are to be won as a fair return for services rendered, or from such voluntary contributions as citizens wish to make, all within a regime regulated by the two principles of justice."[22]

But is this conclusion convincing? Why *must* a society forego collectively supporting its cultural heritage for the sake of (very) marginal increases in the income of some—even the least advantaged—of its citizens or marginal shifts in governmental spending?[23] One answer is that increasing the income of the least advantaged is a more urgent goal than enriching public culture, even if a democratic legislature does not recognize it as such. There are two problems with this answer. First, we

[19] See also Banfield, *The Democratic Muse*, p. 9.
[20] Rawls, *A Theory of Justice*, p. 278. Emphasis added.
[21] Ibid., p. 328.
[22] Ibid., p. 329.
[23] The conjecture that a good deal of our cultural heritage would be destroyed without governmental subsidy is quite plausible given the available evidence. Reasonable people might disagree about how much artistic damage would be done to orchestras, opera, theaters, and museums were *direct* governmental aid ended. It is possible, although not very likely, that higher admissions prices and more private donations would make up the shortfall, but ending the enormously greater amount of indirect governmental subsidies would almost certainly spell disaster for many institutions of the fine arts. Because indirect subsidies (such as the charitable deduction) entail involuntary redistributions just as do direct subsidies, they are ruled out by Rawls's argument as well. (Direct subsidies allow a public institution to decide how to spend taxpayers' money. Indirect subsidies allow private patrons of the arts decide how to spend what is also, in significant part, taxpayers' money.) For a thorough discussion of indirect governmental subsidy of the arts and the likely changes that would ensue from marginal reforms in the structure of those subsidies, see Alan L. Feld, Michael O'Hare, and J. Mark Davidson Schuster, *Patrons Despite Themselves: Taxpayers and Arts Policy* (New York: New York University Press, 1983).

might question whether the urgency of increasing the income of the least advantaged actually competes with enriching public culture. The amount of money needed to support high culture is far too small to involve a significant trade-off with the welfare of the least advantaged.

The second and more serious problem with the Rawlsian critique of cultural subsidies is the implausibility of claiming that a society is unjust if it falls short of *maximizing* the income of the least advantaged. Maximizing income above and beyond basic needs would not be an essential principle of Rawlsian justice were it not for the veil of ignorance, which requires us to assess the interests of the least advantaged by those primary goods that enable (rational) people (whatever historical epoch, nationality, and so on) to pursue whatever ends they may have. Outside of the original position, this claim seems compelling when we focus our attention on the urgent interests of poor people, who lack adequate education, housing, medical care, and disposable income to live a decent life. When we think beyond urgent interests, however, to those human interests that are connected to living not just a decent life but a good life, the claim that justice demands *maximizing* the income of the least advantaged is implausible.

A democratic justification for subsidizing culture does not undercut the urgency of providing for the basic needs of citizens, but neither does the urgency of providing for basic needs undercut a democratic justification for subsidizing culture unless we make one of two assumptions, that (1) citizens have a right to their pre-tax income, or (2) the free market necessarily makes morally better use of money than the government. Rawls rightly rejects the first, libertarian claim in the name of a just distribution of primary goods. But Rawls seems to accept the second claim, thereby becoming a libertarian with regard to secondary goods. We should reject the second claim as well.

Most Americans spend more money on movies than on art museums, although many of us value the culture represented by art museums more. The market does not measure the value of all goods in the proportions that they matter, or are valuable to us. This may be especially true of those valuable things that do not give us pleasure in proportion to their value. We may value the presence of the Smithsonian museums in Washington, D.C. and the Statue of Liberty on Ellis Island very highly, but we might not support them sufficiently by market means because other things—such as good food and movies—generally offer us more pleasure at the moments we seek it. Governmental subsidy provides a means both of making up for the shortcomings of our market behavior and of preventing the private appropriation of cultural objects. It makes sense to say that cultural institutions should be publicly supported because they cannot withstand the test of the market, or because we do not want them to. Like all humanly designed tests, the market only partially measures what matters to us.

Democratic debate and deliberation are a different test, also a partial and imperfect one, of whether cultural institutions should be supported. Because democratic processes ideally complement rather than compete with the market, the standards of value employed within democratic deliberations need not and preferably should not be market standards. The conclusion that democratic governments have a tendency to spend too little on high culture is compatible with the fundamental claim of democratic perfectionism, that state subsidy of culture must be democratically authorized. The results of the democratic deliberations are politically but not morally authoritative, provided they are neither discriminatory nor repressive.

The proviso is important. Nondiscrimination and nonrepression place two major constraints on the legitimate exercise of democratic control over culture as over education. Applied to culture, nondiscrimination requires that democratic governments not exclude citizens from an effective opportunity to participate in shaping the cultural heritage of their society for reasons unrelated to their interest in culture. Nonrepression requires that democratic governments not interfere with the expressive freedom of artists or artistic institutions unless that freedom violates somebody else's basic freedoms. The constraints of cultural nondiscrimination and nonrepression have several significant implications for reorienting governmental policy towards the arts in the United States today.

Influence over Culture

Let's begin with the constraint of cultural nondiscrimination as it affects the distribution of influence over cultural policy. Some forms of governmental subsidy discriminate against poorer citizens more than others, for reasons unrelated to their interest in shaping cultural policy. Consider the charitable deduction, the largest source of subsidy for the arts, which is often applauded for diffusing control over governmental spending. As one defender of the deduction puts it: "One need not be an anarchist to applaud the modest opportunity that this gives the citizen to control the use of funds that will in any event be taken from him."[24]

One need only be a democrat, however, to criticize the charitable deduction for not giving many citizens even a modest opportunity to con-

[24] Boris I. Bittker, "Charitable Contributions: Tax Deductions or Matching Grants?" *Texas Law Review* 28 (1972): 61.

trol the use of public funds, not because they have lower cultural standards or less interest in culture, but because they have less income. By permitting the wealthiest citizens a much larger tax deduction for every dollar that they contribute to the arts, the government gives them a much greater opportunity to control how public tax money is distributed among cultural institutions.[25] A democratic government should aim to equalize the cultural influence of equally interested and able citizens, not to exaggerate the already greater capacity of the wealthy to influence culture.[26] Not all systems of indirect subsidy are equally bad in this regard: a tax credit for charitable contributions, for example, would be considerably less discriminatory.[27] Direct governmental subsidies may be even less discriminatory. The federally funded National Endowment for the Arts succeeds in diffusing control over culture by its policy of funding state arts organizations who then distribute NEA grants among those local projects and institutions that they consider most worthy of support.[28]

The corresponding problem with direct governmental subsidies from a democratic perspective is that the political processes that influence the policies of the NEA may discriminate against the poor just as effectively as does the charitable tax deduction. The poorest citizens, one suspects, have no greater opportunity to influence the NEA than they have to influence spending on the arts by contributing to the Metropolitan Opera. If true, this claim constitutes a critique not of using political processes to determine policy towards the arts but of tolerating degrees of economic (and, one might add, educational) deprivations that render some citizens unable to participate effectively in those processes. At least one important reason why providing income and education for the poor has higher priority than subsidizing culture is that until our society ends poverty and adequately educates citizens, the political processes by which it decides whether to subsidize culture cannot fully live up to their democratic potential.

[25] "[T]he higher the individual donor's taxable income the more of the tax expenditure he is allowed to allocate with each of his own dollars. Charity becomes the province of the wealthy, not only because of their personal tastes and their ability to donate, but also because of the extra tax benefits they are given by the indirect aid system." Feld et al., *Patrons Despite Themselves*, p. 216.

[26] Ibid., pp. 128 and 213-14. For the empirical analysis that supports this conclusion, see pp. 104-127.

[27] And better in other respects as well. For a persuasive case for the greater merit of tax credits over the present charitable deduction as a means of supporting the arts, see ibid., pp. 216-20.

[28] Ibid., p. 125. Cf. Banfield, *The Democratic Muse*, pp. 63-91.

Access to Culture

Nondiscrimination also speaks in favor of increasing access to culture. One should judge some cultural policies better than others on democratic grounds because they afford less wealthy citizens greater access to culture. The audience for art in the United States as in most Western democracies is disproportionately wealthy and well educated.[29] To ask any public arts policy to redress this imbalance would be not only impractical but undesirable. Consider what a cultural policy that took proportional representation as its primary aim would look like. Lincoln Center might sponsor rock concerts so as to attract an audience that was proportionately as poor and uneducated as the population of New York City. Whether or not it were successful, such a policy would entail forsaking the Center's cultural purpose.

In an economically more egalitarian society, the audiences for high culture might be more representative of the general population than they now are, at least with regard to income. But such audiences would probably still be disproportionately well educated. Since going to museums and concerts is one way in which adults continue their education after college, it should neither surprise nor disturb us that art audiences are composed primarily of adults who enjoyed a liberal education in the first place. The principle of nondiscrimination recommends greater access for citizens based on their cultural interest rather than proportional representation of income, ethnic, racial, or any other groups at cultural events. Although increasing access can be expected to make art audiences more representative than they now are, the two aims are separable in both theory and practice.

A democratic culture would be one in which citizens are not discouraged for irrelevant reasons either from influencing or from using cultural institutions. Poverty is the most common source of cultural discrimination, and the source least amenable to correction by cultural institutions. Lowering the already modest admissions prices to museums is unlikely to increase attendance by the poor. Lowering the substantially higher ticket prices of concerts, theater, and opera is more likely to increase middle-class attendance, an important but incomplete accomplishment.

Poverty, however, is not the only source of cultural discrimination that should concern us. Public policy should also encourage greater geographical diffusion of cultural experience. "How can people learn to enjoy the living arts, if no plays, no concert performers and no dancers

[29] Baumol and Bowen, *Performing Arts—The Economic Dilemma*, pp. 71-97.

are available to them?"[30] Viewing an opera on public television is not equivalent to attending a live performance, but it may be the most effective means of making excellent opera performances accessible to citizens regardless of where they live. Channeling federal and state funds to local theater and art groups may produce less excellent performances but more exciting experiences for people who otherwise could never attend a live professional performance.

Nondiscrimination also points in the direction of government support for the controversial practice of funding cultural extravaganzas, such as the King Tut exhibit by the Metropolitan Museum and the Picasso exhibit by the Museum of Modern Art, cultural events that seem to attract many people who know relatively little about art and might not otherwise visit a museum. Edward Banfield takes the federal government to task for funding blockbuster exhibits. By funding such exhibits, he argues, the government contributes to the failure of museums to fulfill their proper function—"to collect and display works of art and, beyond that, to make the experience of art more widely and intensely felt."[31] One might be inclined to suppose that by attracting more people to art museums, cultural extravaganzas contribute to making the experience of art more widely (even if not more intensely) felt, but Banfield's criticism is based on the view that public subsidy of the arts can be justified only if it contributes to "the special state of mind called aesthetic."[32]

Why should more widespread and intense experience of an aesthetic state of mind be all that is relevant to the defense of public support for the arts? Banfield's answer renders his argument against governmental support of art largely a matter of definition and of dubious empirical generalization:

> Art is what engenders in the maker or viewer the special state of mind called aesthetic [the definition]. Conceivably, some or even most arts-related activities serve the public interest and deserve public funding. However, because the purposes of these activities could be served as well or perhaps even better by means not involving art [the empirical generalization], public support for them ought to be justified on grounds other than the value of art.[33]

Public subsidy of art is therefore convicted of injustice and inefficiency almost as soon as the defense closes its case.

---

[30] Ibid., p. 379.
[31] Banfield, *The Democratic Muse*, p. 93. For Banfield's criticism of the NEA and NEH, see pp. 112-16.
[32] Banfield, *The Democratic Muse*, p. 16.
[33] Ibid.

If the public value of art need not necessarily lie in the aesthetic experience that it engenders, then blockbuster exhibits can be defended as supporting the valuable (and valued) experience of connecting citizens to a common, cultural heritage. Less artistic means might sometimes serve a similar purpose, but as long as Americans view art as an important part of their cultural heritage, then a public policy of subsidizing art is not unjust, or even unwise.[34] Public support has contributed to making the art of Tutankhamen, Michelangelo, da Vinci, and Picasso part of our common cultural heritage, rather than a heritage appropriated and appreciated only by the rich.

Cultural Freedom

The nonrepression principle helps refine one of the most common concerns about governmental support—that it not lead to governmental control of the content of art. Anybody who financially contributes to art institutions exercises some control simply by choosing what type of institution to fund. Governments are no different in this regard than private patrons, nor is there any apparent reason why they should be. On democratic grounds, it is preferable that more rather than fewer culturally interested citizens have the opportunity to influence the forms of art that are funded. Democratically accountable agencies at the federal, state, and local levels (such as the NEA, and state and local arts councils) distribute this opportunity more broadly than it would be without any public subsidy or with only indirect subsidies such as the charitable tax deduction. Government subsidies such as these are in themselves benign, although they may lead to repressive forms of control, which violate artistic or cultural freedom.

Like academic freedom, artistic freedom has an institutional and an individual component—it encompasses both the freedom of artists to

[34] This argument satisfies the main requirement that Banfield places on a justification for government support of art—that it rests "on the inherent rather than the incidental values associated with it." (Ibid., p. 204.) But it diverges from Banfield's insofar as it considers a certain kind of cultural experience to be one of the inherent values of art. Art is valuable not just for the aesthetic experience it affords us but also because it is part of our collective cultural heritage. This value helps explain many of our attitudes towards art that otherwise seem irrational, for example, the incomparably higher value that ordinary people along with professional artists and art critics place on viewing the real *Pieta* or *Guernica* rather than on viewing an excellent forgery or reproduction. For a more thorough explanation along these lines of why the real thing radically differs in its aesthetic value from a forgery, see Mark Sagoff, "The Aesthetic Status of Forgeries," in Denis Dutton, ed., *The Forger's Art: Forgery and the Philosophy of Art* (Berkeley: University of California Press, 1983), pp. 131-52; and Mark Sagoff, "On Restoring and Reproducing Art," *The Journal of Philosophy*, vol. 75, no. 9 (September 1978): 453-70.

follow the canons of artistic creativity wherever they lead without fear of social sanction, and the freedom of art institutions to create an environment conducive to artistic freedom. Given the substantial governmental subsidies of art institutions in the United States and Europe over the last century, democratic governments certainly have had ample opportunity to interfere with artistic freedom.[35] Yet they have done so very rarely. The few occasions are so conspicuous partly because they were subject, almost immediately, to critical public scrutiny.[36] Private patrons seem to have interfered with artistic freedom much more frequently, and their interference has been easier to shield from immediate public scrutiny and therefore from effective criticism.[37]

A well-designed governmental policy towards the arts can minimize the chances of cultural repression in several ways. By increasing its own direct subsidies without increasing control over the arts, a democratic government can decrease the dependence of art institutions on private patrons. The less a museum or an opera house must depend on a few wealthy patrons for its financial well-being, the less pressure it will feel to accept aid tied to demands that violate its own artistic standards. Of course, as long as there are relatively few wealthy citizens willing to donate millions to the arts, substantial pressure on art institutions to accept improperly tied aid will remain. Increasing direct public aid to the arts is therefore unlikely to be sufficient to avoid repressive practices. Legislatures can also expose private patronage to closer public scrutiny by placing greater disclosure requirements on tax-deductible donations. This is a doubly desirable policy from a democratic perspective because (1) "the public deserves a clear picture of what is done with money that otherwise would be collected as taxes,"[38] and (2) a clear public picture would pressure private patrons to live up to the principle

---

[35] For an excellent comparative account of governmental support of culture, see Milton C. Cummings, Jr., and Richard S. Katz, eds., *Government and the Arts in the Modern World* (New York: Oxford University Press, 1987). See esp. Kevin V. Mulcahy, "Government and the Arts in the United States," and Milton C. Cummings, Jr. and Richard S. Katz, "Government and the Arts in the Modern World: Trends and Prospects."

[36] For an example of the effectiveness of publicity on preventing government censorship, see Dick Netzer, *The Subsidized Muse: Public Support for Arts in the United States* (Cambridge: Cambridge University Press, 1978), pp. 36-37.

[37] See Feld et al., *Patrons Despite Themselves*, pp. 163-78; and Baumol and Bowen, *Performing Arts—the Economic Dilemma*, p. 375. For evidence concerning the British experience, where direct governmental subsidy is much greater, see John S. Harris, *Government Patronage of the Arts in Great Britain* (Chicago: University of Chicago Press, 1970).

[38] Feld et al., *Patrons Despite Themselves*, p. 215. For ways in which information concerning private donations could be made more accessible to the public, see ibid., pp. 215-16.

of nonrepression.[39] In most cases, the credible threat of adverse publicity is sufficient to prevent private repression. The historical record of democratic support for the arts should also help allay the most common fear that governmental subsidy entails governmental control.[40]

There is a less common concern about economic repression that history cannot allay because the concern rests almost exclusively on a moral conviction. The conviction is that *all* governmental subsidies are repressive because they tax citizens against their will. In so doing, the government takes money away from citizens and spends it on somebody else's preferences. If one accepts the moral standards of this argument, one does not need to look at the consequences of such a policy to realize that it is repressive.

Political philosophers today are accustomed to contrasting this libertarian argument with Rawls's theory of justice. Yet with regard to cultural and other "secondary" goods, Rawlsian justice and libertarianism converge. The arguments in favor of democratic perfectionism and against the Rawlsian critique of cultural subsidies therefore hold with equal force against libertarianism. Although these arguments need not be rehearsed, it may be worth putting the libertarian argument as it applies to governmental support of art in empirical perspective to show how far-fetched it is to call taxation in support of the arts repressive. In 1973, the last year for which complete data on governmental support for the arts in the United States are available, "indirect government aid totaled about $460 million, drawn primarily from federal income tax deductions and property tax exemptions. In contrast, direct aid from government and private sources in 1973 totaled approximately $200 million."[41] The best evidence suggests that the distribution of the burden of this aid for the arts was mildly more progressive than the regular income tax.[42] For the sake of simplicity, let's assume that the burden was spread evenly across all, approximately 100 million, American taxpayers (this increases the burden on our argument). Let's assume furthermore that the contribution from private sources was a relatively small percentage of the $200 million direct aid from public and private sources combined. This would mean that every taxpayer in 1973 who

[39] Better disclosure requirements would also make it more difficult for private contributors to use the indirect subsidy system to defraud the government by overpricing their donations and entering into illegal deals with art institutions, practices that are now almost impossible to uncover unless the Internal Revenue Service decides to conduct an audit. For some of the unethical practices made easy by our present indirect subsidy system, see ibid., pp. 169-77.

[40] See Netzer, *The Subsidized Muse.*

[41] Feld et al., *Patrons Despite Themselves*, p. 212.

[42] Ibid., pp. 90-93, 102-103.

did not support the government's policy of direct *or* indirect aid to the arts was forced to donate $7.00 to support the arts, a sum that could buy two movie tickets.

Taken by itself, this evidence surely would not prove that taxation for the arts is nonrepressive. But we have already offered reasons for not judging cultural subsidies unjust, reasons rooted in the democratic value of distributing the opportunity to participate in the development and enjoyment of a common culture. If we judge a culture more or less free to the degree that it is nondiscriminatory and nonrepressive, then we can conclude that cultural freedom is compatible with public subsidy.

Although a free democratic culture need not be a high culture (one that is marked by the exercise and appreciation of artistic excellence), democratic principles do not stand in the way of the pursuit of high culture. The principle of nondiscrimination does not warrant watering down culture to please more people. Its aim instead is to make high culture accessible to everyone who has the interest and ability to appreciate it. The principle of nonrepression prevents governments from interfering with artistic as it does with academic freedom. It also guides governments in creating an environment that discourages private patrons from exercising improper control over art institutions.

The less common concern may be more warranted: that a high culture will deteriorate in democratic societies unless governments take a substantial interest in supporting expensive forms of art and making them part of a common culture. Although the creation of a more democratic culture is certainly not a sufficient condition for maintaining an artistically high culture, it may be a necessary one in our society. A democratic government cannot supply the sufficient conditions for a high culture, but it may legitimately support some of the necessary ones, if its citizens so choose.

ADULTS AND HIGHER EDUCATION

Many adults want to continue their formal education. These adults are often high-school graduates who either did not go to college or who went to college but did not graduate. The problem is not necessarily that they were poorly educated, but that they were not fully educated according to their present standards. They would like to have a second chance at higher education, but financial and familial responsibilities often stand in the way of their enrolling in a regular college degree program. Should democratic governments support special degree programs for such citizens?

This question raises no special moral problem for a theory of democratic education. Why should adults not be given a second chance to further their formal education? The idea that giving adults a second chance will decrease the motivation of younger people to take full advantage of their first chance is intuitively implausible and without any empirical foundation. Democratic governments should have the discretion to decide whether to support programs of adult education just as they should have the discretion to decide whether to support colleges and universities. The primary obstacle in the way of more adequate support for adult education—other than the democratic will to allocate more money to education—is practical. How can governments support a college-level program of adult education in a way that makes it accessible to those women and men who have to support and care for a family?

The Open University in England provides a promising model of how higher education can be made more accessible to adults without lowering the academic standards of higher education. The Open University supplements extensive correspondence materials and textbooks with weekly television and radio programs and other audio-visual aids, all specially designed by a course team that includes full-time professors as well as specialists in teaching methods and media production. A high-quality college education is thereby made accessible to adults who are employed full-time and are constrained to study mainly at home. Students are also encouraged to meet with tutors and counselors to discuss their work (and also join other students in listening to the television and radio programs) in local study centers. A one-week summer school is the only requirement that takes students away from their work or family, but exemption from this requirement is available on the recommendation of a student's counselor.[43]

The sole admissions requirement to the Open University is age. Adults are admitted on a first-come, first-served basis. (Places are limited by the level of governmental support for the Open University.) Despite the absence of academic requirements for admissions, about 75 percent of those who register for a course succeed in getting credit for it.[44] Almost 60 percent of the hundreds of thousands who enrolled in the Open University during its first ten years (1971-81) graduated, 10

[43] For a more detailed description of how the Open University operates, see John Scupham, "The Open University of the United Kingdom," in Norman MacKenzie, Richmond Postgate, and John Scupham, *Open Learning: Systems and Problems in Post-Secondary Education* (Paris: The UNESCO Press, 1975), pp. 321-64.

[44] N. E. McIntosh and A. Woodley, "The Open University and Second-Chance Education—An Analysis of the Social and Educational Background of Open University Students," in *Paedagogica Europaea: Review of Education in Europe*, vol. 9, no. 2 (1974): "Contemporary Education," pp. 85-86.

percent more than the graduation rate from colleges in the United States.[45] The high success rates are most likely attributable not to lower academic standards but to the greater motivation of Open University students and the extensive support for learning that the Open University provides.[46]

Although it may not be possible to transplant the Open University in all its particulars to American soil, its general structure can teach us several important lessons about the practical requirements of a successful program of adult higher education. First, to provide a second chance to adults with full-time work and family commitments, a program must be more accommodating of those commitments than most degree programs offered by on-campus colleges. Programs that provide more flexibility in choice of time and place of study are more accessible to most adults. Such flexibility does not entail the lowering of academic standards.[47] Secondly, a program that holds out the promise of attracting many more adults to higher education is bound to be expensive to develop. Estimates of the cost of developing each Open University course run higher than a quarter of a million dollars. Although the Open University has turned out to be an efficient way of providing higher education (as a result of its extremely high enrollments and academic success rates), the primary impetus behind establishing such a program must be a commitment not to efficiency but to providing a high quality of higher education to many more adults than now have access to normal college degree programs.[48]

The third and most distinctively democratic lesson to be learned from the Open University is that a program of adult education need not have admissions requirements to maintain high academic standards. The combination of high initial costs and great economies of scale has an important democratic advantage: the Open University can do with-

[45] Fred M. Hechinger, "Will Televised Instruction See Better Days?" *The New York Times,* July 27, 1982.

[46] Cf. the mixed reviews of the televised course instruction by Marghanita Laski, Raymond Williams, and Philip Elliott, *The Listener,* vol. 85, no. 2197 (May 6, 1971): 569-71, 594-96. Reading the criticisms of the social science and humanities courses in these reviews might make one wonder how courses at "closed universities" would fare were they open to similar public scrutiny.

[47] Although this flexibility does make intellectual exchange between students and professors more difficult than it would be in a face-to-face setting. The Open University has been criticized for its hierarchical mode of transmitting knowledge. But even critics appreciate its substantial accomplishments in educating adults who otherwise would not have a second chance. See Rustin, "The Idea of a Popular University: A Historical Perspective," pp. 47-49.

[48] Fred A. Nelson, "The Open University in the United States," *College Board Review,* no. 85 (Fall 1972): 13.

out admissions requirements without lowering its academic standards or discriminating against many adults for economic reasons. The Open University still must exclude some adults to stay within its budget, but the low attrition rate among its enrolled students suggests that a first-come, first-served basis for admissions may be no worse—perhaps even better—than establishing and administering formal academic requirements. Although an equally successful program of adult education in the United States would probably have to be different,[49] the success of the Open University in England suggests that technically and administratively innovative programs might succeed in extending a second chance at higher education considerably further than our more traditional on-campus programs of adult education now do.

ILLITERACY: BACK AGAIN TO BASICS

How to succeed in providing a second chance at primary education for adults who are functionally illiterate presents a harder and more urgent problem. The U.S. census gives credence to the view that "our Nation has a literate population."[50] It reports the proportion of illiterates in 1900 as ten percent; by 1969, the proportion decreases to only one percent.[51] But once we discover that more than 15 percent of the population over age 16 (more than 23 million adult Americans) is not sufficiently literate to read and understand a newspaper, it becomes apparent that the Census's definition of illiteracy—the inability to read and write in any language—is not a meaningful measure of democratic aspirations.[52]

The Practical Problem

The way to overcome adult illiteracy is not apparent. Try to imagine what kind of program would fulfill the aims of the 1966 Adult Educa-

[49] The National University Consortium based at the University of Maryland is much more decentralized and dependent on the faculty and teaching facilities of existing universities than the Open University. Yet it comes closer than any other program of adult education in the United States to fulfilling some of the same purposes. The Consortium pays the Open University royalties to use some of its study materials and television programs.

[50] Roger W. Heyns, "Education and Society: A Complex Interaction," *American Education*, vol. 20, no. 4 (May 1984): 4.

[51] Ibid., p. 4.

[52] Twenty-three million is a conservative estimate. Estimates of functional illiteracy among adults range as high as 65 million, or over 40 percent of adults over the age of 16. For a discussion of the evidence on functional illiteracy and the dispute over measures, see Carmen St. John Hunter with David Harman, *Adult Illiteracy in the United States: A Report to the Ford Foundation* (New York: McGraw-Hill, 1979), pp. 23-56.

tion Act to "enable all adults to continue their education to at least the level of completion of secondary school and make available to them the means to secure training that will enable them to become more employable, productive, and responsible citizens."[53] Over 57 million adults (38 percent of the population over 16) had less than a high-school education and were not enrolled in school in 1976.[54] Even if a substantial proportion—say, half—of these adults were not functionally illiterate, that would leave over 28 million adults for programs of adult education to accommodate.

The practical problem goes beyond large numbers. Literacy programs are aimed at people who are disproportionately poor and unemployed. For people who are "eking out a living at an unstable succession of menial and arduous jobs, . . . going back to school seems an endless uphill struggle. Just learning the three R's means years of weary plugging, night after night, month after month. And then what? What will an eighth-grade education get you? Into the ninth grade is about all."[55] Not surprisingly, poor attendance and high drop-out rates plague most literacy programs. The largest literacy program in the United States—Adult Basic Education (ABE)—is really a group of local programs, jointly financed by federal, state, and local governments, decentrally operated, and often cosponsored by companies, unions, churches, poverty organizations, housing developments, and self-help groups.[56] Although these programs have expanded substantially since ABE began, their total enrollment in 1976 is estimated at 1.7 million, a small proportion of the target population.[57]

Many of the most successful literacy programs are those with captive students. Prisoners, as one study points out, are "particularly promising students." Prisons have "relatively few recruiting problems." Their population "is less affected by family and work demands, and attends more consistently"[58] than other ABE students. Although inductees into the Armed Services are not quite so captive an audience, they also are promising students for some of the same reasons. A follow-up study of

[53] *Adult Education Act*, Section 302, PL 91-230.

[54] *Special Labor Force Report*, no. 186 (Washington, D.C.: U.S. Bureau of Labor Statistics, 1976). Cited in Hunter, *Adult Illiteracy in the United States*, p. 28.

[55] Jack Mezirow, Gordon G. Darkenwald, and Alan B. Know, *Last Gamble on Education* (Washington, D.C.: Adult Education Association, 1975), pp. 37-38.

[56] Hunter, *Adult Illiteracy in the United States*, pp. 63-66.

[57] This figure is probably an overestimate: "There is . . . a high likelihood of duplicate recording procedures; it is hard to determine whether students enrolled in a given program are the same ones recorded previously," and there is also a tendency "to show the highest possible number of 'average daily attenders' to qualify for state funding." Ibid., p. 64.

[58] Ibid., p. 72.

the Special Training Program run by the Army during World War II for illiterate inductees found that it achieved remarkable results for its brief (eight- or twelve-week) duration. Six years after demobilization, men who had entered the Army totally or largely illiterate were still making use of their acquired reading and writing skills.[59] Many reported that the Army program taught them just enough to know how to learn.

We might go a considerable way toward overcoming the practical problem of illiteracy, at least among younger adults, were the Armed Services more willing to recruit illiterate adults and educate them during peacetime.[60] The military is understandably reluctant to do so as long as better-educated recruits are available. Special training programs are costly, time-consuming, and a distraction from the major mission of the military, which is to train an effective fighting force, not to educate illiterate adults.[61]

The Moral Problem

If we cannot rely on prisons or the military to educate illiterate adults, then how should we educate illiterate adults? We are reluctant to compel illiterate adults to go to school, even to schools specially designed for helping them overcome what almost everyone agrees is a serious personal and social liability. Should we force illiterate adults back into schools for the sake of improving their lives and the quality of democratic politics? Or should we resign ourselves to leaving a substantial segment of our citizenry functionally illiterate, thereby perpetuating a cycle in which the poverty and dependency that attends adult illiteracy breeds illiteracy, poverty, and dependency among their children? Neither alternative is appealing, but is there another?

The problem of illiteracy can be viewed as a paradox: we mandate schooling for children because we believe that functional literacy is essential for exercising the rights and responsibilities of democratic citizenship, yet we consider it unjust to force adults who are functionally illiterate (but capable of becoming literate) to continue their education

[59] Eli Ginzberg and Douglas W. Bray, *The Uneducated* (New York: Columbia University Press, 1953), p. 135.

[60] Ibid., pp. 202-221.

[61] This point still stands even after we recognize the limitations of the Armed Force Qualification Test as a screening device: "The test may well be a reasonably good instrument for discerning how literate people will do in certain types of Army training, but it will not help at all in estimating the performance of an illiterate or poorly educated man. There may be relatively few objections to continued use of the test as long as the Congress and the public are willing to permit the Armed Service to reject intelligent, if uneducated, persons. But it is important for the non-expert to recognize how very little the test tells one about the present and potential qualities of those who fail." Ibid., p. 219.

until they achieve some minimal standards of functional literacy. How can functional literacy be at the same time essential and not essential for democratic citizenship? By trying to answer this question, we can gain some additional insights into the moral problem of adult illiteracy and a democratically acceptable means of coping with it.

A common way of dissolving the paradox is to deny that functional literacy is essential for exercising the rights and responsibilities of democratic citizenship. Direct denial is unconvincing in light of the extreme economic, political, and social disadvantages that attend illiteracy,[62] but the claim increases in credibility after examining the criteria typically used to define functional literacy. By UNESCO's definition, for example, a person is functionally literate if she has the knowledge and skills essential for "effective functioning" in her society.[63] We must then ask: What knowledge and skills are needed for getting along well ("effective functioning") in the United States today?

If we assume that getting along well in our society entails (at minimum) the ability to exercise existing rights and responsibilities of democratic citizenship, then any specific set of knowledge and skills will appear either insufficient or unnecessary for democratic citizenship, or both. Unable to settle upon any necessary or sufficient standard of functional literacy, we shall be driven to give up the idea of functional literacy as a standard of democratic citizenship. And having given up the standard of functional literacy, we shall also be driven by logic, even if not by common sense, to give up our commitment to compulsory schooling for children. By examining the strongest arguments that might drive us to these conclusions, I can show why we should resist being driven in this direction.

Consider this list, which includes some of the most common measures of functional literacy:[64]

(1) understanding the help-wanted ads in a local newspaper;
(2) knowing how to fill out a check and address an envelope;
(3) completing sixth grade;

---

[62] For a vivid account of many of these disadvantages, see Jonathan Kozol, *Illiterate America* (Garden City, N.Y.: Doubleday, 1985).

[63] UNESCO's definition is that "a person is literate when he has acquired the essential knowledge and skills which enable him to engage in all those activities in which literacy is required for effective functioning in his group or community, and whose attainments in reading, writing and arithmetic make it possible for him to continue to use these skills towards his own and the community's development." UNESCO, *Statement of the International Committee of Experts on Literacy* (Paris: UNESCO Press, 1962).

[64] These examples are taken from Hunter, *Adult Illiteracy in the United States*, pp. 25-30; and Roger Pattison, *On Literacy: The Politics of the Word from Homer to the Age of Rock* (New York and Oxford: Oxford University Press, 1982), pp. 174-76.

(4) understanding a brief passage describing the function of the Supreme Court;

(5) giving a reasonable interpretation of any section of one's state constitution.

Are adults who succeed only in (1), (2), and (3) able to exercise their rights and responsibilities as American citizens? According to an HEW survey, 90 percent of seventeen-year-olds can read and describe a help-wanted ad in the newspaper, but less than 60 percent are able to understand a brief passage describing the role of the Supreme Court.[65] Unless we radically narrow our ideal of democratic citizenship—to include only the ability to get a job and not the ability to participate effectively in democratic politics—we cannot count the first three accomplishments, or any longer list of similarly economically oriented accomplishments, a sufficient measure of functional literacy.[66] Critics of conventional definitions of functional literacy correctly argue for extending our understanding of what is necessary for "effective functioning" as a citizen in our society.

But when we extend the requirements of functional literacy to include the ability to understand or interpret political ideas, as partially measured by (4) or (5) above, the opposite problem arises.[67] Is understanding a brief passage describing the function of the Supreme Court or interpreting any section of one's state constitution necessary to function effectively as a citizen? Many of us know people unable to interpret any section of their state constitution but quite capable of exercising their rights and responsibilities as a citizen. Although it would be desirable for all citizens to understand the role of the Supreme Court, many who lack this understanding can still function effectively. So we are reluctant to call people who fail such specific tests functional illiterates. Yet we are also reluctant to consider people functionally literate because they have completed sixth grade, can understand a want-ad, or can fill out a check and address an envelope properly.

Even these simpler and more mechanical abilities may not be neces-

---

[65] *What Students Know and Can Do* (Washington, D.C.: Department of Health, Education and Welfare, 1977), pp. 89-97. Cited in Pattison, *On Literacy*, pp. 175-76. Robert Pattison points out that "this was the highest percentage of correct response to any interpretive question in the test, and, typically, the correct reply involves comprehension not so much of a thought as of a social mechanism. From this point onward, critical skills declined, both in reading and writing." Ibid., p. 176.

[66] For a critique of conventional definitions of functional literacy that concentrate on learning mechanical skills, see Pattison, *On Literacy*, pp. 171-78.

[67] You may want to substitute different tests of political understanding if these seem too easy or otherwise inappropriate. Nothing in my argument hinges on choosing these two tests.

sary for carrying out the rights and responsibilities of democratic citizenship. I know someone who can neither read nor write well, but who is very intelligent, holds down a job that does not require reading or writing, learns a great deal about politics from watching television and talking to friends, and relies on family, friends, and professionals for writing his checks, addressing his envelopes, filling out his income-tax forms, and so on. If no set of educational accomplishments is either necessary or sufficient to judge an adult literate, perhaps the problem of adult illiteracy dissolves. If it does dissolve, then we are left with a still more basic problem: How do we justify compulsory education for children in face of the fact that we cannot specify any set of educational accomplishments necessary or sufficient for citizenship?

Some critics argue that we should give up compulsory schooling for children. Compulsory schooling, they suggest, is the unjustified result of the grossly unequal power relation between adults and children.[68] Because the power relation among adults is relatively more equal, adult illiterates have succeeded in blocking the adoption of an equally unjustified policy of continuing compulsory schooling. The moral argument against both policies, however, is similar. Schooling, according to these critics, should not be compulsory for either children or adults because there are no (or only the most minimal) necessary educational conditions for democratic citizenship.

It makes more sense, however, to draw just the opposite conclusion. We are unable to specify necessary or sufficient educational conditions for citizenship not because citizenship is educationally undemanding, but because it is so demanding. So many different intellectual skills are central to the *actual* exercise of democratic citizenship, some of which some adults are capable of acquiring without the aid of formal education, that we cannot assume that the absence of any set of skills renders an adult incapable of exercising her democratic rights and responsibilities. Neither can we assume that there are any sufficient educational conditions for citizenship, since the *ideal* of democratic citizenship is so demanding. Were the only goal of a democratic state to prepare its members for citizenship, its maxim would be, "Mandate the maximum education." Citizens would be forced to spend most of their lives preparing for citizenship rather than exercising it. The state, like Plato's Republic, would claim the authority to make schooling compulsory for

---

[68] See Illich, *Deschooling Society*; William F. Rickenbacker, ed., *The Twelve-Year Sentence* (LaSalle, Ill.: Open Court, 1974). For a philosophically rigorous defense of a similar but more subtle position, see John Harris, "The Political Status of Children," in Keith Graham, ed., *Contemporary Political Philosophy: Radical Studies* (Cambridge: Cambridge University Press, 1982), pp. 35-55.

adults as well as for children on the grounds that citizenship is educationally so demanding.

Who, then, would educate the educators? The best answer again is Plato's, but it is unacceptable. We cannot accept rule by philosopher-kings or -queens unless we reject democracy. Democracy *is* educationally demanding, but its first and foremost demand is that adults be treated as sovereign citizens, not as the students of philosophers or the subjects of kings. This is why we encounter no paradox, only a serious problem, when we acknowledge that democratic states have the authority to make schooling compulsory for children but not for adults who fall below the democratic threshold of education. Since the threshold defines not a fully but an adequately educated citizen, this constraint on democratic authority may leave many adults less than adequately educated. A stricter constraint—mandating the maximum education—is ruled out by our recognition of the primacy of treating adults as sovereign citizens.

This argument helps clarify an uncharacteristically enigmatic passage in *On Liberty*, where Mill rejects legally or morally punishing "grown persons . . . for not taking proper care of themselves" because, as he puts it:

> Society has had absolute power over them during all the early portion of their existence; it has had the whole period of childhood and nonage in which to try whether it could make them capable of rational conduct in life.   . If society lets any considerable number of its members grow up mere children, incapable of being acted on by rational consideration of distant motives, society has itself to blame for the consequences.[69]

Mill seems to load his argument by calling paternalism towards adults "punishment." If compulsory schooling for adults could help adults live better lives, why should we call this kind of paternalism punishment? (We do not, for example, consider the requirement that motorcyclists wear helmets punishment, even if we think it unjustified.) And why should the fact that a state "has itself to blame for the consequences" prevent it from helping adults who suffered those consequences by mandating more free but compulsory schooling for them?[70] It seems strange to insist that a state not try to help adults now because it failed to help when they were children, unless the help is really harm,

[69] *On Liberty*, ch. 4, para. 11. (In John Stuart Mill, *Utilitarianism, On Liberty, Essay on Bentham*, ed. Mary Warnock [New York: New American Library, 1962], pp. 213.)

[70] This argument seems even weaker when one realizes that the public institutions and officials who were responsible for the first failure are probably not those who are now trying to compensate for that failure.

which is what Mill implies by his language but fails to establish by his explicit argument.

Our understanding of the illiteracy problem suggests an argument that supports Mill's language. Dependency is probably the primary harm that attends being functionally illiterate in our society. Illiteracy is humiliating for many adults because it makes them almost totally dependent for their welfare on the good will of other people—of employers to hire them and pay them a decent wage although they have almost no market power, of politicians to take their interests into account although they find it hard to hear their voices in politics, and of literate friends to help them with many of the most basic tasks of everyday life (such as writing checks and filling out applications) although they can often do little in return but to be grateful. But being functionally illiterate *and* under the mandatory tutelage of political authorities would be a state of even greater dependency and humiliation. In this sense, compulsory schooling for illiterate adults would a kind of *political* punishment. It adds the insult of paternalism to the injury of illiteracy.

Is there, then, something short of compulsory schooling that might ameliorate if not solve the problem of adult illiteracy in our society? The most promising possibility would be a national campaign against illiteracy carefully designed to overcome the weaknesses of our present programs, while retaining their two most attractive features: voluntarism and decentralization. The campaign could relieve illiterate adults for a limited period from the financial pressures that interfere with schooling, by paying them a minimum wage for attending a locally sponsored, accredited illiteracy program, whose curriculum includes a significant component of community service. The campaign could attract able teachers to local programs by sponsoring special university scholarships that require, say, two post-graduate years of low-paid service in the national literacy campaign.[71] Such a campaign would, of course, be expensive over the short run. Were it even moderately successful, however, the social benefits of interrupting the intergenerational cycle of illiteracy could easily compensate for the monetary costs.

The problem of adult illiteracy brings us back to the basic issue of the significance of education in a democracy, and requires us to reconsider the rationale for compulsory schooling for children. Schooling should be compulsory for children because it is the primary means by which

[71] A somewhat less costly and more familiar alternative would be to offer special loans, whose principal would be reduced for each year of service in the national literacy campaign.

democratic governments can educate citizens. But schooling must not therefore be compulsory for illiterate adults. If democratic governments fail to educate some of us adequately the first time around, they are not authorized to add political insult to educational injury.[72] Democratic governments must not force adults to be educated, not because their educational needs are necessarily fewer than those of children, but because respect for their freedom and dignity as citizens must be greater. Adult illiteracy poses such a serious problem for a democratic society because the morally acceptable means of overcoming it are so costly, and the costs of not overcoming it are so great. The problem of adult illiteracy underscores the importance of educating citizens adequately the first time around.

[72] Even if the state could single out a few adults who were responsible for their own failure (which it cannot), it would be wrong to punish or publicly to insult them for injuring mainly themselves. Mill's argument on this point is quite clear and correct. See *On Liberty*, ch. 4, paras. 10 and 11 (pp. 212-13).

CONCLUSION

THE PRIMACY OF POLITICAL EDUCATION

"Nor can we regard a republic as disorderly," Machiavelli wrote, "where so many virtues were seen to shine. For good examples are the results of good education, and good education is due to good laws; and good laws in their turn spring from those very agitations which have been so inconsiderately condemned by many."[1] Whether or not Machiavelli was right about Rome, his general argument expresses an important truth about democratic education: good laws, which are the consequence of peaceful political agitation in a democracy, are the source of good education, and good education in turn creates good citizens.

We know, of course, that political agitation does not always produce good laws. In any democracy but one of our imagination, some laws regulating education will be bad laws, like the separate but equal statutes still standing in the 1950s that taught children the wrong lesson about democratic citizenship. Laws that violate the principles of nondiscrimination or nonrepression ought to be overturned in the name of democracy itself. But even laws that lie within the legitimate bounds of democratic authority may fail to institute practices that educate children fully to their rights and responsibilities as citizens. It is all but inevitable that our laws fail in this way, because the democratic ideal of citizenship is so educationally demanding.

DISCRETION IN WORK AND PARTICIPATION IN POLITICS

Democratic education is demanding not just of laws governing schools and other primarily educational and cultural institutions, but also of laws that shape our economic and political institutions. The aims of democratic education will not be fully realized until citizens have additional opportunities to exercise discretion in their daily work and to participate in democratic politics. This point is most often raised today by radical critics of American society, but the insight was widely shared by classical liberals. In *The Wealth of Nations*, for example, Adam Smith commented:

[1] Niccolo Machiavelli, *The Discourses*, in *The Prince and the Discourses* (New York: Modern Library, 1950), book 1, ch. 4, pp. 119-20.

The understandings of the greater part of men are necessarily formed by their ordinary employments. The man whose whole life is spent in performing a few simple operations . . . has no occasion to exert his understanding, or to exercise his invention in finding out expedients for removing difficulties which never occur. He naturally loses, therefore, the habit of such exertion. . . . His dexterity at his own particular trade seems . . . to be acquired at the expense of his intellectual, social, and martial virtues.[2]

Studies of assembly-line workers tend to confirm Smith's conclusion: "factory employment, especially in routine production tasks, does give evidence of extinguishing workers' ambition, initiative, and purposeful direction toward life goals."[3] Other findings suggest that the effects of working conditions extend to the realm of moral education. Many menial workers hold attitudes inimical to the aims of democratic education. They believe that "the most important thing to teach children is absolute obedience to their parents. Young people should not be allowed to read books that are likely to confuse them. People who question the old and accepted ways of doing things usually just end up causing trouble."[4] As one commentator puts it: "[M]enial work tends to breed . . . a sort of blind authoritarian conservatism of the Archie Bunker type."[5]

John Stuart Mill made a similar point with regard to effects of centralized political institutions on human personality: "A democratic constitution, not supported by democratic institutions in detail, but confined to the central government, not only is not political freedom, but often creates a spirit precisely the reverse, carrying down to the lowest grade in society the desire and ambition of political domina-

[2] Adam Smith, *An Inquiry into the Nature and Causes of the Wealth of Nations*, ed. Edwin Cannan (Chicago: University of Chicago Press, 1976), 2: 302-303. For an interesting discussion of the implications of this argument for fostering human autonomy, see Adina Schwartz, "Meaningful Work," *Ethics*, vol. 92 (July 1982): 634-46.

[3] Arthur Kornhauser, *Mental Health of the Industrial Worker: A Detroit Study* (New York: John Wiley and Sons, 1964), p. 252. See also *Work in America: Report of a Special Task Force to the Secretary of Health, Education, and Welfare* (Cambridge, Mass.: MIT Press, 1973), esp. pp. 81-92.

[4] Melvin L. Kohn and Carmi Schooler, "Occupational Experience and Psychological Functioning: An Assessment of Reciprocal Effects," *American Sociological Review*, vol. 38, no. 1 (February 1973): 101. See also Melvin L. Kohn and Carmi Schooler, "Job Conditions and Personality: A Longitudinal Assessment of Their Reciprocal Effects," *American Journal of Sociology*, vol. 87, no. 6 (May 1982): 1257-86; Melvin Kohn, *Class and Conformity: A Study in Values*, 2nd ed. (Chicago: University of Chicago Press, 1977); and Robert Blauner, *Alienation and Freedom* (Chicago: University of Chicago Press, 1964).

[5] Eckstein, "Civic Inclusion and Its Discontents," p. 137.

tion."[6] Like Mill, Tocqueville argued that participatory political institutions have a positive affect on developing democratic character: "Local institutions are to liberty what primary schools are to science; they put it within the people's reach; they teach people to appreciate its peaceful enjoyment and accustom them to make use of it. Without local institutions a nation may give itself a free government, but it has not got the spirit of liberty."[7] Tocqueville's argument can be extended to schools: Without an active democratic politics among its citizens, a nation may give all its children free public schools, but it cannot foster the spirit of democratic education.

Some critics extend these arguments a significant step further. They claim that the educative effects of the organization of industry and government has causal primacy over the effects of more deliberate instruction and enculturation: "Schools ... do not appear to be effective routes out of the ghettos and barrios; rather, improving the lot of ghetto people seems necessary to make them want to use schools for achievement."[8] Variants of this view are widely shared today by scholars if not by citizens. On one interpretation, the view is unexceptionable: Schools will fall far short of achieving their democratic purposes if the living and working conditions of the least advantaged are not improved.[9] But the more controversial claims implicit in this view are more doubtful: that the lives of lower-class children have not been improved by schooling and that our democratic aspirations for schooling should be postponed until the living and working conditions of the least advantaged are improved. Schooling surely is doomed to fall far short of its democratic potential as long as some citizens are poor, their work menial, and their family structure authoritarian. But without the prospects of schooling, most disadvantaged children would be worse off. Better schools do make a difference.[10]

The trade-off between improving the economic lot and improving the education of the least advantaged is, politically as well as morally, a false one. Our political choices are not so stark. Nor are they so easy.

[6] John Stuart Mill, *Principles of Political Economy* [1848, 1871], in *Collected Works*, ed. J. M. Robson (Toronto: University of Toronto Press, 1965), 3: 944.

[7] Alexis de Tocqueville, *Democracy in America*, p. 63. See also John Stuart Mill, "Considerations on Representative Government," in *Essays on Politics and Society*, ed. J. M. Robson (Toronto: University of Toronto, 1977), chs. 3 and 8, pp. 406-412 and 467-69.

[8] Eckstein, "Civic Inclusion and Its Discontents," p. 140.

[9] For an in-depth study of the problems of integrating lower-class black students into the authority structures of high schools in the late 1960s, see Metz, *Classrooms and Corridors*.

[10] See Rutter et al., *Fifteen Thousand Hours*. See also Metz, *Classrooms and Corridors*, pp. 219-40. Metz's study suggests that more participatory schools better integrate lower-class black students, and provide them with a "positive place" in the school.

To improve significantly the working conditions or the schooling of the poor probably requires political pressure from the poor themselves, yet they are the citizens most likely to have been educated in highly authoritarian families and schools, and (therefore?) are those least likely to participate or to be effective (when they do participate) in politics. Even if one could be sure that their working conditions were the primary cause of their limited life chances, it would not be politically wise to focus solely on this single factor, first, because the prospects of political success are limited, and second, because the children who will eventually benefit from economic reforms are generally not the same children who now suffer from poor schooling (and could benefit from educational reforms).

Other critics, who reject the primacy of economics, argue instead for the primacy of politics: "knowledge and the quest for knowledge tend to follow rather than to precede political engagement: give people some significant power and they will quickly appreciate the need for knowledge, but foist knowledge on them without giving them responsibility and they will display only indifference."[11] Were politics primary in this causal sense, we should focus exclusively on increasing political participation; improvements in education would follow.

But why should we believe that politics is primary in this sense? Imagine that the opportunities for democratic participation suddenly expanded. Functionally illiterate adults would, as Benjamin Barber suggests, "appreciate the need for more knowledge." But even today, with considerably more restricted opportunities for political participation, most illiterate adults appreciate—often acutely—their need for more education. What they lack, however, are sufficient means to satisfy their need.

In a more participatory democracy, illiterate adults would probably be more rather than less politically disadvantaged than they are today. Democratic politics puts a high premium on citizens being both knowledgeable and articulate. The crucial question then is not whether illiterate adults would appreciate their need for education in a more democratic society (since they already appreciate it), but whether they would succeed in satisfying their need at the same time as they participated actively and intelligently in politics. The limited evidence that we have from town-meeting democracy gives us no reason to be optimistic.[12]

The visions that claim causal primacy for economics and politics

[11] Barber, *Strong Democracy*, p. 234.
[12] See Jane Mansbridge, *Beyond Adversary Democracy* (New York: Basic Books, 1980).

over education are implausible for yet another reason. We cannot count on a stroke of good economic fortune or on Rousseau's legislator (an "intelligence wholly unrelated to our nature, while knowing it through and through"[13]) to improve the working conditions of the least advantaged or to expand their opportunities for political participation. We must rely on our imperfect democratic politics to generate demands for better living and working conditions and more democratic political institutions. What conceivable change in our economic or political institutions is likely to generate these demands more effectively in the future than improving the education of children today?

The claim that reforms in education would be less useful than reforms in politics may stem from modeling an ideal of democracy too closely on the Greek *polis*, which sustained a high level and quality of democratic participation among its citizens without any formal, publicly supported system of education. We should be wary of using the Greek *polis* as our political model. Since citizenship in Athenian democracy was so exclusive, the *polis* might reasonably expect most parents to educate their children without providing any formal education at public expense.

But even in a democracy as exclusive as Aristotle's Athens, there was good reason to argue for a publicly supported system of education. The wealthiest Athenian citizens hired Sophists to teach their children, among other things, how to gain political advantage for themselves. Regarding such private education as inimical to the constitution of Athenian democracy, Aristotle argued that

> the system of education in a state must . . . be one and the same for all, and the provision of this system must be a matter of public action. It cannot be left, as it is at present, to private enterprise, with each parent making provision privately for his own children, and having them privately instructed as he himself thinks fit. Training for an end which is common should also itself be common.[14]

Far from denying that adults are educated politically when they deliberate democratically, Aristotle suggests that the quality of those deliberations are significantly shaped by the way citizens were educated as children.

We should not therefore conclude that formal education is prior to democratic politics—the claim that adults must be educated before they are fully franchised is just as inimical to democratic principles as the claim that they must be fully franchised before they can be educated as democratic citizens. Democratic politics is one way—probably the

---

[13] Rousseau, *The Social Contract*, book 2, ch. 7 (p. 37).
[14] Aristotle, *The Politics of Aristotle*, bk. 8, ch. 1, 1337a (p. 332).

most effective and certainly the fairest way—in which the educational needs of all citizens, young and old, literate and illiterate, can be recognized and their educational preferences heard. Without recourse to democratic politics, there would be no acceptable means to educate adults and no acceptable means of educating children outside the family. Without the tumult of democratic politics, our educational institutions would not be governed by common values. We discover our common values partly through processes of democratic deliberation by which we agree upon the laws that govern our educational institutions. Take away the processes, and the educational institutions that remain cannot properly be called democratic. Take away the educational institutions, and the processes that remain cannot function democratically.

POLITICAL EDUCATION

Although we cannot conclude that democratic politics has causal primacy over democratic education, we can conclude that "political education"—the cultivation of the virtues, knowledge, and skills necessary for political participation—has moral primacy over other purposes of public education in a democratic society. Political education prepares citizens to participate in consciously reproducing their society, and conscious social reproduction is the ideal not only of democratic education but also of democratic politics, as I shall argue in a moment.

At the level of primary schooling, the primacy of political education supplies a principled argument against tracking, sexist education, racial segregation, and (narrowly) vocational education. Even when these practices improve the academic achievement of students, they neglect the virtues of citizenship, which can be cultivated by a common education characterized by respect for racial, religious, intellectual and sexual differences among students. The moral primacy of political education also supports a presumption in favor of more participatory over more disciplinary methods of teaching. Participatory methods are often the best means of achieving the disciplinary purposes of primary schooling. But even when student participation threatens to produce some degree of disorder within schools, it may be defended on democratic grounds for cultivating political skills and social commitments.

The primacy of political education reorients our expectations of primary schooling away from the distributive goals set by standard interpretations of equal opportunity (such as educating every child for choice among the widest range of good lives) and toward the goal of giving every child an education adequate to participate in the political processes by which choices among good lives are socially structured. The most devastating criticism we can level at primary schools, therefore, is not that they fail to give equally talented children an equal chance to earn the same income or to pursue professional occupations, but that they fail to give all (educable) children an education adequate to take advantage of their political status as citizens.

At the level of higher education, the primacy of political education points away from a singular conception of the university—as an ivory tower, a multiversity, or a community of learning—toward a more pluralistic conception, which accommodates the associational freedoms of a wide variety of universities, all of which uphold academic freedom. Universities serve democracy both as sanctuaries of nonrepression and as associational communities. They also serve as gatekeepers of valuable social offices, and as such they should give priority to the democratic principle of nondiscrimination over efficiency in their admissions procedures.

When we turn our attention away from schools, the idea of the primacy of political education integrates the educational purposes of cultural, economic, and political institutions into a coherent democratic vision. The primary educational purpose of the mass media, industry, and government, like that of schools, is to cultivate the knowledge, skills, and virtues necessary for democratic deliberation among citizens. What distinguishes primary schools, universities, and programs of adult education from the mass media, industry, and other political institutions is that the educational purpose of the former is also their primary social purpose. By contrast, the educational purposes of the mass media, industry, and political institutions are by-products of their other social purposes, the precise content of which are properly subject to democratic determination.

The view that political education is primary—its purpose being to foster the capacities for democratic deliberation essential to conscious social reproduction—does not commit us to considering every outcome of democratic deliberations as correct. Nor does it commit us to accepting democratic authority over every form of education. Rather, it commits us to accepting nondiscriminatory and nonrepressive policies as legitimate even when they are wrong, and to viewing children as neither the mere creatures of their parents nor the mere creatures of a centralized state. Democratic education is best viewed as a shared trust, of parents, citizens, teachers, and public officials, the precise terms of which are to be democratically decided within the bounds of the principles of nondiscrimination and nonrepression.

DEMOCRATIC EDUCATION AND DEMOCRATIC THEORY

How does the ideal of democratic education fit into a democratic theory? If my understanding is correct, our concern for democratic education lies at the core of our commitment to democracy. The ideal of democracy is often said to be collective self-determination. But is there a "collective self" to be determined? Are there not just so many individual selves that must find a fair way of sharing the goods of a society together? It would be dangerous (as critics often charge) to assume that the democratic state constitutes the "collective self" of a society, and that its policies in turn define the best interests of its individual members.

We need no such metaphysical assumption, however, to defend an ideal closely related to that of collective self-determination—an ideal of citizens sharing in deliberatively determining the future shape of their society. If democratic society is the "self" that citizens determine, it is a self that does not define their best interests. There remain independent standards for defining the best interests of individuals and reasons for thinking that individuals, rather than collectivities, are often the best judges of their own interests. To avoid the misleading metaphysical connotations of the concept of collective self-determination, we might better understand the democratic ideal as that of conscious social reproduction, the same ideal that guides democratic education.

The convergence of democratic ideals is not coincidental. Democratic education supplies the foundations upon which a democratic society can secure the civil and political freedoms of its adult citizens without placing their welfare or its very survival at great risk. In the absence of democratic education, risks—perhaps even great risks—will still be worth taking for the sake of respecting the actual preferences of citizens, but the case for civic and political freedom and against paternalism is weaker in a society whose citizens have been deprived of an adequate education (although not as weak as Mill suggested). Democracy thus depends on democratic education for its full moral strength.

The dependency, however, is reciprocal. Were we not already committed to democratic principles, our ideal of education might take a very different form, similar perhaps to that practiced for thirteen centuries in Imperial China, where a centralized state supported schools and designed a highly intricate and seemingly thorough system of examinations that determined access to all state offices. When working at its best, the Chinese educational system allowed for considerable social mobility. Children of rich, well-educated families who could not pass the rigorous examinations lost the high social status of their parents. Lowly peasant children climbed up the academic "ladder of success" to become rich and highly esteemed.[15] The Chinese educational system

[15] See Ping-Ti Ho, *The Ladder of Success in Imperial China: Aspects of Social Mobility, 1368-1911* (New York: Columbia University Press, 1962), esp. pp. 257-62.

thus supported a widespread belief in what one scholar describes as an "academic Horatio Alger myth."[16] Such an educational system would rightly be subject to devastating criticism in our society, but not primarily because the academic Horatio Alger myth would distort social reality as much as did the original, economic version of the Horatio Alger story. The more devastating criticism due such a system would be that a centralized, nondemocratic state usurps control of what rightly belongs to citizens: decisions concerning how the character and consciousness of future citizens take shape outside the home. Democratic sovereignty over education thereby follows at the same time as it reinforces our fundamental political commitments.

Families do not belong to citizens, yet they profoundly affect democratic education, often in adverse ways—when parents predispose their children to violence, religious intolerance, racial bigotry, sexism, and other undemocratic values. Because we so highly value the intimacy of family life and because regulation of parental behavior (within broad bounds) would interfere with that intimacy in repressive ways, the ideal of democratic education does not permit political regulation of the internal life of families. The authority of parents therefore constrains democratic sovereignty over education, although not as absolutely as advocates of the state of families argue.

Respect for the intimacy of the family is consistent with democratic authorization of policies that facilitate changes in the structure of families. Subsidized day care and flexible time for working parents are examples of such policies. By encouraging more egalitarian gender relations, these policies are likely to lead to more democratic education within the family. To the extent that unequal gender roles predispose women to political passivity or deference to men, the ideal of democratic education recommends policies that encourage gender equality, even though it does not permit direct political interference to create more egalitarian families. The ideal of democratic education thus may be morally demanding even when it cannot be politically authoritative. Far from treating the family as a haven in a heartless world, the ideal of democratic education subjects the family to moral scrutiny—but not to political repression. Although political education has primacy among the purposes of public education, public education is bounded by the (private) educational authority of parents.

"The prospect of a theory of education," Kant argued, "is a glorious ideal, and it matters little if we are not able to realise it at once." Kant went on to warn that "we must not look upon the idea as chimerical,

16 Ibid., p. 262.

nor decry it as a beautiful dream, notwithstanding the difficulties that stand in the way of its realisation."[17] Political philosophers are likely to be more receptive to Kant's warning than are policymakers, but we might issue ourselves a parallel warning: that we must not look upon education as a realm ideally to be separated from the tumult of democratic politics. By heeding such a warning, we may develop a less glorious but better grounded theory of both democratic education and democracy.

[17] Kant, *Kant on Education*, p. 8.

CHALLENGES OF CIVIC MINIMALISM, MULTICULTURALISM, AND COSMOPOLITANISM

In this Epilogue, I pursue three issues that have become more prominent since I first wrote *Democratic Education*.[1] The first issue is whether the civic education that is publicly mandated must be minimal so that parental choice can be maximal. The second issue concerns the way in which publicly subsidized schools should respond to the increasingly multicultural character of societies. The third issue is whether democratic education should try to cultivate cosmopolitan or patriotic sentiments among students.

Each of these issues have become more prominent since I first wrote *Democratic Education*. I take the opportunity of this epilogue to approach each issue freshly, as an ongoing challenge to democratic education: the challenge of civic minimalism, multiculturalism, and cosmopolitanism versus patriotism. By responding to each challenge, I try to develop and deepen the conception of democracy and democratic education that informs this book.

CIVIC MINIMALISM: AN ALTERNATIVE TO DEMOCRATIC EDUCATION?

Schooling that is publicly mandated and subsidized by democratic citizens may legitimately pursue civic purposes, which include the teaching of literacy, numeracy, veracity, toleration, and mutual respect. This much is widely acknowledged in most liberal democracies. But no conception of the public purposes of schooling is be-

---

[1] Although I have written about these issues over the past decade in separate essays, what I say here is largely new. The previous essays include "Civic Education and Social Diversity," *Ethics* 105 (April 1995), pp. 557-579; "Challenges of Multiculturalism in Education," in Robert Fullinwider, ed., *Public Education in a Multicultural Society: Policy, Theory, Critique* (Cambridge and New York: Cambridge University Press, 1996), pp. 156-179; "The Challenge of Multiculturalism in Political Ethics," *Philosophy & Public Affairs*, vol. 22, no. 3 (Summer 1993), pp. 171-206; and "Undemocratic Education," in Nancy L. Rosenblum (ed.), *Liberalism and the Moral Life* (Cambridge, Mass.: Harvard University Press, 1989), pp. 71-88.

yond reasonable disagreement. The project of defending a conception of the public purposes of schooling is all the more important because the alternative to articulating a controversial conception is imposing one on other people. This is a recipe for educational tyranny.

How extensive are the civic purposes of schooling? Some liberals argue that the publicly mandated requirements of civic education in schools must be minimal so as to diminish democratic disagreement and increase parental control over schooling. This is "civic minimalism." In this view, requiring anything more than the civic minimum constitutes an illegitimate exercise of political authority on the part of citizens, and therefore should be constitutionally prohibited.[2]

Civic minimalism mandates less public authority over schooling than democratic education recommends. A common corollary is a defense of parental choice over schools, often through a voucher system. Many civic minimalists argue that the government should give every set of parents a stipend to use at the school of their choice, public or private, secular or religious. Some civic minimalists do not defend vouchers, but argue that dissenting parents, especially those who dissent on religious grounds, should be exempted from any educational requirement that cannot be demonstrated to be a necessary part of the civic minimum.

A major attraction of civic minimalism, most advocates argue, is that by virtue of minimizing the civic component of schooling, it can resolve the problem of achieving a consensus about civic education under conditions of reasonable pluralism. Parents can decide for their own children how best to interpret the demands of civic education, its ends as well as its means. Democratic disagreement over public schooling can thereby be minimized.

Civic minimalism amalgamates a defense of parental authority similar to that of the state of families, which I discuss in Chapter Two, with a defense of civic education similar to that of democratic education. Civic educational requirements are justifiable only if they do not exceed the minimum. Beyond the minimal requirements, parental authority must be supreme. Is civic minimalism more defensible than democratic education?

Democratic majorities in some public school districts in the United States support standards of civic education that go beyond those permitted by civic minimalism. Some public school districts, for exam-

---

[2] There is a weaker form of civic minimalism that makes it discretionary rather than mandatory. It recommends that citizens support only the minimum requirements of democratic education for schools, but recognizes the constitutional right of citizens to require more than the minimum. I focus on the stronger form of civic minimalism because the weaker form is not really inconsistent with *Democratic Education*.

ple, support teaching all students about gender nondiscrimination. If civic minimalism says that teaching about gender nondiscrimination exceeds the minimum, it denies democratic citizens the discretion to mandate more than a minimal civic education in schools. It turns to judges to overrule state legislatures, school districts, boards of education, and principals in the name of the constitutional right of parents to determine every feature of their children's schooling except the civic minimum. Civic minimalism presents itself not as a contribution to democratic deliberation, but as an alternative to it.

By contrast, democratic education grants citizens discretion over how to interpret the demands of civic education, consistently with respect for rights. It therefore permits citizens to mandate more than a civic minimum. Parents do not have a general right to override otherwise legitimate democratic decisions concerning the schooling of their children. The conception of democratic education presented in this book offers a moral defense of this position. A long line of court cases supports the idea that a range of democratic discretion over schooling is consistent with the United States Constitution.[3]

How would civic minimalism work in the United States? An

---

[3] Although the precise range is subject to ongoing interpretation and argument, the American judiciary has quite consistently recognized broad democratic authority over public schooling. In *Pierce v. Society of Sisters*, the court recognized "the power of the State reasonably to regulate all schools," 268 US 510 at 534 (1925). Lower courts, therefore, have typically assessed the legitimacy of state regulations of schools, including home schooling, under the rational basis test, which is the easiest test to pass. In *Prince v. Massachusetts*, the court more generally recognized that: "The state's authority over children's activities is broader than over like actions of adults," 321 US 158 at 168 (1944).

One significant limit that the court places on state authority over schooling is to forbid compelling students to profess belief against their convictions. In *Board of Education v. Barnette*, the court does not rest its decision on a right of parents to dictate the content of their children's schooling. It argues that the state's legitimate power of schooling does not extend to compelling a profession of belief. The legitimacy of the laws of the state are limited to those that do not "force citizens to confess by word or act their faith therein," 319 US 624 at 642 (1943).

Even in the exceptional case of *Wisconsin v. Yoder*, where the court exempts Amish children from two years of compulsory schooling on the basis of their parents' right to the free exercise of religion, Justice Burger goes to great lengths to demonstrate that the Amish (by virtue of their highly unusual characteristics) are an almost singular exception to the general rule. Burger concludes the court's opinion by noting that "Nothing we hold is intended to undermine the general applicability of the State's compulsory school-attendance statutes. . . ." 406 US 205 at 236.

This set of issues deserves far more analysis. I have written more about the religious freedom of parents as it relates to the state's authority over schooling in "The Importance of Not Establishing Religion," in Nancy L. Rosenblum, ed., *Religion and the Law* (Princeton: Princeton University Press, forthcoming).

amendment to the Constitution could give parents the constitutional right to dictate the content of schooling for their own children beyond a centrally specified minimum. Although civic minimalists do not accord legitimacy to results of democratic decision making with regard to schooling, a constitutional amendment would require democratic support. This creates a serious problem for civic minimalism.

Competing conceptions of the civic minimum are reasonably contestable. Some will be more minimal than others, but there is no reason to claim that the most minimal will be the constitutionally correct interpretation of the civic minimum. To make matters more complicated, minimalists will not agree on which one is right. Why should it then be beyond democratic disagreement for citizens to claim the constitutional right to legislate more than what anybody claims to be the singularly correct civic minimum? Who in a liberal democracy has the legitimate authority to impose a contestable conception of a civic minimum on all schools in the face of such democratic disagreement?

In order to publicly justify their claim that democratic citizens have no right to mandate a civic education above the minimum, civic minimalists must specify precisely what the civic minimum is and why. Without a substantive defense of a specific civic minimum, minimalism is meaningless. It is a hollow conception into which all citizens, including advocates of democratic education, can put their understanding of civic education and call it the civic minimum.

Civic minimalists therefore need to defend a specific substantive conception of the civic minimum. Some defend no more than the 3R's. Others defend teaching civic virtues such as toleration, racial and gender nondiscrimination, and mutual respect among citizens. Substantive conceptions of the civic minimum are subject to the same sort of reasonable disagreement that minimalists claim is grounds for rejecting democratic education in favor of civic minimalism. The grounds that civic minimalists offer in their own defense is therefore self-defeating since conceptions of the civic minimum are also subject to reasonable disagreement. By its own terms, a civic minimalism that avoids being hollow becomes self-defeating.

Can mandatory minimalism be made more defensible than this? A prominent defense of parental choice, by John Chubb and Terry Moe, argues that it is "not built to enable the imposition of higher-order values on the schools, nor is it driven by a democratic struggle to exercise public authority."[4] Can mandatory minimalism do with-

---

[4] See John E. Chubb and Terry M. Moe, *Politics, Markets, and America's Schools* (Washington, D.C.: Brookings, 1990), p. 189.

out imposing "higher-order values" on schools? It can do so only if it does not say what constitutes a school entitled to public subsidy or accreditation, or if it converts a specific conception of civic minimalism into a higher-order value that is imposed on public schools. Why should citizens mandate schooling for all children if they are constitutionally forbidden to require that mandatory schooling has the civic content they believe is necessary for democratic education? If citizens are constitutionally entitled to expect some civic content from schooling, then they are authorized to impose some values on schools.

Suppose citizens were constitutionally forbidden to impose any values on schools, but they were permitted to give parents the means to educate their own children as they choose. Under these conditions, it makes far more sense for citizens to mandate a general child support subsidy and let parents decide how to spend it on their children. If publicly subsidized schooling cannot have any publicly mandated content, its ceases to make sense as a public good. Civic minimalism implicitly concedes this much by defending a civic minimum.

Parental choice plans must satisfy some standard of mandatory schooling to be publicly defensible. They therefore call for some public oversight over publicly subsidized schools to ensure that schools satisfy the mandatory standards of schooling. Otherwise, a parental choice plan could not even identify what counts as a school for the purpose of satisfying the civic minimum. To avoid being empty, the minimum must be given content. Once given content, it establishes values to be imposed on schools.

Civic minimalists defend their values on grounds that they are more minimal and therefore less controversial than those defended by democratic education. They are presumably right about the relative ease of reaching a social consensus on the positive program of mandating the most minimal requirements, such as the 3R's (reading, writing, and arithmetic). But it does not follow that they can therefore justify the distinctive negative program of civic minimalism, that citizens and their accountable representatives must be prevented from mandating more than the minimum. This claim is at least as controversial as its opposite, that citizens and their accountable representatives may legitimately mandate more than this minimum. Mandating civic minimalism—which entails *preventing* citizens from requiring any more of schools than teaching the 3R's or some other minimum, which is not subject to democratic deliberation—is not a morally neutral or even a morally defensible default position.

To be a defensible alternative to democratic education, civic minimalism must publicly justify denying citizens the legitimate authority to mandate more than a specific civic minimum. If it cannot publicly justify this constitutional restriction and the correlatively broad parental right over schooling, then civic minimalism becomes one of several educational options available to citizens within a system of democratic education.

Democratic education defends decentralization and diversity among public and private, religious and secular schools not as ultimate ends but as means to their achieving educational ends. The civic ends of education need to be publicly defended. Deliberation, which takes place at a variety of levels, including individual schools, local school districts, and state legislatures, is one way of publicly defending the ends of civic education. Citizens and their accountable representatives deliberate about educating children in ways conducive to their becoming free and equal citizens in a democratic society. Schools may teach more than the mandated civic curriculum. Parents may send their children to public or private, religious or secular schools, although only public schools receive complete public subsidy. (I return to consider the problem this creates in a society where some parents cannot afford private schooling.) All schools should be constrained to respect the constitutional rights of students, which include rights against repression and discrimination. Every individual's basic liberties are protected against repression, and every individual's basic opportunities are protected against discrimination. If a school, school board, or state legislature fails to respect individual rights, courts may be authorized to do so.

By contrast, in a regime of civic minimalism, judges and parents together would have almost exclusive control over children's schooling. Judges would enforce the mandated minimum, no more nor less. Parents would control the rest of publicly subsidized schooling. Civic minimalism therefore presumes—before democratic deliberation even begins—that constitutional legitimacy extends only to a single conception of the civic minimum. This presumption has yet to be defended, much less defended in a way that gives clear content to the idea of a civic minimum or in a way that puts it beyond reasonable disagreement. It is therefore presumptuous to denounce democratic decision making over publicly subsidized schools as illegitimate.

What might a morally defensible content of a civic minimum be? The least controversial parts of a civic minimum in the United States—those that can elicit nearly universal agreement among Americans as necessary for every citizen to learn—are probably the 3R's. But it would be morally arbitrary to conclude that the 3R's therefore suffice for civic education in the United States, and that nothing more can be legitimately mandated of schools.

A more popular and promising start for defining the civic minimum is identifying it with what is necessary to make liberal democracy work well. If "well" means fairly or justifiably, then the content of civic minimalism converges with what democratic education identifies as a good civic education. To make liberal democracy work fairly, the civic minimum would include teaching not only the 3R's but also religious toleration and nondiscrimination, racial and gender nondiscrimination, respect for individual rights and legitimate laws, the ability to articulate and the courage to stand up for one's publicly defensible convictions, the ability to deliberate with others and therefore to be open-minded about politically relevant issues, and the ability to evaluate the performance of officeholders.

William Galston defends a civic minimum that generally converges with the principles of democratic education. He defends teaching those virtues that are necessary to make liberal democracy work fairly, which is a high standard, not really a "minimal" one.[5] The implications of this standard are also open to reasonable disagreement. Galston thinks that the standard supports overturning a recent court decision in the case of *Mozert v. Hawkins County Board of Education*. He argues that the Sixth Circuit Court of Appeals failed to recognize a constitutional right of the Mozert parents—based on their right of free exercise of religion—to exempt their children from the mandated reading curriculum of the public school that they attended.[6] Applying the principles of democratic education, I have argued that courts should not overturn the decisions of public school boards on matters of reasonable curricular requirements. The right to free exercise of religion does not entail the right of parents to near-exclusive or comprehensive authority over their children's schooling.[7]

Children, Galston and I agree, are not the mere creatures of the state or their parents. We also agree that the curricular requirements at issue in the *Mozert* case were reasonable ways for the Hawkins County public schools to engage in civic education. The required reading to which the parents objected ranged from a picture of a boy having fun cooking while a girl read to him, to an excerpt from Anne Frank's *Diary of a Young Girl*, to a passage describing a central idea of the Renaissance as belief in the dignity and worth of human beings. None of the requirements entailed forcing the profession of belief by any student (or parent). The disagreement between civic mini-

---

[5] See Galston, *Liberal Virtues* (New York: Cambridge University Press, 1991), esp. pp. 224-227.

[6] *Mozert v. Hawkins County Board of Education*, 827 F.2d 1058.

[7] See "Civic Education and Social Diversity," and "Undemocratic Education."

malism (Galston's interpretation) and democratic education (my interpretation) is about whether the judiciary should set a precedent, based on parents' free exercise of religion, for requiring school boards to exempt children from every part of a public school curriculum—including parts as basic as the reading curriculum—that offends their parents' religious beliefs.

Civic minimalists disagree among themselves even more than Galston disagrees with me. Some criticize Galston's conception as not being minimal enough and, therefore, as not recognizing a far less qualified right to parental control over schooling. Stephen Gilles offers such a critique coupled with an alternative version of civic minimalism, which is no less controversial, but less well defended and less defensible than Galston's.

Gilles recognizes that civic minimalism may not have convincing support in "our existing Constitution, rightly interpreted," but he nevertheless suggests a new way of interpreting the First Amendment right to free speech. He converts parental authority over the content of public schooling into a free speech right: "educational messages to their children, whether delivered directly by parents in the home or indirectly through their agents in the school, should be treated as parental educative speech, and should receive a high level of First Amendment protection similar to that currently afforded to political speech."[8]

The right to free speech, as interpreted by Gilles, requires that judges evaluate educational regulations "in terms of their impacts on parents," rather than on children.[9] The needs, interests, and rights of children fade from this picture, as the free speech rights of parents are converted into authority over other people insofar as it affects their children's education.[10] Instead of focusing on the importance of protecting the needs, interests, or rights of children to an adequate education, Gilles interprets the First Amendment so as to cede control of teachers' speech to parents, thereby maximizing the educational authority of parents over their children.

Like many other advocates of parental power, Gilles presumes it to be a default position and criticizes other positions by saying that they do not command a consensus.[11] But no conception—including that of

[8] Stephen Gilles, "On Educating Children: A Parentalist Manifesto," 63 *University of Chicago Law Review* 937 (Summer 1996), p. 944.

[9] Ibid., p. 1018.

[10] Ibid.

[11] Gilles writes, for example, "there is no consensus in favor of Gutmann's conception of liberal democracy." Ibid., p. 972. I agree. No consensus exists that favors my conception—or any other conception—of liberal democracy, deliberative democracy,

exclusive (or nearly exclusive) parental rights over schooling—can claim a social consensus. There is no better alternative but to defend a controversial substantive conception.

Democratic Education defends the view that (1) parents have extensive authority over the education of their children; (2) consistent with extensive parental authority, citizens may legitimately mandate a civic education that is appropriate to a democracy of free and equal citizenship. It offers an understanding of what kind of civic education is appropriate to a democratic society, and when parents and citizens exceed the limits of their legitimate authority over education. It also welcomes contestation; civic minimalism does not. Democratic education invites citizens to argue about alternative requirements of publicly subsidized schooling, including civic minimalism.

"Choice *is* a panacea," Chubb and Moe say. It is "not like other reforms and should not be combined with them as part of a reformist strategy for improving America's public schools." Choice should be viewed as "a self-contained reform":

> with its own rationale and justification. It has the capacity *all by itself* to bring about the kind of transformation that, for years, reformers have been seeking to engineer in myriad other ways.[12]

The idea that a single sweeping reform can cure all of America's educational ills is as old as the United States itself. What has changed radically over the years is the nature of the panacea that reformers recommend as such. But education remains so complex that no single reform—whether it be in the direction of democratic education or school choice—can promise to be anything close to a panacea. Kant's cautionary claim, with which I began this book, remains as true today as it was when he wrote it: "there are two human inventions which may be considered more difficult than any others—the art of government, and the art of education"[13]

Parental choice still has great appeal, in large part because too many public schools—especially in American inner cities—fail to offer an adequate education to too many children. Democratic education calls for the choice of an effective school for every child who is not now receiving an adequate education in a neighborhood public school. Improving public schools and increasing choice among them

---

or democratic education. But a person who proposes to convert the First Amendment right to free speech into a right of parents to control the speech of everyone who educates their children cannot consistently count lack of consensus as a criticism.

[12] Chubb and Moe, *Politics, Markets, and America's Schools*, p. 217.

[13] Immanuel Kant, *Kant on Education (Ueber Padagogik)*, trans. Annette Churton (Boston: D. C. Heath and Co., 1900), p. 12.

is more defensible than subsidizing private schools in a society that constitutionally separates church and state. But as long as a substantial number of public schools are failing to provide an adequate civic education to a substantial number of children, there will be something to be said for subsidizing private schools that are willing and able to provide these children with an adequate civic education on a nondiscriminatory basis.

Civic standards go beyond the 3R's. They include teaching racial nondiscrimination and religious toleration. Parental choice is therefore most justifiably enhanced in a way that supports racial nondiscrimination and religious toleration, and that does not increase the segregation of most advantaged and least advantaged students. Such segregation is problematic from any civic perspective that recognizes the importance of teaching toleration and mutual respect. Publicly subsidized schools are an appropriate place for children of different socioeconomic, ethnic, racial, and religious backgrounds to learn to respect each other. Students from less educated families also tend to do better by the conventional measures of educational achievement if they attend schools with students from more educated families.[14] Publicly subsidized schools, therefore, should be nondiscriminatory in their admissions.

There is no evidence that choice is a panacea or that effective education can be pursued primarily by switching mechanisms of control from public to private. The efforts at privatizing the Hartford (Connecticut) school system were as disappointing as the efforts at centralizing public control in the Newark (New Jersey) school system. The results of the recent private-public school voucher experiment in Milwaukee (Wisconsin), which wisely targets the least advantaged students in the city, do not support the claim that choice is a panacea. The most reliable studies tentatively suggest that voucher school students show very modest improvements in their mathematics test scores but no improvement in their English test scores over nonvoucher school students.[15] More time is needed to judge the reliability of these

[14] This was a major (although disputed) finding of the path-breaking study by James S. Coleman et al., *Report on Equality of Educational Opportunity* (Washington, D.C.: U.S. Government Printing Office, 1966).

[15] See, for example, Cecilia Elena Rouse, "Private School Vouchers and Student Achievement: An Evaluation of the Milwaukee Parental Choice Program," *The Quarterly Journal of Economics*, May 1998, pp. 552-602; and John F. Witte and Christopher A. Thorn, "Who Chooses? Voucher and Interdistrict Choice Programs in Milwaukee," *American Journal of Education* 104 (May 1996), pp. 186-217. See also John F. Witte, "Reply to Greene, Peterson and Du: 'The Effectiveness of School Choice in Milwaukee: A Secondary Analysis of Data from the Program's Evaluation,'" unpublished paper, August 23, 1996; and Paul E. Peterson, Jay P. Greene, and William

very preliminary findings (which are also contested), but if school systems do nothing more than change mechanisms of control from public to private (or vice versa), the results are bound to be modest at best.

The challenge of adequately educating children who are socially and economically disadvantaged is so great that neither private nor public control, by itself, can promise schools that effectively educate all children for free and equal citizenship. A democratic society needs to offer not only choices among public or private schools, but good choices if it is to fulfill its educational obligations to children. Some kind of competition among schools—both private and public—is educationally productive, even necessary, to prevent schools, like most other public institutions, from atrophying.[16] But it is certainly premature to claim that a voucher plan can solve all the major problems of even a small city school system, let alone all those that beset big city schools.

There is no simple or mechanical substitute, including the "free market," for improving schools and judging them on their educational merits, where those merits include their capacity to contribute to civic education. To what extent do schools succeed in effectively educating every child to literacy, numeracy, economic opportunity, toleration, mutual respect, and the other fundamental skills and virtues of a free and equal citizenry?

When we judge the many school systems of the United States and other contemporary democracies by these standards, they are lacking. But their failings are not attributable primarily to public or private control. When the majority say to parents that they are free to use the public schools at taxpayers' expense or to use any accredited private school at their own expense, they are not being unfair to those who choose private schools for their children. What is unfair is that some citizens are not able to choose a school for their children that provides an adequate education judged by any reasonable standards of civic education, while other citizens can. This problem calls not for paying for private schools but for improving public schools and eliminating the poverty and unemployment that make the task of democratic education such an uphill struggle.

Civic minimalists grant that publicly subsidized and publicly man-

---

Howell, "New Findings from the Cleveland Scholarship Program: A Reanalysis of Data from the Indiana University School of Education Evaluation," unpublished paper, May 6, 1998.

[16] For a balanced overview and analysis of the merits of school choice, see Jeffrey R. Henig, *Rethinking School Choice: Limits of the Market Metaphor* (Princeton: Princeton University Press, 1995).

dated schools should serve civic purposes, and that citizens may therefore mandate teaching the civic minimum. Having granted that publicly subsidized and publicly mandated schools should serve civic purposes, civic minimalists lack good reasons for insisting that the civic purposes of schooling be minimal. A conception of democratic education encourages citizens to support not just minimal but high standards for civic education in schools that do their part to enable all children to enjoy the status of free and equal citizens. Whether those standards are called the civic minimum is far less important than whether—and to what extent—schools succeed in educating all children for free and equal citizenship.

TWO RESPONSES TO MULTICULTURALISM: RECOGNITION AND TOLERATION

Many public schools in the United States once assigned American history texts that referred to Native Americans as savages, neglected the Spanish exploration of the New World, and were almost entirely devoid of voices of African Americans and women. Some even wrote admiringly of the Ku Klux Klan. School days commonly included Protestant prayers, readings from the King James Version of the Bible, and Christian hymns. All children, whatever their religion, were expected to participate.[17]

I mention these practices here, rather than more positive ones, to illustrate two troubling features of a public schooling that does not appropriately recognize multiculturalism. The history books illustrate the first feature: disrespect of experiences of groups that have suffered discrimination. The second feature is reflected in the practices that pressure students to conform to Protestant religious practices: intolerance of dissenting beliefs and practices.

These two features of public schooling are indefensible from any moral and political perspective that would treat individuals as civic equals. Public institutions should manifest and cultivate mutual respect among individuals as free and equal citizens. This aim is basic to almost every democratic ideal. It is explicitly defended by conceptions of both deliberative democracy and political liberalism. A democratic education that is consistent with these conceptions calls for two different responses to multiculturalism, but the two responses

[17] For a recent account of the trends in history textbooks, see Alexander Stille, "The Betrayal of History," *The New York Review of Books*, June 11, 1998, pp. 15-20. For examples of the way non-Protestant school children were treated in public schools, see Diane Ravitch, *The Great School Wars: New York City, 1805-1973* (New York: Basic Books, 1974).

are united by a single principled aim of treating individuals as civic equals.

The first response—in reaction to exclusions of the experiences of entire groups from the curriculum—is publicly recognizing the experiences of oppressed groups, rather than neglecting or denigrating those experiences and thereby exalting those of the dominant group or groups. The second response to a relevantly different set of practices is similarly inspired by a commitment to mutual respect among citizens. The response is toleration—agreeing to disagree about beliefs and practices that are a matter of basic liberty. Toleration substitutes for imposing any single substantive system of beliefs and practices on all students, regardless of their religious or other spiritual convictions. Public recognition and toleration are both appropriate responses to multiculturalism, depending on what is at stake.

To consider whether and why these responses to multiculturalism are defensible, I use the term "multiculturalism" not as a moral perspective in itself (one that defends or denies moral relativism), but rather in a way that does not beg contentious moral questions one way or the other. Multiculturalism, as I use it here, refers to a state of a society and world that contains many cultures (or subcultures) that affect one another by virtue of the interactions of individuals who identify with (or rely upon) these cultures. A culture or subculture, roughly speaking, consists of patterns of thinking, speaking, and acting that are associated with a human community larger than a few families.

As interdependence, communication, and commerce have expanded, most societies have become increasingly multicultural. Cultures are difficult to separate for practical purposes, and often even for analytical purposes, because most individuals rely upon many cultures, not only one, in living their lives.[18] Most individuals are therefore multicultural. Individual identities typically express diverse, inter-dynamic cultures. This does not mean that any individual is completely constituted by even a combination of cultural identities. People creatively constitute their identities, but not de novo. They do so against a background of interactive and continually changing cultural resources.

The debate over how best to respond to multiculturalism too often poses an all-or-nothing choice: Either citizens should tolerate their cultural differences by privatizing them, or they should respect their

[18] For an extended discussion of two models of multiculturalism, and a defense of a model that supports this perspective, see Jeremy Waldron, "Multiculturalism and melange," in Robert Fullinwider, ed., *Public Education in a Multicultural Society* (New York: Cambridge University Press, 1996), pp. 90-118.

cultural differences by publicly recognizing them. The first response is often identified with liberal democratic values and the second response is often identified as opposed to liberal democratic values. But these identifications are misleading. The two responses—toleration and public recognition—need not be (and generally are not) incompatible. Toleration and public recognition are appropriate responses to different issues. Any conception of democracy that is committed to treating people as civic equals should defend both responses.

Liberal democracy, like deliberative democracy, is not opposed to publicly recognizing cultural differences. It is opposed to recognizing collective rights of cultural groups to engage in practices that oppress anyone, including their own members, in the name of cultural difference.[19] Liberal democracy recognizes the rights of individuals to engage in cultural practices that offend other individuals with different cultural identities, as long as the practices do not violate anyone's rights. Toleration and public recognition of cultural differences are two different responses to two different sets of issues that arise because of cultural differences. We should reject the one-eyed visions that defend only one response to all issues of cultural difference.

The response of democratic education to multiculturalism incorporates both toleration and recognition. It rejects the dichotomy "privatize or publicly recognize" because it recognizes two significantly different features of public schooling in multicultural contexts. One feature is the fundamental phenomenon of a world in which all societies and individual identities are increasingly multicultural. Public schooling in a democracy should publicly recognize this phenomenon. Why? To teach United States history largely without reference to the experiences and contributions of Native Americans, African Americans, Latino Americans, and Asian Americans, for example, constitutes an intellectual failure to recognize the contributions of many different cultures—and the contributions of individuals who identify with those cultures—to United States history. This intellectual failure morally damages democracy by conveying a false impression that members of these groups have not contributed significantly to making American politics what it is today.

Something analogous can be said about women's voices being excluded from the curriculum. Women do not constitute a separate cul-

---

[19] For a defense of liberalism's opposition to collective rights based on multiculturalism, see Susan Moller Okin, "Feminism and Multiculturalism: Some Tensions," *Ethics* 108 (July 1998), pp. 661-684. Okin uses the term multiculturalism in a narrower (and more morally loaded) way than I do, which helps explain her claim that feminism and multiculturalism are in tension. She understands multiculturalism as a moral perspective that accords rights to cultural collectivities.

ture, but neither do African Americans. Like other oppressed groups, and partly (but by no means only) due to their oppression, women have some distinct cultural experiences and sensibilities that call for recognition. When history textbooks excluded women's voices and experiences, they conveyed the false impression that women have contributed little or nothing to the political and other cultural resources that should be accessible to everyone in a democratic society. Conveying this impression imposes an extra burden on members of oppressed groups, making it more difficult for them to be empowered to share as civic equals in shaping their society.

Excluding the contribution of different cultures from United States history also constitutes a moral failing in its own right. It does not respect those individuals as equal citizens who identify with less dominant cultures. The most basic premise of democratic education—respect for all individuals as free and equal citizens—calls for a history that recognizes both the oppressions and the social contributions of individuals. To exclude recognition of either because they are associated with less dominant cultures is to disrespect not only those cultures, but also the individuals who identify with them.

Democratic education supports a "politics of recognition" based on respect for individuals and their equal rights as citizens, not on deference to tradition, proportional representation of groups, or the survival rights of cultures.[20] The practice of history textbook publishing in the United States sometimes perverts this politics of recognition. Succumbing to strong market and political pressures, publishers sometimes produce history textbooks that include only positive references to traditional American heroes and only enough references to people of politically prominent ethnicities to achieve proportional representation.[21] These practices are counter-productive to engaging students in learning about the history and politics of their society, an engagement that is essential to teaching the skills and virtues of democratic citizenship and respecting every individual as an equal citizen.[22]

[20] See Charles Taylor, "Multiculturalism and the 'Politics of Recognition,'" in Amy Gutmann, ed., *Multiculturalism: Examining the Politics of Recognition* (Princeton: Princeton University Press, 1994).

[21] See the essay by Alexander Stille, "The Betrayal of History," *The New York Review of Books*, June 11, 1998, pp. 15-20, upon which I rely here.

[22] Stille, "The Betrayal of History," offers examples of such silliness. An eighth-grade history textbook, for example, was rewritten by a major textbook publisher without consulting with the author, so as to credit a Spanish explorer, Bartolomeo Gomez, instead of Henry Hudson, with discovering the Hudson River. As it turns out, Gomez was Portuguese, and there is no evidence that he discovered the Hudson River. See Stille, ibid., p. 15.

Practices like these are not the inevitable product of a democratic process. Democratic processes can be, and in some states actually are, more deliberative and more conducive to developing the deliberative skills of democratic citizenship. Several states, Tennessee and Virginia among them, along with various inner-city public schools and elite private schools have demonstrated this. They were sufficiently impressed to adopt a textbook that can serve as a model for deliberative democratic education. *A History of US* by Joy Hakim presents American history as a series of narratives that are inclusive and accurate. With an engaging and broadly accessible style, its content is relatively complex. Equally important, the narratives highlight the relevance to democratic citizenship of the moral choices that individuals make in politics.[23]

When public school texts and teachers present narratives of moral choices in politics, they set the stage for students to think about those choices as democratic citizens. A multicultural history should not imply—let alone claim—that competing cultural beliefs and practices are equally valuable. There would be little point in understanding competing beliefs and practices if their equal value could simply be assumed. Classrooms that include students from diverse cultural backgrounds can facilitate such understanding, but it is equally important that teaching be well informed, and teachers open-minded to the possibility—and sometimes even the desirability—of reasonable disagreement about the value of competing beliefs and practices.

Open-minded learning in a multicultural setting—to which students bring competing presuppositions and convictions—is a prelude to democratic deliberation in a multicultural society and world. Democratic deliberation, and the open-minded teaching that anticipates it, encourages all citizens to understand and assess competing cultural points of view on matters of mutual concern.

But not all important matters are of mutual concern. Democratic education calls for public recognition, understanding, and assessment when its absence—as in the case of history textbooks that exclude the contributions and experiences of oppressed minorities or women—is disrespectful and discriminatory. But other cultural beliefs and practices—for example, concerning whether or how others worship—are not matters of mutual concern among citizens, or at least not in the same sense. To the extent that there is a mutual concern, it

[23] Hakim's account tells students, for example, that "George Mason of Virginia refused to sign the Constitution because it didn't prohibit the slave trade; but he still remained a life-long slave owner, while South Carolina's John Rutledge argued at the Constitutional Convention in favor of slavery—and then went home and quietly freed his slaves." Recounted in Stille, ibid., p. 20.

is directed not at understanding and assessing competing cultural practices, but at tolerating them. To put the same point somewhat differently, the mutual concern is that citizens tolerate religious differences that do not harm others, not that they assess those differences by a standard of mutual justification. Toleration of diverse ways of worshipping is what is mutually justifiable in a deliberative democracy, not the diverse ways of worshipping themselves. A multicultural world includes competing conceptions of the good life, none of which is mutually justifiable to all the people who would be bound by it were it to become the publicly espoused and enforced doctrine. Such situations call for toleration of competing conceptions of the good life, not public recognition of a single conception.

A second important response of democratic education in a multicultural context is to help students understand the merits (and limits) of tolerating competing conceptions of the good life, and thereby respecting the rights of all individuals to pursue their conception of the good life to the extent that these conceptions are consistent with respecting the equal rights of other individuals. Agreeing to disagree about conceptions of the good life is essential to securing the basic liberty of all individuals. Religious differences have long been among the most salient cultural differences in democratic societies. Deliberative democracy is committed to protecting religious freedom along with other basic liberties, such as freedom of speech. On matters of basic liberty, a democratic education teaches toleration of cultural differences on grounds of reciprocity: mutual respect for the personal integrity of all persons.

An appropriate response of publicly subsidized schooling to cultural differences in the realm of religious worship, for example, is to assess not the merits of our diverse convictions, but rather the merits—and limits—of our agreeing to disagree about diverse convictions on this matter. Multicultural democracies cannot afford to take toleration for granted. Controversies abound in the United States, and in every contemporary democracy, about how far toleration should extend over religious differences.

A democratic education should introduce students to competing perspectives, and it should equip them to deliberate as equal citizens about why and when it is justifiable to agree to disagree over an issue (such as religious worship) and when it is morally necessary to decide collectively on a single substantive policy (such as racial and gender nondiscrimination). The decisions to tolerate religious dissent but not racial or gender discrimination must by their very nature be made collectively, either at the statutory or constitutional level. Reciprocity calls for these decisions to be publicly justified as far as possible to the people who are bound by them.

RECIPROCITY BEYOND BORDERS:
COSMOPOLITANISM AND PATRIOTISM

Reciprocity extends to all individuals, not just to citizens of a single society. Democratic education, therefore, should not limit its vision to a single society. It should encourage students to consider the rights and responsibilities of both a shared citizenship and a shared humanity with all people, regardless of citizenship. The very same value of reciprocity that supports the commitment to cultivate mutual respect in one society, among individuals of many different cultural affiliations, also supports a commitment to cultivate mutual respect beyond the borders of states, among individuals who represent the widest range of citizenships and nationalities.

Cultivating mutual respect entails understanding people not merely as abstractions, upon whom teachers and students project their own conception of what constitutes a good life, but understanding people in their own particularity, with their own lives to lead and their own conceptions of what constitutes a good life. Understanding may or may not lead to acceptance. But understanding in democratic education should precede acceptance or rejection. As importantly, from the perspective of democratic education, understanding opens up previously unknown or misunderstood ways of living and the relationship of those ways of living to politics and public life. Such understanding enriches students' store of civic knowledge.

Although students need to learn a great deal about their own society to function as well-informed citizens, learning only about their own society is not enough to satisfy the moral demands of a democratic education. In an increasingly interdependent world, recognizing the rights of all individuals to live a good life—whatever their citizenship—is just as important as recognizing the rights of one's fellow citizens to live lives to which they are conscientiously committed (as long as they do not violate the equal rights of others). Understanding and assessing foreign societies and ways of life, therefore, presents a similar challenge to understanding and assessing cultural diversity within our own society. The actual practice of a relatively peaceful democratic politics, with all its flaws, however, tends to be more conducive to cultivating mutual respect than does the actual practice of world politics. This is all the more reason for public schools to teach students about the people and politics of societies with which they would otherwise be almost completely unfamiliar, as well as about the history and politics of their own society as it relates to others.[24]

With the ever increasing interdependency of societies, teaching the history and politics of even a single country introduces students to the moral challenge of cultivating mutual respect across borders. One way of cultivating mutual respect while teaching American history and politics is to introduce students to paradigmatic examples of citizens reaching beyond national boundaries in recognition of the equal rights of all people. Martin Luther King's speech opposing the Vietnam War supplies such an example. King presumed to speak from a moral perspective available to all human beings: "[A]ll of us who deem ourselves bound by allegiances and loyalties which are broader and deeper than nationalism and which go beyond our nation's self-defined goals and positions . . . are called to speak for the weak, for the voiceless, for victims of our nation and for those it calls enemy, for no document from human hands can make these humans any less our brothers."[25]

Students should also be encouraged to understand and assess the contributions of political and economic institutions and practices that are not specific to a single society, such as the European Economic Community and the International Monetary Fund. The United Nations' Declaration of Human Rights offers perhaps the best paradigmatic defense of human rights that extends beyond borders. Students should be taught to consider these and other institutionalized relationships among members of different societies, and they should also be exposed to opposing views—for example, of the Vietnam War, EEC, IMF, and the United Nation's Declaration—in a way that encourages them to think about what values are mutually defensible and why. Such reasoning is a prologue to democratic deliberation on an international scale.

Does democratic education therefore support cosmopolitanism

[24] Martha Nussbaum offers four reasons for civic education to focus on the relationship of students to people in other countries. See her "Patriotism and Cosmopolitanism," in Joshua Cohen, ed., *For Love of Country: Debating the Limits of Patriotism* (Boston: Beacon Press, 1996), pp. 11-15. Nussbaum argues for focusing on world citizenship "rather than democratic . . . citizenship," but her explicit arguments converge with mine in suggesting that there need not be such a trade-off, as long as world citizenship is not considered a substitute for democratic citizenship and democratic citizenship is committed to a respect for the dignity and rights of individuals the world over.

[25] Martin Luther King, Jr., "A Time to Break Silence," in James Melvin Washington, ed., *A Testament of Hope: The Essential Writings of Martin Luther King* (New York: Harper & Row, 1986), p. 234.

more than patriotism? Cosmopolitanism and patriotism are used in so many different ways that I should stipulate their meaning before evaluating them from the perspective of democratic education. Cosmopolitanism is often invoked by its advocates as a synonym for moral universalism, and patiotism as a synonym for moral particularism or parochialism. When philosophers defend cosmopolitanism against patriotism by using the terms in this way, they beg the moral question against patriotism. As defined in most dictionaries and as commonly used, cosmopolitanism and patriotism are not moral perspectives. Rather, they are first and foremost sentiments referring to attachments and identifications of the self.

Cosmopolitans are worldly individuals who identify with many places, rather than solely with a single state, as their homeland. Although they are worldly, cosmopolitans cannot avoid discriminating in their attachments. Life is too short to have unlimited attachments. Whether a cosmopolitan's discriminations turn out to be moral and democratic is not foreordained by the fact that they are cosmopolitan. The worldly attachment of cosmopolitans who identify with aristocrats or aesthetes the world over has little to recommend it from a democratic moral perspective.

When philosophers recommend cosmopolitanism over patriotism, they generally are presuming a morally admirable kind of egalitarian cosmopolitan: someone who is attached to human beings wherever they may live and, therefore, is prone to accord equal respect to all human beings, whatever their nationality, ethnicity, religion, race, or gender. It is such an egalitarian attachment to the community of humankind that Anthony Appiah, Martha Nussbaum, and other liberal philosophers defend in the name of cosmopolitanism.[26] It is important to acknowledge, as Appiah does, that not all cosmopolitans are so egalitarian in their attachments.[27] Cosmopolitanism per se does not define an egalitarian attachment to all human beings. The particular kind of cosmopolitan sentiment that is conducive to extending the reach of reciprocity worldwide is one that reflects an egalitarian commitment: an attachment to all human beings regardless of their more particular identities. Egalitarian cosmopolitanism flows from the same moral source as a deliberative democratic education: both are fed by a commitment to equal respect for persons.

Democratic education is therefore compatible with egalitarian cosmopolitanism. Both support extending the reach of reciprocity world-

---

[26] See their respective contributions in Joshua Cohen, ed., *For Love of Country: Debating the Limits of Patriotism* (Boston: Beacon Press, 1996).

[27] Anthony Appiah, "Cosmopolitan Patriots," ibid., p. 23.

wide. Teaching consistently with a moral perspective of democracy means treating students—and expecting students to treat each other and to consider individuals around the world—as having the moral status of civic equals. Democratic education, by virtue of its moral commitment to the equal dignity and civic equality of all individuals, therefore, is conducive to cultivating egalitarian cosmopolitans, even if it does not conceive of the cultivation of egalitarian cosmopolitans as its primary aim. There are multiple ways of being attached to people that are compatible with a democratic commitment to treating all individuals as civic equals. Egalitarian cosmopolitanism is one of those ways.

What, then, is the relationship between democratic education and patriotism? Patriotism, like cosmopolitanism, is a sentiment rather than a moral perspective. Patriotism is commonly defined as love of (and therefore devotion to) country, where country is either a nation or a state. First consider the difference between love of any mass institution, whether it be a nation or a state, and love of a single person, the object of love in its most fundamental form.

Love is a notoriously difficult passion to control. Lovers are relatively unqualified in their loyalty to loved ones. But the danger of such unqualified loyalty in the paradigm case of love—one person's love of another person—pales in comparison to the danger of the unqualified loyalty of millions of people to nations and states. This is the danger of patriotism. Nations and states possess massive institutionalized powers to kill, torture, maim, starve, humiliate, demean, and otherwise deny people the most fundamental prerequisites of a decent life. Nations and states not only frequently threaten to employ these powers, they actually do employ them with terrifying and devastating frequency. Love of country, commonly understood as "my country, right or wrong," is therefore extraordinarily dangerous. A democratic education opposes this kind of patriotism when it encourages students to think about their collective lives in morally principled terms.

Most political philosophers who support patriotism defend another, more particular and less dangerous kind of patriotism: a patriotism that entails love of principle tied to love of country. Republican patriots, as Maurizio Viroli eloquently describes them, love their country because it is a republic that uniquely permits the pursuit of liberty and justice for all.[28] The claim is that love of liberty and love of country (in the form of a republican state) are compatible, indeed

[28] Viroli, *For Love of Country: An Essay on Patriotism and Nationalism* (Oxford: Clarendon Press, 1995).

intimately interconnected, because liberty and justice for all are made possible by a world of republics. Liberty and justice will be forsaken without the active support of citizens, and citizens' active support will not be forthcoming unless they love their country (because liberty and justice are demanding moral causes).

Patriots of the republican sort are therefore persons who love their country because it makes liberty and justice possible. Because republican patriotism is fueled as much by love of justice as by love of country, republican patriots are more discriminating than ordinary patriots in what they will do for their country. They will oppose injustices such as slavery, ethnic cleansing, anti-semitism, racial segregation, and gender discrimination. They will also oppose nationalistic forms of patriotism that subordinate justice to the nationalistic cause of creating states that are thought to be ethnically, religiously, or racially pure. Patriotism of this republican sort is anti-nationalistic, and defined in contrast to nationalism.

But republican patriotism is not therefore without dangers due to its over evaluation of the republic relative to the individuals that constitute it. Republican patriotism does not fully respect the basic liberty of persons. "To be committed to the common liberty of our people," Viroli writes, "means that if our country is unfree we have to work to make it free instead of leaving to look for liberty elsewhere. . . ."[29] Just as faithful lovers do not leave their loved ones except out of necessity, so republican patriots do not leave their countries unless they are forced to do so. "[I]f we are forced to leave," Viroli continues, "we have to continue to work in order to be able to go back to live in freedom with our fellows."[30] In its subordination of the individual to the collectivity, republican patriotism is troubling from a deliberative democratic perspective or any perspective that gives priority to the basic liberties of individuals.

The conception of democracy that informs democratic education gives priority to the basic liberties of individuals. So does the Constitution of the United States. Those basic liberties include the right to leave one's country and settle elsewhere. A public educational system that employed great rhetoric, as republicans recommend, to convince students that "we owe our country our life" would be teaching in a way that violates one of the deliberative aims of democratic education, to subject politically relevant claims to careful public scrutiny.

In the spirit of open-minded inquiry, democratic education should teach students the history and philosophy of patriotism—along with

[29] Ibid., p. 9.
[30] Ibid.

that of cosmopolitanism. Its aim in this regard should be to help students understand these internally complex sentiments of attachment to people and places. But democratic education must resist pressures to inculcate republican patriotism since the inculcation of republican patriotism conflicts with a premise of democratic education—the priority of basic liberties. Internal to republican patriotism is the idea that the subordination of the self to society is obligatory (for the sake of realizing "common liberty"). Moreover, republican patriotism is prone to claims of exclusivity that conflict with the openness of democratic education, as reflected in its assertion that "the cause of liberty against oppression does not need cosmopolitans; it simply needs patriots."[31]

Democracy welcomes diverse ways of identifying with others as civic equals, including the egalitarian cosmopolitanism articulated by Anthony Appiah. Egalitarian cosmopolitans, who respect the equal dignity and basic liberty of all persons, can accept responsibility as citizens of a particular country "to nurture the culture and politics of their homes."[32] Democratic education views this responsibility as one among several morally defensible ways of life, not as a republican requirement that all individuals give their lives for their countries.

Many cultural traditions, not only the European Enlightenment, as Hilary Putnam points out, can (and often do) serve as the source of respect for the equal dignity of all persons. One important contribution of the Enlightenment, which itself is a particular cultural tradition, is the commitment to subjecting inherited moral beliefs to critical inquiry. Putnam defends a kind of "situated intelligence" that is compatible with this (doubly) critical contribution of the Enlightenment. "[W]ithout inherited ways of life," Putnam notes, "there is nothing for criticism to operate on, just as without critical reason there is no way for us to distinguish between what should be saved (perhaps after reinterpretation) and what should be scrapped from our various traditions."[33]

Democratic education welcomes cosmopolitan identities that are egalitarian, but it does not require anybody to be a cosmopolitan. Many people, like Putnam, who are consistently committed to opposing oppression, wherever it exists, do not identify themselves as "citizens of the world."[34] Others, like Appiah and Nussbaum, do. People

[31] Ibid., p. 144.
[32] Anthony Appiah, "Cosmopolitan Patriots," and Hilary Putnam, "Must We Choose?" in For Love of Country: Debating the Limits of Patriotism, pp. 22, 95.
[33] Hilary Putnam, ibid., p. 96.
[34] For a defense of the view that we should be "citizens of the world," see Martha Nussbaum, in For Love of Country: Debating the Limits of Patriotism, pp. 3-17, 131-144.

who do not identify themselves as citizens of the world are not therefore mistaken about their identity. Nor are their identities somehow morally inferior. More likely, they have different (but compatible) ways of understanding the source of their moral commitment, as will almost any group of thoughtful people.

Democratic education has the potential for being far more ecumenical and effective if it does not insist on teaching students that all moral beings must identify themselves in any single way, whether as citizens of the world, Kantian ends-in-themselves, Millean progressive beings, or cosmopolitan patriots. Democratic education instead aims to teach understanding and appreciation of liberty and justice for all from multiple perspectives. There are multiple ways of understanding these values, and there are many self-identifications that converge on the idea that individuals the world over are entitled to the liberties and opportunities necessary to live a good life consistent with their own identities and respecting the equal rights of other individuals. Democratic education welcomes all identifications that are compatible with pursuing liberty and justice for all.

When the aim of democratic education is framed broadly—to encourage the pursuit of liberty and justice for all—it embraces a wide range of attachments and identities at the same time as it recognizes that the moral obligations of citizenship do not stop at state boundaries. It also enables students to expand the horizons of their own lives by learning about lives that otherwise would be less accessible. Teaching students about foreign countries and cultures need not be a recipe for homogenizing the world; it can be consistent with each society's giving the greatest attention to the history, cultures, and politics of its own country.

What then, if anything, makes it legitimate for citizens to support a system of public schooling that focuses disproportionately, although not exclusively, on the histories and cultures of their own country? Particular cultures would not disappear were school curricula to be less discriminating, taking an equal interest in all histories, cultures, and politics of the world. Homogenization of world culture is not a credible consequence of a focus within public schools in the United States on world history rather than American history. But there are at least two other reasons why citizens may legitimately support schooling that focuses disproportionately on the histories, cultures, and politics of their own country.

The first reason is so basic that it is easy to overlook: schooling, even more than life, constitutes too short a timeframe in which to teach everything. Although publicly supported schools could randomly select the history, culture, and politics that they teach, this suggestion is absurd since most citizens appropriately identify more with their own country—its histories, politics, and cultures—than with every other country on the face of the earth. The liberal democratic politics that help protect the equal rights of all individuals builds on particularistic identifications of citizens. Most citizens do not have time to learn as much about all societies as they need to know to be even minimally informed citizens in their own societies. Schooling should make our particularistic cultural identification more well informed and should also demonstrate that particularistic identifications are no excuse whatsoever for oppressing or otherwise denying the equal rights of individuals with other particularistic identifications. Quite the contrary, the fundamental values of liberal democracies oppose oppression and defend the equal rights of all human beings.

A second reason for the focus of schools on domestic history and politics is that this is what citizens can more readily enlist in pursuit of justice, not only within but also beyond their country's borders. Less local forms of politics are increasingly important, but there is still generally more that citizens can do to further the cause of justice by enlisting the assistance of their own country's political institutions. To do so, they must be educated in a way that is conducive to becoming effective citizens of their own society.

These reasons justify teaching students more about the politics, history, and culture of their own society than about any other single society, but they do not justify neglecting the politics, histories, and cultures of other societies. To further reciprocity among all people, schools should convey respect for all people regardless of their nationality, ethnicity, gender, color, class, or religion. This civic aim of democratic education is not minimal. Neither is it optional from a moral perspective.

WORKS CITED

Ackerman, Bruce. *Social Justice in the Liberal State*. New York and London: Yale University Press, 1980.

Adams, Henry. *The Education of Henry Adams*. 1918. Modern Library edition. New York: Modern Library, 1931.

Adler, Richard P., and Ronald J. Faber. "Background: Children's Television Viewing Patterns." In *The Effects of Television Advertising on Children*, ed. by Richard P. Adler, Gerald Slesser, Laurence Krasny Meringoff, Thomas S. Robertson, John R. Rossiter, and Scott Ward, 13-28. Lexington, Mass. and Toronto: Lexington Books, 1980.

Almond, Gabriel, and Sidney Verba. *The Civic Culture: Political Attitudes and Democracy in Five Nations*. Boston: Little, Brown and Co., 1965.

Ambert, Alba N., and Sarah E. Melendez. *Bilingual Education: A Sourcebook*. New York: Garland Publishing, 1985.

Amdur, Robert. "Compensatory Justice: The Question of Costs." *Political Theory*, vol. 7 (May 1979): 229-44.

Angell, George W., ed. *Faculty and Teacher Bargaining: The Impact of Unions on Education*. Lexington, Mass.: D. C. Heath, 1981.

Anghoff, William H. *The College Board Testing Program*. New York: College Entrance Examination Board, 1971.

Appiah, Anthony. "Cosmopolitan Patriots." In *For Love of Country: Debating the Limits of Patriotism*. Ed. by Joshua Cohen, 21-29. Boston: Beacon Press, 1996.

Aristotle. *The Politics of Aristotle*. Ed. and trans. by Ernest Barker. New York: Oxford University Press, 1958.

———. *The Works of Aristotle*. Ed. and trans. by W. D. Ross. Oxford: Oxford University Press, 1928.

Bailyn, Bernard. *Education in the Forming of American Society*. New York: Vintage, 1960.

Banfield, Edward. *The Democratic Muse: The Visual Arts and the Public Interest*. New York: Basic Books, 1984.

Banks, James A. *Multiethnic Education: Theory and Practice*. Boston: Allyn and Bacon, 1981.

Barber, Benjamin. *Strong Democracy: Participatory Politics for a New Age*. Berkeley: University of California Press, 1984.

Bastian, Ann, Norm Fruchter, Marilyn Gittell, Colin Greer, and Kenneth Haskins. *Choosing Equality: The Case for Democratic Schooling.* Philadelphia: Temple University Press, 1986.

Battistoni, Richard M. *Public Schooling and the Education of Democratic Citizens.* Jackson: University Press of Mississippi, 1985.

Baumol, William J., and William G. Bowen. *Performing Arts — The Economic Dilemma.* New York: Twentieth Century Fund, 1966.

Bennett, William J. "Educators in America: The Three R's." Speech before the National Press Club, Washington, D.C., March 27, 1985.

Bentham, Jeremy. *The Works of Jeremy Bentham.* Published under the superintendence of his executor, John Bowring. Edinburgh: W. Tait; London: Simpkin, Marshall and Co., 1843.

Bernstein, Basil. "Education Cannot Compensate for Society." *New Society* (February 26, 1970): 344-77.

Bittker, Boris I. "Charitable Contributions: Tax Deductions or Matching Grants?" *Texas Law Review* 28 (1972): 37-63.

Blatt, Moshe M., and Lawrence Kohlberg. "The Effects of Classroom Moral Discussion Upon Children's Level of Moral Judgment." *Journal of Moral Education,* vol. 4 (1975): 129-62.

Blauner, Robert. *Alienation and Freedom.* Chicago: University of Chicago Press, 1964.

Bok, Derek. *Beyond the Ivory Tower: Social Responsibilities of the Modern University.* Cambridge, Mass.: Harvard University Press, 1982.

Bolton, Roger E. "The Economics and Public Financing of Higher Education: An Overview." In *The Economics and Financing of Higher Education in the United States: A Compendium of Papers,* 11-104. Washington, D.C.: U.S. Government Printing Office, 1969.

Bowen, Howard R. *Financing Higher Education: The Current State of the Debate.* Association of American Colleges, 1974.

Bowles, Samuel, and Herbert Gintis. *Schooling in Capitalist America: Educational Reform and the Contradictions of Economic Life.* New York: Basic Books, 1976

Boyer, Ernest L. *High School: A Report on Secondary Education in America.* New York: Harper and Row, 1983.

Braddock, Jomills Henry II, Robert L. Crain, and James M. McPartland. "A Long-Term View of School Desegregation: Some Recent Studies of Graduates as Adults." *Phi Delta Kappan,* vol. 66, no. 4 (December 1984): 259-64.

Brenemen, David W., and Chester E. Finn, Jr. "An Uncertain Future." In *Public Policy and Private Higher Education,* ed. by

David Brenemen and Charles E. Finn, Jr.,17-48. Washington, D.C.: The Brookings Institution, 1978.

Brenemen, David W., and Susan C. Nelson. *Financing Community Colleges: An Economic Perspective.* Washington, D.C.: The Brookings Institution, 1981.

Brenton, Myron. *What's Happened to Teacher?* New York: Avon Books, 1970.

Brink, André. *Writing in a State of Siege: Essays on Politics and Literature.* New York: Summit Books, 1983.

Burston, W. H., ed. *James Mill on Education.* Cambridge: Cambridge University Press, 1982.

Callahan, Daniel, and Sissela Bok, eds. *Ethics Teaching in Higher Education.* New York: Plenum Press, 1980.

Cantor, Muriel G. "The Role of the Producer in Choosing Children's Television Content." In *Television and Social Behavior: Reports and Papers*, vol. 1, *Media Content and Control*, ed. by George Comstock, Eli A. Rubinstein, and John P. Murray, 259-89. Washington, D.C.: U.S. Government Printing Office, 1972.

Carnegie Commission on the Future of Public Broadcasting. *A Public Trust: The Report of the Carnegie Commission on the Future of Public Broadcasting.* New York: Bantam, 1979.

Carnoy, Martin, and Henry M. Levin. *Schooling and Work in the Democratic State.* Stanford, Calif.: Stanford University Press, 1985.

Cass, Ronald A. *Revolution in the Wasteland: Value and Diversity in Television.* Charlottesville: University of Virginia Press, 1981.

Cavanaugh, Ralph, and Austin Sarat. "Thinking About Courts: Toward and Beyond a Jurisprudence of Judicial Competence." *Law and Society Review*, vol. 14, no. 2 (Winter 1980): 371-420.

Chubb, John E. and Terry M. Moe. *Politics, Markets, and American Schools.* Washington, D.C.: Brookings, 1990.

Clark, Donald H., Arlene Goldsmith, and Clementine Pugh. *Those Children.* Belmont, Calif.: Wadsworth Publishing, 1970.

Cohen, David K., and Bella H. Rosenberg. "Functions and Fantasies: Understanding Schools in Capitalist America." *History of Education Quarterly* (Summer 1977): 113-37.

Coleman, James S., Ernest Q. Campbell, Carol J. Hobson, James McPartland, Alexander M. Mood, Frederic D. Weinfeld, and Robert L. York. *Report on Equality of Educational Opportunity.* Washington, D.C.: U.S. Government Printing Office, 1966.

Coleman, James S., Thomas Hoffer, and Sally Kilgore. *High School Achievement: Public, Catholic, and Private Schools Compared.* New York: Basic Books, 1982.

Comstock, George, Steven Chaffee, Nathan Katzman, Maxwell Mc-Combs, and Donald Roberts. *Television and Human Behavior.* New York: Columbia University Press, 1978.

Comstock, George A., and Eli A. Rubinstein, eds. *Television and Social Behavior: Reports and Papers*, vol. 1, *Media Content and Control.* Washington, D.C.: U.S. Government Printing Office, 1972.

Coons, John E., William H. Clune III, and Stephen D. Sugarman. *Private Wealth and Public Education.* Cambridge, Mass.: Harvard University Press, 1970.

Coons, John E., and Stephen D. Sugarman. *Education by Choice: The Case for Family Control.* Berkeley: University of California Press, 1978.

Crain, Robert L., Jennifer A. Hawes, Randi L. Miller, and Janet R. Peichert. "A Longitudinal Study of a Metropolitan Voluntary Desegregation Plan." Washington, D.C.: National Institute of Education, October 1984.

Crain, Robert L., and Rita E. Mahard. "Desegregation and Black Achievement: A Review of the Research." *Law and Contemporary Problems*, vol. 42, no. 3 (Summer 1978): 17-56.

"Creationism in Schools: The Decision in McLean versus the Arkansas Board of Education." *Science*, vol. 215, no. 4535 (February 19, 1982): 934-43.

Cremin, Lawrence A. American Education: *The National Experience, 1783-1876.* New York: Harper and Row, 1980.

———. *Traditions of American Education.* New York: Basic Books, 1977.

———. *The Transformation of the School: Progressivism in American Education, 1876-1957.* New York: Vintage Books, 1964.

Cummings, Milton C., Jr., and Richard S. Katz, eds. *Government and the Arts in the Modern World.* New York: Oxford University Press, 1986.

Cummings, William K. *Education and Equality in Japan.* Princeton, N.J.: Princeton University Press, 1980.

Dawson, Richard E., and Kenneth Prewitt. *Political Socialization.* Boston: Little, Brown and Co., 1969.

Dewey, John. *"The Child and the Curriculum"* and *"The School and Society."* 1900, 1915. Rev. ed. Chicago: University of Chicago Press, 1956.

———. *Democracy and Education.* 1916. New York: The Free Press, 1966.

Digest of Educational Statistics, 1983-84. Washington, D.C.: U.S. Government Printing Office, 1984.

Do Teachers Make a Difference? Washington, D.C.: U.S. Government Printing Office, 1983.

Durkheim, Emile. *Moral Education.* New York: Free Press, 1961.

Dworkin, Ronald. "DeFunis v. Sweatt." In *Equality and Preferential Treatment,* ed. by Marshall Cohen, Thomas Nagel, and Thomas Scanlon, 63-83. Princeton, N.J.: Princeton University Press, 1977.

Easton, David, and Jack Dennis. *Children in the Political System: Origins of Political Legitimacy.* New York: McGraw-Hill, 1969.

Eaton, William Edward. *The American Federation of Teachers 1916-1961: A History of the Movement.* Carbondale, Ill.: Southern Illinois University Press, 1975.

Eckstein, Harry. "Civic Inclusion and Its Discontents." *Daedalus,* vol. 113, no. 4 (Fall 1984): 107-145.

Elshtain, Jean. "Democracy and the QUBE Tube." *The Nation* (August 7-14, 1982): 108-110.

Elster, Jon. "Marxism, Functionalism and Game Theory." In *Theory and Society,* vol. 11 (1982): 453-82.

———. *Sour Grapes: Studies in the Subversion of Rationality.* Cambridge: Cambridge University Press, 1983.

Ely, John Hart. *Democracy and Distrust: A Theory of Judicial Review.* Cambridge, Mass.: Harvard University Press, 1980.

Epstein, Noel. *Language, Ethnicity and the Schools: Policy Alternatives for Bilingual-Bicultural Education.* Washington, D.C.: Institute for Educational Leadership, 1977.

Feinberg, Joel. *Doing and Deserving.* Princeton, N.J.: Princeton University Press, 1970.

Feld, Alan L., Michael O'Hare, and J. Mark Davidson Schuster. *Patrons Despite Themselves: Taxpayers and Arts Policy.* New York: New York University Press, 1983.

Finley, M. I. *Politics in the Ancient World.* Cambridge: Cambridge University Press, 1983.

Finn, Chester E., Jr. *Scholars, Dollars & Bureaucrats.* Washington, D.C.: The Brookings Institution, 1978.

Fishkin, James S. *Justice, Equal Opportunity, and the Family.* New Haven and London: Yale University Press, 1983.

FitzGerald, Frances. *America Revised: History Schoolbooks in the 20th Century.* New York: Random House, 1980.

Flathman, Richard E., ed. *Concepts in Social and Political Philosophy.* New York: Macmillan, 1973.

Flexner, Abraham. *Universities: American, English, German.* New York and London: Oxford University Press, 1930.

Foote, Susan Bartlett, and Robert H. Mnookin. "The 'Kid Vid' Crusade." *The Public Interest,* no. 61 (Fall 1980): 90-105.

Franklin, Benjamin. *The Writings of Benjamin Franklin.* Ed. by Albert H. Smyth. 10 vols. New York and London: Macmillan, 1905-1907.

Fried, Charles. *Right and Wrong.* Cambridge, Mass.: Harvard University Press, 1978.

Friedman, Milton. *Capitalism and Freedom.* Chicago: University of Chicago Press, 1962.

Friedman, Milton. "The Higher Schooling in America." *The Public Interest* (Spring 1968): 109-112.

———. "The Role of Government in Education." In *Economics and the Public Interest*, ed. by Robert Solo, 123-44. New Brunswick, N.J. Rutgers University Press, 1955.

Fuchs, Ralph F. "Academic Freedom—Its Basic Philosophy, Function, and History." In *Academic Freedom: The Scholar's Place in Modern Society*, ed. by Hans W. Baade and Robinson O. Everett, 1-16. Dobbs Ferry, N.Y.: Oceana Publications, 1964.

Fullinwider, Robert K. *The Reverse Discrimination Controversy: A Moral and Legal Analysis.* Totowa, N.J.: Rowman and Littlefield, 1980.

Galston, William. *Liberal Virtues.* New York: Cambridge University Press, 1991.

Gardner, John W. *Excellence: Can We Be Equal and Excellent Too?* New York: Harper and Brothers, 1961.

Garms, Walter I., James W. Guthrie, and Lawrence C. Pierce. *School Finance: The Economics and Politics of Public Education.* Englewood Cliffs, N.J.: Prentice-Hall, 1978.

General Education in a Free Society: Report of the Harvard Committee. Cambridge, Mass.: Harvard University Press, 1945.

Gibbs, John C. "Kohlberg's States of Moral Judgement: A Constructive Critique." *Harvard Educational Review*, vol. 47, no. 1 (February 1977): 43-61.

Giles, Michael W., Douglas S. Gatlin, and Everett F. Cataldo. "The Impact of Busing on White Flight." *Social Science Quarterly*, vol. 55 (1974): 493-501.

Gilles, Stephen G. "On Educating Children: A Parentalist Manifesto." *University of Chicago Law Review* 63: 937-1032.

Gilligan, Carol. *In a Different Voice: Psychological Theory and Women's Development.* Cambridge, Mass.: Harvard University Press, 1983.

Ginzberg, Eli, and Douglas W. Bray. *The Uneducated.* New York: Columbia University Press, 1953.

Glazer, Nathan. "What Happened at Berkeley." In *The Berkeley Student Revolt: Facts and Interpretations*, ed. by Seymour Martin

Lipset and Sheldon S. Wolin, 285-303. Garden City, N.Y. Doubleday and Co., 1965.

Glock, Charles Y., Robert Wuthnow, Jane Allyn Piliavin, and Metta Spencer. *Adolescent Prejudice*. New York: Harper and Row, 1975.

Goodlad, John I. *A Place Called School: Prospects for the Future*. New York: McGraw-Hill, 1984.

Goodman, Paul. *The Community of Scholars*. New York: Random House, 1962.

Greenstein, Fred I. *Children and Politics*. New Haven: Yale University Press, 1965.

————. "Socialization: Political Socialization." *International Encyclopedia of the Social Sciences*, vol. 14. New York: Macmillan, 1968: 551-55.

Greer, Colin. *The Great School Legend*. New York: Basic Books, 1972.

Grubb, W. Norton, and Stephan Michelson. *States and Schools: The Political Economy of Public School Finance*. Lexington, Mass.: Lexington Books, 1974.

Gutmann, Amy. "The Challenge of Multiculturalism in Political Ethics." *Philosophy & Public Affairs*, vol. 22, no. 3 (Sumer 1993): 171-206.

————. "Challenges of Multiculturalism in Education." In *Public Education in a Multicultural Society*, ed. by Robert Fullinwider, 156-179. New York: Cambridge University Press, 1996.

————. "Children, Paternalism and Education: A Liberal Argument." *Philosophy and Public Affairs*, vol. 9, no. 4 (Summer 1980): 338-58.

————. "Civic Education and Social Diversity." *Ethics* 105 (April 1995): 557-579.

————. "Communitarian Critics of Liberalism." *Philosophy and Public Affairs*, vol. 14, no. 3 (Summer 1985): 308-322.

————. "How Liberal is Democracy." In *Liberalism Reconsidered*, ed. by Douglas MacLean and Claudia Mills, 25-50. Totowa, N.J.: Rowman and Allanheld, 1983.

————. *Liberal Equality*. Cambridge: Cambridge University Press, 1980.

————. "Undemocratic Education." In *Liberalism and the Moral Life*, ed. by Nancy L. Rosenblum, 71-88. Cambridge: Harvard University Press, 1989.

————. "What's the Use of Going to School?: The Problem of Education in Utilitarian and Rights Theories." In *Utilitarianism and Beyond*, ed. by Amartya Sen and Bernard Williams, 261-77. Cambridge: Cambridge University Press, 1982.

Gutmann, Amy, and Dennis Thompson. *Democracy and Disagreement*. Cambridge: Harvard University Press, 1996.

Gutmann, Amy, and Dennis F. Thompson, eds. *Ethics and Politics: Cases and Comments*. Chicago: Nelson-Hall, 1984.

Hansen, W. Lee, and Burton A. Weisbrod. "A New Approach to Higher Education Finance." In *Financing Higher Education: Alternatives for the Federal Government*, ed. by M. D. Orwig, 117-42. Iowa City, Iowa: American College Testing Program, 1971.

Hanushek, Eric A. *Education and Race*. Lexington, Mass.: D. C. Heath and Co., 1972.

Hanushek, Eric A., and John F. Kain. "On the Value of *Equality of Educational Opportunity* as a Guide to Public Policy." In *On Equality of Educational Opportunity*, ed. by Frederick Mosteller and Daniel P. Moynihan, 116-45. New York: Vintage Books, 1972.

Hare, R. M. "Opportunity for What?: Some Remarks on Current Disputes About Equality in Education." *Oxford Review of Education*, vol. 3, no. 3 (1977): 207-216.

Harris, John. "The Political Status of Children." In *Contemporary Political Philosophy: Radical Studies*, ed. by Keith Graham, 35-55. Cambridge: Cambridge University Press, 1982.

Harris, John S. *Government Patronage of the Arts in Great Britain*. Chicago: University of Chicago Press, 1970.

Harris, Louis, and Associates. *A Study of Attitudes Toward Racial and Religious Minorities and Toward Women*. New York: Louis Harris and Associates, 1978.

Hawley, Willis D. "Increasing the Effectiveness of School Desegregation: Lessons from the Research." In *Race and Schooling in the City*, ed. by Adam Yarmolinsky, Lance Liebman, and Corinne S. Schelling, 145-62. Cambridge, Mass.: Harvard University Press, 1981.

Henig, Jeffrey R. *Rethinking School Choice: Limits of the Market Metaphor*. Princeton: Princeton University Press: 1995.

Heyns, Barbara. *Summer Learning and the Effects of Schooling*. New York: Academic Press, 1978.

Heyns, Roger W. "Education and Society: A Complex Interaction." *American Education*, vol. 20, no. 4 (May 1984): 2-5.

Hirst, P. H. "Liberal Education and the Nature of Knowledge." In *Education and the Development of Reason*, ed. R. F. Dearden, P. H. Hirst, and R. S. Peters. London: Routledge and Kegan Paul, 1972.

Hirst, P. H., and R. S. Peters, eds. *The Logic of Education*. London: Routledge and Kegan Paul, 1970.

Ho, Ping-Ti. *The Ladder of Success in Imperial China: Aspects of Social Mobility, 1368-1911*. New York: Columbia University Press, 1962.

Hochschild, Jennifer. *The New American Dilemma: Liberal Democracy and School Desegregation*. New Haven, Conn.: Yale University Press, 1984.

Hofstadter, Richard, and Walter Metzger, eds. *The Development of Academic Freedom in the United States*. New York: Columbia University Press, 1955.

Hoggart, Richard. *An English Temper: Essays on Education, Culture and Communications*. New York: Oxford University Press, 1982.

Hunter, Carmen St. John, with David Harman. *Adult Illiteracy in the United States: A Report to the Ford Foundation*. New York: McGraw-Hill, 1979.

Hutchins, Robert Maynard. *The Higher Learning in America*. New Haven, Conn.: Yale University Press, 1936.

Illich, Ivan. *Deschooling Society*. New York: Harper and Row, 1970.

"In the Matter of Children's Television Programming and Advertising Practices." Docket no. 19142. *Federal Communications Commission 79-851*, December 28, 1979.

Jackson, Philip W. *Life in Classrooms*. New York: Holt, Rinehart and Winston, 1968.

Janowitz, Morris. *The Reconstruction of Patriotism: Education for Civic Consciousness*. Chicago: University of Chicago Press, 1983.

Jencks, Christopher, Marshall Smith, Henry Acland, Mary Jo Bane, David Cohen, Herbert Gintis, Barbara Heyns, and Stephan Michelson. *Inequality: A Reassessment of the Effect of Family and Schooling in America*. New York: Basic Books, 1972.

Jennings, M. Kent, Lee H. Ehman, and Richard G. Niemi. "Social Studies Teachers and Their Pupils." In *The Political Character of Adolescence: The Influence of Families and Schools*, ed. by M. Kent Jennings and Richard G. Niemi, 207-227. Princeton, N.J.: Princeton University Press, 1974.

Jennings, M. Kent, Kenneth P. Langton, and Richard G. Niemi. "Effects of High School Civics Curriculum." In *The Political Character of Adolescence: The Influence of Families and Schools*, ed. by M. Kent Jennings and Richard G. Niemi, 181-206. Princeton, N.J.: Princeton University Press, 1974.

Johns, Roe L., Edgar L. Morphet, and Kern Alexander. *The Economics and Financing of Education*. 4th ed. Englewood Cliffs, N.J.: Prentice-Hall, 1983.

Johnson, David W., and Roger Johnson. *Learning Together and Alone: Cooperation, Competition and Individualization*. Englewood Cliffs, N.J.: Prentice-Hall, 1975.

Jones, A.H.M. *Athenian Democracy*. Oxford: Basil Blackwell, 1957.

Joughin, Louis, ed. *Academic Freedom and Tenure: A Handbook of the American Association of University Professors*. Madison: University of Wisconsin Press, 1969.

Kaestle, Carl F. *The Evolution of an Urban School System: New York City, 1750-1850*. Cambridge, Mass.: Harvard University Press, 1973.

Kant, Immanuel. *Kant on Education*. Trans. by Annette Churton. Boston: D. C. Heath and Co., 1900.

Karier, Clarence, Paul Violas, and Joel Spring. *Roots of Crisis: American Education in the Twentieth Century*. Chicago: Rand McNally, 1973.

Katz, Michael B. *Class, Bureaucracy, and Schools: The Illusion of Educational Change in America*. New York: Praeger, 1971.

Katzman, Martin T. *The Political Economy of Urban Schools*. Cambridge, Mass.: Harvard University Press, 1971.

Katznelson, Ira, and Margaret Weir. *Schooling for All: Class, Race, and the Decline of the American Ideal*. New York: Basic Books, 1985.

Kerr, Clark. *The Uses of the University*. Cambridge, Mass.: Harvard University Press, 1982.

King, Martin Luther. "A Time to Break Silence." In *A Testament of Hope: The Essential Writings of Martin Luther King*. Ed. by James Melvin Washington, 231-244. New York: Harper & Row, 1986.

Kirp, David L. *Just Schools: The Idea of Racial Equality in American Education*. Berkeley: University of California Press, 1982.

Kirp, David, William Buss, and Peter Kuriloff. "Legal Reform of Special Education: Empirical Studies and Procedural Proposals." *California Law Review*, vol. 62, no. 1 January 1974): 40-155.

Kirschenbaum, Howard. "Clarifying Values Clarification: Some Theoretical Issues." In *Moral Education . . . It Comes With the Territory*, ed. by David Purpel and Kevin Ryan, 116-25. Berkeley, Calif.: McCutchan, 1976.

Klitgaard, Robert. *Choosing Elites*. New York: Basic Books, 1985.

Kohlberg, Lawrence. "The Moral Athmosphere of the School." In *The Unstudied Curriculum*, ed. by N. V. Overley, 104-127. Washington, D.C.: Association for Supervision and Curriculum Development, 1970.

Kohlberg, Lawrence, and E. Turiel, "Moral Development and Moral Education." In *Psychology and Educational Practice*, ed. by G. Lesser, 410-65. Chicago: Scott Foresman, 1971.

Kohn, Melvin. *Class and Conformity: A Study in Values.* 2nd ed. Chicago: University of Chicago Press, 1977.

Kohn, Melvin, and Carmi Schooler. "Job Conditions and Personality: A Longitudinal Assessment of Their Reciprocal Effects." *American Journal of Sociology*, vol. 87, no. 6 (May 1982): 1257-86.

————. "Occupational Experience and Psychological Functioning: An Assessment of Reciprocal Effects." *American Sociological Review*, vol. 38, no. 1 (February 1973): 97-118.

Kornhauser, Arthur. *Mental Health of the Industrial Worker: A Detroit Study.* New York: John Wiley and Sons, 1964.

Kozol, Jonathan. *Illiterate America.* Garden City, N.Y.: Doubleday, 1985.

Langton, Kenneth P. *Political Socialization.* New York: Oxford University Press, 1969.

Larson, Magali Sarfatti. *The Rise of Professionalism: A Sociological Analysis.* Berkeley, Calif.: University of California Press, 1977.

Laudan, Larry. "Science at the Bar: Causes for Concern." In *Evolution, Morality and the Meaning of Life*, ed. by Jeffrie G. Murphy, 334-52. Totowa, N.J.: Rowman and Littlefield, 1982.

Levin, Betsy, Thomas Muller, William J. Scanlon, and Michael A. Cohen. *Public School Finance: Present Disparities and Fiscal Alternatives.* Washington, D.C.: The Urban Institute, 1972.

Levy, Frank, Arnold J. Meltsner, and Aaron Wildavsky. *Urban Outcomes: Schools, Streets, and Libraries.* Berkeley: University of California Press, 1974.

Lewin, Roger. "Where is the Science in Creation Science?" *Science*, vol. 215, no. 529 (January 8, 1982): 142-46.

Lightfoot, Sarah Lawrence. *The Good High School: Portraits of Character and Culture.* New York: Basic Books, 1983.

Lilla, Mark T. "Ethos, 'Ethics,' and Public Service." *The Public Interest*, no. 63 (Spring 1981).

Lipset, Seymour Martin. "Political Controversies at Harvard, 1936-1974." In *Education and Politics at Harvard*, ed. by S. M. Lipset and David Riesman, 3-278. New York: McGraw-Hill, 1975.

The Listener, vol. 85, no. 2197 (May 6, 1971). Reviews of televised course instruction by Marghanita Lanski, Raymond Williams, and Philip Elliott.

Locke, John. *Two Treatises of Government.* Intro. by Peter Laslett. New York: Cambridge University Press, 1960.

Lortie, Dan. *School Teacher: A Sociological Study.* Chicago: University of Chicago Press, 1975.

Lukas, J. Anthony. *Common Ground: A Turbulent Decade in the Lives of Three American Families.* New York: Alfred A. Knopf, 1985.

MacCallum, Gerald C., Jr. "Negative and Positive Freedom." *Philosophical Review* 76 (1967): 312-34.

Machiavelli, Niccolo. *The Discourses.* In *The Prince and The Discourses.* 1940. Modern Library edition. New York: The Modern Library (Random House), 1950.

McIntosh, N. E., and A. Woodley. "The Open University and Second-Chance Education—An Analysis of the Social and Educational Background of Open University Students." *Paedagogica Europaea: Review of Education in Europe,* vol. 9, no. 2 (1974): "Contemporary Education," 85-86.

MacIver, Robert M. *Academic Freedom in Our Time.* New York: Columbia University Press, 1955.

Mackey, William. "A Typology for Bilingual Education." In *Bilingual Schooling in the United States: A Source Book for Educational Personnel,* ed. by Francesco Cordasco, 72-90. New York: McGraw-Hill, 1976.

McPherson, Gertrude. *Small Town Teacher.* Cambridge, Mass.: Harvard University Press, 1972.

McPherson, Michael S. "The Demand for Higher Education." In *Public Policy and Private Higher Education,* ed. by David W. Brenemen and Chester E. Finn, Jr., 143-96. Washington, D.C.: The Brookings Institution, 1978.

Mansbridge, Jane. *Beyond Adversary Democracy.* New York: Basic Books, 1980.

Martin, Jane Roland. *Reclaiming a Conversation: The Ideal of the Educated Woman.* New Haven and London: Yale University Press, 1985.

Mayhew, K. C., and A. C. Edwards. *The Dewey School.* New York: Atherton, 1966.

Metz, Mary Haywood. *Classrooms and Corridors: The Crisis of Authority in Desegregated Secondary Schools.* Berkeley: University of California Press, 1978.

Metzger, Walter. "Authority at Columbia." In The *University Crisis Reader: Confrontation and Counterattack,* ed. by Immanuel Wallerstein and Paul Starr, 2 vols., 2: 329-40. New York: Random House, 1971.

Mezirow, Jack, Gordon (G. Darkenwald, and Alan B. Know. *Last Gamble on Education.* Washington, D.C.: Adult Education Association, 1975.

Mill, John Stuart. "Considerations on Representative Government."
    In *Essays on Politics and Society*, ed. by. M. Robson. Vols.
    18-19 of *Collected Works*. Toronto: University of Toronto Press,
    1977.

————. *On Liberty*. In *Utilitarianism, On Liberty, Essay on Ben-
    tham*, ed. by Mary Warnock, 126-250. New York: New Ameri-
    can Library, 1962.

————. *Principles of Political Economy*. 1848, 1871. In *Collected
    Works*, ed. by J. M. Robson, vol 3. Toronto: University of
    Toronto Press, 1965.

Montesquieu. *The Spirit of the Laws*. Trans. by Thomas Nugent.
    London: J. Nourse and P. Vaillant, 1750.

Mosher, Ralph L., and Paul Sullivan. "A Curriculum for Moral Edu-
    cation for Adolescents." in *Moral Education . . . It Comes With
    the Territory*, ed. by David Purpel and Kevin Ryan, 235-51.
    Berkeley, Calif.: McCutchan, 1976.

Murname, Richard J. *The Impact of School Resources on the Learn-
    ing of Inner City Children*. Cambridge, Mass.: Ballinger Publish-
    ing, 1975.

Murphy, Jeffrie G. *Evolution, Morality and the Meaning of Life*.
    Totowa, N.J.: Rowman and Littlefield, 1982.

Murphy, Walter F. "An Ordering of Constitutional Values." *Southern
    California Law Review*, vol. 53, no. 2 (January 1980): 703-760.

Nagel, Thomas. "Symposium on the Public Benefits of the Arts and
    Humanities." *Art and the Law*, vol. 9, no. 2 (1985): 236-39.

National Center for Education Statistics. *Digest of Education Statis-
    tics 1983-84*. Washington, D.C.: U.S. Government Printing Of-
    fice, 1984.

National Commission on Excellence in Education. *A Nation at Risk:
    The Imperative for Educational Reform*. Washington, D.C.: U.S.
    Government Printing Office, 1970.

Neill, A. S. *Summerhill: A Radical Approach to Child Rearing*. New
    York: Hart Publishing, 1960.

Nelson, Fred A. "The Open University in the United States." *College
    Board Review*, no. 85 (Fall 1972): 11-14.

Nelson, Susan C. "Equity and Higher Education Finance: The Case
    of Community Colleges." In *Financing Education: Overcoming
    Inefficiency and Inequity*, ed. by Walter W. McMahon and Terry
    G. Geske, 215-36. Urbana: University of Illinois Press, 1982.

Nelson, William. "Equal Opportunity." *Social Theory and Practice*,
    vol. 10, no. 2 (Summer 1984): 157-84.

Netzer, Dick. *The Subsidized Muse: Public Support for Arts in the
    United States*. Cambridge: Cambridge University Press, 1978.

Nozick, Robert. *Anarchy, State and Utopia*. New York: Basic Books, 1974.

Nussbaum, Martha. "Patriotism and Cosmopolitanism." In *For Love of Country: Debating the Limits of Cosmopolitanism*. Ed. by Joshua Cohen, 2-17, 131-44. Boston: Beacon Press, 1996.

Nyberg, David. *Power Over Power*. Ithaca, N.Y.: Cornell University Press, 1981.

Nyberg, David, and Kieran Egan. *The Erosion of Education: Socialization and the Schools*. New York: Teachers College Press, 1981.

Oaks, Dallin. "A Private University Looks at Government Regulations." *Journal of College and University Law*, vol. 4, no. 1 (February 1976): 1-12.

O'Bryan, Kenneth G. "The Teaching Face: A Historical Perspective." In *Children and the Faces of Television: Teaching, Violence, Selling*, ed. by Edward L. Palmer and Aimee Door, 5-17. New York: Academic Press, 1980.

Okin, Susan Moller. "Feminism and Multiculturalism: Some Tensions." *Ethics* 108 (July 1998): 661-84.

———. *Women in Western Political Thought*. Princeton, N.J.: Princeton University Press, 1979.

Oldenquist, Andrew. "'Indoctrination' and Societal Suicide." *The Public Interest*, no. 63 (Spring 1981): 81-94.

O'Neill, Onora A. "Opportunities, Equalities and Education." *Theory and Decision*, vol. 7 (1976): 275-95.

O'Reilly, Patricia, and Kathryn Borman. "Sexism and Sex Discrimination in Education." *Theory Into Practice*, vol. 23, no. 2 (Spring 1984): 110-16.

Otheguy, Ricardo. "Thinking About Bilingual Education: A Critical Appraisal." *Harvard Educational Review*, vol. 52, no. 3 (August 1982): 301-314.

Owen, David. *None of the Above: Behind the Myth of the Scholastic Aptitude*. Boston: Houghton Mifflin, 1985.

Padilla, Raymond V., ed. *Theory, Technology and Public Policy on Bilingual Education*. Rosslyn, Va.: National Clearinghouse for Bilingual Education, 1983.

Palmer, Edward L., and Aimee Dorr, eds. *Children and the Faces of Television: Teaching, Violence, Selling*. New York: Academic Press, 1980.

Parfit, Derek. *Reasons and Persons*. Oxford: Clarendon Press, 1984.

Pattison, Roger. *On Literacy: The Politics of the Word from Homer to the Age of Rock*. New York and Oxford: Oxford University Press, 1982.

Paulsen, Frederich. *The German Universities and University Study.* 1902. Trans. by F. Thilly and W. W. Elwang. First English edition. New York: C. Scribner's Sons, 1906.

Pechman, Joseph A. "Note on the Intergenerational Transfer of Public Higher-Education Benefits." In *Investment in Education: The Equity-Effciency Quandary*, ed. by Theodore W. Schultz, 256-59. Chicago: University of Chicago Press, 1972.

Peters, R. S. *Authority, Responsibility and Education.* London: George Allen and Unwin, 1973.

———. *Ethics and Education.* London: Allen and Unwin, 1966

———, ed. *The Concept of Education.* London: Routledge and Kegan Paul, 1967.

Peterson, Paul E. *The Politics of School Reform 1870-1940.* Chicago: University of Chicago Press, 1985.

Peterson, Paul E., Jay P. Greene, and William Howell. "New Findings from the Cleveland Scholarship Program: A Reanalysis of Data from the Indiana University School of Education."

Pittenger, John C., and Peter Kuriloff. "Educating the Handicapped: Reforming a Radical Law." *The Public Interest*, no. 66 (Winter 1982): 72-96.

Plato. *Crito.* In *The Last Days of Socrates*, trans. by Hugh Tredennick. Harmondsworth: Penguin Books, 1970.

———. *The Republic of Plato.* Trans. by Allan Bloom. New York: Basic Books, 1978.

Pogrebin, Letty Cottin. *Growing Up Free: Raising Your Child in the 80's.* New York: McGraw-Hill, 1980.

Pool, Ithiel de Sola. *Technologies of Freedom.* Cambridge, Mass.: Harvard University Press, 1983.

Popenoe, Joshua. *Inside Summerhill.* New York: Hart Publishing, 1970.

Popper, Karl. *The Open Society and Its Enemies.* Princeton, N.J.: Princeton University Press, 1971.

Postman, Neil. *Amusing Ourselves to Death: Public Discourse in the Age of Show Business.* New York: Viking, 1985.

Purpel, David, and Kevin Ryan. "It Comes With the Territory: The Inevitability of Moral Education in the Schools." In *Moral Education . . . It Comes With the Territory*, ed. by David Purpel and Kevin Ryan, 44-54. Berkeley, Calif.: McCutchan, 1976.

Putnam, Hilary. "Must We Choose?": In *For Love of Country: Debating the Limits of Patriotism.* Ed. by Joshua Cohen, 91-97. Boston: Beacon Press, 1996.

Raffel, Jeffrey A., Nancy J. Colmer, and Donald J. Berry, "Public Opinion Toward the Public Schools of Northern New Castle

County." Newark, Del.: College of Urban Affairs and Public Policy, 1983.

Ravitch, Diane. *The Great School Wars: New York City, 1805-1973.* New York: Basic Books, 1974.

———. *The Revisionists Revised: A Critique of the Radical Attack on the Schools.* New York: Basic Books, 1978.

———. *The Schools We Deserve: Reflections on the Educational Crises of Our Time.* New York: Basic Books, 1985.

———. *The Troubled Crusade: American Education 1945-1980.* New York: Basic Books, 1983.

Rawls, John. *A Theory of Justice.* Cambridge, Mass.: Harvard University Press, 1971.

Rebell, Michael, and Arthur Block. *Educational Policy Making and the Courts: An Empirical Study of Judicial Activism.* Chicago: University of Chicago Press, 1982.

Rice, Lois D., ed. *Student Loans: Problems and Policy Choices.* New York: College Entrance Examination Board, 1977.

Richards, David A. J. "Equal Opportunity and School Financing: Toward a Moral Theory of Constitutional Adjudication." *University of Chicago Law Review,* vol. 41, no. 1 (Fall 1973): 32-71.

Rickenbacker, William F., ed. *The Twelve-Year Sentence.* LaSalle, Ill.: Open Court, 1974.

Riley, John G. "Testing the Educational Screening Hypothesis." *Journal of Political Economy,* vol. 87, no. 5 (October 1979): 227-52.

Rivlin, Alice. *The Role of the Federal Government in Financing Higher Education.* Washington, D.C.: The Brookings Institution, 1961.

Rodman, Hyman, Susan Lewis, and Saralyn Griffith. *The Sexual Rights of Adolescents.* New York: Columbia University Press, 1984.

Rodriguez, Richard. *Hunger of Memory: The Education of Richard Rodriguez.* Boston: Godine, 1981.

Rosenblum, Nancy L., ed. *Religion and the Law.* Princeton: Princeton University Press, 1999.

Rotberg, Iris C. "Some Legal and Research Considerations in Establishing Federal Policy in Bilingual Education." *Harvard Educational Review,* vol. 52 (May 1982): 148-68.

Rouse, Cecelia Elena. "Private School Vouchers and Student Achievement: An Evaluation of the Milwaukee Parental Choice Program." *The Quarterly Journal of Economics* (May 1998): 552-602.

Rousseau, Jean Jacques. *Emile, or On Education.* Trans. by Barbara Foxley. New York: Everyman, 1972.

———. "J.-J. Rousseau, Citizen of Geneva to Monsieur D'Alembert." In *Politics and the Arts*, trans. by Allan Bloom, 3-137. Ithaca N.Y.: Cornell University Press, 1973.

———. *The Social Contract*. Trans. by G.D.H. Cole. New York: E. P. Dutton, 1950.

Rustin, Michael. "The Idea of the Popular University: A Historical Perspective." In *A Degree of Choice?: Higher Education and the Right to Learn*, ed. by Janet Finch and Michael Rustin, 17-66. Harmondsworth: Penguin Books, 1986.

Rutter, Michael, Barbara Maughan, Peter Mortimore, Janet Ouston, and Alan Smith. *Fifteen Thousand Hours: Secondary Schools and Their Effects on Children*. Cambridge, Mass.: Harvard University Press, 1979.

Sagoff, Mark. "The Aesthetic Status of Forgeries." In *The Forger's Art: Forgery and the Philosophy of Art*, ed. by Dennis Dutton, 131-52. Berkeley: University of California Press, 1983.

———. "On the Aesthetic and Economic Value of Art." *The British Journal of Aesthetics*, vol. 21, no. 4 (Autumn 1981): 131-52.

———. "On Restoring and Reproducing Art." *The Journal of Philosophy*, vol. 75, no. 9 (September 1978): 453-70.

St. John, Nancy. "The Effects of School Desegregation on Children." In *Race and Schooling in the City*, ed. Adam Yarmolinsky, Lance Liebman, and Corinne S. Schelling, 84-103. Cambridge, Mass.: Harvard University Press, 1981.

———. *School Desegregation: Outcomes for Children*. New York: Wiley Interscience, 1975.

Sandel, Michael J. *Liberalism and the Limits of Justice*. New York: Cambridge University Press, 1982.

Sarason, Seymour B. *The Culture of the School and the Problem of Change*. Boston: Allyn and Bacon, 1971.

Scanlon, Thomas. "Symposium on the Public Benefits of the Arts and Humanities." *Art and the Law*, vol. 9, no. 2 (1985): 167-71.

Scheffler, Israel. *Reason and Teaching*. London: Routledge and Kegan Paul, 1973.

Schrag, Francis. "The Right to Educate." *School Review*, vol. 79, no. 3 (May 1971): 359-78.

Schrecker, Ellen. *No Ivory Tower: McCarthyism and the Universities*. New York: Oxford University Press, 1986.

Schultz, Theodore W. *Higher Education: The Equity-Efficiency Quandary*. Arlington, Va.: IDA Economic Papers, 1973.

Schwartz, Adina. "Meaningful Work." *Ethics*, vol. 92 (July 1982): 634-46.

Scupham, John. "The Open University of the United Kingdom." In *Open Learning: Systems and Problems in Post-Secondary Education*, ed. by Norman MacKenzie, Richmond Postgate, and John Scupham, 321-64. Paris: The UNESCO Press, 1975.

Sen, Amartya, and Bernard Williams, eds. *Utilitarianism and Beyond*. Cambridge: Cambridge University Press, 1982.

Sennett, Richard. *The Fall of Public Man*. New York: Vintage Books, 1978.

"Sex Education in Public Schools? — Interview with Jacqueline Kasun." *U.S. News and World Report*, vol. 89, no. 14 (October 1980): 89-90.

Sigel, Roberta S. *Learning About Politics: A Reader in Political Socialization*. New York: Random House, 1970.

Simon, Sidney B. "Values Clarification vs. Indoctrination." *Social Education* (December 1971). Reprinted in *Moral Education . . . It Comes With the Territory*, ed. by David Purpel and Kevin Ryan, 126-35. Berkeley, Calif.: McCutchan, 1976.

Sindler, Allan P. *Bakke, DeFunis, and Minority Admissions: The Quest for Equal Opportunity*. New York: Longman, 1978.

Sizer, Theodore R. *Horace's Compromise: The Dilemma of the American High School*. Boston: Houghton Mifflin, 1984.

Slavin, Robert E. *Cooperative Learning*. New York: Longman, 1982.

———. "Cooperative Learning and Desegregation." In *Effective School Desegregation; Equity, Quality, and Feasibility*, ed. by Willis D. Hawley, 225-44. Beverly Hills, Calif.: Sage, 1981.

Slavin, Robert E., and Nancy A. Madden. "School Practices That Improve Race Relations." *American Educational Research Journal*, vol. 16, no. 2 (Spring 1979): 169-80.

Smith, Adam. *An Inquiry into the Nature and Causes of the Wealth of Nations*. Ed. by Edwin Cannan. 2 vols. Chicago: University of Chicago Press, 1976.

Sonenstein, Freya, and Karen J. Pittman. "The Availability of Sex Education in City School Districts." Research Reports for the Urban Institute, P.O. Box 7273, Dept. C., Washington, D.C., 20044.

———. "The What and Why of Sex Education: Describing and Explaining Program Content and Coverage in City Schools." Research Reports for the Urban Institute, P.O. Box 7273, Dept. C., Washington, D.C., 20044.

Special Committee on the Governing of the University. *The Governing of Princeton University*. Princeton, N.J.: Princeton University, 1970.

Spence, A. Michael. *Market Signaling*. Cambridge, Mass.: Harvard University Press, 1974.

Spender, Dale. *Men's Studies Modified: The Impact of Feminism On the Academic Disciplines*. Oxford: Pergamon Press, 1981.

Spring, Joel H. *American Education: An Introduction to Social and Political Aspects*. 3rd ed. New York: Longman, 1985.

Spring, Joel H. *Education and the Rise of the Corporate State*. Boston: Beacon Press, 1972.

Stairs, Allen. "The Case Against Creationism." *QQ: Report from the Center for Philosophy and Public Policy*, University of Maryland, vol. 2, no. 2 (Spring 1982): 9-11.

Stiglitz, Joseph E. "The Theory of 'Screening,' Education and the Distribution of Income." *American Economic Review*, vol. 65, no. 3 (June 1975): 283-300.

Stille, Alexander. "The Betrayal of History." *New York Review of Books*, June 11, 1998: 15-20.

Surgeon General's Scientific Advisory Committee on Television and Social Behavior. *Television and Growing Up: The Impact of Televised Violence*. Report to the Surgeon General. Washington, D.C.: U.S. Government Printing Office, 1972.

Swearingen, Roger. *The World of Communism*. New York: Houghton Mifflin, 1962.

Tarcov, Nathan. *Locke's Education for Liberty*. Chicago: University of Chicago Press, 1984.

Taylor, Charles. *Multiculturalism: Examining the Politics of Recognition*. Ed. by Amy Gutmann. Princeton: Princeton University Press, 1994.

Thernstrom, Abigail M. "E Pluribus Plura — Congress and Bilingual Education." *The Public Interest*, vol. 60 (Summer 1980): 3-22.

Thompson, Dennis F. "Bureaucracy and Democracy." In *Democratic Theory and Practice*, ed. by Graeme Duncan, 235-50. New York: Cambridge University Press, 1983.

———. "Democracy and the Governing of the University." *Annals of the American Academy of Political and Social Science*, vol. 404 (November 1972): 157-70.

———. "Political Theory and Political Judgement." *PS*, vol. 17, no. 2 (Spring 1984): 193-97.

———. "Reasoning, Religion and the Court." In *Public Policy*, ed. by John D. Montgomery and Albert O. Hirschman, vol. 21, 358-92. Cambridge, Mass.: Harvard University Press, 1967.

Tocqueville, Alexis de. *Democracy in America*. 1848. Trans. by George Lawrence, ed. by J. P. Mayer. Anchor Books edition. Garden City, N.Y.: Doubleday and Co., 1969.

Tuckman, Howard P., and Edward Whalen, eds. *Subsidies to Higher Education: The Issues*. New York: Praeger, 1980.

Tyack, David B. *The One Best System: A History of American Urban Education.* Cambridge, Mass.: Harvard University Press, 1974.

Tyack, David B., and Elisabeth Hansot. *Managers of Virtue: Public School Leadership in America, 1820-1980.* New York: Basic Books, 1982.

UNESCO. *Statement of the International Committee of Experts on Literacy.* Paris: UNESCO Press, 1962.

U.S. Bureau of the Census. "Characteristics of the Population Below the Poverty Level: 1983." *Current Population Reports,* Series P-60, no. 148.

Viroli, Maurizio. *For Love of Country: An Essay on Patriotism and Nationalism.* Oxford: Clarendon Press, 1995.

Waldron, Jeremy. "Multiculturalism and melange." In *Public Education in a Multicultural Society:* 90-118. New York: Cambridge University Press, 1996.

Walzer, Michael. "Philosophy and Democracy." *Political Theory,* vol. 9, no. 3 (August 1981): 379-99.

———. *Spheres of Justice.* New York: Basic Books, 1983.

Wasserstrom, Richard. "Preferential Treatment." In *Philosophy and Social Issues: Five Studies,* 51-82. Notre Dame, Ind. and London: University of Notre Dame Press, 1980.

Watkins, Bruce A., Aletha Huston-Stein, and John C. Wright. "Effects of Planned Television Programming." In *Children and the Faces of Television: Teaching, Violence, Selling,* ed. by Edward L. Palmer and Aimee Dorr, 49-69. New York: Academic Press, 1980.

Weatherly, Richard A. *Reforming Special Education: Policy Implementation From State to Street Level.* Cambridge, Mass.: MIT Press, 1979.

Webster, Noah. "On the Education of Youth in America." In *Essays on Education in the Early Republic,* ed. by Frederick Rudolph, 41-77. Cambridge, Mass.: Harvard University Press, 1965.

Weinberg, Meyer. "The Relationship between School Desegregation and Academic Acheivement: A Review of the Research." *Law and Contemporary Problems,* vol. 39, no. 2 (Spring 1975): 240-70.

Welter, Rush. *Popular Education and Democratic Thought in America.* New York: Columbia University Press, 1962.

———. "Reason, Rhetoric, and Reality in American Educational History." *The Review of Education,* vol. 2 (January/February 1976): 91-99.

Wesley, Edgar. *NEA: The First Hundred Years.* New York: Harper and Brothers, 1957.

"The What and Why of Sex Education in the Nation's Schools." *The Urban Institute: Policy and Research Report*, vol. 14, no. 3 (December 1984): 8-9.

Whitehead, Alfred North. *The Aims of Education and Other Essays.* 1929. New York: The Free Press, 1967.

Williams, Bernard. *Ethics and the Limits of Philosophy.* Cambridge, Mass.: Harvard University Press, 1985.

———. "The Truth in Relativism." In *Moral Luck*, 132-43. New York: Cambridge University Press, 1981.

Wilson, John. *Preface to the Philosophy of Education.* London: Routledge and Kegan Paul, 1979.

Wise, Arthur E. *Legislated Learning: The Bureaucratization of the American Classroom.* Berkeley: University of California Press, 1979.

Witte, John F. "Reply to Greene, Peterson, and Du: 'The Effectiveness of School Choice in Milwaukee: A Secondary Analysis of Data from the Program's Evaluation.'" Unpublished paper: August 23, 1996.

Witte, John F., and Christopher A. Thorn. "Who Chooses? Voucher and Interdistrict Choice Programs in Milwaukee." *American Journal of Education* 104 (May 1996): 186-217.

Wolf, Susan. "Asymmetrical Freedom." *The Journal of Philosophy* (1980): 151-66.

Wolff, Robert Paul. *The Ideal of the University.* Boston: Beacon Press, 1969.

Wolpin, Kenneth. "Education and Screening." *American Economic Review*, vol. 67, no. 5 (December 1977): 949-58.

Work in America: Report of a Special Task Force to the Secretary of Health, Education, and Welfare. Cambridge, Mass.: MIT Press, 1973.

Yudof, Mark G. *When Government Speaks: Politics, Law, and Government Expression in America.* Berkeley: University of California Press, 1983.

Zaitchik, Alan. "On Deserving to Deserve." *Philosophy and Public Affairs*, vol. 6 (Summer 1977): 370-88.

Zeigler, L. Harmon, M. Kent Jennings, and G. Wayne Peak. *Governing American Schools: Political Interaction in Local School Districts.* North Scituate, Mass.: Duxbury, 1974.

INDEX